TOP 10 OF EVERYTHING 2011

TOP 10 OF EVERYTHING 2011

Russell Ash

hamlyn

CONTENTS

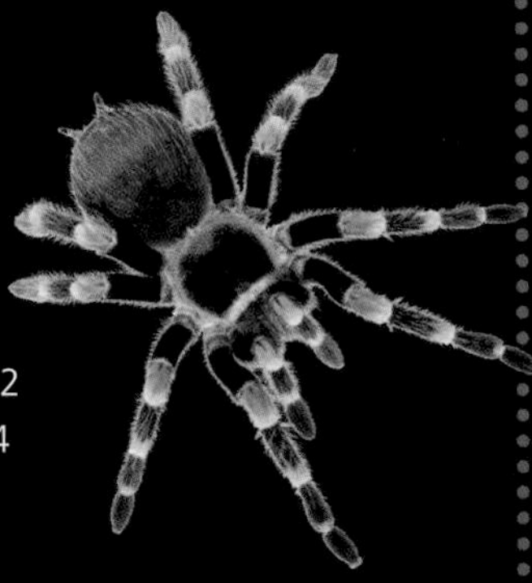

Produced for Hamlyn by
Palazzo Editions Ltd
2 Wood Street, Bath, BA1 2JQ

Publishing director: Colin Webb
Art director: Bernard Higton
Managing editor: Sonya Newland
Picture researcher: Sophie Hartley

An Hachette UK Company
www.hachette.co.uk

First published in Great Britain in 2010 by
Hamlyn, a division of
Octopus Publishing Group Ltd
Endeavour House, 189 Shaftesbury Avenue,
London, WC2 8JY

www.octopusbooks.co.uk

ISBN 978-0-600-61743-3

A CIP catalogue record for this book is available from the British Library.

Printed and bound in Spain.

10 9 8 7 6 5 4 3 2 1

INTRODUCTION

CATCH-22

Joseph Heller's novel *Catch-22* is one of many places in which the number 22 crops up. It is also the atomic number of titanium, there are 22 cards in a Tarot pack, and Grover Cleveland was unusual in being both the 22nd and the 24th US president. A 22-calibre gun has a bore of .22 of an inch, the USAF stealth fighter is designated the *F-22 Raptor*, f22 is the smallest aperture on a camera, there are 22 letters in the Hebrew alphabet and, since 1974, 22 has been the number of stars in the Paramount film logo. In sport, there are 22 balls in snooker, 22 yards in a cricket pitch, John O'Shea – Manchester United's No. 22 – is the only Premier League footballer to play all in 11 positions, and 22 was the number of consecutive motor-racing champions' cars, Lewis Hamilton's McLaren-Mercedes (2008) and Jenson Button's Brawn-Mercedes (2009). And this is the 22nd annual edition of *Top 10 of Everything*.

CHANGE

I am sometimes asked to sign and dedicate copies of *Top 10* to a newborn child as a time-capsule of the year in which it was born. Not only are the changes mirrored in it over the past 22 years enormous – hardly a single list has remained unchanged – but I am all too aware of how much they change in a single year. Many entirely new lists are introduced each year. In this we have features and lists that reveal the most-played songs, the longest-lived and the richest people of all time, land speed records (including one on ice!); the biggest online retailers and social networks, the most-followed people on Twitter and the top iPhone apps; the latest film, book, music and other award-winners; the top singles of every decade since the charts began, the highest-earning vampire films and the worst film flops; every building to hold the title 'tallest building in the world', the tallest bridges and the longest tunnels; the most common first names, the longest place names and the countries with the greatest declining populations; the most common murder weapons, the shortest wars, the first and the worst air crashes, the fattest people and the tallest trees; the fastest people in the world, the greatest Paralympic champions; the most intelligent and the most aggressive dogs, the deadliest spiders, the heaviest dinosaurs and the worst volcanoes. Alongside these, and almost in contradiction to the ongoing global economic crisis, the lists in *Top 10* show that works of art continue to command high prices and record football transfer fees are still being paid, the largest cruise ships ever built are entering service, and *Avatar* has become the first film ever to earn more than $2 billion at the world box office.

CHECKLISTS

As always, all the *Top 10* lists are quantifiable – measurable in some way or other: the biggest, smallest, first, last, tallest, deepest, sunniest, dullest, or chronologically the first or last. All the lists thus offer more than just the No. 1, and provide a perspective in which to compare the subjects of the list. There are no 'bests', other than bestsellers, and 'worsts' are of disasters, military losses and murders, where they are measured by numbers of victims. Unless otherwise stated, film lists are based on cumulative global earnings, irrespective of production or marketing budgets and – as is standard in the movie industry – inflation is not taken into account, which

means that recent releases tend to feature disproportionately prominently. Countries are independent countries, not dependencies or overseas territories. All the lists are all-time and global unless a specific year or territory is noted. If the UK does not figure in a country-based list, it is generally added as an extra entry.

CREDITS

My sources encompass international organizations, commercial companies and research bodies, specialized publications and a network of experts around the world who have generously shared their knowledge. As always, I happily acknowledge their important contribution (see page 255 for a full list of credits), along with that of everyone who has been involved with the book at all stages of its development on this and the previous annual editions.

CRYSTAL BALL

As another innovation, the introduction to each of the 10 sections of *Top 10* looks into the future and to a significant event in 2011. As we enter this year, all we can be sure of is that the Top 10 lists that define it will reflect further remarkable changes.

CONTACTS

I hope you enjoy the book. Your comments, corrections and suggestions for new lists are always welcome. Please contact me via the publishers or visit the *Top 10 of Everything* website (top10ofeverything.com) or my own (RussellAsh.com).

Russell Ash

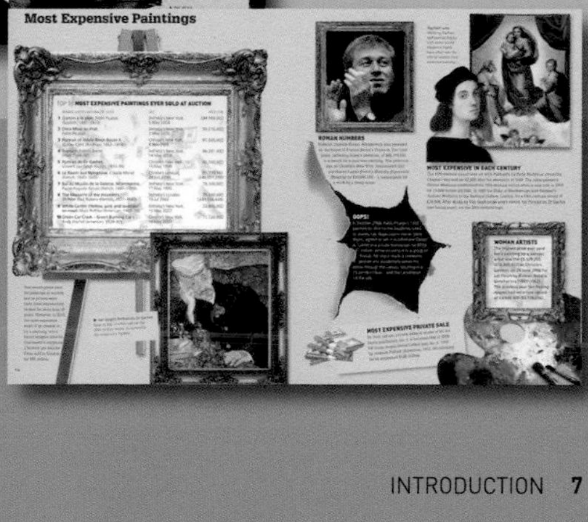

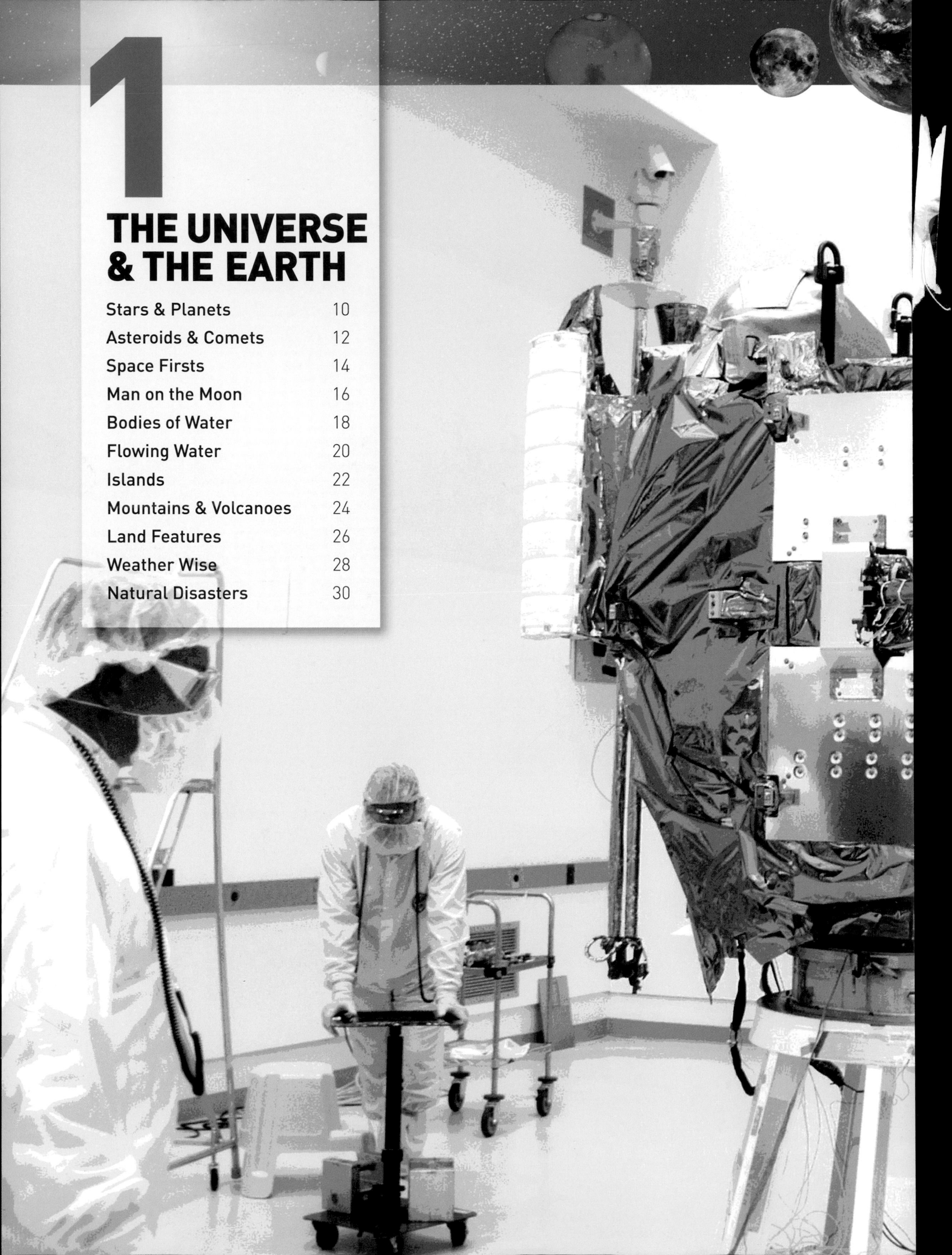

1

THE UNIVERSE & THE EARTH

MESSENGER TO MERCURY

Launched on 3 August 2004, NASA's *MESSENGER* (MErcury Surface, Space ENvironment, GEochemistry and Ranging) probe is scheduled to reach Mercury, a distance of 155.06 million km (96.35 million miles) from Earth, and enter orbit at a height of 200 km (124 miles) on 18 March 2011. *Mariner 10* (1974–75), the only other space probe to approach Mercury, did not orbit. *MESSENGER* has already performed flybys of Venus (2006) and Mercury (2008), but it is expected that its year-long orbit will transmit unprecedented images and data, including investigations of the planet's surface composition, volcanoes and magnetic core.

STARS & PLANETS

TOP 10 **LARGEST BODIES IN THE SOLAR SYSTEM**

BODY / MAX. DIAMETER (KM/MILES) / SIZE COMPARED WITH EARTH

1 **Sun**
1,392,140 / 865,036
109.136

2 **Jupiter**
142,984 / 88,846
11.209

3 **Saturn**
120,536 / 74,898
9.449

4 **Uranus**
51,118 / 31,763
4.007

TOP 10 **LARGEST PLANETARY MOONS**

MOON / PLANET / DIAMETER (KM/MILES)

1. **Ganymede** / Jupiter (5,262.4 / 3,269.9)
Discovered by Galileo in 1610, Ganymede is thought to have a surface of ice about 97 km (60 miles) thick.

2. **Titan** / Saturn (5,150.0 / 3,200.1)
Titan has a dense atmosphere containing nitrogen, ethane and other gases that shroud its surface.

3. **Callisto** / Jupiter (4,820.6 / 2,995.4)
Callisto is heavily pitted with craters, perhaps more so than any other body in the Solar System.

4. **Io** / Jupiter (3,642.6 / 2,263.4)
Io has a crust of solid sulphur, with massive volcanic eruptions hurling sulphurous material 300 km (186 miles) into space.

5. **Moon** / Earth (3,476.2 / 2,160.0)
Our own satellite is the fifth largest in the Solar System and, to date, the only one to have been explored by humans.

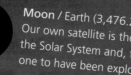

6. **Europa** / Jupiter (3,121.6 / 1,939.7)
Europa's ice-covered surface is apparently smooth and crater-free, but is covered with black lines.

7. **Triton** / Neptune (2,706.8 / 1,681.9)
Triton is the only known satellite in the Solar System that revolves around its planet in the opposite direction to the planet's rotation.

8. **Titania** / Uranus (1,577.8 / 980.4)
Titania was discovered by William Herschel (who had discovered the planet six years earlier) in 1787, and has a snowball-like surface of ice.

9. **Rhea** / Saturn (1,528.0 / 947.6)
Rhea was discovered in 1672 by the astronomer Jean-Dominique Cassini. Its icy surface is pitted with enormous craters.

10. **Oberon** / Uranus (1,522.8 / 946.2)
Oberon was discovered by Herschel at the same time as Titania and given the name of her fairy-king husband.

THE LARGEST STAR

VY Canis Majoris, a red hypergiant star some 4,900 light years from Earth, is estimated to be 2,100 times the diameter and a billion times the volume of the Sun. Light, which takes about eight minutes to travel from the Sun to Earth, would take eight hours to travel round its circumference.

5 Neptune
49,528 / 30,775
3.883

7 Venus
12,104 / 7,521
0.949

9 Ganymede
5,262 / 3,270
0.413

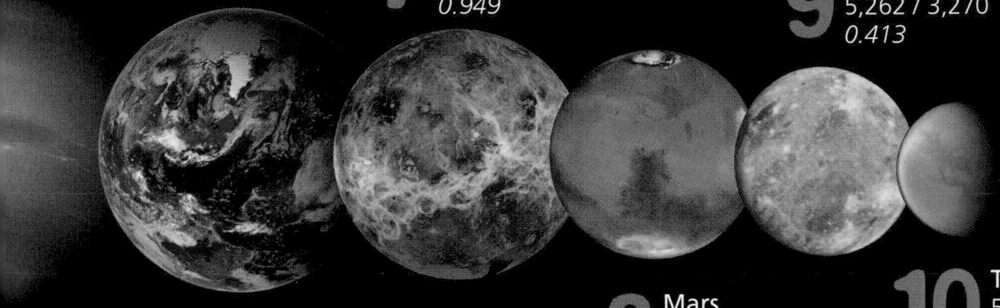

6 Earth
12,756 / 7,926
1.000

8 Mars
6,805 / 4,228
0.533

10 Titan
5,150 / 3,200
0.404

TOP 10 LONGEST DAYS IN THE SOLAR SYSTEM

	BODY*	DAYS	LENGTH OF DAY# HRS	MINS	SECS
1	Venus	243	0	26	56
2	Mercury	58	15	30	32
3	Sun	25†			
4	Pluto	6	9	17	34
5	Mars		24	37	23
6	Earth		23	56	4.1
7	Uranus		17	14	24
8	Neptune		16	6	36
9	Saturn		10	29	32
10	Jupiter		9	55	33

* Excluding satellites
\# Period of rotation, based on Earth day
† Variable

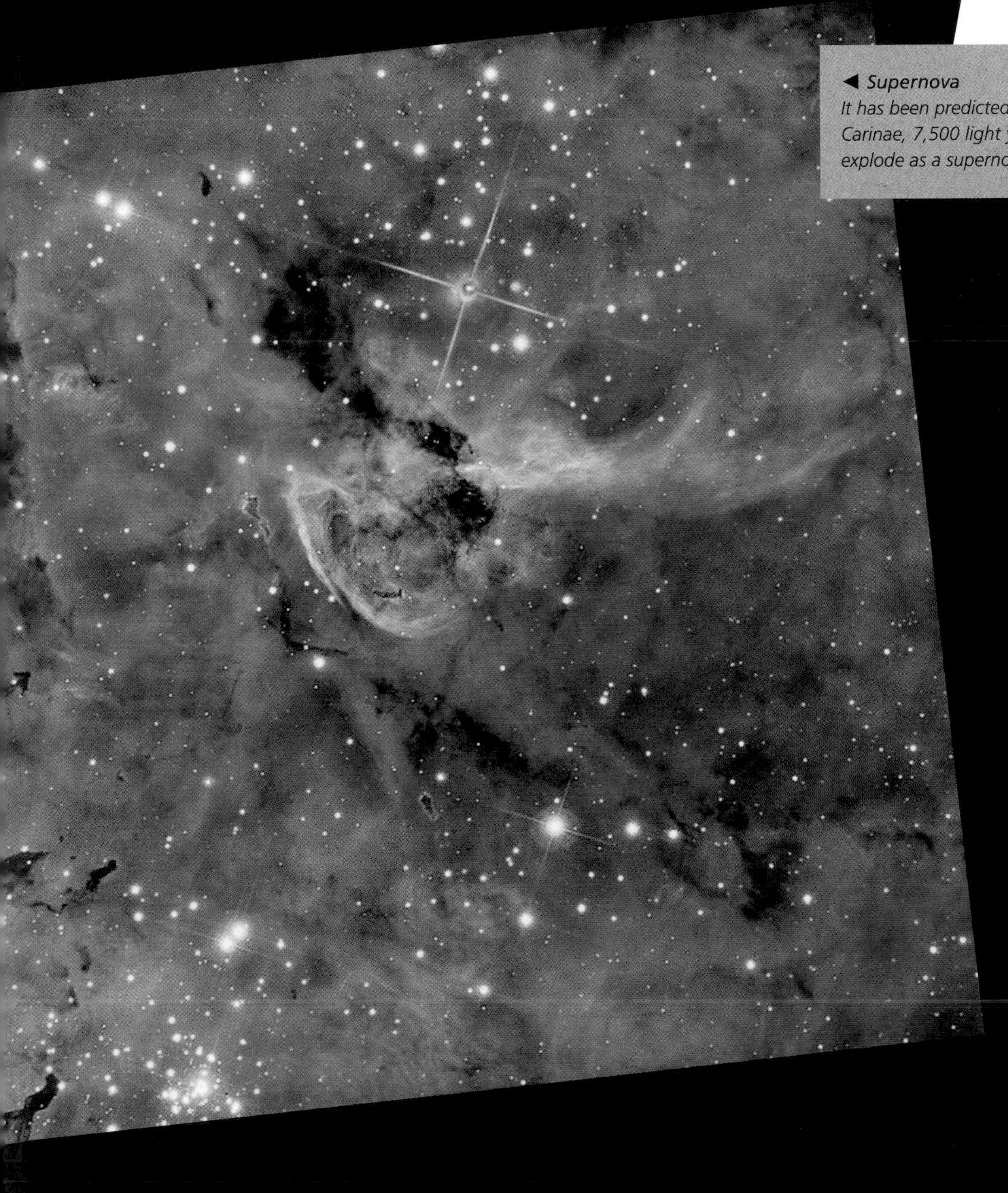

◀ *Supernova*
It has been predicted that massive star Eta Carinae, 7,500 light years from Earth, will explode as a supernova.

TOP 10 MOST MASSIVE STARS

STAR / MASS* / LOCATION

1. **LBV 1806-20** 130–200
   Milky Way
2. **Peony Nebula Star** 175
   Milky Way
3. **HD 269810** 150
   Large Magellanic Cloud
4. **Eta Carinae** 100–150
   Carina
5. **Pistol Star** 80–150
   Milky Way
6. **Arches cluster** 100–130
   Milky Way
7. **HD 93129A** 120
   Milky Way
8. **Pismis 24-1 A** 100–120
   NGC 6357
9. **HD 93250** 118
   Carina
10. **A1** 116
   NGC 3603

* Compared with Sun – solar mass, the mass of the Sun (about two nonillion [10^{30}] kg), or 332,950 times the mass of the Earth.

TOP 10 **LARGEST ASTEROIDS**

	NAME	NO.	DISCOVERED	MEAN DIAMETER* KM	MILES
1	Ceres	1	1 Jan 1801	952	592
2	Pallas	2	28 Mar 1802	544	338
3	Vesta	4	29 Mar 1807	529	329
4	Hygeia	10	12 Apr 1849	431	268
5	Interamnia	704	2 Oct 1910	326	203
6	Europa	52	4 Feb 1858	301	187
7	Davida	511	30 May 1903	289	180
8	Sylvia	87	16 May 1866	286	178
9	Cybele	65	8 Mar 1861	273	170
10	Eunomia	15	29 Jul 1899	268	167

* Most asteroids are irregular in shape

▲ *Asteroid belt*
Astronomers have recently discovered a narrow asteroid belt filled with rocks and dust surrounding a distant star, which may suggest a planetary system.

TOP 10 **ASTEROIDS DUE TO COME CLOSEST TO EARTH**

NAME/DESIGNATION / DUE DATE* / DISTANCE (KM/MILES)

* Closest point to Earth

1 Aphosis 13 Apr 2029 34,677 / 21,547
2 2005 YU55 8 Nov 2011 159,322 / 98,998
3 2000 WO107 2 Dec 2169 242,797 / 150,867
4 2000 WN5 26 Jun 2028 249,828 / 155,235
5 1998 OX4 22 Jan 2148 299,794 / 186,283
6 1999 AN10 7 Aug 2027 388,954 / 241,684
7 1998 MZ 26 Nov 2116 411,394 / 255,6280
8 1997 XF11 28 Oct 2136 413,189 / 256,743
9 2003 QC10 24 Sep 2066 508,034 / 315,677
10 2001 GQ2 27 Apr 2100 508,632 / 316,049

As of 18 January 2010, NASA's Near Earth Object Program listed 6,684 objects, including 1,086 asteroids with a diameter of approximately 1 km (0.6 mile) or more, and many thousands of smaller ones that approach Earth's orbit and could potentially impact with our planet, with the PHAs (Potentially Hazardous Asteroids) listed here predicted to make the closest approaches. Among recent visitors, asteroid 2004 XP14 approached to within 432,487 km (268,734 miles) on 3 July 2006, and we lived to tell the tale.

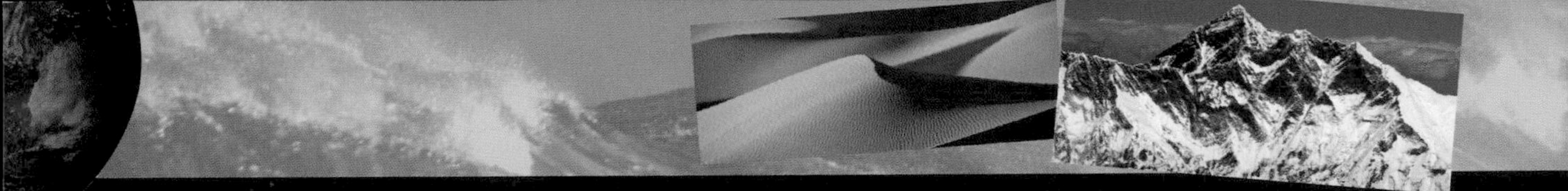

THE 10 **MOST RECENT OBSERVATIONS OF HALLEY'S COMET**

1 **1986**
The Japanese *Suisei* probe passed within 151,000 km (93,827 miles) of its 15-km (9-mile) nucleus on 8 March 1986, revealing a whirling nucleus within a hydrogen cloud. The Soviet probes *Vega 1* and *Vega 2* passed within 8,890 km (5,524 miles) and 8,030 km (4,990 miles) respectively. The European Space Agency's *Giotto* passed as close as 596 km (370 miles). All were heavily battered by dust particles, and it was concluded that Halley's Comet is composed of dust bonded by water and carbon-dioxide ice.

2 **1910**
With widespread predictions of disaster, many people were convinced that the world would come to an end. American author Mark Twain, who had been born at the time of the 1835 appearance and believed that his fate was linked to that of the comet, died when it reappeared this year.

3 **1835**
Widely observed, but noticeably dimmer than in 1759.

4 **1759**
The comet's first return, as predicted by Halley, and thus proving his calculations correct.

5 **1682**
Observed in Africa and China, and extensively in Europe, where it was viewed from 5–19 September by Edmond Halley, who predicted its return.

6 **1607**
Seen extensively in China, Japan, Korea and Europe, described by German astronomer Joannes Kepler and its position accurately measured by amateur Welsh astronomer Thomas Harriot.

7 **1531**
Observed in China, Japan and Korea, and in Europe 13–23 August by Peter Appian, a German geographer and astronomer, who noted that comets' tails point away from the Sun.

8 **1456**
Observed in China, Japan and Korea, and by the Turkish army that was threatening to invade Europe. When the Turks were defeated by papal forces, it was seen as a portent of victory.

9 **1378**
Observed in China, Japan, Korea and Europe.

10 **1301**
Seen in Iceland, parts of Europe, China, Japan and Korea.

▲ ***Deep impact***
In 2005, NASA's Deep Impact *mission released an impactor into comet Tempel 1, relaying photographs of its surface.*

TOP 10 **MOST FREQUENTLY SEEN COMETS**

	COMET*	YEARS BETWEEN APPEARANCES
1	Encke 1	3.29
2	NEAT (Near Earth Asteroid Tracking) 22	4.20
3	Wilson-Harrington#	4.29
4	Helfenzrieder 1	4.35
5	Catalina 3	4.42
6	Garradd 4	4.50
7	LINEAR (Lincoln Near-Earth Asteroid Research) 53	4.63
8	LINEAR 30	4.85
9	LINEAR 46	4.86
10=	Grigg-Skjellerup 1	4.98
=	NEAT 10	4.98

* Excluding sungrazer comets
# Identified as a comet and an asteroid

Source: NASA, Planetary Data System Small Bodies Node

Our most frequent visitor is Encke's Comet, named after the German astronomer Johann Franz Encke (1791–1865), who in 1818 calculated the period of its elliptical orbit. It made its 61st observed return, reaching perihelion (closest to the Sun) on 6 August 2010.

Background: Halley's Comet
Last observed from Earth in 1986, Halley's Comet will next be seen in 2061.

SPACE FIRSTS

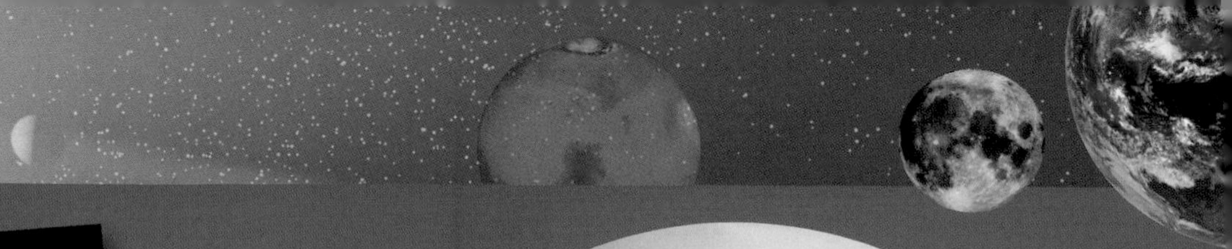

◄ *Sputnik 2*
The second satellite launch of 1957 carried Laika, the first animal to orbit Earth, paving the way for human spaceflight in 1961.

THE 10 **FIRST PLANETARY PROBES**

	PROBE*	PLANET	ARRIVAL#
1	Venera 4	Venus	18 Oct 1967
2	Venera 5	Venus	16 May 1969
3	Venera 6	Venus	17 May 1969
4	Venera 7	Venus	15 Dec 1970
5	Mariner 9 (USA)	Mars	13 Nov 1971
6	Mars 2	Mars	27 Nov 1971
7	Mars 3	Mars	2 Dec 1971
8	Venera 8	Venus	22 Jul 1972
9	Venera 9	Venus	22 Oct 1975
10	Venera 10	Venus	25 Oct 1975

* All USSR unless otherwise stated
\# Successfully entered orbit or landed

This list excludes 'flybys' – probes that passed by but did not land on the surface of another planet. *Pioneer 10* (USA), for example, flew past Jupiter on 3 December 1973, but did not land. *Venera 4* was the first unmanned probe to land on a planet and *Venera 9* the first to transmit pictures from a planet's surface. *Mariner 9* was the first to orbit another planet. Other *Mariner* probes did not land and are now either in orbit around the Sun or have travelled beyond the Solar System.

THE 10 **FIRST ARTIFICIAL SATELLITES**

SATELLITE / COUNTRY / LAUNCH DATE

1. **Sputnik 1** USSR
   4 Oct 1957
2. **Sputnik 2** USSR
   3 Nov 1957
3. **Explorer 1** USA
   1 Feb 1958
4. **Vanguard** USA
   17 Mar 1958
5. **Explorer 3** USA
   26 Mar 1958
6. **Sputnik 3** USSR
   15 May 1958
7. **Explorer 4** USA
   26 Jul 1958
8. **SCORE** USA
   18 Dec 1958
9. **Vanguard 2** USA
   17 Feb 1959
10. **Discoverer 1** USA
   28 Feb 1959

THE 10 **FIRST MEN TO ORBIT EARTH**

NAME (AGE) / ORBITS / DURATION (DAY:HR:MIN) / SPACECRAFT / COUNTRY / DATE

1 **Yuri A. Gagarin** (27) 1
0:1:48 Vostok I, USSR
12 Apr 1961

2 **Gherman S. Titov** (25) 17
1:1:18 Vostok II, USSR
6–7 Aug 1961

3 **John H. Glenn** (40) 3
0:4:55 Friendship 7, USA
20 Feb 1962

4 **Malcolm S. Carpenter** (37) 3
0:4:56 Aurora 7, USA
24 May 1962

5 **Andrian G. Nikolayev** (32) 64
3:22:22 Vostok III, USSR
11–15 Aug 1962

6 **Pavel R. Popovich** (31) 48
2:22:56 Vostok IV, USSR
12–15 Aug 1962

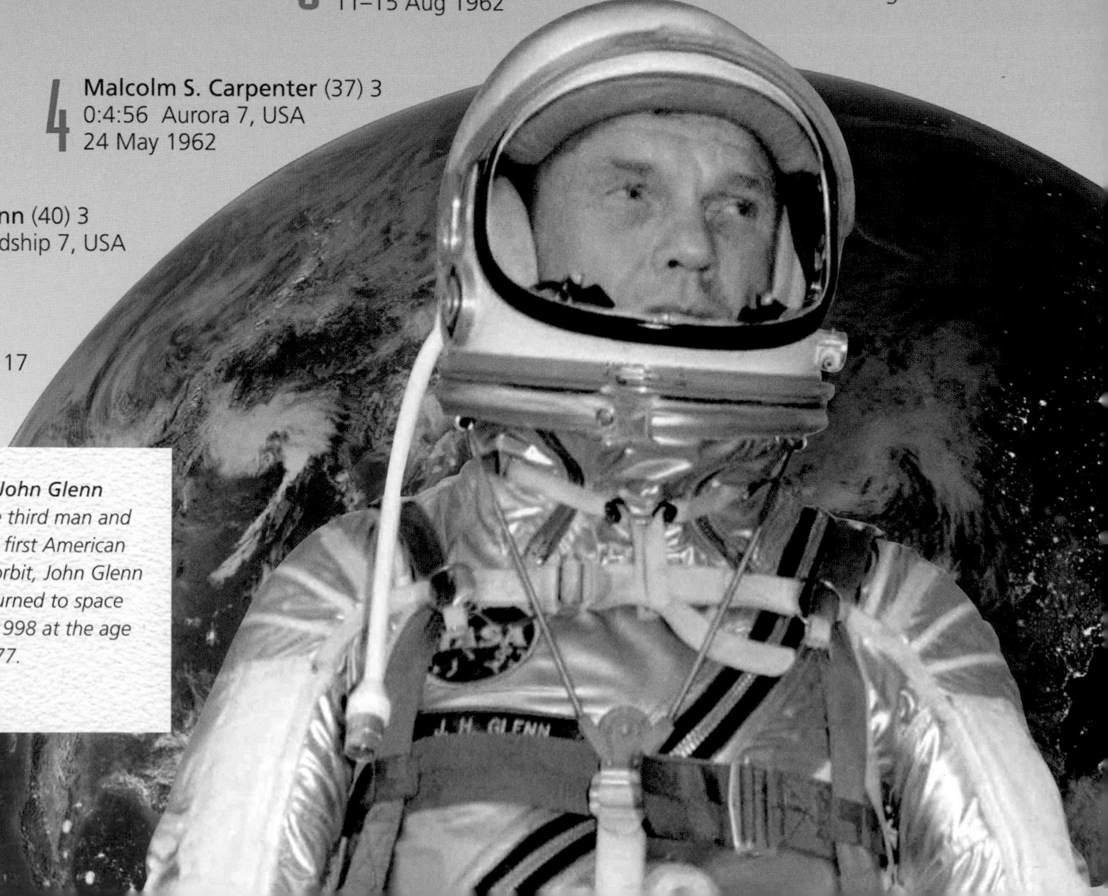

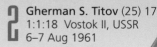

► *John Glenn*
The third man and the first American in orbit, John Glenn returned to space in 1998 at the age of 77.

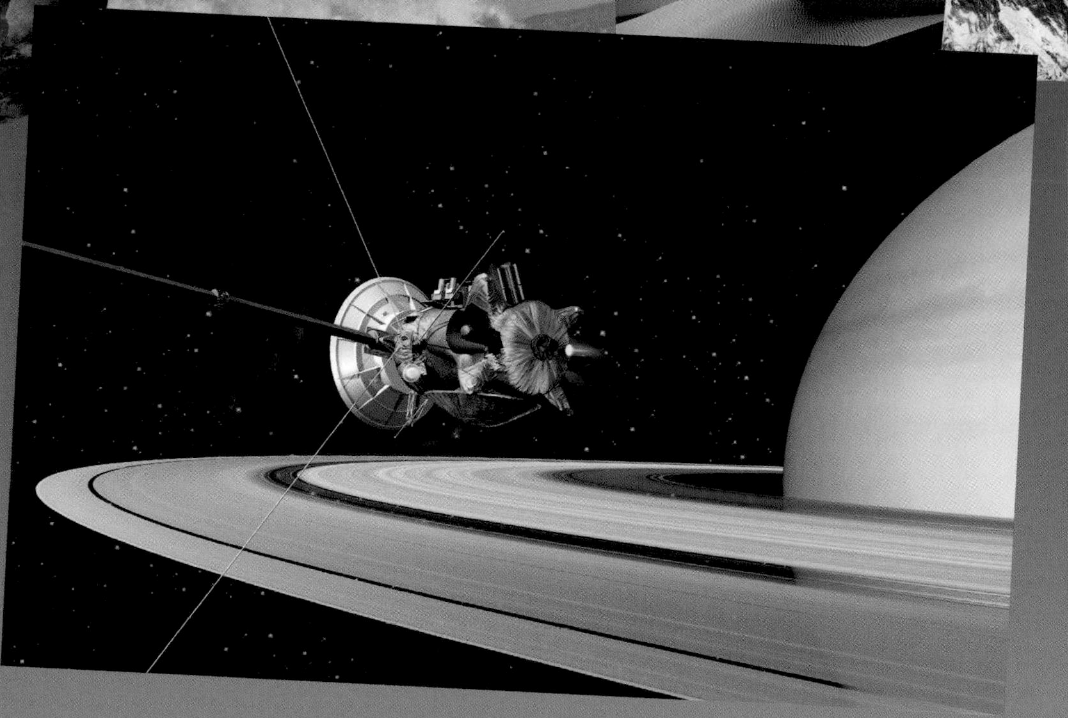

◀ *Return to Saturn*
In 2004, 25 years after Pioneer 11's flyby, Cassini entered orbit round the planet.

THE 10 **FIRST WOMEN TO ORBIT EARTH**

NAME (AGE) / ORBITS / DURATION (DAY:HR:MIN) / SPACECRAFT / COUNTRY / DATE

1. Valentina V. Tereshkova (26) 48
2:22:50 Vostok 6, USSR
16–19 Jun 1963
2. Svetlana Y. Savitskaya (34) 126
7:21:52 Soyuz T7, USSR
19 Aug 1982
3. Sally K. Ride (32) 97
6:2:24 Challenger STS-7, USA
18–24 Jun 1983
4. Judith A. Resnik (35) 97
6:0:56 Discovery STS-41-D, USA
30 Aug–5 Sep 1984
5. Kathryn D. Sullivan (33) 133
8:5:24 Challenger STS-41-G, USA
5–13 Oct 1984
6. Anna L. Fisher (35) 127
7:23:45 Discovery STS-51-A, USA
8–16 Nov 1984
7. Margaret R. Seddon (37) 110
6:23:55 Discovery STS-51-D, USA
12–19 Apr 1985
8. Shannon W. Lucid (42) 112
7:1:39 Discovery STS-51-G, USA
17–24 Jun 1985
9. Bonnie J. Dunbar (36) 112
7:0:45 Challenger STS-61-A, USA
30 Oct–6 Nov 1985
10. Mary L. Cleave (42) 109
6:21:5 Atlantis STS-61-B, USA
26 Nov–3 Dec 1985

THE 10 **FIRST BODIES TO HAVE BEEN VISITED BY SPACECRAFT**

	BODY / SPACECRAFT / COUNTRY	DATE
1	**Moon** Luna 1, USSR	2 Jan 1959
2	**Venus** Venera 1, USSR	19 May 1961
3	**Sun** Pioneer 5, USA	10 Aug 1961
4	**Mars** Mariner 4, USA	14 Jul 1965
5	**Jupiter** Pioneer 10, USA	3 Dec 1973
6	**Mercury** Mariner 10, USA	29 Mar 1974
7	**Saturn** Pioneer 11, USA	1 Sep 1979
8	**Comet Giacobini-Zinner** International Sun-Earth Explorer 3 (International Cometary Explorer), Europe/USA	11 Sep 1985
9	**Uranus** Voyager 2, USA	30 Jan 1986
10	**Halley's Comet** Vega 1, USSR	6 Mar 1986

Only the first spacecraft successfully to approach or land on each body is included.

7. Walter M. Schirra (39) 6
0:9:13 Sigma 7, USA
3 Oct 1962
8. Leroy G. Cooper (36) 22
1:10:19 Faith 7, USA
15–16 May 1963
9. Valeri F. Bykovsky (28) 81
4:23:7 Vostok V, USSR
14–19 Jun 1963
10. = Konstantin P. Feoktistov (38) 16
= Vladimir M. Komarov (37) 16
= Boris B. Yegorov (26) 16
1:0:17 Voskhod 1, USSR
12–13 Oct 1964

▶ Pioneer *message*
Metal plaques on Pioneers 10 and 11 space probes were designed to convey a visual message to extra-terrestrials who might encounter them.

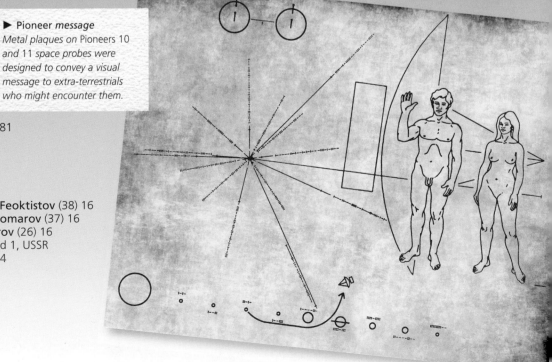

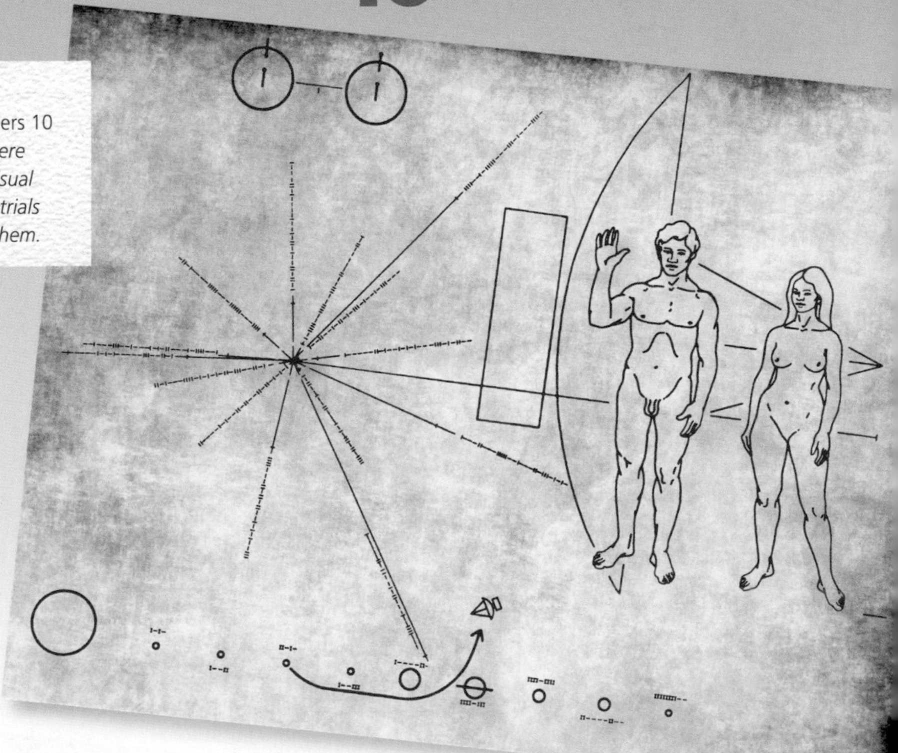

THE 10 **FIRST MOONWALKERS**

	ASTRONAUT	BIRTH DATE	SPACECRAFT	TOTAL EVA* HR:MIN	MISSION DATES
1	Neil A. Armstrong	5 Aug 1930	Apollo 11	2:32	16–24 Jul 1969
2	Edwin E. 'Buzz' Aldrin	20 Jan 1930	Apollo 11	2:15	16–24 Jul 1969
3	Charles Conrad Jr	2 Jun 1930 (d. 8 Jul 1999)	Apollo 12	7:45	14–24 Nov 1969
4	Alan L. Bean	15 Mar 1932	Apollo 12	7:45	14–24 Nov 1969
5	Alan B. Shepard	18 Nov 1923 (d. 21 Jul 1998)	Apollo 14	9:23	31 Jan–9 Feb 1971
6	Edgar D. Mitchell	17 Sep 1930	Apollo 14	9:23	31 Jan–9 Feb 1971
7	David R. Scott	6 Jun 1932	Apollo 15	19:08	26 Jul–7 Aug 1971
8	James B. Irwin	17 Mar 1930 (d. 8 Aug 1991)	Apollo 15	18:35	26 Jul–7 Aug 1971
9	John W. Young	24 Sep 1930	Apollo 16	20:14	16–27 Apr 1972
10	Charles M. Duke Jr	3 Oct 1935	Apollo 16	20:14	16–27 Apr 1972

* Extra-Vehicular Activity – time spent out of the lunar module on the Moon's surface

Six US *Apollo* missions resulted in successful Moon landings (*Apollo 13*, 11–17 April 1970, was aborted after an oxygen tank exploded). During the last of these (*Apollo 17*, 7–19 December 1972), Eugene A. Cernan (b. 14 March 1934) and Harrison H. Schmitt (b. 3 July 1935) became the only other astronauts to date who have walked on the surface of the Moon, both spending a total of 22:04 in EVA. Cernan is noted as the 'Last Man on the Moon'; coincidentally, both he and 'First Man' Neil Armstrong attended the same university – Purdue, Indiana.

▶ *Man on the Moon*
Buzz Aldrin, the second person to set foot on the Moon, accompanied Armstrong in the first moonwalk, for 2 hours 31 minutes 40 seconds.

▲ *Mission badges*
Every NASA mission, including the six Moon landings, had a specially designed badge.

▲ *Apollo 11 crew*
Armstrong (left) and Aldrin (right) were the first to set foot on the Moon. Michael Collins (centre) piloted the Command Module.

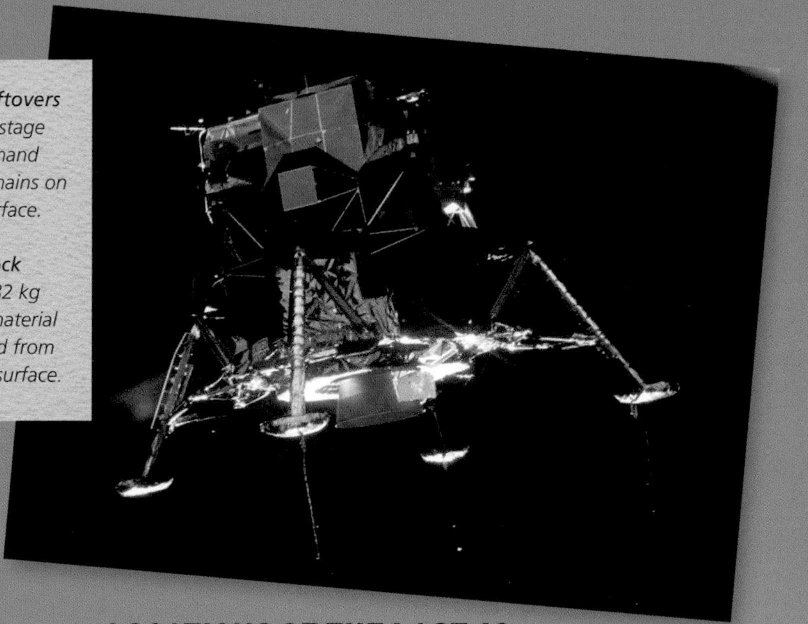

► *Lunar leftovers*
The landing stage of the Command Modules remains on the lunar surface.

◄ *Moon rock*
A total of 382 kg (842 lb) of material was collected from the Moon's surface.

TOP 10 **MOST COMMON ELEMENTS ON THE MOON**

ELEMENT / %

1 Oxygen 40.0 **2** Silicon 19.2 **3** Iron 14.3
4 Calcium 8.0 **5** Titanium 5.9 **6** Aluminium 5.6
7 Magnesium 4.5 **8** Sodium 0.33
9 Potassium 0.14 **10** Chromium 0.002

This list is based on the analysis of the 20.77 kg (45.8 lb) of rock samples brought back to Earth by the crew of the 1969 *Apollo 11* lunar mission. One of the minerals they discovered was named Armalcolite in honour of the three astronauts **Arm**strong, **Al**drin and **Col**lins.

LOCATIONS OF THE LAST 10 APOLLO COMMAND MODULES

Apollo 8
Chicago Museum of Science and Industry, Chicago, Illinois, USA

Apollo 9
San Diego Aerospace Museum, San Diego, California, USA

Apollo 10
Science Museum, London, UK

Apollo 11
The National Air and Space Museum, Washington, DC, USA

Apollo 12
Virginia Air and Space Center, Hampton, Virginia, USA

Apollo 13
Kansas Cosmosphere and Space Center, Hutchinson, Kansas, USA (formerly at Musée de l'Air, Paris, France)

Apollo 14
Astronaut Hall of Fame, Titusville, Florida, USA

Apollo 15
USAF Museum, Wright-Patterson Air Force Base, Dayton, Ohio, USA

Apollo 16
US Space and Rocket Center, Huntsville, Alabama, USA

Apollo 17
NASA Johnson Space Center, Houston, Texas, USA

THE FIRST UNMANNED MOON LANDINGS

The first four Soviet *Luna* and five NASA *Ranger* spacecraft sent to the Moon in 1959–65 were destroyed. *Luna 9*, a 99-kg (218-lb) package of scientific equipment, was the first to make a soft landing and transmit photographic images back to Earth. Subsequent *Luna* missions *16*, *20* and *24* not only landed successfully, but collected soil samples and returned to Earth. *Luna 24*, which returned to Earth on 22 August 1976, was the last-ever soft landing of a spacecraft on the Moon, although others, such as the *SELENE* main orbiter (Japan, 10 June 2009) have ended their missions by impacting on the surface.

Apollo 14 astronaut **Alan B. Shepard** made the first golf shot on the Moon on 6 February 1971 using a 6-iron head attached to a rock-sample collector handle. The head is in the US Golf Association Hall of Fame, New Jersey, but the balls still lie in a lunar bunker. These are not the only evidence of human visits: since there is no wind on the Moon, the astronauts' footprints will be visible for thousands of years.

◄ *Space Ranger*
Ranger *missions relayed photographic data prior to the Moon landings.*

BODIES OF WATER

TOP 10 OCEANS AND SEAS WITH THE GREATEST VOLUME

NAME / APPROX. VOLUME (CU KM/CU MILES)

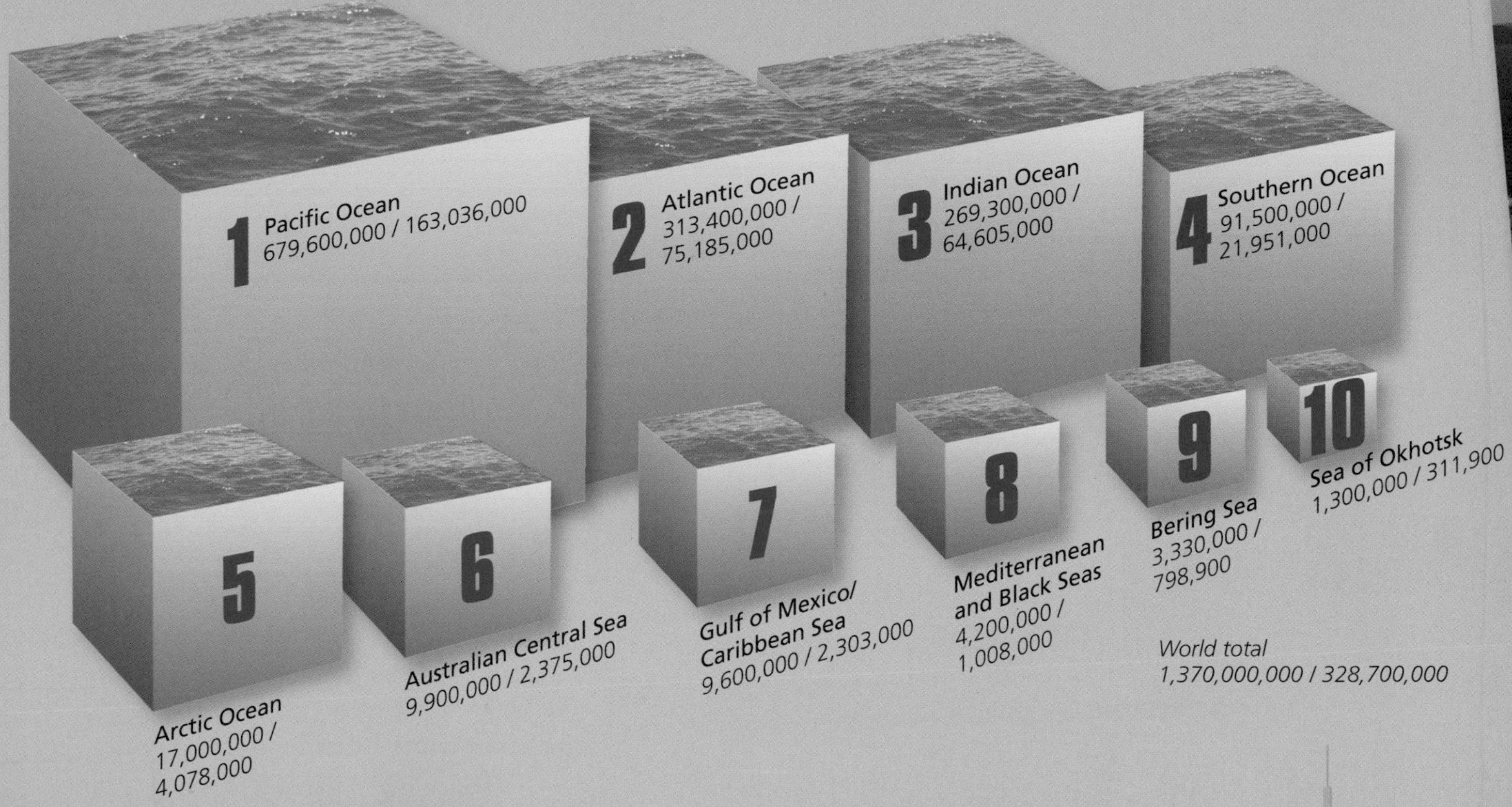

THE 10 SHALLOWEST OCEANS AND SEAS

SEA*/OCEAN	AVERAGE DEPTH M	AVERAGE DEPTH FT
10 Arctic Ocean	1,038.4	3,407
9 Sea of Okhotsk, Pacific Ocean	972.9	3,192
8 Gulf of California, Pacific Ocean	723.9	2,375
7 Red Sea, Indian Ocean	537.6	1,764
6 East China Sea, Indian Ocean	188.9	620
5 Persian Gulf, Indian Ocean	99.9	328
4 North Sea, Atlantic Ocean	93.8	308
3 Hudson Bay, Atlantic Ocean	92.9	305
2 Baltic Sea, Atlantic Ocean	54.8	180
1 Yellow Sea, Pacific Ocean	36.8	121

The depths of the six shallowest seas compared to the Empire State Building

* Excludes landlocked seas

◀ *Gulf of California*
The shallowness of parts of the Gulf make it a haven for kayaking and diving.

The Yellow Sea has a maximum depth of 152 m (500 ft). Its name comes from the colour of mineral deposits from the rivers that discharge into it that would disperse in deeper water. Environmentally unstable, ice fields form during the winter, while shifting sandbanks make it treacherous to shipping.

▲ *Lake Nasser*
Abu Simbel, an important archaeological site, was relocated to high ground before the creation of Nasser, Africa's largest manmade lake.

TOP 10 **LARGEST MANMADE LAKES BY SURFACE AREA**

LAKE	LOCATION	AREA SQ KM	AREA SQ MILES
1 Volta	Ghana	8,502	3,286
2 Smallwood	Canada	6,527	2,520
3 Kujbyshevskoe	Russia	6,450	2,490
4 Kariba	Zimbabwe, Zambia	5,580	2,154
5 Bukhtarma	Kazakhstan	5,490	2,120
6 Bratskoye	Russia	5,470	2,112
7 Nasser	Egypt, Sudan	5,248	2,026
8 Rybinsk	Russia	4,580	1,768
9 Caniapiscau	Canada	4,318	1,667
10 Raúl Leoni (Guri)	Venezuela	4,250	1,641

TOP 10 **FRESHWATER LAKES WITH THE GREATEST VOLUME OF WATER**

LAKE	LOCATION	VOLUME CU KM	VOLUME CU MILES
1 Baikal	Russia	22,995	5,517
2 Tanganyika	Burundi/Tanzania/ Dem. Rep. of Congo/Zambia	18,304	4,391
3 Superior	Canada/USA	12,174	2,921
4 Michigan/Huron	USA/Canada	8,449	2,642
5 Nyasa (Malawi)	Malawi/Mozambique/ Tanzania	6,140	1,473
6 Victoria	Kenya/Tanzania/Uganda	2,518	604
7 Great Bear	Canada	2,258	542
8 Great Slave	Canada	1,771	425
9 Ontario	Canada/USA	1,539	369
10 Ladoga	Russia	903	217

THE 10 **DEEPEST FRESHWATER LAKES**

LAKE / LOCATION / GREATEST DEPTH (M/FT)

10 **Tahoe**
California/Nevada, USA
501 / 1,643

9 **Sarezskoye** (Sarez)
Tajikistan
505 / 1,657

8 **Hornindals**
Norway
514 / 1,686

7 **Toba**
Sumatra, Indonesia
529 / 1,736

6 **Matana**
Celebes, Indonesia
590 / 1,936

5 **Crater**
Oregon, USA
594 / 1,949

4 **Great Slave**
Canada
614 / 2,014

3 **Malawi**
Malawi/Mozambique/Tanzania
706 / 2,316

2 **Tanganyika**
Burundi/Tanzania/
Dem. Rep. of Congo/Zambia
1,471 / 4,826

1 **Baikal**
Russia
1,741 / 5,712

Source: International Lake Environment Committee Foundation – ILEC

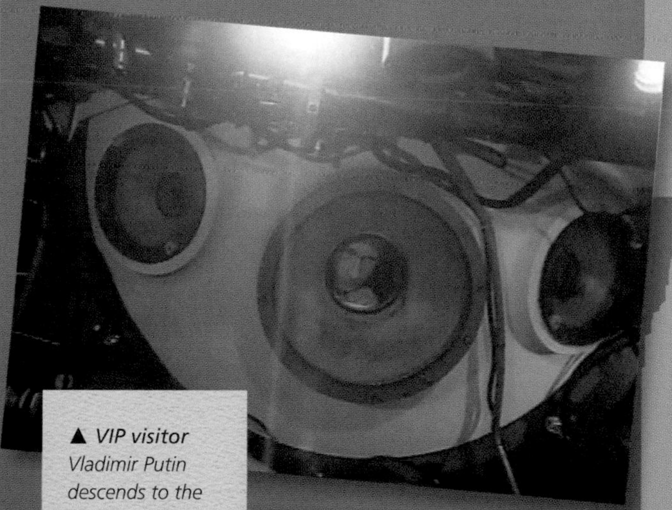

▲ *VIP visitor*
Vladimir Putin descends to the bottom of Lake Baikal in a Mir-2 submarine, 2009.

► *Lake Baikal is 4.5 times deeper than the height of the Empire State Building.*

FLOWING WATER

TOP 10 GREATEST* WATERFALLS

	WATERFALL	COUNTRY	AVERAGE FLOW CU M/SEC	AVERAGE FLOW CU FT/SEC
1	**Inga**	Dem. Rep. of Congo	42,476	1,500,000
2	**Livingstone**	Dem. Rep. of Congo	35,113	1,240,000
3	**Boyoma** (Stanley)	Dem. Rep. of Congo	16,990	600,000
4	**Khône**	Laos	10,783	410,000
5	**Celilo**	USA	5,415	191,215
6	**Salto Pará**	Venezuela	3,540	125,000
7	**Paulo Afonso**	Brazil	2,832	100,000
8	**Niagara** (Horseshoe)	Canada/USA	2,407	85,000
9	**Iguaçu**	Argentina/Brazil	1,746	61,660
10	**Victoria**	Zambia/Zimbabwe	1,088	38,430

* Based on volume of water

With an average flow rate of 13,000 cu m/sec (459,090 cu ft/sec) and a peak of 50,000 cu m/sec (1,765,000 cu ft/sec), the Guaíra, or Salto das Sete Quedas, between Brazil and Paraguay, once occupied 2nd place in this list, and the Urubupungá, with a discharge rate of 2,747 cu m/sec (97,000 cu ft/sec) was in 6th position, but following the completion of the Itaipú dam in 1982, both are now 'lost'.

◄ *Iguaçu Falls*
The rate of flow of the Iguaçu Falls varies from as little as 300 cu m/s in times of drought to a peak of 6,500 cu m/s.

TOP 10 WIDEST WATERFALLS

	WATERFALL / RIVER	COUNTRY	WIDTH M	WIDTH FT
1	**Khône**, Mekong River	Laos	10,783	35,376
2	**Pará**, Rio Caura	Venezuela	5,608	18,400
3	**Livingstone**, Congo River	Congo	4,828	15,840
4	**Celilo**, Columbia River	USA	3,219	10,560
5	**Kongou**, Ivindo River	Gabon	3,200	10,500
6	**Iguaçu**, Rio Iguaçu	Argentina/Brazil	2,700	8,858
7	**Patos e Maribondo**, Rio Grande	Brazil	2,012	6,600
8	**Victoria**, Zambezi River	Zimbabwe/Zambia	1,737	5,700
9	**Boyoma**, Lualaba River	Congo	1,372	4,500
10	**Niagara**, Niagara River	USA/Canada	1,203	3,948

► *Bering glacier*
The longest outside Antarctica, the Bering glacier is retreating as a result of global warming, releasing some 30 cu km of water annually.

▲ *Amazon*
A floating Peruvian village on the Amazon, the world's greatest river system.

TOP 10 LONGEST RIVERS

	RIVER / LOCATION	KM	MILES
1	**Nile** Burundi, Dem. Rep. of Congo, Egypt, Eritrea, Ethiopia, Kenya, Rwanda, Sudan, Tanzania, Uganda	6,650	4,132
2	**Amazon** Bolivia, Brazil, Colombia, Ecuador, Peru, Venezuela	6,400	3,976
3	**Yangtze** (Chang Jiang) China	6,300	3,915
4	**Mississippi-Missouri** USA	6,275	3,899
5	**Yenisei-Angara-Selenga** Mongolia, Russia	5,539	3,441
6	**Huang He** (Yellow) China	5,464	3,395
7	**Ob-Irtysh** China, Kazkhakstan, Russia	5,410	3,362
8	**Congo-Chambeshi** Angola, Burundi Cameroon, Dem. Rep. of Congo, Rep. of Congo, Central African Republic, Rwanda, Tanzania, Zambia	4,700	2,920
9	**Amur-Argun** China, Mongolia, Russia	4,444	2,761
10	**Lena** Russia	4,400	2,734

TOP 10 GREATEST* RIVER SYSTEMS

RIVER SYSTEM	CONTINENT	AVERAGE DISCHARGE AT MOUTH CU M/SEC	CU FT/SEC
1 Amazon	South America	219,000	7,733,912
2 Congo (Zaïre)	Africa	41,800	1,476,153
3 Yangtze (Chang Jiang)	Asia	31,900	1,126,538
4 Orinoco	South America	30,000	1,059,440
5 Paraná	South America	25,700	907,587
6 Yenisei-Angara	Asia	19,600	692,168
7 Brahmaputra (Tsangpo)	Asia	19,200	678,042
8 Lena	Asia	17,100	603,881
9 Madeira-Mamoré	South America	17,000	600,349
10 Mississippi-Missouri	North America	16,200	572,098

* Based on rate of discharge at mouth

TOP 10 LONGEST GLACIERS

GLACIER / LOCATION	LENGTH KM	MILES
1 Lambert Antarctica	400	249
2 Bering Alaska, USA	190	118
3 Beardmore Antarctica	160	99
4 Byrd Antarctica	136	85
5 Nimrod Antarctica	135	84
6 Amundsen Antarctica	128	80
7 Hubbard Alaska, USA	122	76
8 Slessor Antarctica	120	75
9 Denman Antarctica	112	70
10 Recovery Antarctica	100	62

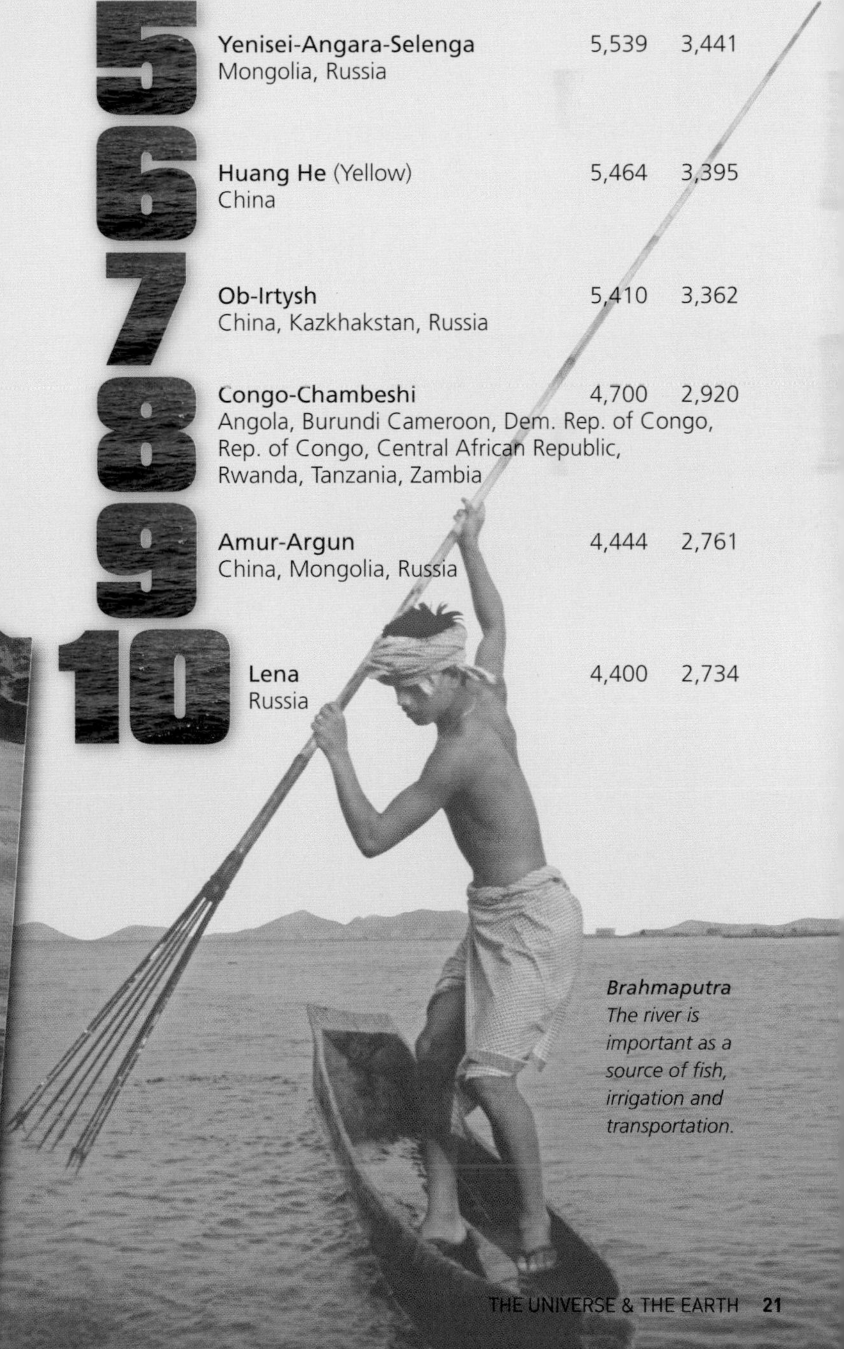

Brahmaputra
The river is important as a source of fish, irrigation and transportation.

ISLANDS

THE 10 SMALLEST ISLAND COUNTRIES

	COUNTRY / LOCATION	AREA SQ KM	SQ MILES
1	**Nauru**, Pacific Ocean	21.2	8.2
2	**Tuvalu**, Pacific Ocean	26.0	10.0
3	**Marshall Islands**, Pacific Ocean	181.3	70.0
4	**St Kitts and Nevis**, Caribbean Sea	261.0	100.8
5	**Maldives**, Indian Ocean	298.0	115.1
6	**Malta**, Mediterranean Sea	316.0	122.0
7	**Grenada**, Caribbean Sea	344.0	132.8
8	**St Vincent and the Grenadines**, Caribbean Sea	389.0	150.2
9	**Barbados**, Caribbean Sea	431.0	166.4
10	**Antigua and Barbuda**, Caribbean Sea	442.6	170.9

TOP 10 HIGHEST ISLANDS

	ISLAND / LOCATION / HIGHEST POINT	HIGHEST ELEVATION M	FT
1	**New Guinea**, Indonesia/Papua New Guinea, Puncak Jaya (Mount Carstensz)	4,884	16,023
2	**Hawaii**, USA, Mauna Kea	4,205	13,795
3	**Borneo**, Indonesia/Malaysia, Mount Kinabalu	4,101	13,454
4	**Taiwan**, China, Jade Mountain (Yu Shan)	3,952	12,965
5	**Sumatra**, Indonesia, Mount Kerinci	3,805	12,480
6	**Ross**, Antarctica, Mount Erebus	3,794	12,447
7	**Honshu**, Japan, Mount Fuji	3,776	12,388
8	**New Zealand**, Aorakim (Mount Cook)	3,755	12,319
9	**Lombok**, Indonesia, Mount Rinjani	3,726	12,224
10	**Tenerife**, Spain, Pico de Teide	3,718	12,198

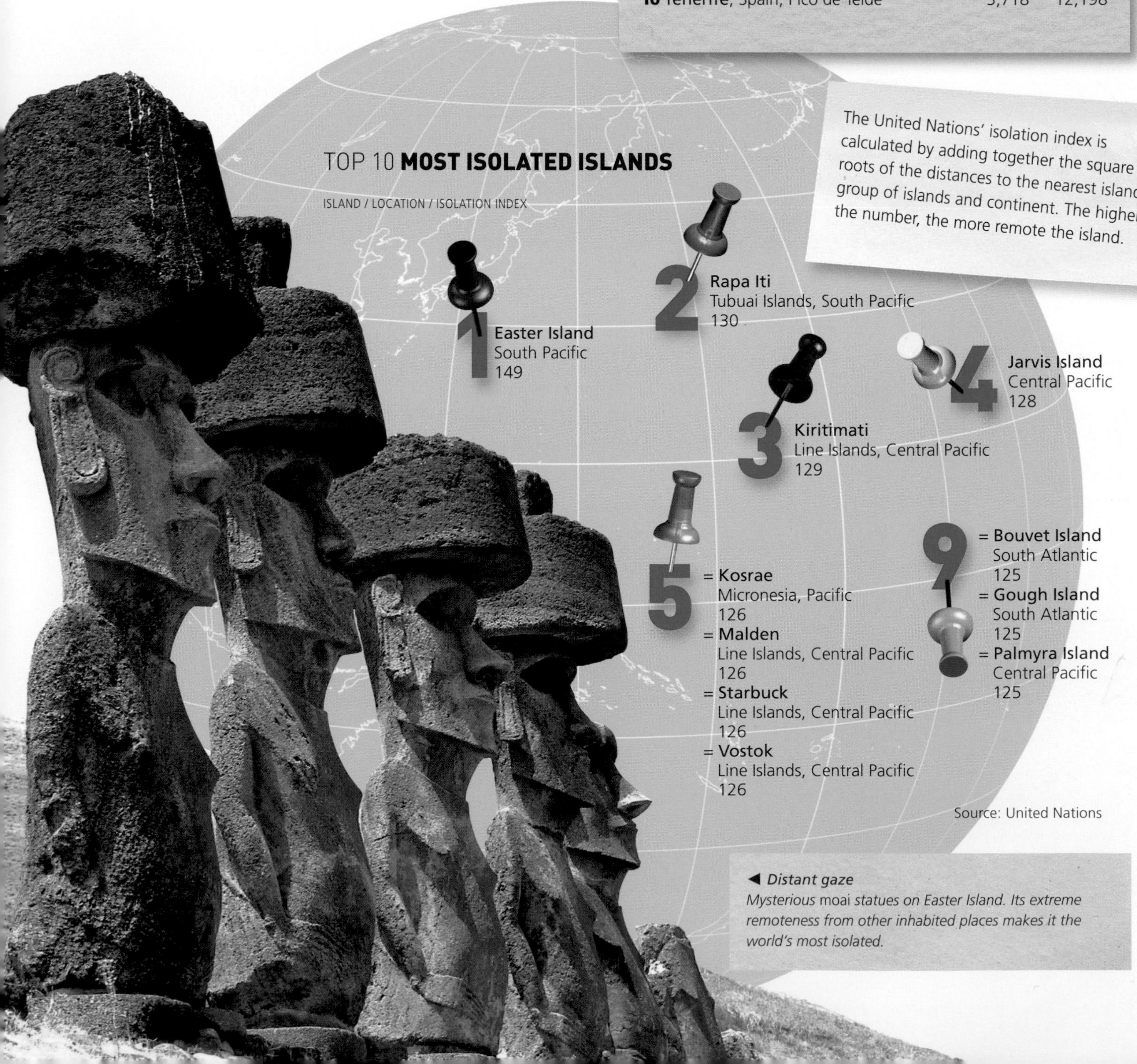

TOP 10 MOST ISOLATED ISLANDS

The United Nations' isolation index is calculated by adding together the square roots of the distances to the nearest island, group of islands and continent. The higher the number, the more remote the island.

ISLAND / LOCATION / ISOLATION INDEX

1 **Easter Island**
South Pacific
149

2 **Rapa Iti**
Tubuai Islands, South Pacific
130

3 **Kiritimati**
Line Islands, Central Pacific
129

4 **Jarvis Island**
Central Pacific
128

5 = **Kosrae**
Micronesia, Pacific
126

= **Malden**
Line Islands, Central Pacific
126

= **Starbuck**
Line Islands, Central Pacific
126

= **Vostok**
Line Islands, Central Pacific
126

9 = **Bouvet Island**
South Atlantic
125

= **Gough Island**
South Atlantic
125

= **Palmyra Island**
Central Pacific
125

Source: United Nations

◄ *Distant gaze*
Mysterious moai statues on Easter Island. Its extreme remoteness from other inhabited places makes it the world's most isolated.

TOP 10 LARGEST ISLANDS

	ISLAND / LOCATION	AREA* SQ KM	SQ MILES
1	**Greenland** (Kalaatdlit Nunaat)	2,175,600	840,004
2	**New Guinea**, Papua New Guinea/ Indonesia	785,753	303,381
3	**Borneo**, Indonesia/Malaysia/Brunei	748,168	288,869
4	**Madagascar**	587,713	226,917
5	**Baffin Island**, Canada	503,944	194,574
6	**Sumatra**, Indonesia	443,065	171,068
7	**Honshu**, Japan	227,413	87,805
8	**Great Britain**	218,077	84,200
9	**Victoria Island**, Canada	217,292	83,897
10	**Ellesmere Island**, Canada	196,236	75,767

* Mainlands, including areas of inland water, but excluding offshore islands

▲ *Exotic island*
Borneo is one of the world's largest islands and one of the most biodiverse, its rainforests supporting exotic plants such as the giant Rafflesia.

Australia is regarded as a continental land mass rather than an island, otherwise it would rank first, at 7,618,493 sq km (2,941,517 sq miles), or 35 times the size of Great Britain.

TOP 10 LARGEST DIVIDED ISLANDS

	ISLAND	DIVIDED BETWEEN	AREA SQ KM	SQ MILES
1	New Guinea	Indonesia/Papua New Guinea	785,753	303,380
2	Borneo	Indonesia/Malaysia/Brunei	748,168	288,869
3	Cuba	Cuba/USA (Guantanamo Bay)	110,861	42,803
4	Ireland	Ireland/UK	81,638	31,520
5	Hispaniola	Dominican Republic/Haiti	73,929	28,544
6	Tierra del Fuego	Chile/Argentina	47,401	18,301
7	Timor	Indonesia/East Timor	28,418	10,972
8	Cyprus	Greece/Turkey	9,234	3,565
9	Sebatik Island	Indonesia/Malaysia	452	174
10	Usedom (Uznan)	Germany/Poland	445	171

While most islands are either countries or parts of larger (usually, though not always, adjacent) countries, there are some that are divided between two or more countries. In some instances this results from or remains the cause of political disputes, as with Ireland and Cyprus, for example. Märket (33,000 sq m/355,209 sq ft), split between Finnish-administered Åland and Sweden, is the world's smallest shared sea island.

▼ *Border patrol*
Until recently, Ireland experienced the political tensions that often characterize divided islands.

MOU[illegible]TAINS & VOLCA[illegible]OES

TOP 10 HIGHEST MOUNTAINS

MOUNTAIN / LOCATION / FIRST ASCENT / TEAM NATIONALITY / HEIGHT* (M/FT)

1	**Everest**, Nepal/China 29 May 1953 British/New Zealand 8,850 / 29,035
2	**K2 (Chogori)**, Pakistan/China 31 Jul 1954, Italian 8,611 / 28,251
3	**Kangchenjunga**, Nepal/India 25 May 1955, British 8,586 / 28,169
4	**Lhotse** Nepal/China 18 May 1956, Swiss 8,516 / 27,940
5	**Makalu I** Nepal/China 15 May 1955, French 8,485 / 27,838
6	**Cho Oyu** Nepal/China 19 Oct 1954, Austrian 8,188 / 26,864
7	**Dhaulagiri I** Nepal 13 May 1960, Swiss/Austrian 8,167 / 26,795
8	**Manaslu I (Kutang I)**, Nepal 9 May 1956, Japanese 8,163 / 26,781
9	**Nanga Parbat (Diamir)**, Pakistan 3 Jul 1953, German/Austrian 8,125 / 26,657
10	**Anapurna I** Nepal 3 Jun 1950, French 8,091 / 26,545

* Height of principal peak; lower peaks of the same mountain are excluded

TOP 10 LONGEST MOUNTAIN RANGES

	RANGE / LOCATION	LENGTH KM	LENGTH MILES
1	**Andes** South America	7,242	4,500
2	**Rocky Mountains** North America	6,035	3,750
3	**Himalayas/Karakoram/ Hundu Kush** Asia	3,862	2,400
4	**Great Dividing Range** Australia	3,621	2,250
5	**Trans-Antarctic Mountains** Antarctica	3,541	2,200
6	**Brazilian East Coast Range** Brazil	3,058	1,900
7	**Sumatran/Javan Range** Sumatra, Java	2,897	1,800
8	**Tien Shan** China	2,253	1,400
9	**Eastern Ghats** India	2,092	1,300
10 =	**Altai** Asia	2,012	1,250
=	**Central New Guinean Range** Papua New Guinea	2,012	1,250
=	**Urals** Russia	2,012	1,250

This Top 10 includes only ranges that are continuous (the Sumatran/Javan Range is divided only by a short interruption between the two islands).

▲ ***Rocky Mountain High***
Running from British Columbia, Canada, to New Mexico, USA, the Rockies rank as one of the world's longest ranges.

▼ ***Peak mountain***
Everest was identified as the world's highest mountain in 1856.

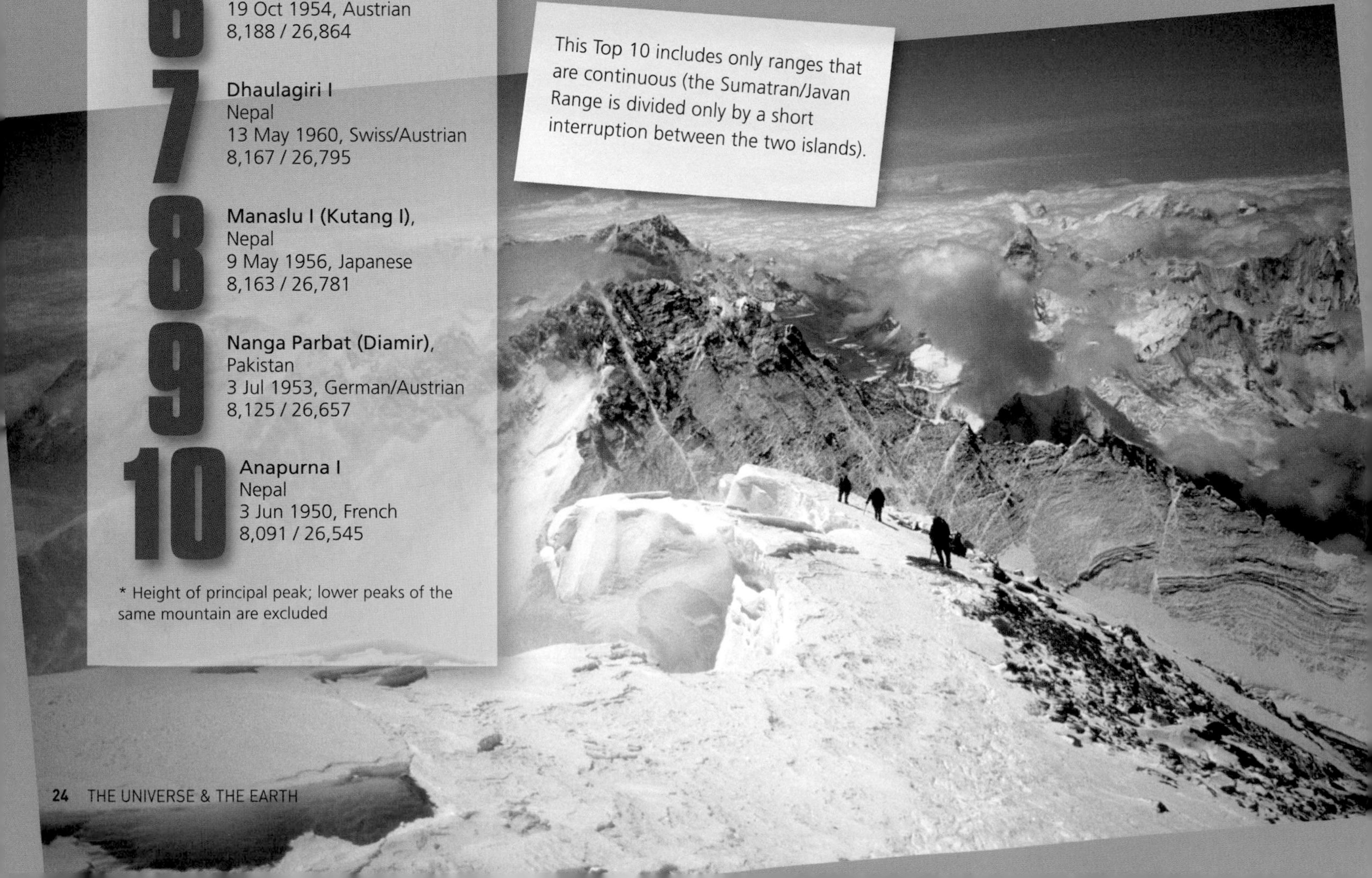

TOP 10 **HIGHEST MOUNTAINS IN EUROPE**

	MOUNTAIN	COUNTRY	HEIGHT* M	FT
1	Mont Blanc	France/Italy	4,807	15,771
2	Monte Rosa	Switzerland	4,634	15,203
3	Zumsteinspitze	Italy/Switzerland	4,564	14,970
4	Signalkuppe	Italy/Switzerland	4,555	14,941
5	Dom	Switzerland	4,545	14,911
6	Liskamm	Italy/Switzerland	4,527	14,853
7	Weisshorn	Switzerland	4,505	14,780
8	Täschorn	Switzerland	4,491	14,733
9	Matterhorn	Italy/Switzerland	4,477	14,688
10	Mont Maudit	France/Italy	4,466	14,649

* Height of principal peak; lower peaks of the same mountain are excluded

All 10 of Europe's highest mountains are in the Alps; there are, however, at least 15 mountains in the Caucasus (the mountain range that straddles Europe and Asia) that are taller than Mont Blanc. The highest of them, the west peak of Mount Elbrus, measures 5,642 m (18,510 ft).

DECADE VOLCANOS

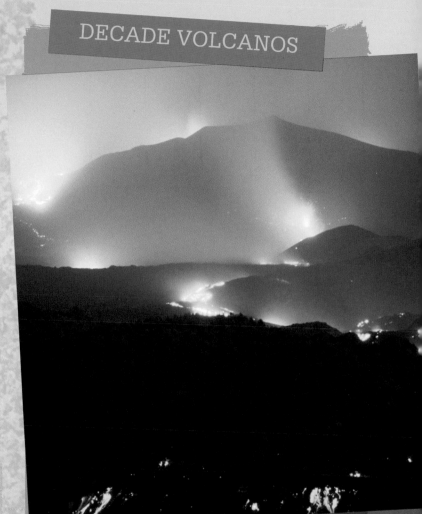

► *Mount Etna*
One of the volcanoes on the Decade Volcano list, Mount Etna, Sicily, poses an ongoing threat to the local population.

The Decade Volcano programme of the International Association of Volcanology and Chemistry of the Earth's Interior has nominated 16 active volcanoes as of particular importance. The programme studies the volcanoes on the list, assesses the level of risk posed by their eruption and formulates plans for action in the event of such occurrences.

Avachinsky-Koryaksky, Kamchatka, Russia
Nevado de Colima, Mexico
Mount Etna, Sicily, Italy
Galeras, Nariño, Colombia
Mauna Loa, Hawaii, USA
Mount Merapi, Indonesia
Mount Nyiragongo, Dem. Rep. of Congo
Mount Rainier, Washington, USA
Sakurajima, Japan
Santamaria/Santiaguito, Guatemala
Santorini, Greece
Taal Volcano, Luzon, Philippines
Teide, Canary Islands, Spain
Ulawun, Papua New Guinea
Mount Unzen, Japan
Vesuvius, Italy

TOP 10 **HIGHEST ACTIVE VOLCANOES***

	VOLCANO / LOCATION	LAST ERUPTION	HEIGHT M	FT
1	**Tupungatito**, Chile/Argentina	1987	6,570	21,555
2	**Pular**, Chile	1990	6,233	20,449
3	**San Pedro**, Chile	1960	6,145	20,161
4	**Aracar**, Argentina	1993	6,082	19,954
5	**Guallatiri**, Chile	1985	6,071	19,918
6	**Tacora**, Chile	1937	5,980	19,619
7	**Sabancaya**, Peru	2003	5,967	19,576
8	**Cotopaxi**, Ecuador	1942	5,911	19,393
9	**Putana**, Chile	1972	5,890	19,324
10	**San Jose**, Chile	1960	5,856	19,213

* Eruption during past 100 years

LAND FEATURES

THE 10 DEEPEST DEPRESSIONS

	DEPRESSION / LOCATION	MAX. DEPTH BELOW SEA LEVEL M	FT
1	**Dead Sea**, Israel/Jordan	400	1,312
2	**Sea of Galilee**, Israel	209	686
3	**Lake Assal**, Djibouti	155	511
4	**Turfan Depression**, China	154	505
5	**Qattâra Depression**, Egypt	133	436
6	**Mangyshlak Peninsula**, Kazakhstan	132	433
7	**Danakil (Afar) Depression**, Ethiopia	117	383
8	**Laguna del Carbón**, Argentina	105	344
9	**Death Valley**, California, USA	86	282
10	**Salton Sink**, California, USA	72	235

TOP 10 LARGEST DESERTS

	DESERT / LOCATION	APPROX. AREA SQ KM	SQ MILES
1	**Sahara**, northern Africa	9,100,000	3,513,530
2	**Arabian**, south-west Asia	2,330,000	899,618
3	**Gobi**, central Asia	1,295,000	500,002
4	**Patagonian**, Argentina/Chile	673,000	259,847
5	**Great Basin**, USA	492,000	189,962
6	**Great Victoria**, Australia	424,000	163,707
7	**Chihuahuan**, Mexico/USA	362,600	140,000
8	**Great Sandy**, Australia	360,000	138,997
9	**Karakum**, Turkmenistan	350,000	135,136
10	**Sonoran**, Mexico/USA	311,000	120,078

▲ ***Salty sea***
The salinity of the low-lying Dead Sea – 8.6 times that of the average ocean – means that bathers are unusually buoyant.

TOP 10 LARGEST METEORITE CRATERS

	CRATER / LOCATION	DIAMETER KM	MILES
1	**Vredefort**, South Africa	300	186
2	**Sudbury**, Ontario, Canada	250	155
3	**Chicxulub**, Yucatan, Mexico	170	107
4	=**Manicougan**, Quebec, Canada	100	62
	=**Popigai**, Russia	100	62
6	=**Acraman**, Australia	90	56
	=**Chesapeake Bay**, Virginia, USA	90	56
8	**Puchezh-Katunki**, Russia	80	50
9	**Morokweng**, South Africa	70	43
10	**Kara**, Russia	65	40

Source: Earth Impact Database, Planetary and Space Science Centre, University of New Brunswick

CANYONS AND GORGES

According to how it is defined, there are various candidates for the title of 'largest' canyon or gorge. Based on the greatest difference between the height of the adjacent mountains and the river valley, the Kali Gandaki Gorge, at 5,500 to 6,800 m (18,044 to 22,231 ft), is the deepest. The Yarlung Zangbo Grand Canyon, China, 496 km (308 miles) long and 5,382 m (17,657 ft) at its deepest. The Grand Canyon, Arizona, is less deep, but is as much as 29 km (18 miles) wide and 446 km (277 miles) long, while the Copper Canyon, Mexico, is a series of six canyons that in total is longer and deeper than the Grand Canyon.

Kali Gorge
By some measures, Kali Gandaki Gorge, Nepal, is the world's deepest.

THE 10 **DEEPEST CAVES**

	CAVE SYSTEM / LOCATION	DEPTH M	FT
1	**Krubera (Voronja)**, Georgia	2,191	7,188
2	**Illyuzia-Mezhonnogo-Snezhnaya**, Georgia	1,753	5,751
3	**Lamprechtsofen Vogelschacht Weg Schacht**, Austria	1,632	5,354
4	**Gouffre Mirolda**, France	1,626	5,335
5	**Réseau Jean Bernard**, France	1,602	5,256
6	**Torca del Cerro del Cuevon/ Torca de las Saxifragas**, Spain	1,589	5,213
7	**Sarma**, Georgia	1,543	5,062
8	**Shakta Vjacheslav Pantjukhina**, Georgia	1,508	4,948
9	**Sima de la Conisa/Torca Magali**, Spain	1,507	4,944
10	**Cehi 2**, Slovenia	1,502	4,928

In 2001 cave explorers discovered a branch of the Voronja, or 'Crow's Cave', Georgia, and established its depth at 1,710 m (5,610 ft). Subsequent penetrations have extended its known depth as equivalent to seven times the height of the Eiffel Tower.

▲ ***Mammoth Cave***
Discovered in 1797, a National Park (1941) and World Heritage site (1981), the Mammoth Cave system is the world's longest.

TOP 10 **LONGEST CAVES**

CAVE / LOCATION / TOTAL KNOWN LENGTH (KM/MILES)

1 **Mammoth Cave System**
Kentucky, USA
590.6 / 367

2 **Jewel Cave**
South Dakota, USA
233.1 / 145

3 **Optimisticeskaja**
Ukraine
230.1 / 143

4 **Wind Cave**
South Dakota, USA
212.5 / 132

5 **Lechuguilla Cave**
New Mexico, USA
203.6 / 127

6 **Hölloch**
Switzerland
195.9 / 122

7 = **Fisher Ridge System**
Kentucky, USA
180.0 / 112

= **Sistema Ox Bel Ha***
Mexico
180.0 / 112

9 **Sistema Sac Actun***
Mexico
175.7 / 109

10 **Siebenhengste-hohgant**
Switzerland
171.5 / 107

* Underwater cave

WEATHER WISE

TOP 10 HOTTEST PLACES

	LOCATION*	HIGHEST TEMPERATURE °C	°F
1	**Al'Azīzīyah**, Libya	58.0	136.4
2	**Greenland Ranch**, Death Valley, USA	56.7	134.0
3	=**Ghudamis**, Libya	55.0	131.0
	=**Kebili**, Tunisia	55.0	131.0
5	**Tombouctou**, Mali	54.5	130.1
6	=**Araouane**, Mali	54.4	130.0
	=**Mammoth Tank**#, California, USA	54.4	130.0
8	**Tirat Tavi**, Israel	54.0	129.0
9	**Ahwāz**, Iran	53.5	128.3
10	**Agha Jārī**, Iran	53.3	128.0

* Maximum of two places per country listed
# Former weather station

TOP 10 SUNNIEST PLACES*

	LOCATION#	% OF MAX. POSSIBLE	AVERAGE ANNUAL HOURS SUNSHINE
1	**Yuma**, Arizona, USA	91	4,127
2	**Phoenix**, Arizona, USA	90	4,041
3	**Wadi Halfa**, Sudan	89	3,964
4	**Bordj Omar Driss**, Algeria	88	3,899
5	**Keetmanshoop**, Namibia	88	3,876
6	**Aoulef**, Algeria	86	3,784
7	**Upington**, South Africa	86	3,766
8	**Atbara**, Sudan	85	3,739
9	**Mariental**, Namibia	84	3,707
10	**Bilma**, Niger	84	3,699

* Highest yearly sunshine total, averaged over a long period of years
# Maximum of two places per country listed

Source: Philip Eden

▲ *Dakhla Oasis*
Despite the extreme aridity, the Oasis survives by drawing on underground water.

TOP 10 PLACES WITH THE FEWEST RAINY DAYS

	LOCATION*	NO. OF RAINY DAYS#
1	**Arica**, Chile	1 day every 6 years
2	**Asyût**, Egypt	1 day every 5 years
3	**Dakhla Oasis**, Egypt	1 day every 4 years
4	**Al'Kufrah**, Libya	1 day every 2 years
5	=**Bender Qaasim**, Somalia	1 day per year
	=**Wadi Halfa**, Sudan	1 day per year
7	**Iquique**, Chile	2 days per year
8	=**Dongola**, Sudan	3 days per year
	=**Faya-Largeau**, Chad	3 days per year
	=**Masirāh Island**, Oman	3 days per year

* Maximum of two places per country listed
# Lowest number of days with rain per year, averaged over a long period of years

Source: Philip Eden

◀ *Mount Waialeale*
Rain falls on the Hawaiian volcano on 92 per cent of the days of the year, an average equivalent to the total height of 6.5 adults.

TOP 10 **PLACES WITH THE MOST RAINY DAYS**

LOCATION*	RAINY DAYS PER ANNUM#
1 Waialeale, Hawaii, USA	335
2 Marion Island, South Africa	312
3 Pohnpei, Federated States of Micronesia	311
4 Andagoya, Colombia	306
5 Macquarie Island, Australia	299
6 Gough Island, Tristan da Cunha group, South Atlantic	291
7 Palau, Federated States of Micronesia	286
8 Heard Island, Australia	279
9 Camp Jacob, Guadeloupe	274
10 Atu Nau, Alaska, USA	268

* Maximum of two places per country listed
# Annual rainfall total, averaged over a long period of years
Source: Philip Eden

TOP 10 **WETTEST PLACES – AVERAGE**

	LOCATION*	AVERAGE ANUAL RAINFALL# MM	IN
1	**Cherrapunji**, India	12,649	498.0
2	**Mawsynram**, India	11,872	467.4
3	**Waialeale**, Hawaii, USA	11,455	451.0
4	**Debundscha**, Cameroon	10,277	404.6
5	**Quibdó**, Colombia	8,989	353.9
6	**Bellenden Ker Range**, Australia	8,636	340.0
7	**Andagoya**, Colombia	7,137	281.0
8	**Henderson Lake**, British Columbia, Canada	6,502	256.0
9	**Kikori**, Papua New Guinea	5,916	232.9
10	**Tavoy**, Myanmar	5,451	214.6

* Maximum of two places per country listed
# Annual rainfall total, averaged over a long period of years
Source: Philip Eden

TOP 10 **MOST INTENSE DOWNPOURS***

	LOCATION	RAINFALL MM	IN	TIME PERIOD
1	**Unionville**, Maryland, USA	31	1.23	1 minute
2	**Füssen**, Germany	126	4.96	8 minutes
3	**Plumb Point**, Jamaica	198	7.80	15 minutes
4	**Curtea De Arges**, Romania	206	8.10	20 minutes
5	**Holt**, Montana, USA	305	12.0	1 hour
6	**Belouve**, Réunion	1,346	53.0	12 hours
7	**Chilaos**, Réunion	1,870	73.6	24 hours
8	**Chilaos**, Réunion	2,489	98.0	2 days
9	**Cherrapunji**, India	9,296	366.0	1 month
10	**Cherrapunji**, India	22,454	884	6 months

* Highest rainfall total recorded in selected time periods
Source: Philip Eden

THE 10 WORST VOLCANIC ERUPTIONS

	LOCATION	DATE	ESTIMATED NO. KILLED
1	Tambora, Indonesia	5–12 Apr 1815	92,000

The cataclysmic eruption of Tambora on the island of Sumbawa killed about 10,000 islanders immediately, with a further 82,000 dying subsequently from disease and famine resulting from crops being destroyed. An estimated 1.7 million tonnes of ash was hurled into the atmosphere.

2	Krakatoa, Sumatra/Java	26–27 Aug 1883	36,380

After a series of eruptions over the course of several days, the uninhabited island of Krakatoa exploded with what may have been the biggest bang ever heard by humans, audible up to 4,800 km (3,000 miles) away.

3	Mont Pelée, Martinique	8 May 1902	27,000

After lying dormant for centuries, Mont Pelée began to erupt in April 1902. Assured that there was no danger, the residents of the main city, St Pierre, stayed in their homes and were there when, at 7.30 a.m. on 8 May, the volcano burst apart.

4	Nevado del Ruiz, Colombia	13 Nov 1985	22,940

The Andean volcano gave warning signs of erupting, but by the time it was decided to evacuate the local inhabitants, it was too late.

5	Mount Etna, Sicily	11 Mar 1669	<20,000

Europe's largest volcano (3,280 m/10,760 ft) has erupted frequently, but the worst instance occurred in 1669, when the lava flow engulfed the town of Catania, according to some accounts killing as many as 20,000.

6	Mount Etna, Sicily	1169	>15,000

Large numbers died in Catania cathedral, where they believed they would be safe, and more were killed when a tsunami caused by the eruption hit the port of Messina.

7	Unzen, Japan	1 Apr 1792	14,300

During a period of intense volcanic activity in the area, the island of Unzen (or Unsen) completely disappeared, killing all its inhabitants.

8	Laki, Iceland	Jan–Jun 1783	9,350

Iceland is one the most volcanically active places on Earth, but being sparsely populated, eruptions seldom result in major loss of life. The worst exception occurred at the Laki volcanic ridge, culminating on 11 June with the largest ever recorded lava flow.

9	Kelut, Indonesia	19 May 1919	5,110

Dormant since 1901, Kelut erupted without warning, ejecting a crater lake that killed inhabitants by drowning or in resultant mudslides. The volcano remains active, erupting as recently as 2007.

10	Galunggung, Indonesia	8 Oct 1882	4,011

Galunggung erupted suddenly, spewing boiling mud, burning sulphur, ash and rocks before finally exploding, destroying a total of 114 villages. A further eruption in 1982 killed 68 people.

THE 10 WORST FAMINES

	COUNTRY	YEAR(S)	ESTIMATED DEATHS
1	China	1958–61	36,000,000
2	China	1907	24,000,000
3	India	1896–1902	19,000,000
4	India	1769–71	15,000,000
5	China	1876–79	13,000,000
6	India	1876–79	10,000,000
7	Europe	1315–17	7,500,000
8	USSR	1932–33	6,000,000
9	= USSR	1921–22	5,000,000
	= China	1936	5,000,000

▼ *Mont Pelée*
The 1902 eruption of Mont Pelée, Martinique, annihilated St Pierre, killing all but two inhabitants, along with the passengers and crew of ships moored in its port.

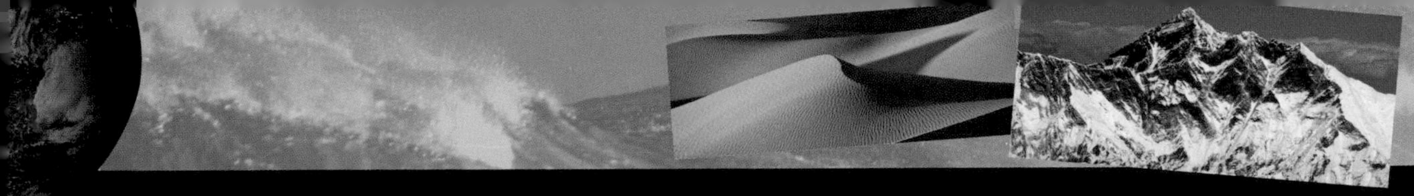

THE 10 **WORST EARTHQUAKES**

	LOCATION	DATE	ESTIMATED NO. KILLED
1	**Near East/Mediterranean**	20 May 1202	1,100,000
2	**Shenshi**, China	2 Feb 1556	820,000
3	**Calcutta**, India	11 Oct 1737	300,000
4	**Antioch**, Syria	20 May 526	250,000
5	**Tang-shan**, China	28 Jul 1976	242,419
6	**Port-au-Prince**, Japan	12 Jan 2010	230,000
7	**Nan-Shan**, China	22 May 1927	200,000
8	**Yeddo**, Japan	30 Dec 1703	190,000
9	**Kansu**, China	16 Dec 1920	180,000
10	**Messina**, Italy	28 Dec 1908	160,000

There are some discrepancies between the 'official' death tolls in many of the world's worst earthquakes and the estimates of other authorities: a figure of 750,000 is sometimes quoted for the Tang-shan earthquake of 1976. Several other earthquakes in China and Turkey resulted in the deaths of 100,000 or more.

THE 10 **WORST AVALANCHES AND LANDSLIDES***

	LOCATION	INCIDENT	DATE	ESTIMATED NO. KILLED
1	**Alps**, Italy	Avalanche	Oct 218 BC	18,000
2	**Yungay**, Peru	Landslide	31 May 1970	17,500
3	**Marmolada**, Italian Alps	Avalanche	13 Dec 1916	10,000
4	**Huarás**, Peru	Avalanche	13 Dec 1941	5,000
5	**Nevada Huascaran**, Peru	Avalanche	10 Jan 1962	3,500
6	**Chiavenna**, Italy	Landslide	4 Sep 1618	2,427
7	**Plurs**, Switzerland	Avalanche	4 Sep 1618	1,496
8	**Goldau Valley**, Switzerland	Landslide	2 Sep 1806	800
9	**Medellin**, Colombia	Landslide	27 Sep 1987	683
10	**Chungar**, Peru	Avalanche	19 Mar 1971	600

* Excluding those where most deaths resulted from flooding, earthquakes, volcanoes, etc., associated with landslides

This list is headed by the catastrophe that befell Carthaginian troops under Hannibal as they descended the Alps, probably in the region of the Col de la Traversette, a pass between France and Italy, when 18,000 men, 2,000 horses and a number of elephants fell victim to a series of avalanches on a single day.

▼ *Kobe earthquake*
The casualty figures resulting from the earthquake that struck Kobe, Japan, at 5.46 a.m. on 17 January 1995 were exceptionally precisely monitored by the rescue authorities, indicating something of the severity of a quake affecting a densely populated urban area.

2

LIFE ON EARTH

UNITED NATIONS INTERNATIONAL YEAR OF FORESTS

As a result of a UN Resolution in 2006, the year 2011 has been designated International Year of Forests. A series of events in the world's forests – including conferences, tree-planting days and exhibitions – will be staged to increase awareness, promote global action of and reinforce sustainable forest management and development, and conserve and protect the whole range of Earth's forests for the benefit of current and future generations. Forests are economically important directly or indirectly in supporting up to a quarter of the world's population and are the habitat of two-thirds of the world's species, while deforestation is considered a major cause of global warming.

◀ ***Battle of the giants***
Although Tyrannosaurus rex (12.8 m/42 ft and 6.8 tonnes) is the best-known carnivorous dinosaur, another Cretaceous monster, Spinosaurus (18 m/59 ft and 9 tonnes), was larger.

TOP 10 **LONGEST DINOSAURS EVER DISCOVERED**

	NAME	ESTIMATED LENGTH (M)
1	Puertasaurus	35–40
2	Sauroposeidon	34
3	Supersaurus	33–34
4	Bruhathkayosaurus	28–34
5	=Hudiesaurus	30
	=Turiasaurus	30
7	Giraffatitan	25–30
8	=Argyrosaurus	20–30
	=Diplodocus	20–30
10	Argentinosaurus	22–26

1 Puertasaurus — 35–40
Provisional estimates by palaeontologist Fernando Novas place this as the longest dinosaur yet discovered.

2 Sauroposeidon — 34
It has been estimated that this creature was probably the tallest ever to walk on Earth, able to extend its neck to 18 m (60 ft).

3 Supersaurus — 33–34
Claims of a length of up to 40 m (130 ft) have been made by some authorities.

4 Bruhathkayosaurus — 28–34
As with claims of its record-breaking weight, those of a length of up to 44 m (145 ft) remain questionable.

5 =Hudiesaurus — 30
Although known only from incomplete remains found in China, it may have been one of the longest of all sauropods.

=Turiasaurus — 30
This long sauropod was named after Turia, the Latin name of Teruel, Spain, where it was found.

7 Giraffatitan — 25–30
This lightly built but long dinosaur was found in Tanzania. A skeleton in the Humboldt Museum, Berlin, is the longest dinosaur on display.

8 =Argyrosaurus — 20–30
This dinosaur from the late Cretaceous period is believed to have stood 8 m (26 ft) tall.

=Diplodocus — 20–30
As it was long and thin, Diplodocus was a relative lightweight in the dinosaur world. It was also probably one of the most stupid dinosaurs, having the smallest brain in relation to its body size. Diplodocus was given its name (which means 'double beam') in 1878 by US palaeontologist Othniel C. Marsh.

10 Argentinosaurus — 22–26
Estimates of the length of Argentinosaurus vary, some earlier claims putting it at up to 35 m (110 ft).

THE 10 **SMALLEST DINOSAURS**

	DINOSAUR	MAX. SIZE CM	IN
1	Micropachycephalosaurus	50	20
2	Saltopus	59	23
3	=Fruitadens	60	24
	=Microceratops	60	24
	=Yandangornis	60	24
6	Bambiraptor	69	27
7	Microraptor	83	33
8	Lesothosaurus	90	35
9	=Sinosauropteryx	98	39
	=Wannanosaurus	99	39

Micropachycephalosaurus is ironically the longest name for the smallest dinosaur. Discovered in Argentina, Mussaurus (meaning 'mouse lizard') is the smallest complete dinosaur skeleton found, but all known specimens are of infants.

◀ ***Microraptor***
Among the smallest known dinosaurs, chicken-sized Microraptor had feathered wings and is believed to have been capable of gliding flight.

▼ ***Diplodocus***
Once considered the longest of all dinosaurs, Diplodocus has been overtaken by new discoveries.

TOP 10 **HEAVIEST DINOSAURS EVER DISCOVERED**

NAME	ESTIMATED WEIGHT (TONNES)
1 Bruhathkayosaurus	126
2 Amphicoelias	122
3 Puertasaurus	80–100
4 Argentinosaurus	60–88
5 Argyrosaurus	80
6 Antarctosaurus	69
7 Sauroposeidon	50–60
8 Paralititan	59
9 Turiasaurus	40–48
10 Supersaurus	35–40

1 Bruhathkayosaurus — 126
Fossil remains of this dinosaur were found in southern India. Some authorities have estimated it as having weighed as much as 220 tonnes, greater than that of a blue whale, but such claims have been questioned.

2 Amphicoelias — 122
Its massive size, with a length of some 25 m (82 ft) has been extrapolated from vertebrae fragments discovered in Colorado in 1877, but since lost.

3 Puertasaurus — 80–100
Its huge size has been estimated from partial remains found in Patagonia in 2001.

4 Argentinosaurus — 60–88
An Argentinean farmer discovered a 1.8 m (6 ft) bone in 1988. It was found to be the shinbone of a previously unknown dinosaur, which was given the name Argentinosaurus.

5 Argyrosaurus — 80
This South American dinosaur's name means 'silver lizard'.

6 Antarctosaurus — 69
This name, which means 'southern lizard', was coined in 1929 by German palaeontologist Friedrich von Huene. The creature's thigh bone alone measures 2.3 m (7 ft 6 in) and a total length of 18 m (60 ft) has been estimated. Some authorities have put its weight as high as 80 tonnes.

7 Sauroposeidon — 50–60
Known only from vertebrae discovered in Oklahoma in 1994, its name means 'earthquake lizard-god'.

8 Paralititan — 59
Remains discovered in 2001 in the Sahara Desert in Egypt suggest that it was a giant plant-eater.

9 Turiasaurus — 40–48
The largest dinosaur yet discovered in Europe, remains of Turiasaurus were unearthed in Spain in 2003.

10 Supersaurus — 35–40
Fragments of Supersaurus were unearthed in Colorado in 1972. Another more complete specimen, known as 'Jimbo', has been discovered in Wyoming and is undergoing examination.

Weights and lengths of dinosaurs have often been estimated from only a few surviving fossilized bones, and there is much dispute even among experts about these. This Top 10 is based on the most reliable recent evidence and indicates the probable ranges, but as more and more information is assembled, these are undergoing constant revision. Some dinosaurs, such as Diplodocus, had squat bodies but extended necks, which made them extremely long but not necessarily immensely heavy.

◀ ***Bruhathkayosaurus***
Although only partial remains have been discovered, it is claimed to be the largest of all dinosaurs. Even the lower end of the size estimates put its weight at greater than that of a Boeing 757 airliner.

E DANGERED ANI ALS

▲ *Red List*
Found in India and adjoining countries, the red panda is on the IUCN's Red List.

TOP 10 **COUNTRIES WITH THE MOST THREATENED MAMMAL SPECIES**

COUNTRY / TOTAL NO. OF THREATENED MAMMALS

1	Indonesia	185
2	Mexico	101
3	India	96
4	Brazil	82
5	China	74
6	Malaysia	70
7	Madagascar	63
8	Thailand	57
9	Australia	55
10	Vietnam	54
	UK	*5*

Source (all lists): International Union for Conservation of Nature, *2009 Red List of Threatened Species*

TOP 10 **COUNTRIES WITH THE MOST THREATENED BIRD SPECIES**

COUNTRY / TOTAL NO. OF THREATENED BIRDS

1	Brazil	124
2	Indonesia	114
3	Peru	94
4	Colombia	90
5	China	82
6	India	75
7	USA	74
8	Ecuador	71
9	New Zealand	69
10	Philippines	67
	UK	*2*

▶ *Iguana*
The Galapagos marine iguana is listed among Ecuador's vulnerable animals.

TOP 10 **COUNTRIES WITH THE MOST THREATENED REPTILE AND AMPHIBIAN SPECIES**

			THREATENED	
	COUNTRY	REPTILES	AMPHIBIANS	TOTAL
1	Mexico	95	211	306
2	Colombia	15	211	226
3	Ecuador	11	171	182
4	China	29	87	116
5	Peru	6	97	103
6	India	25	65	90
7	USA	32	56	88
8	=Australia	40	47	87
	=Madagascar	20	67	87
10	Malaysia	21	47	68
	UK	*0*	*0*	*0*

The IUCN Red List system classifies the degree of threat posed to wildlife on a sliding scale from Vulnerable (high risk of extinction in the wild) through Endangered (very high risk of extinction in the wild), to Critically Endangered (facing an extremely high risk of extinction in the wild), with mammals in these countries under threat in any of these categories.

▲ *Danger zone*
Once common in China and neighbouring countries, poaching and habitat loss have caused the snow leopard population, now classed as 'endangered', to decline to an estimated 2,500.

◀ *Under threat*
Among Brazil's 124 threatened bird species, the harpy eagle is found only in remote parts of the Amazon basin.

TOP 10 **COUNTRIES WITH THE MOST THREATENED ANIMAL SPECIES***

	COUNTRY	MAMMALS	BIRDS	REPTILES	AMPHIBIANS	FISH	INVERTEBRATES	TOTAL
1	USA	37	74	32	56	175	585	959
2	Australia	55	49	40	47	96	462	749
3	Indonesia	185	114	27	32	138	244	740
4	Mexico	101	55	95	211	127	63	652
5	Philippines	39	67	35	48	63	213	465
6	India	96	75	25	65	64	115	440
7	Colombia	52	90	15	211	37	30	435
8	China	74	82	29	87	91	32	395
9	Brazil	82	124	22	30	80	45	383
10	Ecuador	43	71	11	171	18	62	376
	UK	*5*	*2*	*0*	*0*	*41*	*10*	*58*

* Identified by the IUCN as Critically Endangered, Endangered or Vulnerable

THE 10 **MOST THREATENED SPECIES OF ANIMAL**

CLASS / SPECIES EVALUATED / SPECIES THREATENED*

1. Amphibians 6,285 / 1,895
2. Fish 4,443 / 1,414
3. Birds 9,998 / 1,223
4. Mammals 5,490 / 1,142
5. Molluscs 2,306 / 1,036
6. Insects 2,619 / 711
7. Crustaceans 1,735 / 606
8. Reptiles 1,677 / 469
9. Corals 856 / 235
10. Arachnids 32 / 18

Total (including classes not in Top 10): 35,508 / 8,782

* Identified by the IUCN as Critically Endangered, Endangered or Vulnerable

► *Red eye*
Although the red-eyed tree frog of Central America is not considered endangered, some 1,895 amphibian species are regarded as threatened.

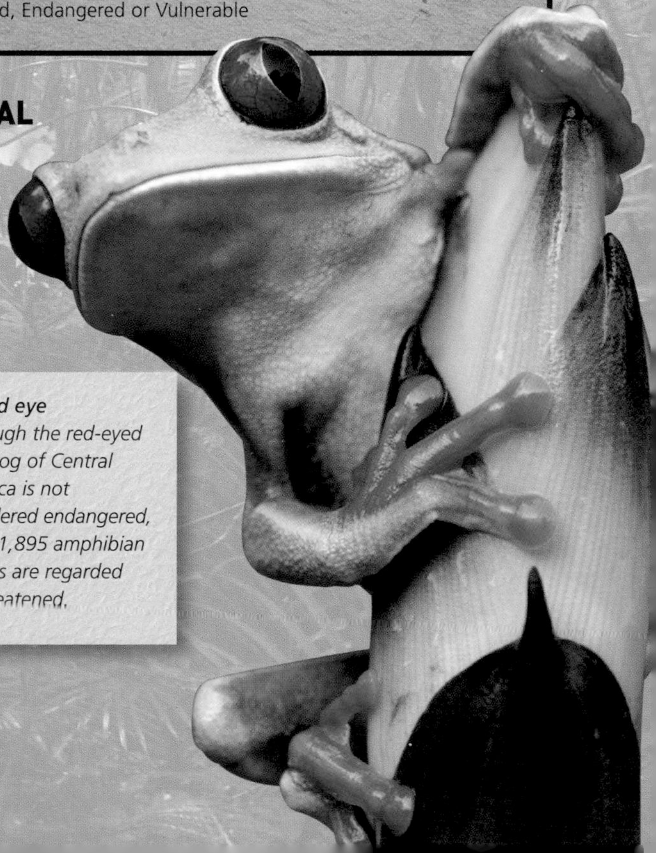

Land Animal Giants

Hippopotamus

White rhinoceros

American buffalo

TOP 10 **HEAVIEST LAND MAMMALS**

MAMMAL* / SCIENTIFIC NAME	LENGTH M	LENGTH FT	WEIGHT KG	WEIGHT LB
1 African elephant (*Loxodonta africana*)	7.5	24.6	7,500	16,534
2 Hippopotamus (*Hippopotamus amphibius*)	5.0	16.4	4,500	9,920
3 White rhinoceros (*Ceratotherium simum*)	4.2	13.7	3,600	7,937
4 Giraffe (*Giraffa camelopardalis*)	4.7	15.4	1,930	4,255
5 American buffalo (*Bison bison*)	3.5	11.4	1,000	2,205
6 Moose (*Alces alces*)	3.1	10.1	825	1,820
7 Grizzly bear (*Ursus arctos*)	3.0	9.8	780	1,720
8 Arabian camel (dromedary) (*Camelus dromedarius*)	3.45	11.3	690	1,521
9 Siberian tiger (*Panthera tigris altaica*)	3.3	10.8	360	793
10 Gorilla (*Gorilla gorilla gorilla*)	2.0	6.5	275	606

* Heaviest species per genus; exclusively terrestrial, excluding seals, etc.

Giraffe

The list excludes domesticated cattle and horses. It also avoids comparing close kin such as the African and Indian elephants, highlighting instead the sumo stars within distinctive large mammal groups such as the bears, deer, big cats, primates and bovines (ox-like mammals).

The elephant is 357,000 times as heavy as smallest mammal, the pygmy shrew.

African elephant

HEAVIEST PRIMATES

It may be argued that exceptionally obese humans weighing up to 636 kg (1,400 lb) are the heaviest primates of all time, but in the 'normal' range, the lowland gorilla (*Gorilla gorilla gorilla*) is the heaviest primate at 135–275 kg (297–606 lb). The mountain gorilla (*Gorilla beringei beringei*) is smaller, at 70–200 kg (154–440 lb).

BIG BABIES

Newborn African lion (*Panthera leo*) cubs weigh 1,650 g (3 lb 10 oz) – less than 1/300th of the of adult weight of 150–250 kg (330–550 lb). If a human grew at the same rate, an adult would weigh over 2.1 tonnes (4,630 lb).

JUMBO SIZED

As well as the heaviest, the African elephant is the longest quadruped at 7.3 m (24 ft), with the southern elephant seal (*Mirounga leonina*) a close second at 6.9 m (22.5 ft). The elephant also has the heaviest brain of any terrestrial mammal, at 6,000 g (13 lb 4 oz). This compares with the adult human average of 1,350 g (3 lb) – although all are eclipsed by the 7,800 g (17 lb 3 oz) of the sperm whale. Discounting examples of horses' tails that have been trained to more than 6 m (20 ft), the Asian elephant has the longest tail, at 10 cm (4 in); that of the African elephant is shorter, at 130 cm (51 in).

LARGEST CARNIVORES

The southern elephant seal can weigh as much as 3,500 kg (7,716 lb), three times the weight of a family car. Its close kin include the 1,200-kg (2,646-lb) walrus and the 1,100-kg (2,425-lb) Steller sea lion. Many mammal species in the order *Carnivora*, or meat-eaters, are omnivorous and around 40 specialize in eating fish or insects. The polar bear is the largest land carnivore if shoulder height (when the animal is on all fours) is taken into account: it tops an awesome 1.6 m (5.3 ft), compared with the 1.2 m (4 ft) of its nearest rival, the grizzly bear.

WINGED WONDERS

▲ *Great white pelican*
One of the heaviest birds that is capable of flight.

► *Northern cassowary*
The flightless bird weighs in second after the ostrich, at around 58 kg (128 lb).

TOP 10 **HEAVIEST FLIGHTED BIRDS**

		WINGSPAN		WEIGHT		
	BIRD* / SCIENTIFIC NAME	CM	IN	KG	LB	OZ
1	Mute swan (*Cygnus olor*)	238	93.7	22.50	49	6
2	Kori bustard (*Ardeotis kori*)	270	106.3	19.00	41	8
3	=Andean condor (*Vultur gryphus*)	320	126.0	15.00	33	1
	=Great white pelican (*Pelecanus onocrotalus*)	360	141.7	15.00	33	1
5	Eurasian black vulture (*Aegypius monachus*)	295	116.1	12.50	27	5
6	Sarus crane (*Grus antigone*)	280	110.2	12.24	26	9
7	Himalayan griffon (vulture) (*Gyps himalayensis*)	310	122.0	12.00	26	5
8	Wandering albatross (*Diomedea exulans*)	350	137.8	11.30	24	9
9	Steller's sea eagle (*Haliaeetus pelagicus*)	265	104.3	9.00	19	8
10	Marabou stork (*Leptoptilos crumeniferus*)	287	113.0	8.90	19	6

* By species

Heaviest Flightless Birds
The ostrich, at about 156 kg (343 lb 9 oz) the heaviest living flightless bird, was outweighed by the almost 500-kg (1,102-lb 5-oz) elephant bird (*Aepyornis maximus*) that became extinct in Madagascar 350 years ago, and the similarly gigantic emu-like *Dromornis* of Australia.

TOP 10 **BIRDS WITH THE LARGEST WINGSPANS**

BIRD* / SCIENTIFIC NAME / MAX. WINGSPAN (CM/IN)

1 Wandering albatross#
(*Diomedea exulans*)
370 / 146

2 Great white pelican
(*Pelecanus onocrotalus*)
360 / 141

3 Andean condor
(*Vultur gryphus*)
320 / 126

4 Himalayan griffon
(*Gyps himalayensis*)
310 / 122

5 Eurasian black vulture
(*Aegypius monachus*)
295 / 116

6 Marabou stork
(*Leptoptilos crumeniferus*)
287 / 113

7 Lammergeier
(*Gypaetus barbatus*)
282 / 111

* By species
# Royal albatross, a close relative, is the same size

▲ *Southern royal albatross*
Ringed specimens have proved that these are the longest-lived birds.

TOP 10 **MOST COMMON GARDEN BIRDS IN THE UK**

	BIRD	% OF GARDEN SPECIES SEEN (2009)	AVERAGE PER GARDEN (2009)
1	House sparrow	62.23	3.70
2	Starling	50.10	3.21
3	Blackbird	94.59	2.84
4	Blue tit	81.53	2.45
5	Chaffinch	55.53	2.01
6	Woodpigeon	65.32	1.85
7	Collared dove	55.67	1.44
8	Great tit	58.65	1.40
9	Robin	85.50	1.36
10	Long-tailed tit	29.19	1.34

Source: Royal Society for the Protection of Birds

In the RSPB's Big Garden Birdwatch 2009 survey – the biggest conducted anywhere in the world – 552,000 participants recorded 8.5 million birds of 73 species in the UK, the long-tailed tit entering the Top 10 for the first time in the survey's 30-year history, with an 88 per cent increase on the number observed in 2008.

TOP 10 **LONGEST-LIVED RINGED WILD BIRDS**

	BIRD / SCIENTIFIC NAME	AGE* YEARS	MONTHS
1	Southern royal albatross (*Diomedea epomophora*)	50	0
2	Fulmar (*Fulmarus glacialis*)	40	11
3	Manx shearwater (*Puffinus puffinus*)	37	0
4	Gannet (*Morus bassanus*)	36	4
5	Oystercatcher (*Haematopus ostralegus*)	36	0
6	White (Fairy) tern (*Gygis alba*)	35	11
7	Common eider (*Somateria mollissima*)	35	0
8	Lesser black-backed gull (*Larus fuscus*)	34	10
9	Pink-footed goose (*Anser brachyrhynchus*)	34	2
10	Great frigate bird (*Fregata minor*)	33	9

* Elapsed time between marking and report

Only by ringing can the true age of a wild bird be monitored. Hard rings, likely to last as long as the bird, started to be used about 50 years ago. Land-based songbirds do not live as long as the slow-breeding seabirds.

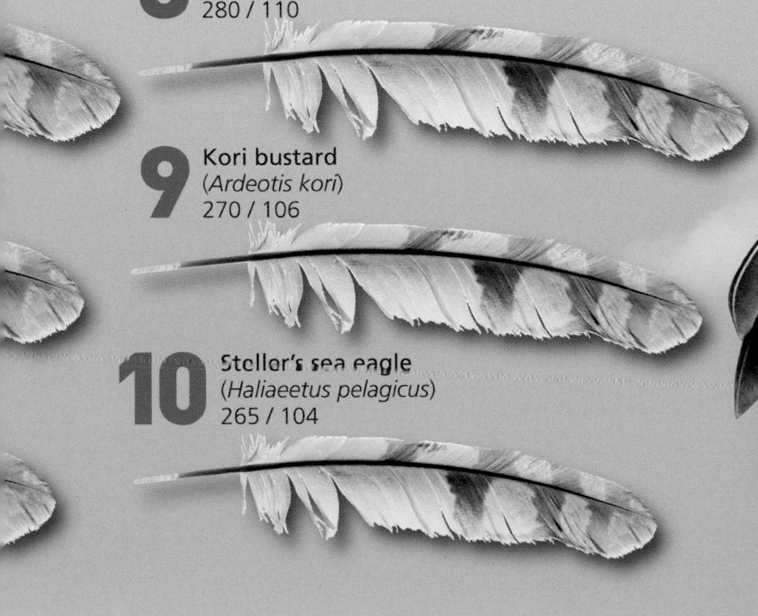

8 Sarus crane
(*Grus antigone*)
280 / 110

9 Kori bustard
(*Ardeotis kori*)
270 / 106

10 Steller's sea eagle
(*Haliaeetus pelagicus*)
265 / 104

▲ *Big wings*
The Himalayan griffon vulture has a wingspan of over 3 m (10 ft) and weighs up to 12 kg (26.4 lb).

▼ *Giant clam*
One of the longest molluscs, its relatives are among the longest-lived, with claims of lifespans up to 400 years.

TOP 10 LONGEST MOLLUSCS*

	MOLLUSC / SCIENTIFIC NAME	CLASS	LENGTH MM	LENGTH IN
1	Giant squid (*Architeuthis sp.*)	Cephalopod	16,764	660#
2	Giant clam (*Tridacna gigas*)	Marine bivalve	1,300	51
3	Australian trumpet (*Syrinx aruanus*)	Marine snail	770	30
4	Hexabranchus sanguineus	Sea slug	520	20
5	Carinaria cristata	Heteropod	500	19
6	Steller's coat of mail shell (*Cryptochiton stelleri*)	Chiton	470	18
7	Freshwater mussel (*Cristaria plicata*)	Freshwater bivalve	300	11
8	Giant African snail (*Achatina achatina*)	Land snail	200	7
9	Tusk shell (*Dentalium vernedi*)	Scaphopod	138	5
10	Apple snail (*Pila werneri*)	Freshwater snail	125	4

* Largest species within each class
\# Estimated – actual length unknown

ACTUAL SIZE

THE 10 MOST VENOMOUS REPTILES AND AMPHIBIANS

	CREATURE*	TOXIN	FATAL AMOUNT (MG)#
1	Indian cobra	Peak V	0.009
2	Mamba	Toxin 1	0.02
3	Brown snake	Texilotoxin	0.05
4	=Inland taipan	Paradotoxin	0.10
	=Mamba	Dendrotoxin	0.10
6	Taipan	Taipoxin	0.11
7	=Indian cobra	Peak X	0.12
	=Poison arrow frog	Batrachotoxin	0.12
9	Indian cobra	Peak 1X	0.17
10	Krait	Bungarotoxin	0.50

* Excluding bacteria
\# Quantity required to kill an average-sized human adult

TOP 10 LONGEST SNAKES

	SNAKE / SCIENTIFIC NAME	MAX. LENGTH M	MAX. LENGTH FT
1	Reticulated (royal) python (*Python reticulatus*)	10.0	32
2	Anaconda (*Eunectes murinus*)	8.5	28
3	Indian python (*Python molurus molurus*)	7.6	25
4	Diamond python (*Morelia spilota spilota*)	6.4	21
5	King cobra (*Opiophagus hannah*)	5.8	19
6	Boa constrictor (*Boa constrictor*)	4.9	16
7	Bushmaster (*Lachesis muta*)	3.7	12
8	Giant brown snake (*Oxyuranus scutellatus*)	3.4	11
9	Diamondback rattlesnake (*Crotalus atrox*)	2.7	9
10	Indigo or gopher snake (*Drymarchon corais*)	2.4	8

► *Inland taipan*
The Australian snake is rarely seen, but is one of the most venomous on Earth.

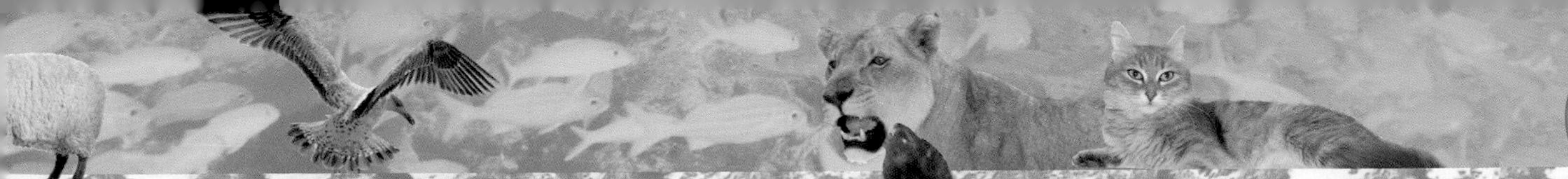

TOP 10 DEADLIEST SPIDERS

	SPIDER / SCIENTIFIC NAME	RANGE
1	Banana spider (*Phonenutria nigriventer*)	Central and South America
2	Sydney funnel web (*Atrax robustus*)	Australia
3	Wolf spider (*Lycosa raptoria/erythrognatha*)	Central and South America
4	Black widow (*Latrodectus species*)	Widespread
5	Violin spider/recluse spider (*Loxesceles reclusa*)	Widespread
6	Sac spider (*Cheiracanthium punctorium*)	Central Europe
7	Tarantula (*Eurypelma rubropilosum*)	Neotropics
8	Tarantula (*Acanthoscurria atrox*)	Neotropics
9	Tarantula (*Lasiodora klugi*)	Neotropics
10	Tarantula (*Pamphobeteus species*)	Neotropics

ACTUAL SIZE

◀ *Black death*
The deadly female black widow spider has a distinctive red hourglass pattern on its back.

▼ *Tarantula*
Though large, the South American goliath tarantula presents little danger to humans.

ACTUAL SIZE

◀ *Millipede*
Only one species comes close to its literal translation of '1,000 feet'.

TOP 10 CREATURES WITH THE MOST LEGS

	CREATURE / SCIENTIFIC NAME	LEGS
1	Millipede (*Illacme plenipes*)	750
2	Centipede (*Himantarum gabrielis*)	354
3	Centipede (*Haplophilus subterraneus*)	178
4	Millipedes*	30
5	Symphylans	24
6	Caterpillars*	16
7	Woodlice	14
8	Crabs, shrimps	10
9	Spiders	8
10	Insects	6

* Most species

TOP 10 LARGEST SPIDERS

	SPIDER / SCIENTIFIC NAME	LEG SPAN MM	IN
1	Huntsman spider (*Heteropoda maxima*)	300	11.8
2	Brazilian salmon pink (*Lasiodora parahybana*)	270	10.6
3	Brazilian ginat tawny red (*Grammostola mollicoma*)	260	10.2
4	=Goliath tarantula or bird-eating spider (*Theraphosa blondi*)	254	10.0
	=Wolf spider (*Cupiennius sallei*)	254	10.0
6	=Purple bloom bird-eating (*Xenesthis immanis*)	230	9.1
	=Xenesthis monstrosa	230	9.1
8	Hercules baboon (*Hysterocrates hercules*)	203	8.0
9	Hysterocrates sp.	178	7.0
10	Tegenaria parietin	140	5.5

MARINE MARVELS

THE 10 **TYPES OF SHARK THAT HAVE ATTACKED AND KILLED THE MOST HUMANS**

SHARK / SPECIES / UNPROVOKED ATTACKS* / TOTAL / FATALITIES#

1 **Great white** (*Carcharodon carcharias*) 244 / 65
2 **Tiger** (*Galeocerdo cuvier*) 88 / 27
3 **Bull** (*Carcharhinus leucas*) 82 / 25
4 **Requiem** (*Carcharhinus sp.*) 39 / 7
5 **Blue** (*Prionace glauca*) 13 / 4
6 **Sand tiger** (*Carcharias taurus*) 32 / 3
7 =**Blacktip** (*Carcharhinus limbatus*) 28 / 1
=**Shortfin mako** (*Isurus oxyrinchus*) 8 / 1
Oceanic whitetip (*Carcharhinus longimanus*) 5 / 1
=**Dusky** (*Carcharhinus obscurus*) 3 / 1
=**Galapagos** (*Carcharhinus galapagensis*) 1 / 1

* 1580–2008
\# Where fatalities are equal, entries are ranked by total attacks

Source: International Shark Attack File, Florida Museum of Natural History

▲ ***Jaws of death***
The great white shark has earned a fearsome reputation as a killer.

TOP 10 **LONGEST-LIVED MARINE ANIMALS***

ANIMAL / SCIENTIFIC NAME / LIFE SPAN (YEARS)

1 **Quahog** (marine clam)
(*Arctica islandica*)
220

2 **Bowhead whale**
(*Balaena mysticetus*)
200

3 = **Alligator snapping turtle**
(*Macrochelys temminckii*)
150

= **Whale shark**
(*Rhincodon typus*)
150

5 **Sea anemone**
(*Actinia mesembryanthemum*, etc.)
90

6 **European eel**
(*Anguilla anguilla*)
88

7 **Lake sturgeon**
(*Acipenser fulvescens*)
82

8 **Freshwater mussel**
(*Palaeoheterodonta* – various)
80

9 **Dugong**
(*Dugong dugon*)
73

10 **Spiny dogfish**
(*Squalus acanthias*)
70

* Longest-lived of each genus listed

This is based on known life spans, excluding one-off extreme claims, such as that of a 405-year-old quahog caught off Iceland in 2007.

► ***Mollusc Methuselah***
Annual growth rings suggest that some quahogs may live for even longer than their official 220-year record.

▶ *Speed in the water*
The streamlined sailfish measures 3 m (10 ft) in length and is the fastest fish in the ocean.

TOP 10 **FASTEST FISH**

	FISH / SCIENTIFIC NAME	MAX. RECORDED SPEED KM/H	MPH
1	Sailfish (*Istiophorus platypterus*)	112	69
2	Striped marlin (*Tetrapturus audax*)	80	50
3	Wahoo (peto, jack mackerel) (*Acanthocybium solandri*)	77	48
4	Southern bluefin tuna (*Thunnus maccoyii*)	76	47
5	Blue shark (*Prionace glauca*)	69	43
6	= Bonefish (*Albula vulpes*)	64	40
	= Swordfish (*Xiphias gladius*)	64	40
8	Atlantic needlefish (*Strongylura marina*)	60	37*
9	= Four-winged flying fish (*Hirundichthys affinis*)	56	35*
	= Tarpon (ox-eye herring) (*Megalops cyprinoides*)	56	35*

* 'Flying' or leaping through air

Only the fastest of each genus is included, but many other sharks come close to these speeds – the great white shark (of *Jaws* fame) is easily capable of 48 km/h (30 mph), almost six times as fast as the fastest human swimmer.

TOP 10 **HEAVIEST FRESHWATER FISH CAUGHT**

	FISH / SCIENTIFIC NAME	ANGLER / LOCATION / DATE	WEIGHT KG	LB	OZ
1	White sturgeon (*Acipenser transmontanus*)	Joey Pallotta III, Benicia, California, 9 Jul 1983	212.28	468	0
2	Alligator gar (*Atractosteus spatula*)	Bill Valverde, Rio Grande, Texas, 2 Dec 1951	126.55	279	0
3	Nile perch (*Lates niloticus*)	William Toth, Lake Nasser, Egypt, 20 Dec 2000	104.33	230	0
4	Beluga sturgeon (*Huso huso*)	Ms Merete Lehne, Guryev, Kazakhstan, 3 May 1993	101.97	224	13
5	Mekong giant catfish (*Pangasianodon gigas*)	Rob Maylin, Gillhams Fishing Resort, Thailand, 28 May 2008	83.97	185	2
6	Blue catfish (*Ictalurus furcatus*)	Timothy E. Pruitt, Mississippi River, Alton, Illinois, 21 May 2005	56.25	124	0
7	Flathead catfish (*Pylodictis olivaris*)	Ken Paulie, Elk City Reservoir, Kansas, 14 May 1998	55.79	123	0
8	Redtail catfish (*Phractocephalus hemioliopteru*)	Gilberto Fernandes, Rio Amazonas, Brazil, 28 Dec 2008	55.00	121	4
9	Chinook salmon (*Oncorhynchus tshawytscha*)	Les Anderson, Kenai River, Alaska, 17 May 1985	44.20	97	4
10	Giant tigerfish (*Hydrocynus goliath*)	Raymond Houtmans, Zaïre River, Kinshasa, Zaïre (now Democratic Republic of Congo), 9 Jul 1988	44.00	97	0

Source: International Game Fish Association

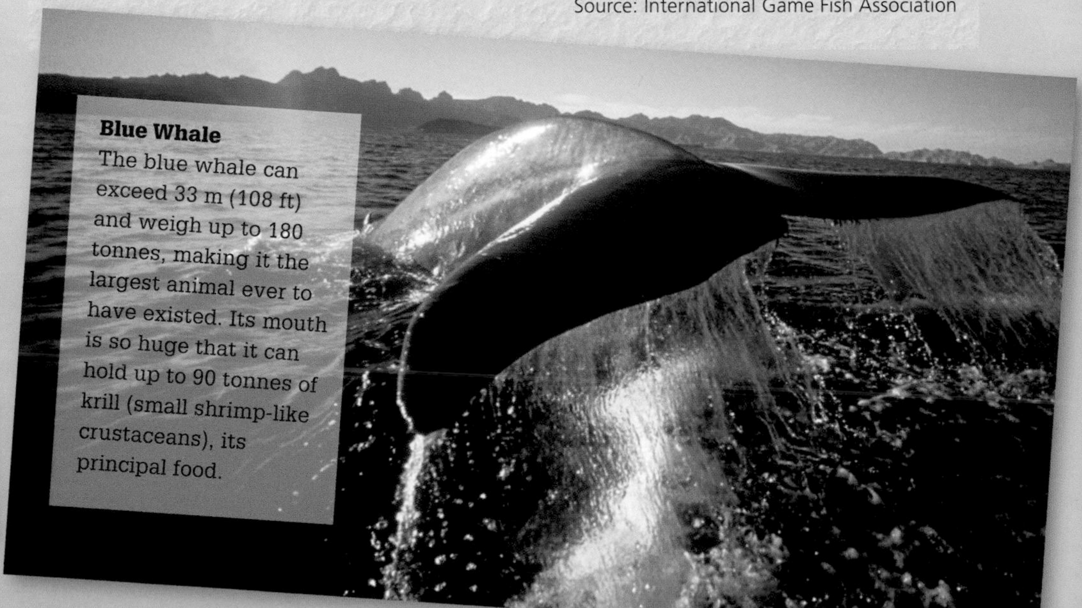

Blue Whale
The blue whale can exceed 33 m (108 ft) and weigh up to 180 tonnes, making it the largest animal ever to have existed. Its mouth is so huge that it can hold up to 90 tonnes of krill (small shrimp-like crustaceans), its principal food.

CATS & DOGS

TOP 10 PEDIGREE CAT BREEDS IN THE UK

BREED / NO. REGISTERED BY CAT FANCY (2008)

1 British shorthair 6,463
2 Siamese 3,404
3 Bengal 2,598
4 Burmese 2,371
5 Persian 2,332
6 Ragdoll 2,289
7 Maine coon 2,095
8 Birman 1,673
9 Norwegian forest 1,375
10 Oriental short hair 1,110

Source: The Governing Council of the Cat Fancy

This Top 10 comprises 84 per cent of the total of 30,604 cats registered with the Governing Council of the Cat Fancy in 2008.

▲ *Ex-top cat*
Formerly the UK's No. 1 breed, the Persian's status has declined in the 21st century, but it remains highly esteemed among feline aficionados.

TOP 10 PET CAT POPULATIONS

COUNTRY / ESTIMATED PET CAT POPULATION (2009)

1 USA 79,695,000
2 Russia 17,800,000
3 Brazil 17,262,000
4 Japan 11,300,000
5 China 10,726,000
6 France 10,550,000
7 UK 10,450,000
8 Ukraine 8,895,000
9 Canada 8,583,100
10 Germany 8,050,000

Top 10 population 183,311,100

Source: Euromonitor International

TOP 10 CAT FILMS

FILM	YEAR
1 Garfield: The Movie*	2004
2 Cats & Dogs	2001
3 Garfield: A Tail of Two Kitties*	2006
4 The Cat in the Hat	2003
5 Oliver & Company*	1988
6 The Aristocats*	1970
7 Homeward Bound: The Incredible Journey	1993
8 Homeward Bound II: Lost in San Francisco	1996
9 That Darn Cat	1997
10 The Cat from Outer Space	1978

* Animated or part animated

◄ *Moggy movie*
Based on the comic strip by Jim Davis, Garfield made a successful transition to a film in which he was created by CGI, while the other characters were real.

TOP 10 PET DOG POPULATIONS

COUNTRY / ESTIMATED PET DOG POPULATION (2009)

1. USA 65,791,000
2. Brazil 33,745,300
3. China 27,034,000
4. Mexico 17,859,300
5. Japan 13,618,000
6. Russia 12,270,000
7. Philippines 9,651,500
8. Ukraine 8,517,000
9. France 8,495,000
10. South Africa 7,449,000

UK 6,500,000
Top 10 population 204,430,100

Source: Euromonitor International

◄ *Labrador*
The Labrador retriever is the world's favourite pedigree dog.

TOP 10 PEDIGREE DOG BREEDS IN THE UK

BREED / NO. REGISTERED BY THE KENNEL CLUB (2008)

1. Labrador retriever 45,233
2. Cocker spaniel 22,508
3. English springer spaniel 14,899
4. German shepherd dog (Alsatian) 11,903
5. Cavalier King Charles spaniel 11,226
6. Staffordshire bull terrier 10,744
7. Golden retriever 9,159
8. Border terrier 9,145
9. Boxer 7,353
10. West Highland white terrier 7,330

Source: The Kennel Club

TOP 10 MOST INTELLIGENT DOG BREEDS

BREED

1. Border collie
2. Poodle
3. German shepherd (Alsatian)
4. Golden retriever
5. Doberman pinscher
6. Shetland sheepdog
7. Labrador retriever
8. Papillon
9. Rottweiler
10. Australian cattle dog

Source: Stanley Coren, *The Intelligence of Dogs* (Scribner, 1994)

American psychology professor and pet trainer Stanley Coren devised a ranking of 133 breeds of dogs after studying their responses to a range of IQ tests, as well as the opinions of judges in dog obedience tests.

▲ *Clever collie*
The Border collie is ranked first for its innate intelligence.

THE 10 MOST AGGRESSIVE DOGS

BREED

1. Dachshund
2. Chihuahua
3. Jack Russell terrier
4. Akita
5. Australian cattle dog
6. Pit bull
7. Beagle
8. English springer spaniel
9. Border collie
10. German shepherd

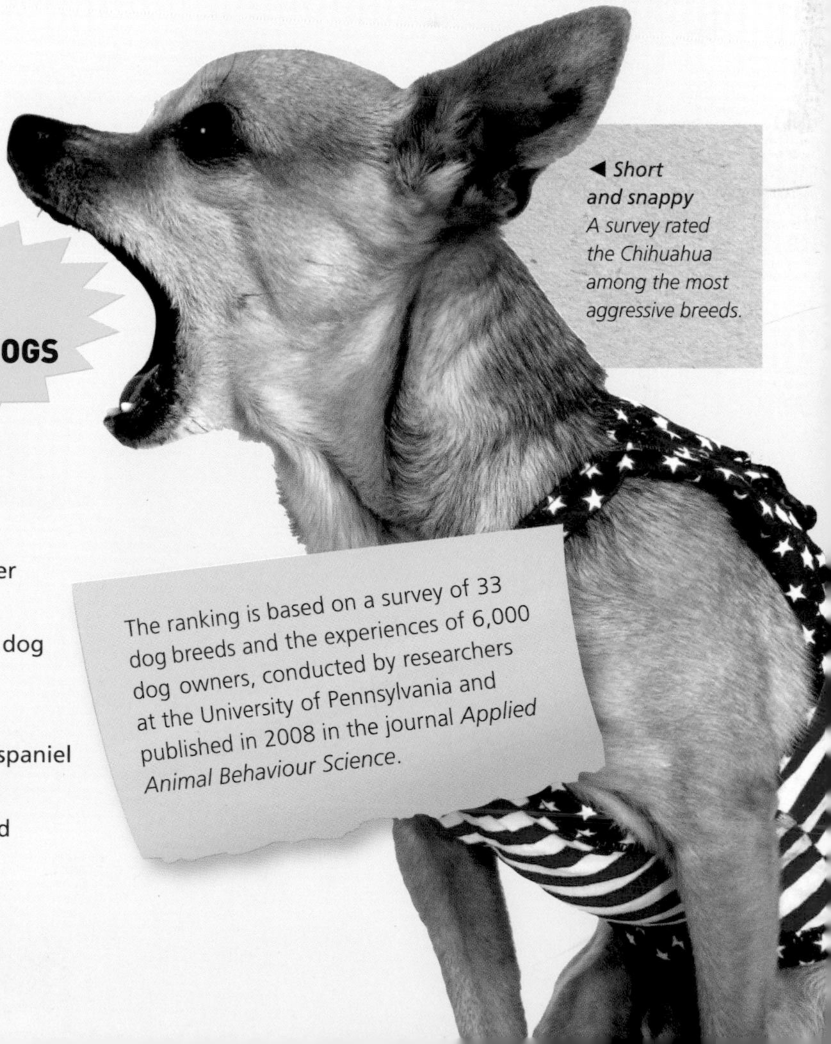

◄ *Short and snappy*
A survey rated the Chihuahua among the most aggressive breeds.

The ranking is based on a survey of 33 dog breeds and the experiences of 6,000 dog owners, conducted by researchers at the University of Pennsylvania and published in 2008 in the journal *Applied Animal Behaviour Science*.

FARM ANIMALS

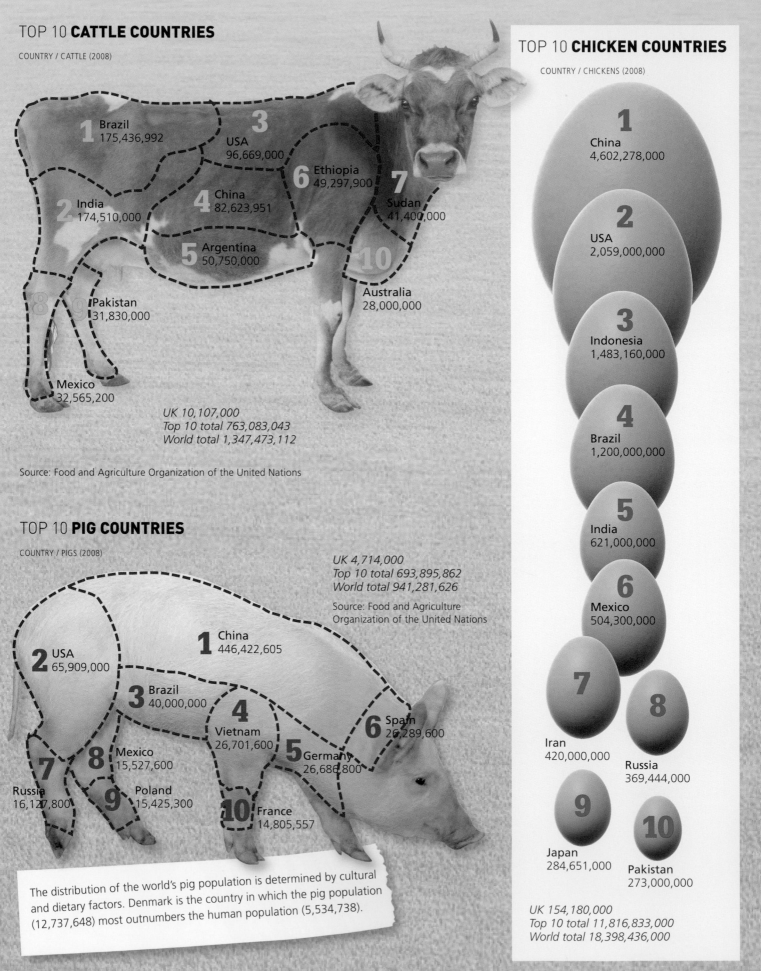

TOP 10 CATTLE COUNTRIES

COUNTRY / CATTLE (2008)

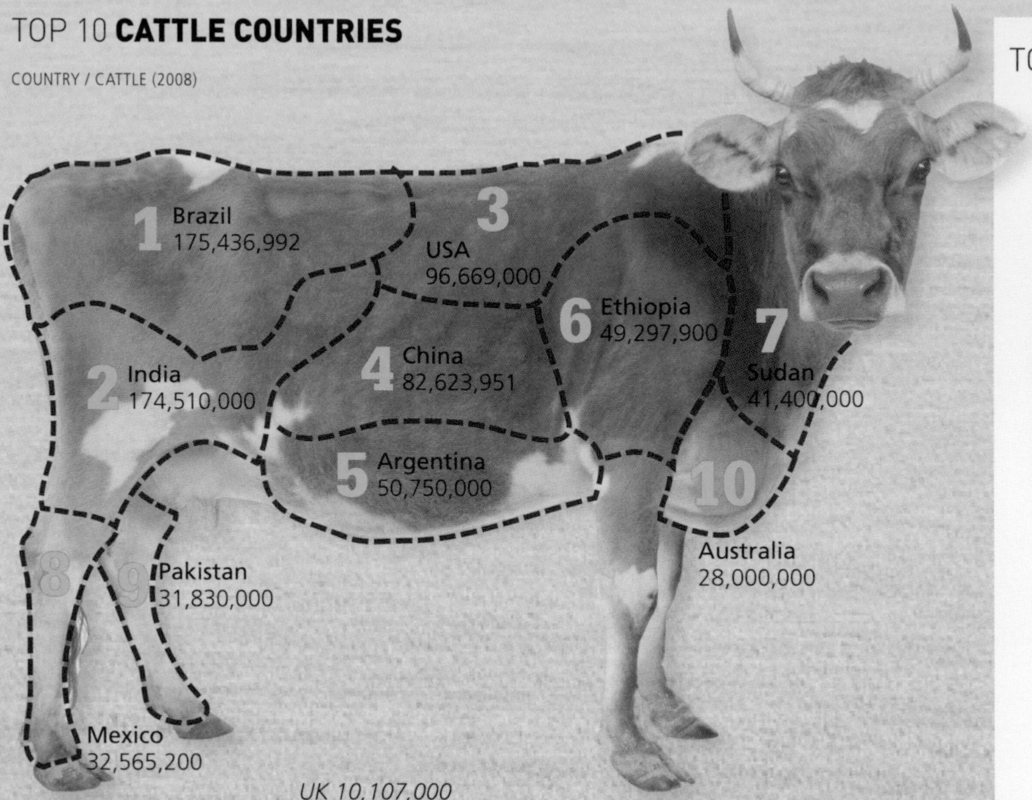

UK 10,107,000
Top 10 total 763,083,043
World total 1,347,473,112

Source: Food and Agriculture Organization of the United Nations

TOP 10 CHICKEN COUNTRIES

COUNTRY / CHICKENS (2008)

UK 154,180,000
Top 10 total 11,816,833,000
World total 18,398,436,000

TOP 10 PIG COUNTRIES

COUNTRY / PIGS (2008)

UK 4,714,000
Top 10 total 693,895,862
World total 941,281,626

Source: Food and Agriculture Organization of the United Nations

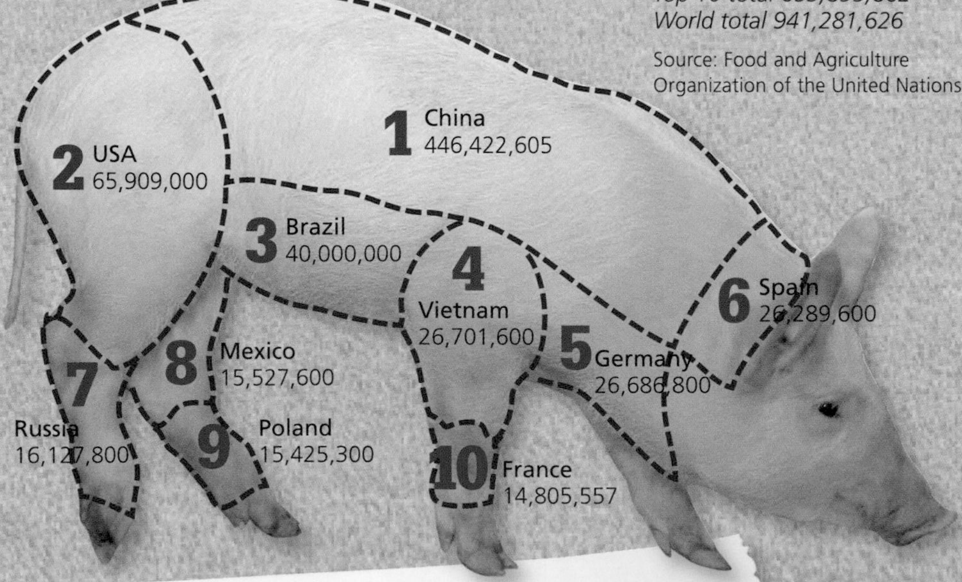

The distribution of the world's pig population is determined by cultural and dietary factors. Denmark is the country in which the pig population (12,737,648) most outnumbers the human population (5,534,738).

TOP 10 **DUCK COUNTRIES**

COUNTRY / DUCKS (2008)

Love a duck
Two-thirds of the world's 1.1 billion ducks are in China, where it is a popular menu item.

1. China 761,250,000
2. Vietnam 67,800,000
3. Indonesia 36,931,000
4. India 35,000,000
5. Bangladesh 23,000,000
6. France 22,848,000
7. Malaysia 16,000,000
8. Thailand 14,048,000
9. Myanmar 11,144,000
10. South Korea 11,000,000

UK 2,227,000 World total 1,108,354,000

TOP 10 **SHEEP COUNTRIES**

COUNTRY / SHEEP (2008)

1. China 136,436,203
2. Australia 79,000,000
3. India 64,989,000
4. Iran 53,800,000
5. Sudan 51,100,000
6. New Zealand 34,087,864
7. Nigeria 33,874,300
8. UK 33,131,000
9. Pakistan 27,111,000
10. South Africa 25,232,593

Top 10 total 538,761,960
World total 1,078,178,799

TOP 10 **TYPES OF LIVESTOCK**

ANIMAL / WORLD STOCKS (2008)

1. Chickens 18,398,436,000
2. Cattle 1,347,473,112
3. Ducks 1,108,354,000
4. Sheep 1,078,178,799
5. Pigs 941,281,626
6. Goats 861,901,978
7. Turkeys 472,635,000
8. Geese and guinea fowl 351,373,000
9. Buffaloes 180,702,923
10. Horses 58,770,171

The 24,799,106,609 animals accounted for by the Top 10 outnumber the world's human population by almost four to one.

CROPS

TOP 10 **CEREAL CROPS**

CROP / PRODUCTION 2008 (TONNES)

1	Maize	822,712,527
2	Wheat	689,945,712
3	Rice (paddy)	685,013,374
4	Barley	157,644,721
5	Sorghum	65,534,273
6	Millet	35,651,146
7	Oats	25,784,608
8	Rye	17,750,767
9	Triticale (wheat/rye hybrid)	14,020,842
10	Mixed grain	4,515,561

Source (all lists): Food and Agriculture Organization of the United Nations

TOP 10 **RICE-GROWING COUNTRIES**

COUNTRY / PRODUCTION 2008 (TONNES)

1 China 193,354,175

2 India 148,260,000

3 Indonesia 60,251,072

4 Bangladesh 46,905,000

5 Vietnam 38,725,100

6 Myanmar 30,500,000

7 Thailand 30,466,918

8 Philippines 16,815,500

9 Brazil 12,100,138

10 Japan 11,028,750

TOP 10 **FRUIT CROPS**

CROP / PRODUCTION 2008 (TONNES)

1 Watermelons 99,194,223

2 Bananas 90,705,922

3 Apples 69,603,640

4 Grapes 67,708,587

TOP 10 **VEGETABLE CROPS**

CROP* / PRODUCTION 2008 (TONNES)

1. Sugar cane 1,743,092,995
2. Potatoes 314,140,107
3. Sugar beets 230,952,636
4. Soybeans 227,585,414
5. Tomatoes# 129,649,883
6. Sweet potatoes 110,128,298
7. Cabbages and other brassicas 69,664,185
8. Onions (dry) 66,829,917
9. Yams 51,728,233
10. Cucumbers and gherkins 44,321,303

* Excluding cereals; including only vegetables grown for human and animal consumption
# Botanically it is a fruit, but, based on its use in cooking, for legal and import duty purposes certain countries consider it a vegetable

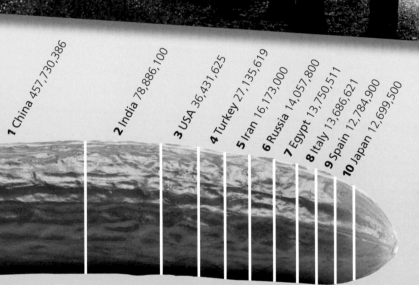

TOP 10 **NON-FOOD CROPS**

	CROP	PRODUCTION 2008 (TONNES)
1	Cotton	65,985,197
2	Rubber	10,605,618
3	Coffee	8,235,190
4	Tobacco	6,881,434
5	Tea	4,735,961
6	Jute	2,837,519
7	Linseed	2,199,537
8	Castor oil seed	1,580,603
9	Coir	1,111,270
10	Flax	935,172

▼ *Rubber plantation*
Despite the growth of synthetic alternatives, natural rubber remains a major crop.

TOP 10 **VEGETABLE-PRODUCING COUNTRIES**

COUNTRY / PRODUCTION* 2008 (TONNES)

* Including watermelons; only vegetables grown for human consumption, excluding crops from private gardens

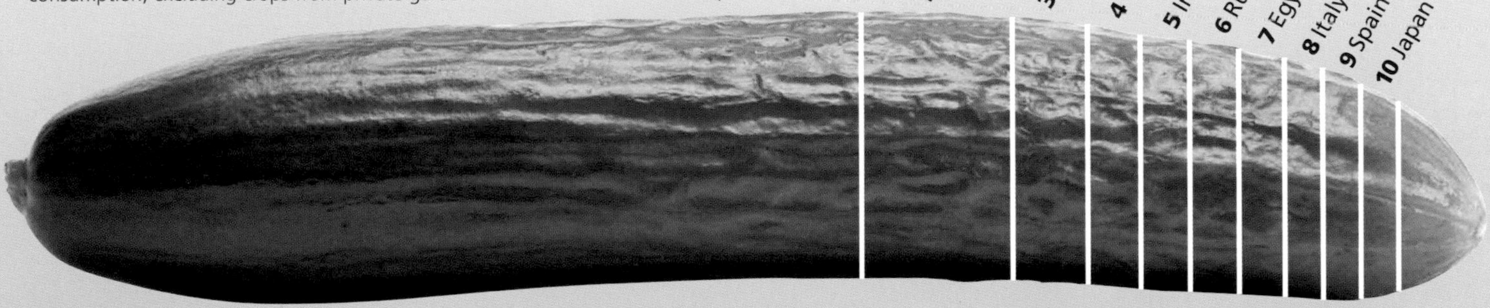

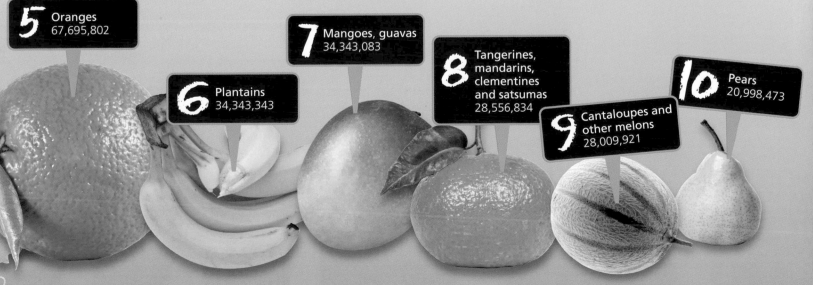

TREES & FORESTS

▲ *Canada Sustainable forestry in Canada, where one-third of the country is forested, ensures that the total area does not fluctuate.*

TOP 10 **COUNTRIES WITH THE LARGEST AREAS OF FOREST**

	COUNTRY	SQ KM	% OF TOTAL	SQ MILES
1	Russia	8,087,900	47.9	3,122,756
2	Brazil	4,776,980	57.2	1,844,402
3	Canada	3,101,340	33.6	1,197,434
4	USA	3,030,890	33.1	1,170,233
5	China	1,972,900	21.2	761,741
6	Australia	1,636,780	21.3	631,964
7	Dem. Rep. of Congo	1,336,100	58.9	515,871
8	Indonesia	884,950	48.8	341,681
9	Peru	687,420	53.7	265,414
10	India	677,010	22.8	261,395
	UK	*28,450*	*11.8*	*10,985*
	World total	*39,520,250*	*30.3*	*15,258,855*

Source: Food and Agriculture Organization of the United Nations, *Global Forest Resources Assessment 2005*

TOP 10 **COUNTRIES WITH THE LARGEST AREAS OF TROPICAL FOREST**

		AREA	
	COUNTRY	SQ KM	SQ MILES
1	Brazil	3,012,730	1,163,222
2	Dem. Rep. of Congo	1,350,710	521,512
3	Indonesia	887,440	343,029
4	Peru	756,360	292,032
5	Bolivia	686,380	265,012
6	Venezuela	556,150	214,730
7	Columbia	531,860	205,352
8	Mexico	457,650	176,700
9	India	444,500	171,622
10	Angola	375,640	145,035
	World total	*14,076,490*	*5,434,964*

Source: Food and Agriculture Organization of the United Nations, *State of the World's Forests, 2005*

TOP 10 **DEFORESTING COUNTRIES***

COUNTRY / ANNUAL FOREST LOSS 2000–05 (SQ KM/SQ MILES)

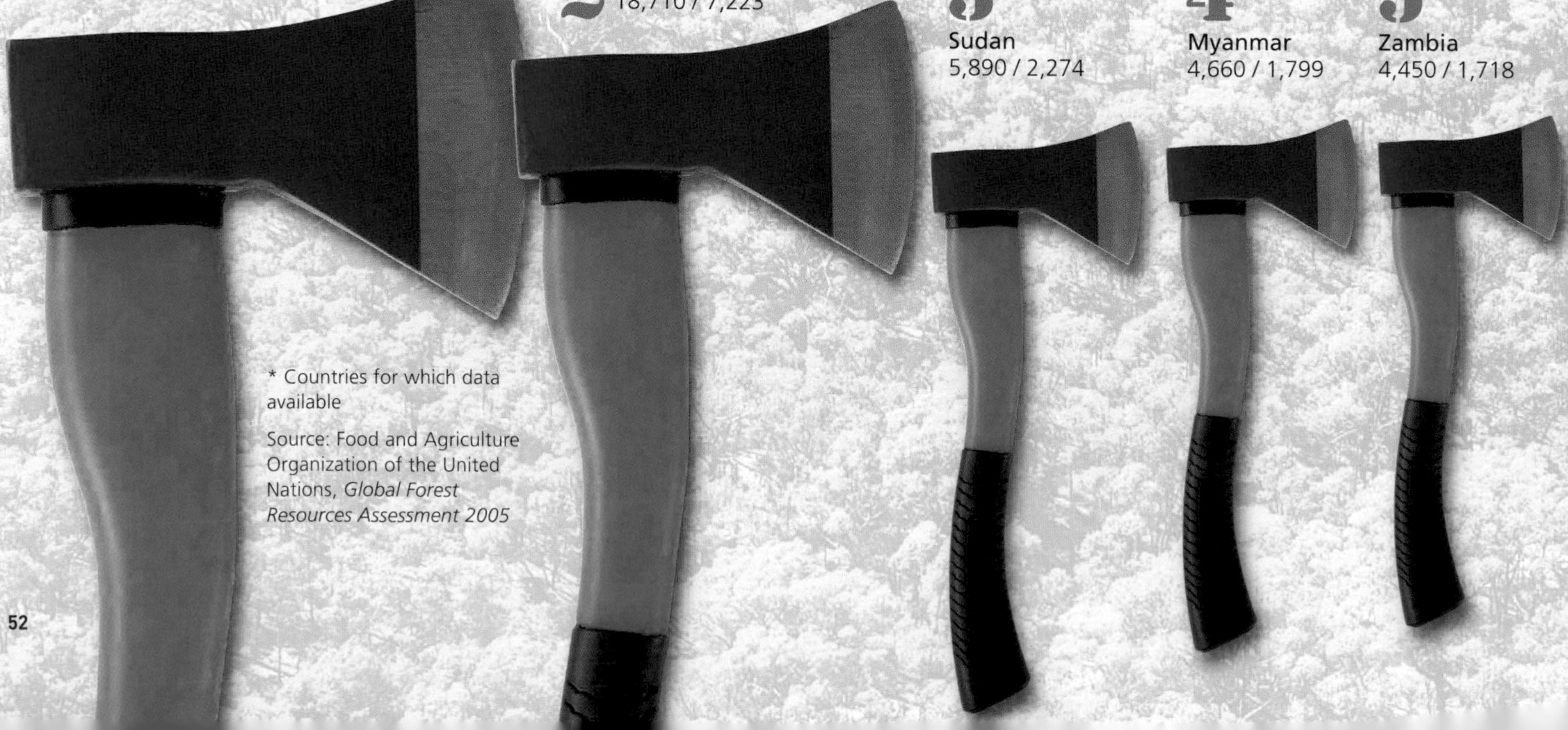

1 Brazil 31,030 / 11,980

2 Indonesia 18,710 / 7,223

3 Sudan 5,890 / 2,274

4 Myanmar 4,660 / 1,799

5 Zambia 4,450 / 1,718

* Countries for which data available

Source: Food and Agriculture Organization of the United Nations, *Global Forest Resources Assessment 2005*

TOP 10 **BIGGEST OAK TREES IN THE UK***

	LOCATION	GIRTH CM	FT	IN
1	=**Chaceley**, Gloucestershire	1,210	39	8
	=**Fredville Park**, Kent	1,210	39	8
3	**Melbury Park**, Dorset	1,188	39	0
4	**Private land**, Powys, Wales	1,175	38	7
5	**Kentchurch Court Park**, Herefordshire	1,137	37	4
6	**Eastwood Park**, Gloucestershire	1,128	37	0
7	**Penshurst**, Kent	1,118	36	8
8	**Hazelgrove**, Somerset	1,074	35	3
9	**Sherwood Forest**, Nottinghamshire	1,062	34	10
10	**Pulverbatch**, Shropshire	1,037	34	0

* Complete living single oaks, excluding dead or hollow trunks and split remains

Source: The Tree Register of the British Isles

Tallest Trees in the UK

Britain's tallest tree is a Douglas fir planted in 1849 by Archie Fletcher on the Dunans Estate, Scotland, at 63.79 m (209 ft 4 in) – 12 m (39 ft) taller than Nelson's Column. In 2009 its precise height was confirmed when it was climbed by a team from Sparsholt College, Hampshire.

Some 42,510 sq km (16,413 sq miles) of forest were lost in South America each year between 2000 and 2005, 40,400 sq km (15,598 sq miles) in Africa and 38,400 sq km (14,826 sq miles) in Asia. The total global loss during the period was 439,020 sq km (169,506 sq miles). In the same period, certain countries adopted reforestation programmes, including China, which added 40,580 sq km (15,668 sq miles) – an area the size of Switzerland. The net global loss was thus reduced to 365,850 sq km (141,255 sq miles), or 0.18 per cent of the total world forest area.

6 Tanzania 4,120 / 1,590

7 Nigeria 4,100 / 1,583

8 Dem. Rep. of Congo 3,190 / 1,231

9 Zimbabwe 3,130 / 1,208

10 Venezuela 2,880 / 1,111

► ***Deforestation***
Soybean fields occupy former forest land in Brazil. Since 1970, 724,587 sq km (279,765 sq miles) of forest, three times the size of the UK, has been lost.

3 THE HUMAN WORLD

22ND WORLD SCOUT JAMBOREE

A World Scout Jamboree has been held every four years since 1920, when the event took place in Olympia, London. It was presided over by Robert Baden-Powell, who had founded the Scouting movement in 1907, and was attended by 8,000 Scouts from 34 countries. It has since been staged in countries in Europe, North and South America, Asia and Australasia. The 22nd Jamboree – the world's biggest gathering of Scouts – will be held on a 2.25-sq km (1-sq mile) campsite in Rinkaby, Sweden, throughout July and August 2011, with 30,000 Scouts attending.

THE 10 **MOST OBESE COUNTRIES – ADULTS**

COUNTRY	% OF OBESE ADULTS* MEN	WOMEN
1 Tonga	46.6	70.3
2 Samoa	32.9	63.0
3 Nauru	55.7	60.5
4 Qatar	34.6	45.3
5 Saudi Arabia	26.4	44.0
6 Lebanon	36.3	38.3
7 Panama	27.9	36.1
8 Paraguay	22.9	35.7
9 Albania#	22.8	35.6
10 Mexico	24.4	34.5
England	*23.6*	*24.4*
Scotland	*24.9*	*26.5*
Wales	*20.0*	*21.0*

* Ranked by percentage of obese women (those with a BMI greater than 30) in those countries and latest year for which data available
# Urban population

Source: International Obesity Task Force (IOTF)

TOP 10 **COSMETIC SURGERY PROCEDURES IN THE UK, 2009**

PROCEDURE	NO.
1 Breast augmentation (women)	8,537
2 Blepharoplasty (eyelid surgery) (women)	4,827
3 Breast reduction (women)	4,122
4 Face/neck lift (women)	4,005
5 Abdominoplasty (women)	3,268
6 Liposuction (women)	3,010
7 Rhinoplasty (women)	2,959
8 Brow lifts (women)	1,324
9 Rhinoplasty (men)	877
10 Otoplasty (ear correction) (women)	807

Source: British Association of Aesthetic Plastic Surgeons

THE 10 **MOST OVERWEIGHT COUNTRIES – CHILDREN**

	COUNTRY	% OF OVERWEIGHT CHILDREN* BOYS	GIRLS
1	Bahrain	29.9	42.4
2	USA	35.1	36.0
3	Portugal	29.5	34.3
4	Spain	35.0	32.0
5	Kuwait	30.0	31.8
6	= Australia	25.0	30.0
	= New Zealand	30.0	30.0
8	England	29.0	29.3
9	Bolivia#	15.6	27.5
10	Sweden	17.6	27.4

* Ranked by percentage of overweight girls (those with a BMI greater than 25) in those countries and latest year for which data available
# Urban population

Source: International Obesity Task Force (IOTF)

▲ ***Fat of the land***
Children attending a 'fat camp' in the USA, where childhood obesity continues to increase.

TOP 10 **LONGEST BONES IN THE HUMAN BODY**

	BONE	AVERAGE LENGTH CM	IN
1	**Femur** (thighbone – upper leg)	50.50	19.88
2	**Tibia** (shinbone – inner lower leg)	43.03	16.94
3	**Fibula** (outer lower leg)	40.50	15.94
4	**Humerus** (upper arm)	36.46	14.35
5	**Ulna** (inner lower arm)	28.20	11.10
6	**Radius** (outer lower arm)	26.42	10.40
7	**7th rib**	24.00	9.45
8	**8th rib**	23.00	9.06
9	**Innominate bone** (hipbone – half pelvis)	18.50	7.28
10	**Sternum** (breastbone)	17.00	6.69

These are average dimensions of the bones of an adult male measured from their extremities (ribs are curved, and the pelvis measurement is taken diagonally). The same bones in the female skeleton are usually 6 to 13 per cent smaller, with the exception of the sternum, which is virtually identical.

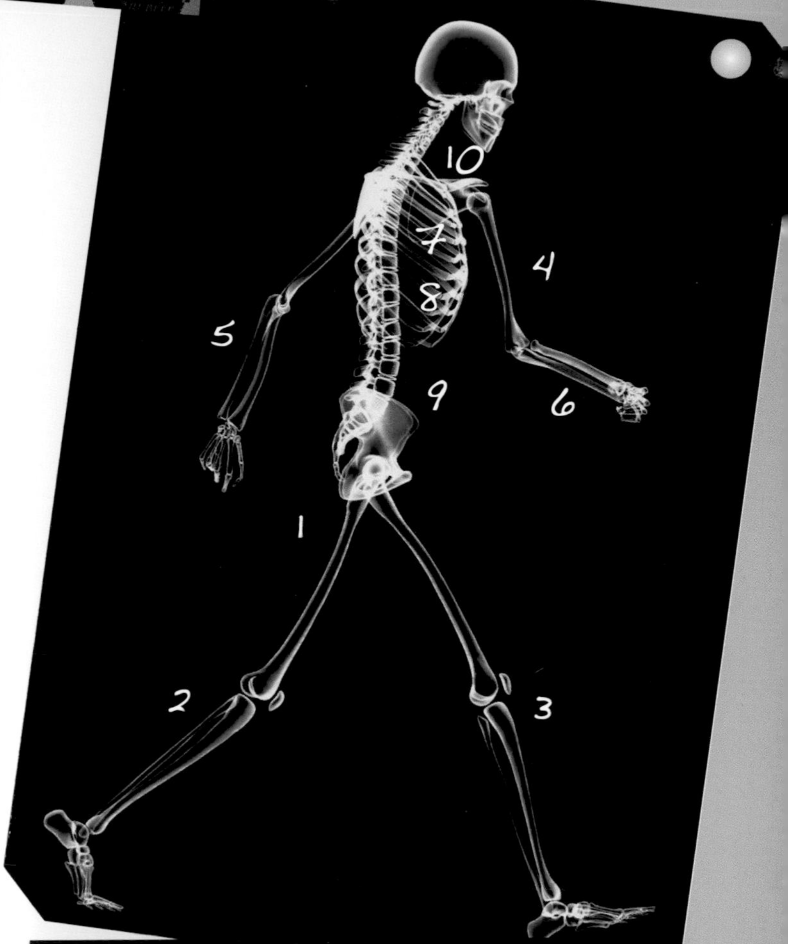

THE 10 **MOST COMMON ELEMENTS IN THE HUMAN BODY**

	ELEMENT	SYMBOL	AVERAGE ADULT* TOTAL G	OZ
1	Oxygen#	O	48,800	1,721
2	Carbon	C	18,400	649
3	Hydrogen#	H	8,000	282
4	Nitrogen	N	2,080	73
5	Calcium	Ca	1,120	39.5
6	Phosphorus	P	880	31.0
7	=Potassium	K	160	5.6
	=Sulphur	S	160	5.6
9	Sodium	Na	112	4.0
10	Chlorine	Cl	96	3.4

* 80 kg male
\# Mostly combined as water

The Top 10 elements account for more than 99 per cent of the total, the balance comprising minute quantities of metallic elements including iron – enough (4.8 g/ 0.17 oz) to make a 15-cm (6-in) nail – as well as zinc, tin and aluminium.

TOP 10 **LARGEST HUMAN ORGANS**

	ORGAN		AVERAGE WEIGHT G	OZ
1	**Skin**		10,886	384.0
2	**Liver**		1,560	55.0
3	**Brain**	male	1,408	49.7
		female	1,263	44.6
4	**Lungs**	*right*	*580*	*20.5*
		left	*510*	*18.0*
		total	1,090	38.5
5	**Heart**	male	315	11.1
		female	265	9.3
6	**Kidneys**	*right*	*140*	*4.9*
		left	*150*	*5.3*
		total	290	10.2
7	**Spleen**		170	6.0
8	**Pancreas**		98	3.5
9	**Thyroid**		35	1.2
10	**Prostate**	male only	20	0.7

This list is based on average post-mortem weights, although organs far in excess of the average have been recorded, including male brains of over 2 kg (4.4 lb). The skin is regarded by many as an organ. As it can constitute 16 per cent of a body's total weight, or 10,886 g (384 oz) in a person weighing 68 kg (150 lb), it heads the Top 10.

FROM THE CRADLE TO THE GRAVE

TOP 10 COUNTRIES WITH THE HIGHEST LIFE EXPECTANCY

	COUNTRY	LIFE EXPECTANCY AT BIRTH (2011)
1	Andorra	82.4
2	Japan	82.3
3	Singapore	82.1
4	Australia	81.8
5	Canada	81.4
6	France	81.2
7	=Sweden	81.1
	=Switzerland	81.1
9	=Israel	81.0
	=San Marino	81.0
	UK	*79.3*
	World average	*66.7*

Source: US Census Bureau, International Data Base

TOP 10 YEARS WITH MOST BIRTHS IN THE UK

	YEAR	BIRTHS
1	1920	1,194,068
2	1903	1,183,627
3	1904	1,181,770
4	1902	1,174,639
5	1908	1,173,759
6	1906	1,170,622
7	1905	1,163,535
8	1899	1,163,279
9	1901	1,162,975
10	1900	1,159,922

Source: National Statistics

Although not an independent country, Macau, a Special Administrative Region of China, reports a life expectancy of 84.4 years, placing it ahead of all countries in the Top 10.

TOP 10 COUNTRIES WITH THE LOWEST BIRTH RATE

	COUNTRY	ESTIMATED BIRTH RATE (LIVE BIRTHS PER 1,000, 2011)
1	Japan	7.3
2	Italy	7.9
3	Germany	8.2
4	Singapore	8.5
5	South Korea	8.6
6	=Austria	8.7
	=Czech Republic	8.7
8	=Bosnia and Herzegovina	8.9
	=Slovenia	8.9
	=Taiwan	8.9

Source: US Census Bureau, International Data Base

TOP 10 COUNTRIES WITH THE HIGHEST BIRTH RATE

COUNTRY / ESTIMATED BIRTH RATE (LIVE BIRTHS PER 1,000, 2011)

Source: US Census Bureau, International Data Base

	COUNTRY	ESTIMATED BIRTH RATE
1	Niger	50.5
2	Uganda	47.5
3	Mali	45.6
4	Burkina Faso	43.6
5	Ethiopia	43
6	Angola	42.97
7	Somalia	42.9
8	Dem. Rep. of Congo	41.8
9	Liberia	41.1
10	Malawi	40.9

TOP 10 MOST COMMON CAUSES OF DEATH

	CAUSE	WORLD DEATHS PER ANNUM
1	Cardiovascular diseases	14,942,817
2	Cancer	6,491,958
3	Respiratory infections	3,594,289
4	Respiratory diseases	3,307,337
5	STD/HIV/AIDS	2,770,004
6	Perinatal conditions	2,199,236
7	Digestive diseases	1,757,219
8	Diarrhoeal diseases	1,671,281
9	Tuberculosis	1,399,765
10	Traffic accidents	1,064,052

TOP 10 COUNTRIES WITH THE HIGHEST DEATH RATE

	COUNTRY	ESTIMATED DEATH RATE (DEATHS PER 1,000, 2011)
1	Angola	23.4
2	Lesotho	22.0
3	Zambia	21.0
4	Liberia	20.2
5	Mozambique	19.6
6	Central African Republic	17.5
7	Afghanistan	17.4
8	South Africa	17.1
9	Nigeria	16.1
10	Ukraine	15.7
	UK	*10.0*
	World average	*8.3*

Source: US Census Bureau, International Data Base

THE 10 COUNTRIES WITH THE LOWEST DEATH RATE

	COUNTRY	ESTIMATED DEATH RATE (DEATHS PER 1,000, 2011)
1	United Arab Emirates	2.1
2	Kuwait	2.3
3	= Qatar	2.4
	= Saudi Arabia	2.4
5	Jordan	2.7
6	= Brunei	3.4
	= Libya	3.4
8	Oman	3.6
9	= Maldives	3.7
	= Solomon Islands	3.7
	= Syria	3.7

Source: US Census Bureau, International Data Base

◀ *Burkina Faso*
African countries are notable for having the world's highest birth rates. Burkina Faso's population increased from 11.8 million in 2000 to 16.2 million in 2010.

THE 10 COUNTRIES WITH THE LOWEST LIFE EXPECTANCY

	COUNTRY	LIFE EXPECTANCY AT BIRTH (2011)
1	Angola	38.8
2	Zambia	39.1
3	Lesotho	40.8
4	Mozambique	41.6
5	Liberia	42.2
6	Afghanistan	45.0
7	Swaziland	48.7
8	South Africa	49.3
9	Zimbabwe	49.6
10	Somalia	50.4

Source: US Census Bureau, International Data Base

With the exception of Afghanistan, all the countries in this Top 10 are in sub-Saharan Africa, pointing to the prevalence of AIDS in these countries.

Oldest Ever

TOP 10 **OLDEST PEOPLE**

	NAME / COUNTRY	BORN	DIED	AGE YRS	MTHS	DAYS
1	**Jeanne Calment** (France)	21 Feb 1875	4 Aug 1997	122	5	14
2	**Sarah Knauss** (USA)	24 Sep 1880	30 Dec 1999	119	3	6
3	**Lucy Hannah** (USA)	16 Jul 1875	21 Mar 1993	117	8	5
4	**Marie-Louise Meilleur** (Canada)	29 Aug 1880	16 Apr 1998	117	7	18
5	**María Capovilla** (Ecuador)	14 Sep 1889	27 Aug 2006	116	11	13
6	**Tane Ikai** (Japan)	18 Jan 1879	12 Jul 1995	116	5	24
7	**Elizabeth Bolden** (USA)	15 Aug 1890	11 Dec 2006	116	3	26
8	**Maggie Barnes** (USA)	6 Mar 1882	19 Jan 1998	115	10	13
9	**Christian Mortensen*** (Denmark/USA)	16 Aug 1882	25 Apr 1998	115	8	9
10	**Charlotte Hughes** (UK)	1 Aug 1877	17 Mar 1993	115	7	16

* Oldest male – all others female

DISPUTED CLAIMS

The Top 10 list is based on the longevity of supercentenarians (those aged over 110) for whom there is undisputed evidence of their birthdate. It excludes alleged oldest man Shigechiyo Izumi (Japan), as there is doubt as to whether he was born in 1865 or 1880, and Carrie C. White (USA), whose 1874 birthdate cannot be verified.

▲ Monumental achievement
Pictured here with her great-great-great-grandson, oldest American Sarah Knauss was just six when the Statue of Liberty was unveiled.

◄ French vintage
Verifiably the oldest person of all time, French supercentenarian Jeanne Calment claimed to have met the artist Vincent van Gogh.

OLDEST MEN

For a month before his death at the age of 113, British World War I veteran Henry Allingham (6 June 1896–18 July 2009) was the world's oldest living man, and remains Britain's oldest ever man. His age does not, however, qualify him for the list of 10 oldest men ever, which – discounting disputed claims – is headed by Danish-American Christian Mortensen (1882–1998), the first man verifiably to celebrate both a 114th and 115th birthday.

IT AIN'T NECESSARILY SO...

A number of Biblical patriarchs are credited with extreme ages, led by Methuselah, the grandfather of the similarly long-lived Noah (above), who is said to have survived for 350 years after the Flood. Although depicted as ancient, a mere 120 years was claimed for Moses.

	PATRIARCH / AGE	
1	Methuselah	969
2	Jared	962
3	Noah	950
4	Adam	930
5	Seth	912
6	Kenan	910
7	Enos	905
8	Mahalalel	895
9	Lamech	777
10	Shem	600

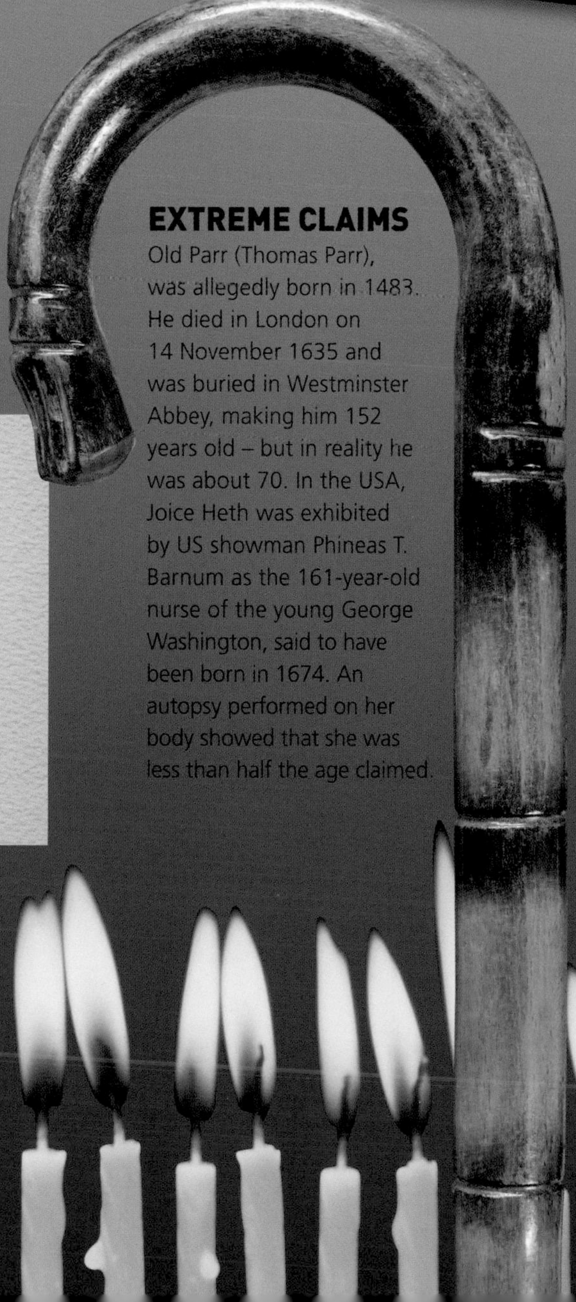

EXTREME CLAIMS

Old Parr (Thomas Parr), was allegedly born in 1483. He died in London on 14 November 1635 and was buried in Westminster Abbey, making him 152 years old – but in reality he was about 70. In the USA, Joice Heth was exhibited by US showman Phineas T. Barnum as the 161-year-old nurse of the young George Washington, said to have been born in 1674. An autopsy performed on her body showed that she was less than half the age claimed.

OLDEST IN THE UK

Margaret Ann Neve (18 May 1792–4 April 1903) of Guernsey was the first supercentenarian ever recorded. At one time the world's oldest living person, her life spanned the 18th, 19th and 20th centuries. Charlotte Hughes (1 August 1877–17 March 1993) is Britain's oldest, at 115 years 228 days, and Florie Baldwin (born 31 March 1896) is the oldest living (as at 1 April 2010).

MARRIAGE & DIVORCE

TOP 10 COUNTRIES WHERE MOST MEN MARRY

	COUNTRY	% OF MEN MARRIED BY AGE 50*
1	=Chad	100.0
	=The Gambia	100.0
3	Guinea	99.7
4	=Mali	99.6
	=Niger	99.6
6	=Bangladesh	99.3
	=Mozambique	99.3
8	Cameroon	99.2
9	Nepal	99.1
10	=Central African Republic	99.0
	=Eritrea	99.0
	=Tajikistan	99.0
	UK	*91.2*

* In latest year for which data available

Source: United Nations

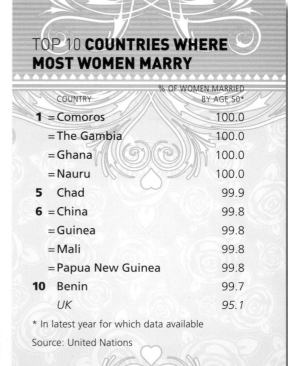

▲ *Marriage in Mali*
The marriage rate for Malian men is among the world's highest. The country also has one of the highest rates for 15–19-year-old girls, 72 per cent of whom marry.

TOP 10 COUNTRIES WHERE MOST WOMEN MARRY

	COUNTRY	% OF WOMEN MARRIED BY AGE 50*
1	=Comoros	100.0
	=The Gambia	100.0
	=Ghana	100.0
	=Nauru	100.0
5	Chad	99.9
6	=China	99.8
	=Guinea	99.8
	=Mali	99.8
	=Papua New Guinea	99.8
10	Benin	99.7
	UK	*95.1*

* In latest year for which data available

Source: United Nations

TOP 10 **COUNTRIES WITH THE HIGHEST MARRIAGE RATES**

	COUNTRY	MARRIAGES PER 1,000 PER ANNUM*
1	Barbados	13.1
2	Vietnam	12.1
3	Ethiopia	10.2
4	Seychelles	9.9
5	Jordan	9.7
6	Iran	8.9
7	=Algeria	8.8
	=Mauritius	8.8
9	Jamaica	8.3
10	USA	8.0
	UK	*5.1*

* In 2005 or latest year in those countries for which data available

Source: United Nations

► *Vietnamese wedding*
By the age of 50, only 3.3 per cent of the population of Vietnam has never married.

The countries that figure among those with the lowest rates represent a range of cultures and religions, which either condone or condemn divorce to varying extents, thus affecting its prevalence or otherwise. In some countries, legal and other obstacles make divorce difficult or costly, while in certain societies, such as Jamaica, where the marriage rate is also low, partners often separate without the formality of divorce.

TOP 10 **MONTHS FOR MARRIAGES IN ENGLAND AND WALES**

	MONTH	MARRIAGES
1	August	37,128
2	September	34,544
3	July	34,501
4	June	26,410
5	May	21,965
6	April	17,876
7	October	16,697
8	December	13,562
9	November	10,891
10	March	10,763

THE 10 **COUNTRIES WITH THE LOWEST DIVORCE RATES**

	COUNTRY	DIVORCE RATE PER 1,000*
1	Guatemala	0.12
2	Belize	0.17
3	Mongolia	0.28
4	Libya	0.32
5	Georgia	0.40
6	Chile	0.42
7	St Vincent and the Grenadines	0.43
8	Jamaica	0.44
9	Armenia	0.47
10	Turkey	0.49

* In those countries/latest year for which data available

Source: United Nations

THE 10 **COUNTRIES WITH THE HIGHEST DIVORCE RATES**

	COUNTRY	DIVORCE RATE PER 1,000*
1	Russia	5.30
2	Aruba	5.27
3	USA	4.19
4	Ukraine	3.79
5	Belarus	3.77
6	Moldova	3.50
7	Cuba	3.16
8	Czech Republic	3.11
9	Lithuania	3.05
10	South Korea	3.05
	UK	*2.58*

* In those countries/latest year for which data available

Source: United Nations

NAMES TO CONJURE WITH

TOP 10 FIRST NAMES IN ENGLAND AND WALES, 2008

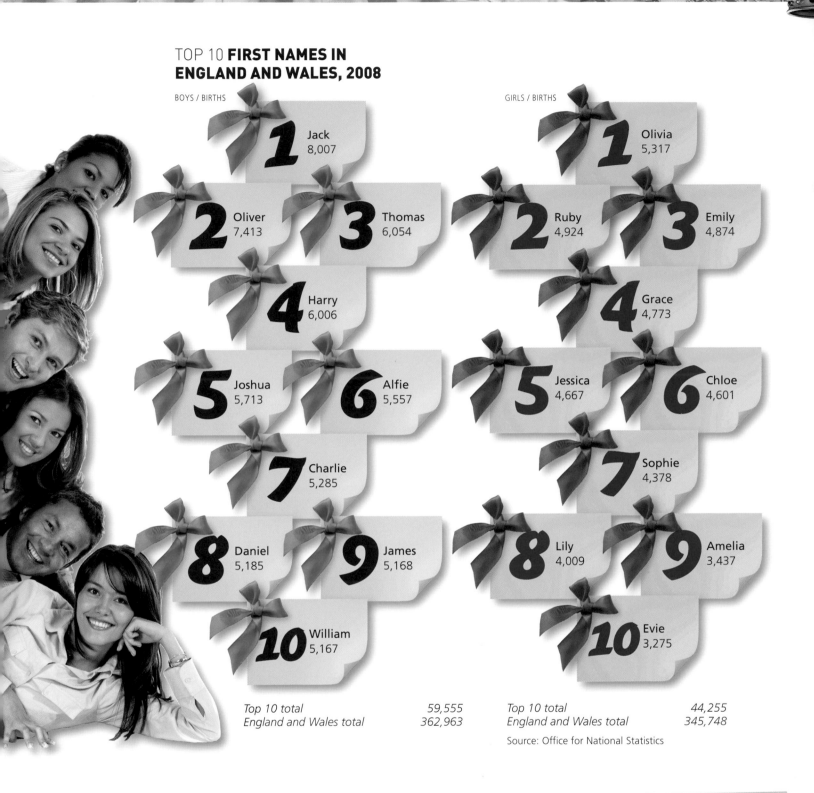

BOYS / BIRTHS		
1	Jack	8,007
2	Oliver	7,413
3	Thomas	6,054
4	Harry	6,006
5	Joshua	5,713
6	Alfie	5,557
7	Charlie	5,285
8	Daniel	5,185
9	James	5,168
10	William	5,167
	Top 10 total	*59,555*
	England and Wales total	*362,963*

GIRLS / BIRTHS		
1	Olivia	5,317
2	Ruby	4,924
3	Emily	4,874
4	Grace	4,773
5	Jessica	4,667
6	Chloe	4,601
7	Sophie	4,378
8	Lily	4,009
9	Amelia	3,437
10	Evie	3,275
	Top 10 total	*44,255*
	England and Wales total	*345,748*

Source: Office for National Statistics

TOP 10 MOST COMMON NAMES IN ENGLAND AND WALES

	NAME	NO.
1	David Jones	15,763
2	David Smith	14,341
3	John Smith	12,793
4	David Williams	11,392
5	Michael Smith	10,516
6	John Jones	10,021
7	John Williams	8,738
8	=Paul Smith	8,348
	=Peter Smith	8,348
10	David Evans	8,103

A survey of first name and surname combinations based on the National Health Service Register reveals more variation among female first names, resulting in none making the Top 10: the closest runner-up is Margaret Smith, with 7,640 examples, followed by Margaret Jones with 7,068.

TOP 10 **FIRST NAMES IN NORTHERN IRELAND, 2008**

	BOYS	BIRTHS
1	Jack	342
2	Matthew	290
3	Daniel	270
4	Ryan	264
5	James	260
6	Joshua	195
7	Conor	186
8	=Dylan	181
	=Thomas	181
10	=Charlie	176
	Ethan	176
	Top 10 total	*2,521*
	Northern Ireland total	*12,535*

	GIRLS	BIRTHS
1	Katie	281
2	Sophie	221
3	Grace	217
4	Jessica	206
5	Emma	205
6	Lucy	198
7	Emily	192
8	Chloe	179
9	Eva	178
10	Hannah	172
	Top 10 total	*2,049*
	Northern Ireland total	*12,717*

Source: Northern Ireland Statistics & Research Agency

TOP 10 **SURNAMES IN SCOTLAND**

	NAME	FREQUENCY*
1	Smith	4,291
2	Brown	3,030
3	Wilson	2,876
4	Campbell	2,657
5	Stewart	2,626
6	Thomson	2,616
7	Robertson	2,536
8	Anderson	2,297
9	Macdonald	1,844
10	Scott	1,839

* Number recorded in sample of 335,000 births and deaths, 1999–2001

Source: General Register Office for Scotland

TOP 10 **FIRST NAMES IN SCOTLAND, 2008**

GIRLS / BIRTHS

1	Sophie	632
2	Emily	433
3	Olivia	421
4	Chloe	404
5	Emma	401
6	Lucy	391
7	Ava	383
8	Katie	360
9	Erin	355
10	Hannah	344

Top 10 total 4,124
Scotland total 29,470

BOYS / BIRTHS

1	Jack	692
2	Lewis	611
3	Daniel	475
4	Liam	445
5	=James	444
	=Ryan	444
7	Callum	368
8	Logan	359
9	Matthew	349
10	Cameron	332

Top 10 total 4,519
Scotland total 30,571

Source: General Register Office for Scotland

THE 10 **SHORTEST-SERVING US PRESIDENTS**

	PRESIDENT	PERIOD IN OFFICE YEARS	MONTHS	DAYS
1	William H. Harrison (1841)*	–	–	30
2	James A. Garfield (1881)*	–	6	15
3	Zachary Taylor (1849–50)*	1	4	5
4	Warren G. Harding (1921–23)*	2	4	29
5	Gerald R. Ford (1974–77)	2	5	11
6	Millard Fillmore (1850–53)	2	5	25
7	John F. Kennedy (1961–63)*	2	10	2
8	Chester A. Arthur (1881–85)	3	5	13
9	Andrew Johnson (1865–69)	3	10	17
10	John Tyler (1841–45)	3	11	0

* Died in office

Ninth and second-oldest president William Harrison caught pneumonia while delivering an inaugural address in the rain on 4 March 1841. The longest on record, its 8,400 words took him 1 hour 45 minutes to deliver. He was ill throughout his record shortest term in office, and became the first US president to die in office and the first to die in the White House. Outside these 10, all other presidents have served either one or the now-maximum two full four-year terms – three in the case of Franklin D. Roosevelt.

THE 10 **WOMEN MOST RECENTLY ELECTED AS PRESIDENTS**

	PRESIDENT	COUNTRY	TOOK OFFICE
1	Dalia Grybauskaitė	Lithuania	12 Jul 2009
2	Cristina Fernández de Kirchner	Argentina	10 Dec 2007
3	Pratibha Patil	India	25 Jul 2007
4	Michelle Bachelet	Chile	11 Mar 2006
5	Ellen Johnson-Sirleaf	Liberia	16 Jan 2006
6	Megawati Sukarnoputri	Indonesia	23 Jul 2001*
7	Gloria Macapagal-Arroyo	Philippines	20 Jan 2001
8	Tarja Halonen	Finland	1 Mar 2000
9	Mireya Moscoso	Panama	1 Sep 1999#
10	Vaira Vīķe-Freiberga	Latvia	8 Jul 1999†

* Left office 20 October 2004
\# Left office 1 September 2004
† Left office 7 July 2007

TOP 10 **LONGEST-SERVING PRESIDENTS TODAY**

	PRESIDENT	COUNTRY	TOOK OFFICE
1	Colonel Mu'ammar Gaddafi*	Libya	1 Sep 1969
2	Ali Abdullah Saleh	Yemen	18 Jul 1978#
3	Teodoro Obiang Nguema Mbasogo	Equatorial Guinea	3 Aug 1979
4	José Eduardo dos Santos	Angola	21 Sep 1979
5	Hosni Mubarak	Egypt	6 Oct 1981
6	Paul Biya	Cameroon	7 Nov 1982
7	Yoweri Museveni	Uganda	29 Jan 1986
8	Zine El Abidine Ben Ali	Tunisia	2 Oct 1987
9	Blaise Compaoré	Burkina Faso	15 Oct 1987
10	Robert Mugabe	Zimbabwe	31 Dec 1987

* Since a reorganization in 1979, Colonel Gaddafi has held no formal position, but continues to rule under the ceremonial title of 'Leader and Guide of the Revolution'
\# Became president of North Yemen; of combined country since 22 May 1990

► ***Leading leaders***
Two Arab rulers, Saleh of Yemen (left) and Gaddafi of Libya (right) are the world's current (as at 9 February 2010) longest-serving national leaders, with a total of over 72 years in office between them.

TOP 10 **LONGEST-REIGNING MONARCHS***

	MONARCH	COUNTRY	REIGN	AGE AT ACCESSION	REIGN YRS	MTHS	DAYS
1	King Louis XIV	France	14 May 1643–1 Sep 1715	5	72	3	18
2	King John II	Liechtenstein	12 Nov 1858–11 Feb 1929	18	70	2	30
3	Emperor Franz-Josef	Austria-Hungary	2 Dec 1848–21 Nov 1916	18	67	11	19
4	Queen Victoria	UK	20 Jun 1837–22 Jan 1901	18	63	7	2
5	James I	Aragon	12 Sep 1213–27 Jul 1276	5	62	10	15
6	Emperor Hirohito	Japan	25 Dec 1926–7 Jan 1989	25	62	0	13
7	Emperor K'ang Hsi	China	5 Feb 1661–20 Dec 1722	7	61	10	15
8	King Sobhuza II#	Swaziland	22 Dec 1921–21 Aug 1982	22	60	7	30
9	Emperor Ch'ien Lung	China	18 Oct 1735–9 Feb 1796	25	60	3	22
10	King Christian IV	Denmark	4 Apr 1588–21 Feb 1648	11	59	10	17

* During past 1,000 years, excluding earlier rulers of dubious authenticity and current rulers
# Paramount chief until 1967, when Great Britain recognized him as king with the granting of internal self-government

This list excludes rulers of the ancient world with unsubstantiated claims of reigns of up to 95 years. Queen Elizabeth II is coming up on the rail: she acceded on 6 February 1952, so as at 6 February 2010 passed the 58-year mark.

TOP 10 **MONARCHIES WITH THE MOST SUBJECTS***

COUNTRY / MONARCH / ACCESSION / POPULATION (2011)

1 Britain#
Elizabeth II (1952)
132,645,981

2 Japan
Akihito (1989)
126,475,664

3 Thailand
Bhumibol Adulyadej (1946)
66,796,787

4 Spain
Juan Carlos I (1975)
40,560,943

5 Morocco
Mohammed VI (1999)
31,968,361

6 Saudi Arabia
Abdullah (2005)
29,709,239

7 Nepal
Gyanendra Bir Bikram Shah Dev (2001)
29,391,883

8 Malaysia
Mizan Zainal Abidin (2006)
26,607,887

9 Netherlands
Beatrix (1980)
16,847,007

10 Cambodia
Norodom Sihamoni (1999)
15,019,430

* By population
# Total of British Commonwealth realms with monarch as Head of State

Source: US Census Bureau

► Long to reign over us
On the throne for 58 years, Elizabeth II reigns over two per cent of the world's population.

ORGANIZATIONS

▲ *Scout jamboree*
Baden-Powell coined the term jamboree for the first world meeting in 1920, when 8,000 assembled in London.

TOP 10 **COUNTRIES WITH THE HIGHEST SCOUT MEMBERSHIP**

	COUNTRY	SCOUTING FOUNDED	MEMBERSHIP*
1	Indonesia	1912	8,103,835
2	USA	1909	5,970,203
3	India	1909	2,423,686
4	Philippines	1923	1,872,525
5	Thailand	1911	1,360,869
6	Bangladesh	1972	896,118
7	Pakistan	1947	526,403
8	UK	1907	499,323
9	Kenya	1910	262,146
10	South Korea	1922	214,363

* Latest available year
Source: World Organization of the Scout Movement

Following an experimental camp held from 29 July to 9 August 1907 on Brownsea Island, Dorset, England, Sir Robert Baden Powell (1857–1941), a former general in the British army, launched the Scouting Movement.

TOP 10 **LARGEST TRADE UNIONS IN THE UK**

	UNION	MEMBERSHIP* MALE	FEMALE	TOTAL
1	**Unite** (formed 2007 by merger of Amicus and Transport and General Workers' Union)	1,201,103	356,789	1,557,892
2	**UNISON**	408,600	953,400	1,362,000
3	**GMB** (formerly General, Municipal Boilermakers and Allied Trades Union)	324,529	276,602	601,131
4	**Royal College of Nursing** (RCN)	34,875	356,261	391,136
5	**Union of Shop, Distributive and Allied Workers** (USDAW)	156,984	213,779	370,763
6	**Public and Commercial Services Union** (PCS)	120,049	180,175	300,224
7	**National Union of Teachers** (NUT)	69,751	224,184	293,935
8	**National Association of Schoolmasters Union of Women Teachers** (NASUWT)	76,865	198,046	274,911
9	**Communications Workers Union** (CWU)	184,395	46,573	230,968
10	**Union of Construction, Allied Trades and Technicians** (UCATT)	128,728	2,131	130,859

* 2010 or latest year for which data available
Source: TUC

There are 185 trade unions in the UK, with a total membership of 7,656,156. In recent years many smaller unions, such as the Card Setting Machine Tenters Society, disbanded as the industries they represented disappeared.

TOP 10 **COUNTRIES WITH THE HIGHEST GIRL GUIDE AND GIRL SCOUT MEMBERSHIP**

	COUNTRY / GUIDING FOUNDED	MEMBERSHIP (2006)
1	USA 1912	3,578,760
2	India 1911	1,305,028
3	Philippines 1919	713,777
4	UK 1909	552,603
5	Kenya 1920	158,810
6	Canada 1910	116,206
7	Nigeria 1919	113,726
8	Uganda 1914	112,371
9	Italy 1912	83,601
10	Poland 1910	76,718

Source: World Association of Girl Guides and Girl Scouts

TOP 10 **UK CHARITIES BY INCOME**

	CHARITY	INCOME (£)
1	The Children's Investment Fund Foundation	494,870,000
2	Cancer Research UK	419,610,000
3	CITB-ConstructionSkill	323,650,000
4	Wellcome Trust	305,000,000
5	Anchor Trust	276,420,000
6	Oxfam	219,800,000
7	UFI Charitable Trust	216,890,000
8	British Heart Foundation	183,210,000
9	The Gatsby Charitable Foundation	180,760,000
10	Peabody Trust	168,130,000

TOP 10 **UK CHARITIES BY DONATIONS**

CHARITY / DONATIONS (£)

1 Wellcome Trust 790,700,000

2 The British Council 621,580,000

3 Nuffield Health 588,020,000

4 Cancer Research UK 475,770,000

5 The Arts Council England 445,080,000

6 The National Trust 396,920,000

7 CITB-Construction Skill 335,340,000

8 Charities Aid Foundation 321,420,000

9 Oxfam 298,400,000

10 Anchor Trust 267,400,000

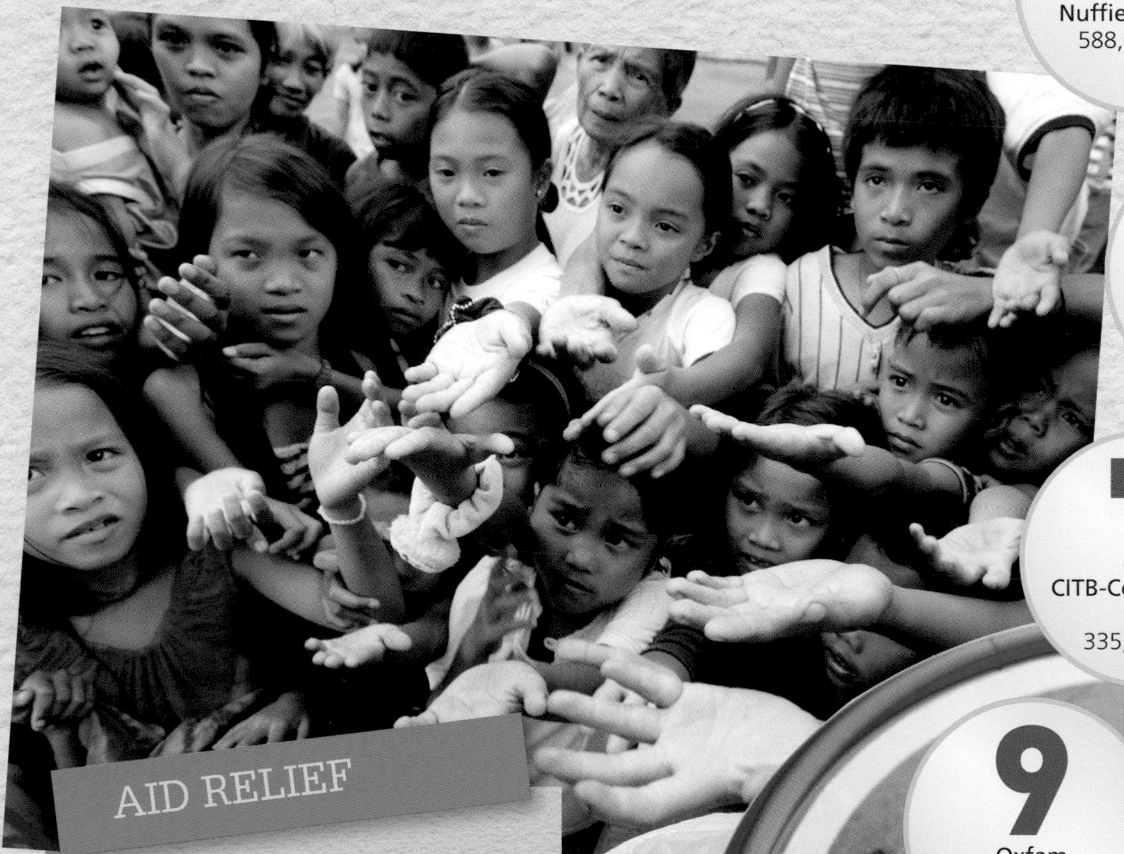

AID RELIEF

Although high-profile events such as Live Aid (1985) have focused the world's attention on famine and poverty, the work of international charities and aid organizations such as Oxfam are at the forefront of humanitarian aid, providing food, economic and other support, while many target health issues including combating epidemics such as malaria and AIDS, with funding from governmental and other organizations, corporations and individual donors.

WAR ON LAND

▲ *Stalingrad*
The 200-day Battle of Stalingrad was the bloodiest of all time.

THE 10 **BATTLES WITH MOST CASUALTIES**

	BATTLE	WAR / DATE	CASUALTIES*
1	Stalingrad	World War II, 1942–43	2,000,000
2	Somme River I	World War I, 1916	1,073,900
3	Po Valley	World War II, 1945	740,000
4	Moscow	World War II, 1941–42	700,000
5	Verdun	World War I, 1916	595,000
6	Gallipoli	World War I, 1915	500,000
7	Artois-Loos	World War I, 1915	428,000
8	Berezina	War of 1812	400,000
9	38th Parallel	Korean War, 1951	320,000
10	Somme River II	World War I, 1918	300,000

* Estimated total of military and civilian dead, wounded and missing

Total numbers of casualties in the Battle of Stalingrad are at best estimates, but it was undoubtedly one of the longest and almost certainly the bloodiest battles of all time. Fought between German (with Hungarian, Romanian and Italian troops also under German command) and Soviet forces, it continued from 19 August 1942 to 2 February 1943, with huge losses on both sides.

THE 10 **WORST US CIVIL WAR BATTLES**

	BATTLE	DATE	CASUALTIES*
1	Gettysburg	1–3 Jul 1863	51,116
2	Seven Day Battles	25 Jun–1 Jul 1862	36,463
3	Chickamauga	19–20 Sep 1863	34,624
4	Chancellorsville/ Fredericksburg	1–4 May 1863	30,099
5	Wilderness#	5–7 May 1862	25,416
6	Manassas/Chantilly	27 Aug–2 Sep 1862	25,340
7	Stone's River	31 Dec 1862–1 Jan 1863	24,645
8	Shiloh	6–7 Apr 1862	23,741
9	Antietam	17 Sep 1862	22,726
10	Fort Donelson	13–16 Dec 1862	19,455

* Killed, missing and wounded
# Confederate totals estimated

▼ *Gettysburg*
The Union victory at Gettysburg, Pennsylvania, caused severe casualties on both sides.

THE 10 **WORST BATTLES OF THE NAPOLEONIC WARS**

	BATTLE / COUNTRY	DATE	CASUALTIES*
1	**Leipzig**, Germany	16–19 Oct 1813	120,000
2	**Wagram**, Austria	5–6 Jul 1809	79,000
3	**Borodino**, Russia	7 Sep 1812	68,000
4	**Waterloo**, Belgium	18 Jun 1815	52,000
5	**Aspern-Essling**, Austria	21–22 May 1815	44,500
6	**Eylau**, Poland	7–8 Feb 1807	43,000
7	**Lutzen**, Germany	2 May 1813	36,000
8	**Friedland**, Poland	14 Jun 1807	33,000
9	**Beresina**, Russia	26–28 Nov 1812	28,000
10	**Bautzen**, Germany	20–21 May 1813	20,000

* Estimated total killed or wounded

◀ *Borodino*
Napoleon was victorious, but total French and Russian casualties were the worst of the campaign.

TOP 10 **TANKS OF WORLD WAR II**

	TANK / YEAR INTRODUCED	COUNTRY	WEIGHT (TONS)	NO. PRODUCED
1	**M4A3 Sherman** (1942)	USA	31.0	41,530
2	**T34 Model 42** (1940)	USSR	28.5	35,120
3	**T34/85** (1944)	USSR	32.0	29,430
4	**M3 General Stuart** (1941)	USA	12.2	14,000
5	**Valentine II** (1941)	UK	17.5	8,280
6	**M3A1 Lee/Grant** (1941)	USA	26.8	7,400
7	**Churchill VII** (1942)	UK	40.0	5,640
8	=**Panzer IVD** (pre-war)	Germany	20.0	5,500
	=**Panzer VG** (1943)	Germany	44.8	5,500
10	**Crusader I** (1941)	UK	19.0	4,750

The tank named after US Civil War General William Tecumseh Sherman was used in large numbers by both US and British troops during World War II. It carried a crew of five and could cruise over a distance of 230 km (143 miles) at up to 40 km/h (25 mph).

THE 10 **SHORTEST WARS**

	WAR / DATES	DURATION
1	**Anglo-Zanzibar** 27 Aug 1896	38 mins
2	**Six-Day** 5–10 Jun 1967	6 days
3	**Indo-Pakistani** 3–16 Dec 1971	13 days
4	**Serbo-Bulgarian** 14–28 Nov 1885	14 days
5	**Georgian-Armenian** 7–31 Dec 1918	24 days
6	**Sino-Vietnamese** 17 Feb–16 Mar 1979	27 days
7	**Greco-Turkish** 10 Apr–20 May 1897	30 days
8	**Second Balkan** 16 Jun–18 Jul 1913	32 days
9	**Polish-Lithuanian** 1 Sep–7 Oct 1920	37 days
10	**Falklands** 2 Apr–14 Jun 1982	42 days

At 9.02 a.m. on 27 August 1896, after Sa'id Khalid bin Barghash proclaimed himself ruler of Zanzibar, the British fleet declared war, opening fire on the Sultan's palace, which was destroyed and some 500 people killed. The shortest-ever war ended at 9.40 a.m., when Khalid surrendered.

► ***Six-Day War***
Israel's land and air war on three fronts (Egypt, Jordan and Syria) achieved a swift and decisive victory.

WAR IN THE AIR

► *Battle of Britain*
In the period 10 July to 31 October 1940 Germany lost 1,887 aircraft and 2,698 aircrew.

THE 10 **WORST ALLIED BATTLE OF BRITAIN LOSSES**

	NATIONALITY	PILOTS	KILLED
1	RAF (British/other Commonwealth)	1,822	339
2	Polish	141	29
3	Canadian	88	20
4	Australian	21	14
5	New Zealander	73	11
6	=Fleet Air Arm	56	9
	=South African	21	9
8	Czech	86	8
9	Belgian	26	6
10	American	7	1

TOP 10 **AIR ACES OF WORLD WAR I**

	PILOT	NATIONALITY	KILLS CLAIMED*
1	Rittmeister Manfred Albrecht Freiherr von Richthofen#	German	80
2	Capitaine René Paul Fonck	French	75
3	Maj. William Avery Bishop	Canadian	72
4	Maj. Edward Corringham 'Mick' Mannock#	British	68
5	=Maj. Raymond Collishaw	Canadian	62†
	=Oberleutnant Ernst Udet	German	62
7	Maj. James Thomas Byford McCudden#	British	57
8	=Capt. Anthony Wetherby Beauchamp-Proctor	South African	54
	=Capt. Donald Roderick MacLaren	Canadian	54
	=Capitaine George Marie Ludovic Jules Guynemer#	French	54

* Approximate – some kills disputed
# Killed in action
† Including two in Russian Civil War, 1919

TOP 10 **FASTEST FIGHTER AIRCRAFT OF WORLD WAR II**

	AIRCRAFT	COUNTRY	MAX. SPEED KM/H	MPH
1	Messerschmitt Me 163	Germany	959	596
2	Messerschmitt Me 262	Germany	901	560
3	Heinkel He 162A	Germany	890	553
4	P-51-H Mustang	USA	784	487
5	Lavochkin La11	USSR	740	460
6	Spitfire XIV	UK	721	448
7	Yakolev Yak-3	USSR	719	447
8	P-51-D Mustang	USA	708	440
9	Tempest VI	UK	705	438
10	Focke-Wulf FW190D	Germany	700	435

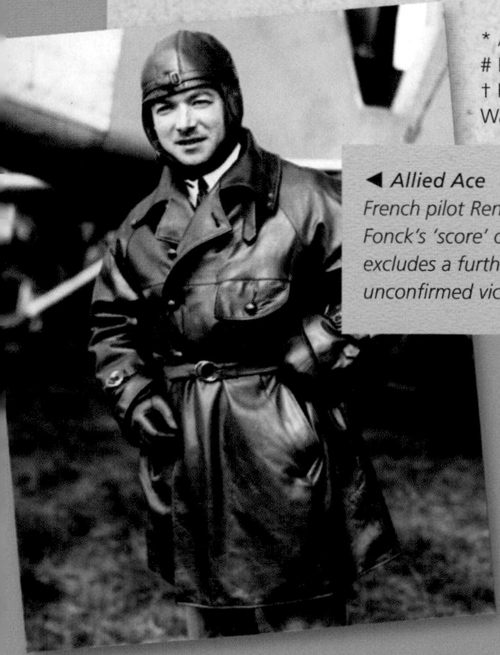

◄ *Allied Ace*
French pilot René Fonck's 'score' of 75 excludes a further 52 unconfirmed victories.

▼ *Messerschmitt Me 163*
Also known as the Komet, the Messerschmitt Me 163 was a short-range, rocket-powered interceptor brought into service in 1944–45, during which this aircraft scored a number of victories over its slower Allied rivals.

Aircraft losses
Estimates of military equipment losses, especially of aircraft, remain highly speculative.

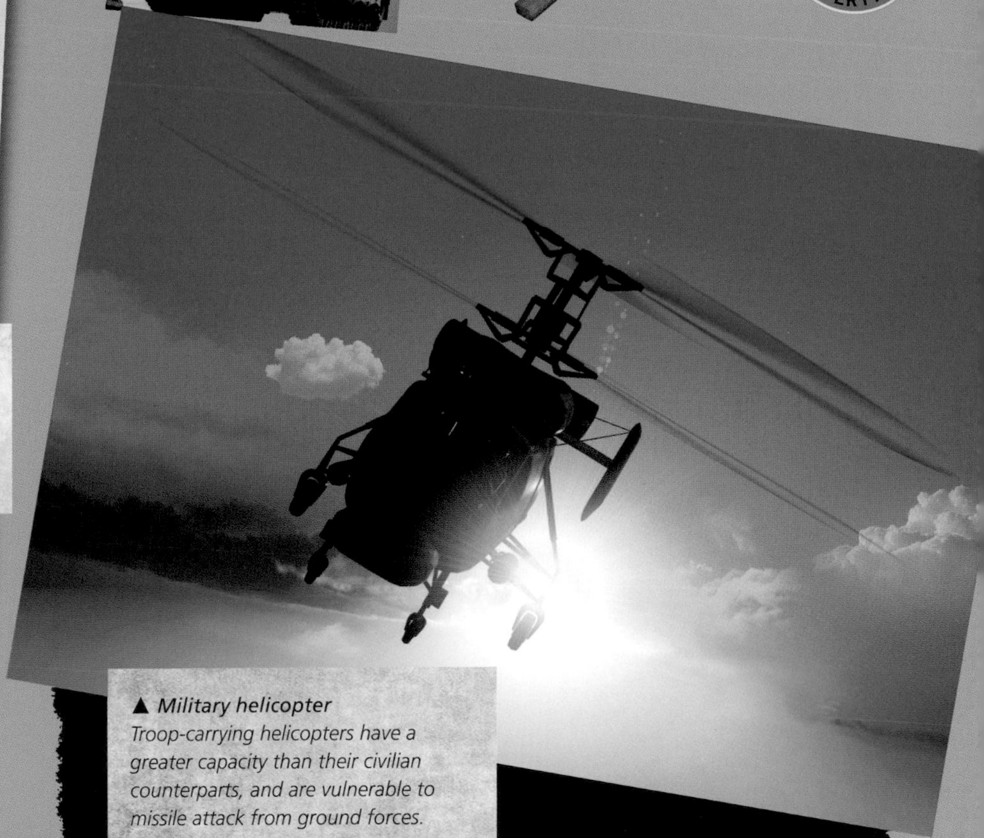

▲ *Military helicopter*
Troop-carrying helicopters have a greater capacity than their civilian counterparts, and are vulnerable to missile attack from ground forces.

THE 10 **COUNTRIES SUFFERING THE GREATEST AIRCRAFT LOSSES IN WORLD WAR II**

COUNTRY / AIRCRAFT LOST

1. Germany 116,584
2. USSR 106,652
3. USA 59,296
4. Japan 49,485
5. UK 33,090
6. Australia 7,160
7. Italy 5,272
8. Canada 2,389
9. France 2,100
10. New Zealand 684

Reports of aircraft losses vary considerably from country to country, some of them including aircraft damaged, lost due to accidents or scrapped, as well as those destroyed during combat.

THE 10 **WORST MILITARY HELICOPTER DISASTERS**

	LOCATION / DATE / INCIDENT	NO. KILLED
1	**Near San Andres de Bocay,** Nueva Segovia, Nicaragua, 9 Dec 1982. A Mil Mi-8 shot down by Sandinistian rebels crashed in a mountainous area. Some 75 of those killed were children.	84
2	**Near She'ar Yeshuv,** Israel, 4 Feb 1997. Two Sikorsky CHD-53D helicopters collided.	73
3	**Near Lata,** Georgia, 14 Dec 1992. A Mil Mi-8T was shot down by a missile.	61
4 =	**Near Moc Hoa,** South Vietnam, 12 Dec 1974. A Boeing/Vertol CH-47 was shot down by a missile.	54
=	**Near Jericho,** Jordan, 10 May 1977. A Sikorsky CH-53D crashed shortly after takeoff.	54
6	**Near Quang Tri,** South Vietnam, 11 Jul 1972. A Sikorsky CH-53D was reported to have been shot down.	52
7 =	**Near An Loc,** South Vietnam, 13 Jun 1972. A Boeing/Vertol CH-47 was shot down by ground fire.	47
=	**Near Stepanakert,** Azerbaijan, 28 Jan 1992. A Mil Mi-8 was shot down by a missile and exploded in mid-air.	47
9	**Near Mannheim,** West Germany, 11 Sep 1982. A Boeing/Vertol CH-47C carrying British, French and German skydivers broke up, crashed and exploded.	46
10	**Near Karakent,** Azerbaijan, 1 Nov 1991. A Mil Mi-8 was shot down.	40

▲ *World War II convoy*
Despite sailing in convoys with warship escorts to protect them, merchant shipping suffered severe losses.

THE 10 COUNTRIES SUFFERING THE GREATEST MERCHANT-SHIPPING LOSSES IN WORLD WAR I

	COUNTRY	VESSELS SUNK NO.	TONNAGE
1	UK	2,038	6,797,802
2	Italy	228	720,064
3	France	213	651,583
4	USA	93	372,892
5	Germany	188	319,552
6	Greece	115	304,992
7	Denmark	126	205,002
8	Netherlands	74	194,483
9	Sweden	124	192,807
10	Spain	70	160,383

THE 10 COUNTRIES SUFFERING THE GREATEST MERCHANT-SHIPPING LOSSES IN WORLD WAR II

	COUNTRY	VESSELS SUNK NO.	TONNAGE
1	UK	4,786	21,194,000
2	Japan	2,346	8,618,109
3	Germany	1,595	7,064,600
4	USA	578	3,524,983
5	Norway	427	1,728,531
6	Netherlands	286	1,195,204
7	Italy	467	1,155,080
8	Greece	262	883,200
9	Panama	107	542,772
10	Sweden	204	481,864

During 1939–45, Allied losses in the Atlantic alone totalled 3,843 ships. June 1942 was the worst period of the war, with 131 vessels lost in the Atlantic and a further 42 elsewhere.

THE 10 COUNTRIES SUFFERING THE GREATEST NUMBER OF WARSHIP LOSSES IN WORLD WAR II

	COUNTRY	WARSHIPS SUNK
1	UK	213
2	Japan	198
3	USA	105
4	Italy	97
5	Germany	60
6	USSR	37
7	Canada	17
8	France	11
9	Australia	9
10	Norway	2

► *Pearl Harbor*
The Japanese attack of 7 December 1941 sunk or disabled battleships and destroyers of the US fleet.

▶ *USS* Iowa
One of the largest class of US World War II battleships, Iowa also saw service in the Korean War.

TOP 10 **U-BOAT COMMANDERS OF WORLD WAR II**

	COMMANDER / U-BOATS COMMANDED	SHIPS SUNK
1	Otto Kretschmer U-23, U-99	45
2	Wolfgang Luth U-9, U-138, U-43, U-181	44
3	Joachim Schepke U-3, U-19, U-100	39
4	Erich Topp U-57, U-552	35
5	Victor Schutze U-25, U-103	34
6	Heinrich Leibe U-38	30
7	Karl F. Merten U-68	29*
8	Günther Prien U-47	29*
9	Johann Mohr U-124	29*
10	Georg Lassen U-160	28

* Gross tonnage used to determine ranking order

Günther Prien performed the remarkable feat of penetrating the British naval base at Scapa Flow on 14 October 1939, and sinking the Royal Navy battleship *Royal Oak*.

TOP 10 **LARGEST BATTLESHIPS OF WORLD WAR II**

	NAME	COUNTRY	STATUS	OVERALL LENGTH M	OVERALL LENGTH FT	TONNAGE
1	=Musashi	Japan	Sunk 24 Oct 1944	263	862	72,809
	=Yamato	Japan	Sunk 7 Apr 1945	263	862	72,809
3	=Iowa	USA	Decommissioned 26 Oct 1990	270	887	55,710
	=Missouri	USA	Decommissioned 31 Mar 1992	270	887	55,710
	=New Jersey	USA	Decommissioned 8 Feb 1991	270	887	55,710
	=Wisconsin	USA	Decommissioned 30 Sep 1991	270	887	55,710
7	=Bismarck	Germany	Sunk 27 May 1941	251	823	50,153
	=Tirpitz	Germany	Sunk 12 Nov 1944	251	823	50,153
9	=Jean Bart	France	Survived WWII, scrapped 1969	247	812	47,500
	=Richelieu	France	Survived WWII, scrapped 1968	247	812	47,500

◀ *Ace of the deep*
Germany's leading ace, Otto Kretschmer, sunk the greatest tonnage of any U-boat commander of World War II.

THE 10 **SUBMARINE FLEETS WITH GREATEST LOSSES IN WORLD WAR II**

	COUNTRY	SUBMARINES SUNK
1	Germany	787
2	Japan	130
3	USSR	103
4	Italy	85
5	UK	77
6	USA	50
7	France	23
8	Netherlands	10
9	Norway	5
10	Greece	4

21ST-CENTURY MILITARY

TOP 10 COUNTRIES WITH THE HIGHEST MILITARY EXPENDITURE AS A PERCENTAGE OF GDP

#	COUNTRY	GDP*
1	Oman	11.40
2	= Qatar	10.00
	= Saudi Arabia	10.00
4	= Iraq	8.60
	= Jordan	8.60
6	Israel	7.30
7	Yemen	6.60
8	Armenia	6.50
9	Eritrea	6.30
10	Macedonia	6.00
	UK	*2.40*

* In latest year for which data available

Source: *CIA World Factbook 2010*

TOP 10 COUNTRIES WITH THE MOST BATTLE TANKS

#	COUNTRY	TANKS
1	Russia	28,381
2	USA	7,821
3	China	7,580
4	Turkey	4,205
5	Syria	4,100
6	India	3,978
7	Ukraine	3,784
8	Egypt	3,680
9	Israel	3,650
10	North Korea	3,500
	UK	*393*

TOP 10 COUNTRIES WITH THE MOST SUBMARINES

#	COUNTRY	SUBMARINES
1	USA	73
2	China	63
3	Russia	56
4	= North Korea	26
	= South Korea	26
6	= India	16
	= Japan	16
	= UK	16
9	Germany	14
10	Turkey	13

The USS *Holland*, commissioned in 1900, was the US Navy's first military submarine and HMS *Holland 1* (1901) the British Navy's first.

THE 10 SMALLEST ARMED FORCES*

#	COUNTRY	ESTIMATED TOTAL ACTIVE FORCES
1	Antigua and Barbuda	170
2	Seychelles	450
3	Barbados	610
4	Gambia	800
5	Bahamas	860
6	Luxembourg	900
7	Belize	1,050
8	Guyana	1,100
9	Cape Verde	1,200
10	East Timor	1,250

* Includes only those countries that declare a defence budget

Source: The International Institute for Strategic Studies, *The Military Balance 2005–2006*

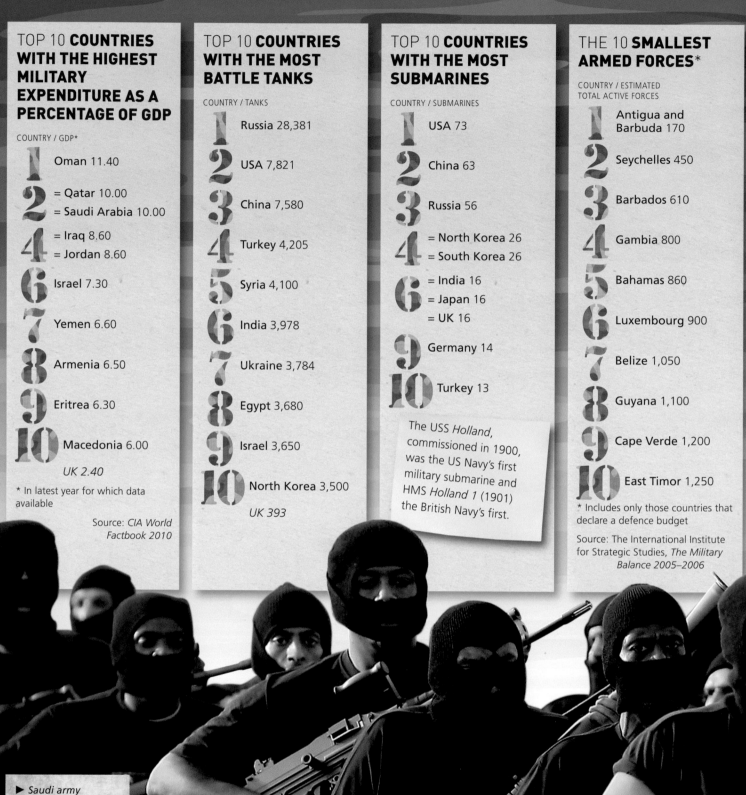

► *Saudi army*
Saudi Arabia's military expenditure was equivalent to 15.2 per cent of GDP in 1988, but remains among the world's highest.

▲ *Fire power*
China's status as a global power is reflected in its vast armed force, the world's largest.

TOP 10 **LARGEST ARMED FORCES**

COUNTRY	ESTIMATED ACTIVE FORCES ARMY	NAVY	AIR	TOTAL
1 China	1,600,000	255,000	330,000	2,285,000*
2 USA	662,232	335,822	334,342	1,580,255#
3 India	1,129,900	58,350	127,200	1,325,000†
4 North Korea	950,000	46,000	110,000	1,106,000
5 Russia	360,000	142,000	160,000	1,027,000§
6 South Korea	560,000	68,000	64,000	692,000
7 Pakistan	550,000	22,000	45,000	617,000
8 Iran	350,000	18,000	30,000	523,000‡
9 Turkey	402,000	48,600	60,000	510,600
10 Egypt	340,000	18,500	30,000	468,500¶
UK	*95,780*	*30,880*	*33,620*	*160,280*

* Includes 100,000 Strategic Missile Forces # Includes 204,261 Marine Corps and 43,598 Coast Guard
† Includes 9,950 Coast Guard § Includes 35,000 Airbone Army, 80,000 Strategic Deterrent Forces and 250,000 Command and Support
‡ Includes 125,000 Islamic Revolutionary Guard Corps
¶ Includes 80,000 Air Defence Command

Source: The International Institute for Strategic Studies, *The Military Balance 2010*

Several countries also have substantial reserves on standby: South Korea's has been estimated at some 4.5 million plus 3.5 million Paramilitary, Vietnam's at 5 million and China's 510,000. North Korea has the highest number of troops in relation to its population – 46 per 1,000.

TOP 10 **ARMS MANUFACTURERS**

COMPANY / COUNTRY / SALES 2007 (US$)

1. **Boeing** (USA) 30,500,000,000
2. **BAE Systems** (UK) 29,900,000,000
3. **Lockheed Martin** (USA) 29,400,000,000
4. **Northrop Grumman** (USA) 24,600,000,000
5. **General Dynamics** (USA) 21,500,000,000
6. **Raytheon** (USA) 19,500,000,000
7. **EADS** (Europe) 13,100,000,000
8. **L-3 Communications** (USA) 11,200,000,000
9. **Finmeccanica** (Italy) 9,900,000,000
10. **Thales** (France) 9,400,000,000

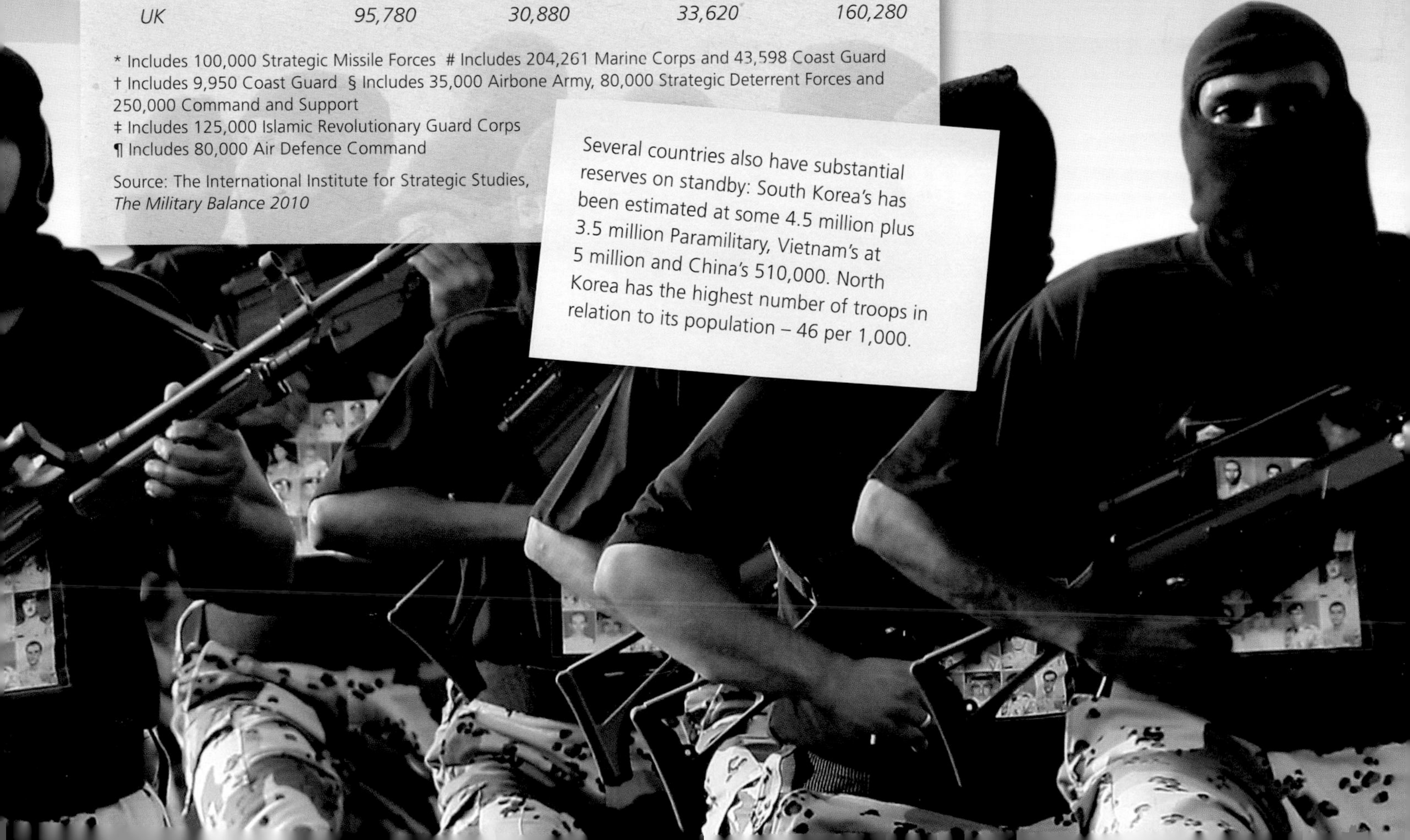

CRIMINAL RECORDS

THE 10 **MOST COMMON MURDER WEAPONS AND METHODS IN ENGLAND AND WALES**

WEAPON/METHOD	VICTIMS (2007–08) MEN	WOMEN	TOTAL
1 Sharp instrument	212	58	270
2 Hitting and kicking	140	23	163
3 Blunt instrument	44	22	66
4 Strangulation	16	41	57
5 Shooting	47	6	53
6 Unknown	30	22	52
7 Burning	14	13	27
8 Poison or drugs	16	4	20
9 Motor vehicle	9	3	12
10 Drowning	5	1	6
Other (unspecified)	*22*	*15*	*37*
Total	*555*	*208*	*763*

Source: Home Office

THE 10 **COUNTRIES WITH THE HIGHEST REPORTED CRIME RATES**

COUNTRY / REPORTED CRIMES PER 100,000 POPULATION

1. Dominica 11,382
2. New Zealand 10,588
3. Finland 10,153
4. Denmark 9,283
5. Chile 8,823
6. UK 8,555
7. Montserrat 8,040
8. USA 8,007
9. The Netherlands 7,958
10. South Africa 7,719

Source: United Nations

THE 10 **MOST COMMON CRIMES IN ENGLAND AND WALES**

CRIME	NO. RECORDED (2008–09)
1 Theft and handling stolen goods (excl. car theft)	1,080,655
2 Criminal damage	936,729
3 Violence against the person	903,993
4 Car theft (incl. theft from vehicles)	592,117
5 Burglary (excl. domestic)	296,952
6 Domestic burglary	284,445
7 Drug offences	242,907
8 Fraud and forgery	163,283
9 Robbery	80,104
10 Sexual offences	51,488

Source: Home Office, *Crime in England and Wales 2008/09*

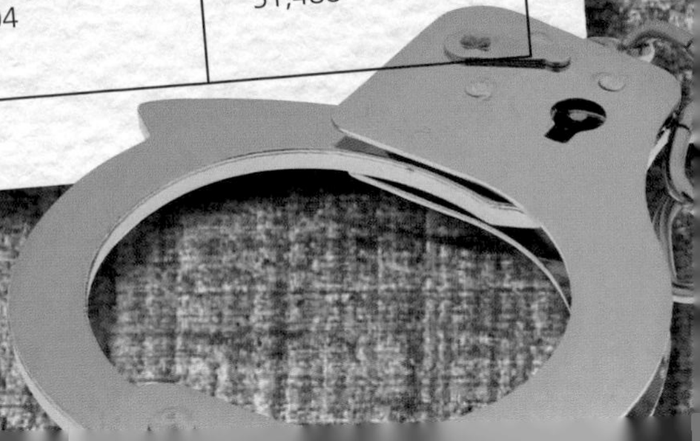

THE 10 COUNTRIES WITH THE HIGHEST PRISON POPULATIONS

COUNTRY	PRISONERS PER 100,000 POPULATION	TOTAL PRISONERS*
1 USA	760	2,310,984
2 China	119	1,565,771
3 Russia	624	884,523
4 Brazil	242	469,546
5 India	33	373,271
6 Mexico	207	227,735
7 Thailand	303	199,607
8 South Africa	329	163,108
9 Iran	222	158,351
10 Ukraine	314	144,380
England and Wales	*153*	*84,180*

* As at date of most recent data

Source: International Centre for Prison Studies

THE 10 CRIMINALS LONGEST ON THE FBI'S '10 MOST WANTED' LIST

FUGITIVE (FBI NO.) / CRIME	ADDED TO LIST	REMOVED FROM LIST	PERIOD ON LIST YRS	MTHS	DAYS
1 Donald Eugene Webb (375) Alleged cop killer	4 May 1981	31 Mar 2007	25	10	27
2 Victor Manuel Gerena (386) Armed robbery	14 May 1984	*	25	10	18
3 Charles Lee Heron (265) Murder	9 Feb 1968	18 Jun 1986	18	4	9
4 Frederick J. Tenuto (14) Murder	24 May 1950	9 Mar 1964	13	9	14
5 Katherine Ann Power (315) Bank robbery	17 Oct 1970	15 Jun 1984	13	7	29
6 Glen Stewart Godwin (447) Murder	7 Dec 1996	*	13	3	25
7 Arthur Lee Washington Jr (427) Attempted murder	18 Oct 1989	27 Dec 2000	11	2	19
8 Osama bin Laden (456) Terrorism, murder	7 Jun 1999	*	10	9	25
9 David Daniel Keegan (78) Murder, robbery	21 Jun 1954	13 Dec 1963	9	5	22
10 James Eddie Diggs (36) Alleged murder	27 Aug 1952	14 Dec 1961	9	3	17

* Still at large as at 1 April 2010

Source: FBI

The Federal Bureau of Investigation officially launched its celebrated '10 Most Wanted' list on 14 March 1950. Since then almost 500 criminals have figured on it. Names appear until individuals are captured, die or charges are dropped.

▶ *'Most wanted'*
Osama bin Laden (right) has been on the FBI's 'Most Wanted' list since 7 June 1999. Longest-listed uncaptured fugitive Victor Gerena (far right) has a $1 million price on his head.

WORLD RELIGIONS

▲ *Islamic majority*
Although not an Islamic state, Indonesia is home to the largest Muslim population.

TOP 10 **LARGEST MUSLIM POPULATIONS**

	COUNTRY	MUSLIMS
1	Indonesia	172,401,505
2	Pakistan	159,231,188
3	India	155,477,386
4	Bangladesh	135,647,471
5	Iran	69,804,213
6	Turkey	69,309,707
7	Egypt	66,796,916
8	Nigeria	63,999,191
9	Algeria	32,171,532
10	Morocco	30,015,036

Source (all lists): World Christian Database

TOP 10 **LARGEST JEWISH POPULATIONS**

	COUNTRY	JEWS
1	USA	5,302,245
2	Israel	4,852,767
3	France	609,905
4	Argentina	491,789
5	Canada	418,315
6	UK	282,306
7	Germany	224,963
8	Russia	187,916
9	Ukraine	182,425
10	Brazil	140,925
	Top 10 total	*12,693,556*
	World total	*14,206,582*

The Diaspora, or scattering of Jewish people, has established Jewish communities in almost every country in the world. In 1939 the estimated total Jewish population was 17 million. Some six million fell victim to Nazi persecution, reducing the figure to about 11 million, since when it has grown to more than 14 million.

▼ *Jewish nation*
Israel's Jewish population is less than that of the United States, but is the only country where it comprises the majority.

▼ *Sacred lake*
Pilgrims bathe in the Puskar Lake, India, where Hindus comprise the majority of the population.

TOP 10 **LARGEST HINDU POPULATIONS**

	COUNTRY	HINDUS
1	India	832,056,362
2	Nepal	18,725,504
3	Bangladesh	14,792,995
4	Indonesia	4,286,550
5	Sri Lanka	2,515,776
6	Pakistan	2,084,990
7	Malaysia	1,607,947
8	USA	1,337,734
9	South Africa	1,140,817
10	Myanmar	818,250
	UK	*604,436*
	Top 10 total	*879,366,925*
	World total	*885,074,141*

TOP 10 **LARGEST BUDDHIST POPULATIONS**

	COUNTRY	BUDDHISTS
1	China	181,925,031
2	Japan	71,780,867
3	Thailand	54,653,836
4	Vietnam	41,825,435
5	Myanmar	35,488,634
6	Sri Lanka	12,999,238
7	Cambodia	11,901,352
8	India	7,789,140
9	South Korea	7,234,415
10	Laos	2,995,972
	UK	*191,482*
	Top 10 total	*428,593,920*
	World total	*444,864,181*

Hindus constitute some 73.34 per cent of the population of India and 69.11 per cent of that of Nepal, but it is a minority religion in Bangladesh and Indonesia, where it comprises 9.65 and 1.90 per cent of the countries' respective populations.

TOP 10 **LARGEST SIKH POPULATIONS**

	COUNTRY	SIKHS
1	India	21,274,191
2	UK	384,906
3	Canada	330,773
4	USA	269,862
5	Thailand	51,032
6	Saudi Arabia	45,336
7	Malaysia	42,481
8	Pakistan	40,627
9	Australia	35,171
10	Kenya	32,566
	Top 10 total	*22,506,945*
	World total	*22,782,827*

► *Chinese Buddhism*
The Tian Tang Buddha, Hong Kong: Buddhism has maintained its followers in China, making it the foremost religion in an officially atheist state.

CHRISTIANITY & THE BIBLE

TOP 10 LONGEST BOOKS IN THE BIBLE*

	BOOK	CHAPTERS	VERSES	WORDS
1	Psalms	150	2,461	43,743
2	Jeremiah	52	1,364	42,659
3	Ezekiel	48	1,273	39,407
4	Genesis	50	1,533	38,267
5	Isaiah	66	1,292	37,044
6	Numbers	36	1,288	32,902
7	Exodus	40	1,213	32,602
8	Deuteronomy	34	959	28,461
9	II Chronicles	36	822	26,074
10	Luke	24	1,151	25,944

* King James Bible (Old and New Testaments)

THE 10 NAMES MOST MENTIONED IN THE BIBLE

	NAME / TOTAL	
1	Jesus (973)/Christ (555)	1,528
2	David	1,011
3	Moses	828
4	Saul	389
5	Jacob	358
6	Aaron	319
7	Solomon	288
8	Joseph	228
9	Abraham	231
10	Joshua	241

* Occurrences in verses in the King James Bible (Old and New Testaments), including possessive uses, such as 'Joseph's'

▲ *In the beginning...*
Biblical scenes in a 13th-century manuscript. In the past 560 years, the Bible has become the world's bestselling book.

▲ *Christianity in China*
Restrictions on religion in China have been relaxed since the Cultural Revolution, with membership of Chinese house churches and other Christian organizations estimated at over 100 million.

TOP 10 LARGEST CHRISTIAN POPULATIONS

	COUNTRY	CHRISTIANS
1	USA	245,930,675
2	Brazil	170,213,252
3	Russia	114,510,266
4	China	101,997,935
5	Mexico	99,945,687
6	Philippines	75,520,618
7	Nigeria	64,226,200
8	Germany	59,364,498
9	Dem. Rep. of Congo	56,019,573
10	India	51,881,253
	UK	*48,735,779*
	Top 10 total	*1,039,609,957*
	World total	*2,159,141,594*

Source: World Christian Database

The Christian populations of these countries comprise almost half the world total. Christian communities exist in almost every country, but precise estimates of nominal membership (declared religious persuasion) rather than active participation (regular attendance at a place of worship) are inevitably vague.

TOP 10 **LONGEST-REIGNING POPES**

	POPE	PERIOD IN OFFICE	DURATION YRS	MTHS	DAYS
1	Pius IX	16 Jun 1846–7 Feb 1878	31	7	22
2	John Paul II	16 Oct 1978–2 Apr 2005	26	5	17
3	Leo XIII	20 Feb 1878–20 Jul 1903	25	5	0
4	Pius VI	15 Feb 1775–29 Aug 1799	24	6	14
5	Adrian I	1 Feb AD 772–25 Dec AD 795	23	10	24
6	Pius VII	14 Mar 1800–20 Aug 1823	23	5	6
7	Alexander III	7 Sep 1159–30 Aug 1181	21	11	23
8	Sylvester I	31 Jan AD 314–31 Dec AD 335	21	11	0
9	Leo I	29 Sep AD 440–10 Nov AD 461	21	1	12
10	Urban VIII	6 Aug 1623–29 Jul 1644	20	11	23

Popes are usually chosen from the ranks of cardinals, who are customarily men of mature years, so it is unusual for a pope to remain in office for more than 20 years. Pius IX, the longest-serving pope, was 85 years old at the time of his death. The longest-lived in the Top 10 was Leo XIII at 93. It is sometimes claimed, though with little evidence, that Pope Agatho was at least 100 when he was elected and died in AD 681 at the age of 106.

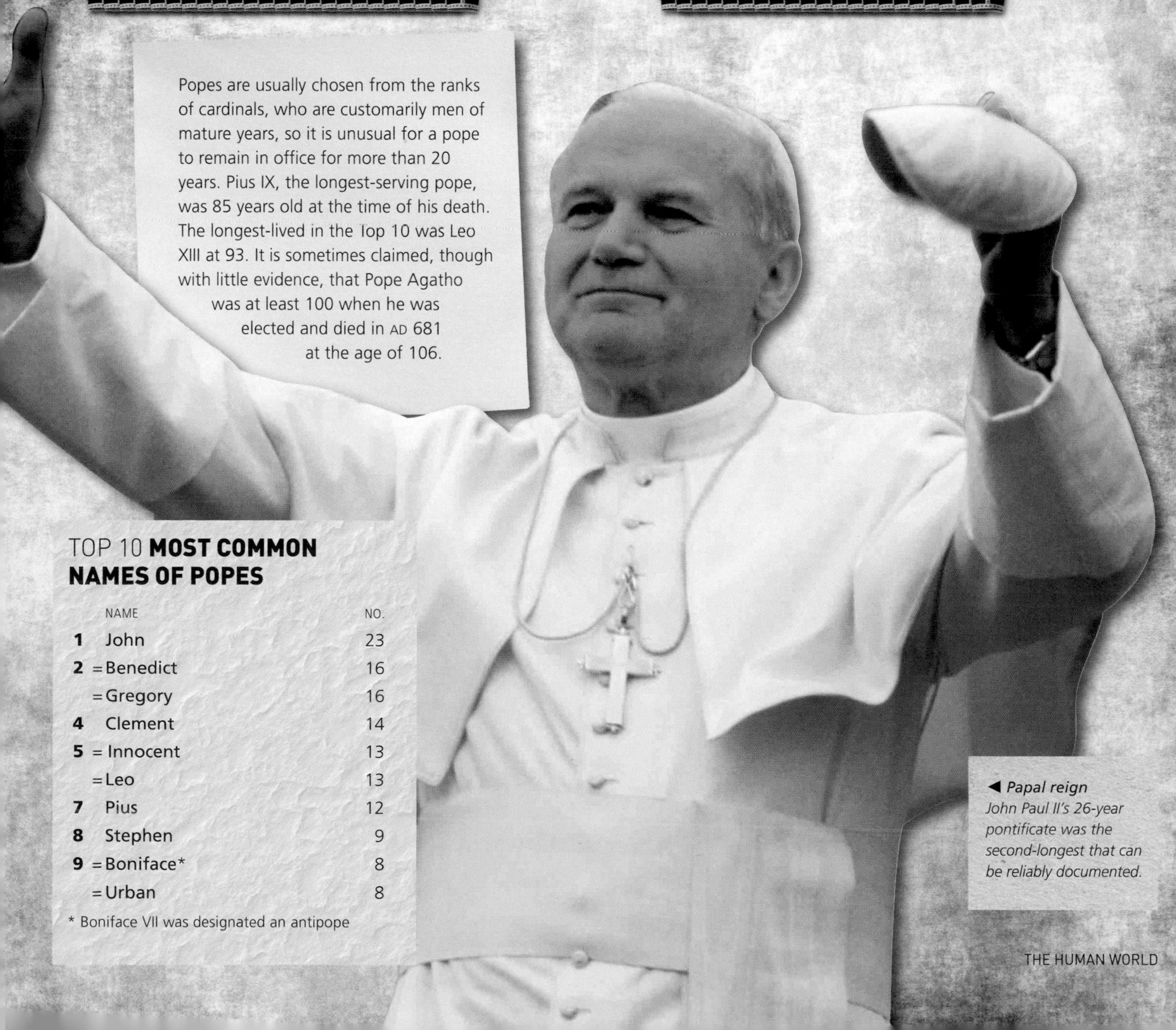

TOP 10 **MOST COMMON NAMES OF POPES**

	NAME	NO.
1	John	23
2	=Benedict	16
	=Gregory	16
4	Clement	14
5	=Innocent	13
	=Leo	13
7	Pius	12
8	Stephen	9
9	=Boniface*	8
	=Urban	8

* Boniface VII was designated an antipope

◀ ***Papal reign***
John Paul II's 26-year pontificate was the second-longest that can be reliably documented.

4
TOWN & COUNTRY

FREEDOM TOWER

Formerly called – and often still nicknamed – 'Freedom Tower', but officially One World Trade Center, the skyscraper on the site of the World Trade Center twin towers will be topped out (structurally completed) in 2011, the 10th anniversary of the terrorist attacks that destroyed them on 11 September 2001. The 105-storey building will have a roof height of 417 m (1,368 ft), identical to that of the original structure it replaces and commemorates, and an overall height, including its spire, of 541.3 m (1,776 ft), its height in feet symbolizing the year of the Declaration of Independence.

THE 10 SMALLEST COUNTRIES

COUNTRY / AREA (SQ KM/SQ MILES)

1. Vatican City 0.44 / 0.17
2. Monaco 1.95 / 0.75
3. Nauru 21.20 / 8.18
4. Tuvalu 25.63 / 9.89
5. San Marino 61.20 / 23.63
6. Liechtenstein 160.00 / 61.77
7. Marshall Islands 181.43 / 70.05
8. St Kitts and Nevis 269.40 / 104.01
9. Maldives 298.00 / 115.05
10. Malta 315.10 / 121.66

TOP 10 LONGEST BORDERS

	COUNTRY	TOTAL BORDERS KM	MILES
1	China	22,117	13,642
2	Russia	20,017	12,437
3	Brazil	14,691	9,128
4	India	14,103	8,763
5	USA	12,034	7,477
6	Kazakhstan	12,012	7,463
7	Dem. Rep. of Congo	10,730	6,667
8	Argentina	9,665	6,005
9	Canada	8,893	5,525
10	Mongolia	8,220	5,107

Source: CIA, *The World Factbook 2010*

This list represents the cumulative totals of each country's individual land borders. The 12,248 km (7,610 miles) of the USA's borders include those shared with Canada, 6,416 km (3,986 miles) of which comprise the longest continuous border in the world, the 2,477-km (1,539-mile) boundary between Canada and Alaska.

TOP 10 COUNTRIES WITH THE LONGEST COASTLINES

	COUNTRY	TOTAL COASTLINE LENGTH KM	MILES
1	Canada	202,080	125,566
2	Indonesia	54,716	33,999
3	Russia	37,653	23,396
4	Philippines	36,289	22,559
5	Japan	29,751	18,486
6	Australia	25,760	16,007
7	Norway	25,148	15,626
8	USA	19,924	12,380
9	New Zealand	15,134	9,404
10	China	14,500	9,010

Source: CIA, *The World Factbook 2010*

Including all its islands, the coastline of Canada is more than six times as long as the distance round the Earth at the Equator (40,076 km/24,9012 miles). If Greenland (44,087 km/27,394 miles) were an independent country it would rank 3rd.

◀ ***Microstate***
San Marino, along with Vatican City and Liechtenstein, is one of three landlocked European countries among the 10 smallest.

► *Landlocked*
Kazakhstan is the 9th largest country, and the largest landlocked state in the world.

TOP 10 **LARGEST COUNTRIES**

	COUNTRY	AREA SQ KM	AREA SQ MILES	% OF WORLD TOTAL
1	Russia	17,098,242	6,601,669	11.5
2	Canada	9,984,670	3,855,103	6.7
3	USA	9,629,091	3,717,813	6.5
4	China	9,596,961	3,704,408	6.4
5	Brazil	8,514,877	3,287,613	5.7
6	Australia	7,692,024	2,969,907	5.2
7	India	3,287,263	1,269,219	2.3
8	Argentina	2,780,400	1,073,519	2.0
9	Kazakhstan	2,724,900	1,052,090	1.8
10	Sudan	2,505,813	967,500	1.7
	UK	*242,900*	*93,784*	*0.16*
	World total	*148,939,063*	*57,505,700*	*100.0*

Source: United Nations Statistics Division

This list is based on the total area of a country within its borders, including offshore islands, inland water such as lakes and rivers, and reservoirs. It may thus differ from versions in which these are excluded. Antarctica has an approximate area of 13,200,000 sq km (5,096,549 sq miles), but is discounted as it is not considered a country. The countries in the Top 10 collectively comprise 50 per cent of the total Earth's surface.

TOP 10 **LARGEST LANDLOCKED COUNTRIES**

	COUNTRY / NEIGHBOURS	AREA SQ KM	AREA SQ MILES
1	Kazakhstan China, Kyrgyzstan, Russia, Turkmenistan, Uzbekistan	2,717,300	1,049,156
2	Mongolia China, Russia	1,564,116	603,908
3	Niger Algeria, Benin, Burkina Faso, Chad, Libya, Mali, Nigeria	1,266,699	489,075
4	Chad Cameroon, Central African Republic, Libya, Niger, Nigeria, Sudan	1,259,201	486,180
5	Mali Algeria, Burkina Faso, Côte d'Ivoire, Guinea, Mauritania, Niger, Senegal	1,219,999	471,044
6	Ethiopia Djibouti, Eritrea, Kenya, Somalia, Sudan	1,127,127	435,186
7	Bolivia Argentina, Brazil, Chile, Paraguay, Peru	1,098,580	424,164
8	Zambia Angola, Dem. Rep. of Congo, Malawi, Mozambique, Namibia, Tanzania, Zimbabwe	752,614	290,585
9	Afghanistan China, Iran, Pakistan, Tajikistan, Turkmenistan, Uzbekistan	647,500	250,001
10	Central African Republic Cameroon, Chad, Congo, Dem. Rep. of Congo, Sudan	622,984	240,535

WORLD POPULATION

▲ *Population change*
India's burgeoning population surges as China's one-child policy pays dividends: demographic predictions for 2025 put India at 1,396,046,308, overtaking China with 1,394,638,699. In third place, the USA, which reached 300 million in 2007, is set to top 400 million in 2039.

2010

TOP 10 **MOST POPULATED COUNTRIES IN 2010**

	COUNTRY	ESTIMATED POPULATION (2010)
1	China	1,347,563,498
2	India	1,173,108,018
3	USA	310,232,863
4	Indonesia	242,968,342
5	Brazil	201,103,330
6	Pakistan	177,276,594
7	Bangladesh	158,065,841
8	Nigeria	152,217,341
9	Russia	139,390,205
10	Japan	126,804,433
	UK	*61,284,806*
	Top 10 total	*4,028,730,465*
	World	*6,845,146,634*

Source (all lists): US Census Bureau, International Data Base

2050

TOP 10 **MOST POPULATED COUNTRIES IN 2050**

	COUNTRY	ESTIMATED POPULATION (2050)
1	India	1,656,553,632
2	China	1,424,161,948
3	USA	439,010,253
4	Indonesia	313,020,847
5	Ethiopia	278,283,137
6	Pakistan	276,428,758
7	Nigeria	264,262,405
8	Brazil	260,692,493
9	Bangladesh	233,587,279
10	Dem. Rep. of Congo	189,310,849
	UK	*63,977,435*
	Top 10 total	*5,335,311,601*
	World total	*9,316,823,185*

Estimates of national populations in 2050 present a striking change, as long-time world leader China is eclipsed by India, a reversal that is projected to take place around the year 2025. By 2050, the UK's ranking in the world population league table is expected to have dropped from 22nd to 27th.

TOP 10 **MOST DENSELY POPULATED COUNTRIES, 2010**

	COUNTRY	AREA (SQ KM)	ESTIMATED POPULATION (2010)	POPULATION PER SQ KM
1	Monaco	1.95	33,095	16,971.8
2	Singapore	683	4,701,069	6,883.0
3	Vatican City	0.44	932	2,118.2
4	Maldives	300	395,650	1,318.8
5	Malta	316	406,771	1,287.3
6	Bahrain	665	738,004	1,109.8
7	Bangladesh	133,910	139,390,205	1,040.9
8	Taiwan	32,261	23,024,956	713.7
9	Mauritius	1,849	1,294,104	699.9
10	Nauru	21	14,264	679.2
	UK	*241,590*	*61,284,806*	*253.6*
	World	*132,519,533*	*6,845,146,634*	*51.7*

Other territories with high population densities include Gibraltar with a population of 28,877 occupying 6 sq km (4,812.8 people per sq km); and the Gaza Strip, with its population of 1,604,238 occupying a land area of 381 sq km (4,210.6 people per sq km).

THE 10 **LEAST DENSELY POPULATED COUNTRIES, 2010**

	COUNTRY	AREA (SQ KM)	ESTIMATED POPULATION (2010)	POPULATION PER SQ KM
1	Mongolia	1,554,731	3,086,918	1.98
2	Namibia	825,418	2,128,471	2.58
3	Australia	7,617,930	21,515,754	2.82
4	Suriname	161,470	486,618	3.01
5	Iceland	100,250	308,910	3.08
6	Mauritania	1,030,400	3,205,060	3.11
7	Botswana	585,370	2,029,307	3.47
8	Libya	1,759,540	6,461,454	3.67
9	Canada	9,093,507	33,759,742	3.71
10	Guyana	196,850	748,486	3.80

► ***Mongolia***
Only two territories, Greenland (0.026 per sq km) and the Falkland Islands (0.26), have lower population densities than Mongolia.

THE 10 **COUNTRIES WITH THE GREATEST POPULATION DECLINE, 2005–50**

COUNTRY / ESTIMATED POPULATION (2010/2050) / % DECLINE

1 Bulgaria
7,148,785
4,651,477
34.93%

2 Estonia
1,291,170
861,913
33.25%

3 Latvia
2,217,969
1,544,073
30.38%

4 Japan
126,804,433
93,673,826
26.13%

5 Ukraine
45,415,596
33,573,842
26.07%

6 Russia
139,390,205
109,187,353
21.67%

7 Lithuania
3,545,319
2,787,516
21.37%

8 Slovenia
2,003,136
1,596,947
20.28%

9 Belarus
9,612,632
7,738,613
19.50%

10 Poland
38,463,689
32,084,570
16.58%

LONGEST PLACE NAMES

TOP 10 **LONGEST PLACE NAMES IN THE UK***

NAME / LETTERS

1. **Gorsafawddachaidraigddanheddogleddollônpenrhyn-areurdraethceredigion** (see Top 10 Longest Place Names, No. 3) 67
2. **Llanfairpwllgwyngyllgogerychwyrndrobwllllantysiliogogogoch** (see Top 10 Longest Place Names, No. 4) 58
3. **Sutton-under-Whitestonecliffe,** North Yorkshire 27
4. **Llansantffraid-ym-mechain**, Powys 23
5. **Llanfihangel-yng-Ngwynfa,** Powys 22
6. = **Llanfihangel-y-Creuddyn**, Ceredigion
   = **Llanfihangel-y-traethau**, Gwynedd
   21
8. **Cottonshopeburnfoot**, Northumberland 19
9. = **Blakehopeburnhaugh**, Northumberland
   = **Coignafeuinternich**, Highlands
   18

* Single and hyphenated only

Runners up include Claddach-baleshare and Claddach-knockline, both in North Uist, Outer Hebrides, each having 17 letters. Next come Combeinteignhead, Doddiscombsleigh, Moretonhampstead, Stokeinteignhead and Woolfardisworthy (pronounced 'Woolsery'), all of which are in Devon and have 16 letters. The longest multiple name in England is North Leverton with Habblesthorpe, Nottinghamshire (30 letters), followed by Sulhampstead Bannister Upper End, West Berkshire (29).

TOP 10 **LONGEST PLACE NAMES***

NAME / LETTERS

1 **Krung Thep Mahanakhon Amon Rattanakosin Mahinthara Ayuthaya Mahadilok Phop Noppharat Ratchathani Burirom Udomratchaniwet Mahasathan Amon Piman Awatan Sathit Sakkathattiya Witsanukam Prasit** 168
It means 'The city of angels, the great city, the eternal jewel city, the impregnable city of God Indra, the grand capital of the world endowed with nine precious gems, the happy city, abounding in an enormous Royal Palace that resembles the heavenly abode where reigns the reincarnated god, a city given by Indra and built by Vishnukarn'. When the poetic name of Bangkok, capital of Thailand, is used, it is usually abbreviated to 'Krung Thep' (city of angels).

2 **Taumatawhakatangihangakoauauotamateaturipukakapikimaungahoronukupokaiwhenuakitanatahu** 85
This is the longer version (the other has a mere 83 letters) of the Maori name of a hill in New Zealand. It translates as 'The place where Tamatea, the man with the big knees, who slid, climbed and swallowed mountains, known as land-eater, played on the flute to his loved one'.

3 **Gorsafawddachaidraigddanheddogleddollônpenrhyn-areurdraethceredigion** 67
A name contrived by the Fairbourne Steam Railway, Gwynedd, North Wales, for publicity purposes and in order to outdo its rival, No. 4. It means 'The Mawddach station and its dragon teeth at the Northern Penrhyn Road on the golden beach of Cardigan Bay'.

4 **Llanfairpwllgwyngyllgogerychwyrndrobwllllantysiliogogogoch** 58
This is the place in Gwynedd famed especially for the length of its railway tickets. It means 'St Mary's Church in the hollow of the white hazel near to the rapid whirlpool of the church of St Tysilo near the Red Cave'.

TOP 10 COUNTRIES WITH THE LONGEST OFFICIAL NAMES

	OFFICIAL NAME*	COMMON NAME IN ENGLISH	LETTERS
1	Al-Jumh riyyah al-Isl miyyah al-M r t niyyah République Islamique de Mauritanie Mauritania	Mauritania	71
2	al-Jam h riyyah al-'Arabiyyah al-L biyyah aš-Ša biyyah al-Ištir kiyyah al-'U m	Libya	65
3	al Jumhuriyya al Jazaa'iriyya al Dimuqratiyya ash Sha'biyya	Algeria	50
4	United Kingdom of Great Britain and Northern Ireland	United Kingdom	45
5	= Jumhuriyat al-Qumur al Ittihadiyah al-Islamiyah	The Comoros	41
	= Sri Lanka Prajatantrika Samajavadi Janarajaya	Sri Lanka	41
7	República Democrática de São Tomé e Príncipe	São Tomé and Príncipe	38
8	Federation of Saint Christopher and Nevis	Saint Kitts and Nevis	36
9	Federal Democratic Republic of Ethiopia	Ethiopia	35
10	= al-Mamlakah al-Urdunniyah al-Hashimiyah	Jordan	34
	= Sathalanalat Paxathipatai Paxaxôn Lao	Laos	34

* Some official names have been transliterated from languages that do not use the Roman alphabet; their length may vary according to the method used

▲ ***Mauritanian mouthful***
Mauritania's full name occupies a substantial portion of the country's passports.

5 **El Pueblo de Nuestra Señora la Reina de los Ángeles de la Porciúncula** 57
The site of a Franciscan mission and the full Spanish name of Los Angeles; it means 'The town of Our Lady the Queen of the Angels of the Little Portion'. Nowadays it is customarily known by its initial letters, 'LA', making it also one of the shortest-named cities in the world.

6 **Chargoggagoggmanchaugagoggchaubunagungamaug** 43
A lake near Webster, Massachusetts. Its Indian name, loosely translated, is claimed to mean 'You fish on your side, I'll fish on mine, and no one fishes in the middle'. It is said to be pronounced 'Char-gogg-a-gogg [pause] man-chaugg-a-gog [pause] chau-bun-a-gung-a maug'.

7 = **Lower North Branch Little Southwest Miramichi** 40
Canada's longest place name – a short river in New Brunswick.
= **Villa Real de la Santa Fé de San Francisco de Asis**
The full Spanish name of Santa Fe, New Mexico.

9 **Te Whakatakanga-o-te-ngarehu-o-te-ahi-a-Tamatea** 38
The Maori name of Hammer Springs, New Zealand; like the second name in this list, it refers to a legend of Tamatea, explaining how the springs were warmed by 'the falling of the cinders of the fire of Tamatea'.

10 **Meallan Liath Coire Mhic Dhubhghaill** 32
The longest multiple name in Scotland, a place near Aultanrynie, Highland, alternatively spelled Meallan Liath Coire Mhic Dhughaill (30 letters).

* Including single-word, hyphenated and multiple names

URBAN EXTREMES

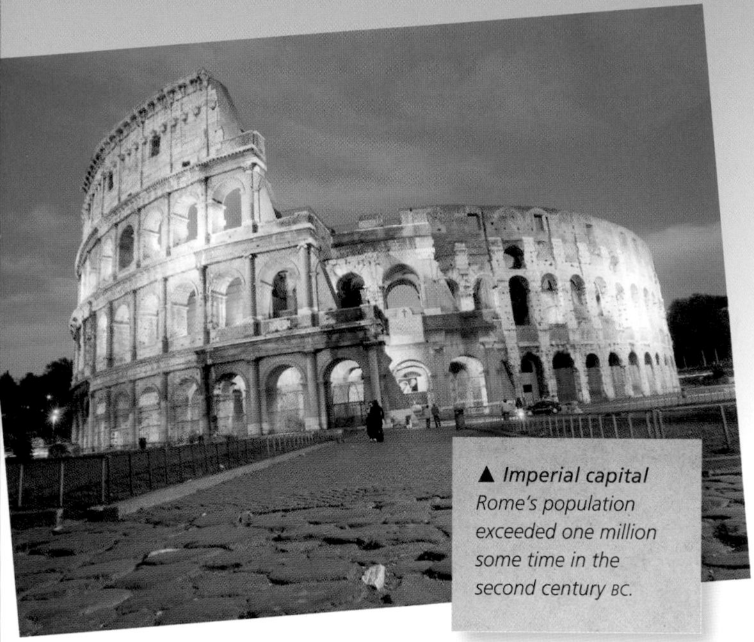

▲ *Imperial capital*
Rome's population exceeded one million some time in the second century BC.

THE 10 **FIRST CITIES WITH POPULATIONS OF MORE THAN ONE MILLION**

CITY / COUNTRY

1. **Rome**, Italy
2. **Alexandria**, Egypt
3. **Angkor**, Cambodia
4. **Hangchow** (Hangzhou), China
5. **London**, UK
6. **Paris**, France
7. **Peking** (Beijing), China
8. **Canton** (Guangzhou), China
9. **Berlin**, Prussia
10. **New York**, USA

Following Rome and Alexandria, Angkor and Hangchow reached one million by about AD 900 and 1200 respectively, but subsequently declined, Angkor being completely abandoned in the 15th century.

TOP 10 **CITIES WITH THE HIGHEST PROPORTION OF A COUNTRY'S POPULATION**

CITY / COUNTRY / % OF TOTAL COUNTRY POPULATION

1	= **Hong Kong**	100.0
	= **Singapore**	100.0
3	**Kuwait City**, Kuwait	69.9
4	**San Juan**, Puerto Rico	66.0
5	**Montevideo**, Uruguay	45.9
6	**Tel Aviv**, Israel	45.0
7	**Beirut**, Lebanon	44.3
8	**Panama City**, Panama	37.6
9	**Yerevan**, Armenia	36.5
10	**Tripoli**, Libya	35.4

▼ *Hong Kong*
Hong Kong is a special administrative region of China, rather than a 'country', but is often included as such in demographic statistics.

TOP 10 **MOST POPULATED PURPOSE-BUILT CAPITAL CITIES***

	CAPITAL / COUNTRY	BECAME CAPITAL	POPULATION#
1	**Brasília**, Brazil	1960	2,606,885
2	**Islamabad**, Pakistan	1967	1,740,000
3	**Naypyidaw**, Myanmar	2005	925,000
4	**Nouakchott**, Mauritania	1957	881,000
5	**Abuja**, Nigeria	1991	778,567
6	**Washington, DC**, USA	1800	591,833
7	**Canberra**, Australia	1927	345,257
8	**New Delhi**, India	1912	302,363
9	**Belmopan**, Belize	1970	16,400
10	**Melekeok**, Palau	2006	271

* Since 1800
\# 2008 or latest available year

▼ Uptown
Lhasa was formerly the highest capital city in the world, an honour now enjoyed by La Paz.

TOP 10 **COUNTRIES WITH THE MOST MILLION-PLUS CITIES**

COUNTRY / CITIES WITH POPULATIONS OF OVER 1 MILLION	
1	China 79*
2	USA 52
3	India 48
4	Brazil 21
5	Russia 15
6	Japan 13
7	= Germany 11
	= Mexico 11
9	= Pakistan 8
	= UK 8

* 84 including Taiwan

There are 479 cities or urban agglomerations with populations of more than one million in over 100 different countries.

TOP 10 **HIGHEST TOWNS AND CITIES***

	CITY / COUNTRY	HEIGHT M	FT
1	**La Rinconada**, Peru	5,100	16,732
2	**Wenzhuan**, Tibet, China	5,099	16,730
3	**El Alto**#, Bolivia	4,150	13,615
4	**Potosí**, Bolivia	4,090	13,419
5	**Oruro**, Bolivia	3,702	12,146
6	**Lhasa**†, Tibet, China	3,684	12,087
7	**Apartaderos**, Venezuela	3,505	11,502
8	**Cusco**, Peru	3,360	11,024
9	**Huancayo**, Peru	3,271	10,732
10	**Alma**, Colorado, USA	3,158	10,361

* Excluding hamlets and small settlements
\# A suburb of La Paz; the main city – the world's highest capital – is at 3,632 m (11,916 ft)
† Former capital of independent Tibet

TOP 10 **MOST POPULOUS CITIES**

	CITY / COUNTRY	POPULATION
1	**Tokyo**, Japan	34,000,000
2	=**Guangzhou**, China	24,200,000
	=**Seoul**, South Korea	24,200,000
4	**Mexico City**, Mexico	23,400,000
5	**Delhi**, India	23,200,000
6	**Mumbai** (Bombay), India	22,800,000
7	**New York**, USA	22,200,000
8	**São Paulo**, Brazil	21,000,000
9	**Manila**, Philippines	19,600,000
10	**Shanghai**, China	18,400,000
	Top 10 total	*223,300,000*

Source: Th. Brinkhoff: The Principal Agglomerations of the World, http://www.citypopulation.de
© Thomas Brinkhoff 2010-01-23

SKYSCRAPERS

TOP 10 **TALLEST HABITABLE BUILDINGS IN 2011**

	BUILDING / LOCATION / YEAR COMPLETED / STOREYS	HEIGHT M	FT
1	**Burj Khalifa**, Dubai, UAE 2009 / 162	818	2,684
2	**Abraj Al Bait Towers**, Mecca, Saudi Arabia 2010 / 76	595	1,952
3	**Taipei 101**, Taipei, Taiwan, China 2004 / 101	509	1,671
4	**Shanghai World Financial Center** Shanghai, China 2008 / 101	492	1,614
5	**International Commerce Centre**, Hong Kong, China 2010 / 118	484	1,588
6	**Petronas Towers**, Kuala Lumpur, Malaysia 1998 / 88	452	1,483
7	**Willis** (formerly Sears) **Tower**, Chicago, USA 1974 / 108	442	1,451
8	**West Tower**, Guangzhou, China 2009 / 110	432	1,417*
9	**Jin Mao Building**, Shanghai, China 1998 / 88	421	1,381
10	**Trump International Hotel & Tower**, Chicago, USA 2009 / 96	415	1,362

* Helipad takes height to 437.5 m (1,435 ft)

► *Petronas Towers*
The accelerating pace of skyscraper building means the Petronas towers held the world record for only five years.

THE 10 **LAST HABITABLE BUILDINGS TO HOLD THE TITLE OF 'WORLD'S TALLEST'**

	BUILDING / LOCATION / YEAR	HEIGHT M	FT
1	**Burj Khalifa**, Dubai, UAE, 2009	818	2,684
2	**Taipei 101**, Taiwan, China, 2004	509	1,671
3	**Petronas Towers**, Malaysia, 1998	452	1,483
4	**Willis** (formerly Sears) **Tower**, Chicago, USA, 1974	442	1,451
5	**1 World Trade Center** New York, USA, 1972	417	1,368
6	**Empire State Building**, New York, USA, 1931	381	1,250
7	**Chrysler Building**, New York, USA, 1930	319	1,046
8	**Trump Building** (formerly Bank of Manhattan Trust Building, 40 Wall Street, New York), USA 1930	283	927
9	**Woolworth Building**, New York, USA, 1913	241	792
10	**Metropolitan Life Tower**, New York, USA, 1909	213	700

Highest rise
The Burj Khalifa at its opening ceremony in 2010 (left) and towering above the city (right) indicates the extent to which the 'world's tallest' title has been overtaken.

In accordance with the Council on Tall Buildings and Urban Habitat's rules, height is measured from ground level of the main entrance to the architectural tip of the building, including its spire.

TOP 10 TALLEST HABITABLE* BUILDINGS DEMOLISHED

	BUILDING / LOCATION	YEAR COMPLETED	YEAR DESTROYED	STOREYS	HEIGHT M	HEIGHT FT
1	1 World Trade Center, New York, USA	1972	2001	110	417.0	1,368
2	2 World Trade Center, New York, USA	1973	2001	110	415.4	1,363
3	Singer Building, New York, USA	1908	1968	47	186.5	612
4	7 World Trade Center, New York, USA	1987	2001	47	173.7	570
5	Morrison Hotel, Chicago, USA	1926	1965	45	160.3	526
6	Deutsche Bank, New York, USA	1974	2010	39	157.6	517
7	One Meridian Plaza, Philadelphia, USA	1972	1999	38	150.0	492
8	City Investing Building, New York, USA	1908	1968	33	148.1	486
9	The Ritz-Carlton, Hong Kong, China	1993	2009	31	141.9	466
10	Hennessy Centre, Hong Kong, China	1983	2007	41	139.7	458

* Excluding masts, chimneys, churches, etc.

◀ *World Trade Center*
The events of 9/11 resulted in both tragic loss of lives and the destruction of an iconic part of the New York skyline.

TOP 10 HIGHRISE CITIES, 2010

CITY / NO. OF BUILDINGS OVER 100 M / TOTAL HEIGHT (M)

1. Hong Kong, China — 2,354 / 333,836
2. New York City, USA — 794 / 109,720
3. Tokyo, Japan — 556 / 73,008
4. Dubai, UAE — 403 / 66,248
5. Shanghai, China — 430 / 59,958
6. Bangkok, Thailand — 355 / 48,737
7. Chicago, USA — 341 / 48,441
8. Guangzhou, China — 294 / 42,865
9. Seoul, South Korea — 282 / 39,308
10. Kuala Lumpur, Malaysia — 244 / 34,035

Mighty Structures

TOP 10 TALLEST TELECOMMUNICATIONS TOWERS

	TOWER / LOCATION	YEAR COMPLETED	HEIGHT* M	FT
1	**Tokyo Sky Tree**, Tokyo, Japan	2011#	634.0	2,080
2	**Guangzhou TV & Sightseeing Tower**, Guangzhou, China	2009#	610.0	2,001
3	**CN Tower**, Toronto, Canada	1975	555.0	1,821
4	**Ostankino Tower**†, Moscow, Russia	1967	537.0	1,762
5	**Broadcasting, Telephone and TV-tower**, Xian, China	2009	470.0	1,542
6	**Oriental Pearl Broadcasting Tower**, Shanghai, China	1995	467.9	1,535
7	**Borj-e Milad Telecommunications Tower**, Tehran, Iran	2007	435.0	1,427
8	**Menara Telecom Tower**, Kuala Lumpur, Malaysia	1996	421.0	1,381
9	**Tianjin Radio and Television Tower**, Tianjin, China	1991	415.2	1,362
10	**Indosiar Television Tower**, Jakarta, Indonesia	2006	395.0	1,296

* To tip of antenna
\# Under construction – scheduled completion
† Severely damaged by fire 27 August 2000, restored and reopened 2004

All the towers listed are self-supporting, rather than masts braced with guy wires, and all have observation facilities. A flurry of tower construction in recent years has evicted the Eiffel Tower (1889 – 324 m/ 1,063 ft), which long headed the list, from the Top 10.

MASTS

Built in 1963, the KVLY-TV mast (formerly KTHI-TV mast), Fargo, North Dakota, USA, held the record as the world's tallest structure until 1974, when it was overtaken by the 646.38-m (2,120.67-ft) Warsaw radio mast. When this collapsed during maintenance work on 8 August 1991, the KVLY-TV regained the record until the Burj Khalifa became the world's tallest structure, but it remains the tallest mast.

TALLEST LIGHTHOUSE

Built in 1961 and refurbished and reopened in 2009, the Yokohama Marine Tower, Japan, is 106 m (348 ft) tall.

◀ *Sky high*
When completed, the Tokyo Sky Tree will be the world's tallest self-supporting steel tower.

EIFFEL TOWER

The Eiffel Tower held the record as world's tallest structure from 31 March 1889, when it overtook the 169-m (555-ft) Washington Monument, until 27 May 1930, when it was itself overtaken by the Chrysler Building.

TALLEST OFFSHORE STRUCTURES

When it was built in 1989, Shell Petroleum's $500-million Bullwinkle oil platform (seen here being towed horizontally into position in the Gulf of Mexico) was the tallest offshore structure in the world, measuring 529.1 m (1,736 ft), with 412.4 m (1,353 ft) below the waterline. It has since been overtaken by the 609.9-m (2,001-ft) Petronius platform in the same oilfield.

◀ ***Towering success***
It has been calculated that from 1889 to 2009 249,976,000 tourists visited the Eiffel Tower.

TOP 10 TALLEST RELIGIOUS BUILDINGS

	BUILDING / LOCATION	YEAR COMPLETED	HEIGHT M	FT
1	**Hassan II Mosque**, Casablanca, Morocco	1993	210.0	689
2	**Sagrada Família**, Barcelona, Spain	2026*	170.0	558
3	**Mole Antonelliana**#, Turin, Italy	1889	167.5	550
4	**Ulm Cathedral**, Ulm, Germany	1890	161.5	530
5	**Our Lady of Peace Basilica**, Yamoussoukro, Côte d'Ivoire	1990	158.0	518
6	**Cologne Cathedral**, Cologne, Germany	1880	157.4	516
7	**Tianning Pagoda**, Changzhou, China	2007	154.0	505
8	**Notre-Dame Cathedral**, Rouen, France	1876	151.0	495
9	**St Nicholas**, Hamburg, Germany	1847	147.3	483
10	**Notre Dame Cathedral**, Strasbourg, France	1439	144.0	472

* Under construction – scheduled completion
# Designed as a synagogue, now a museum

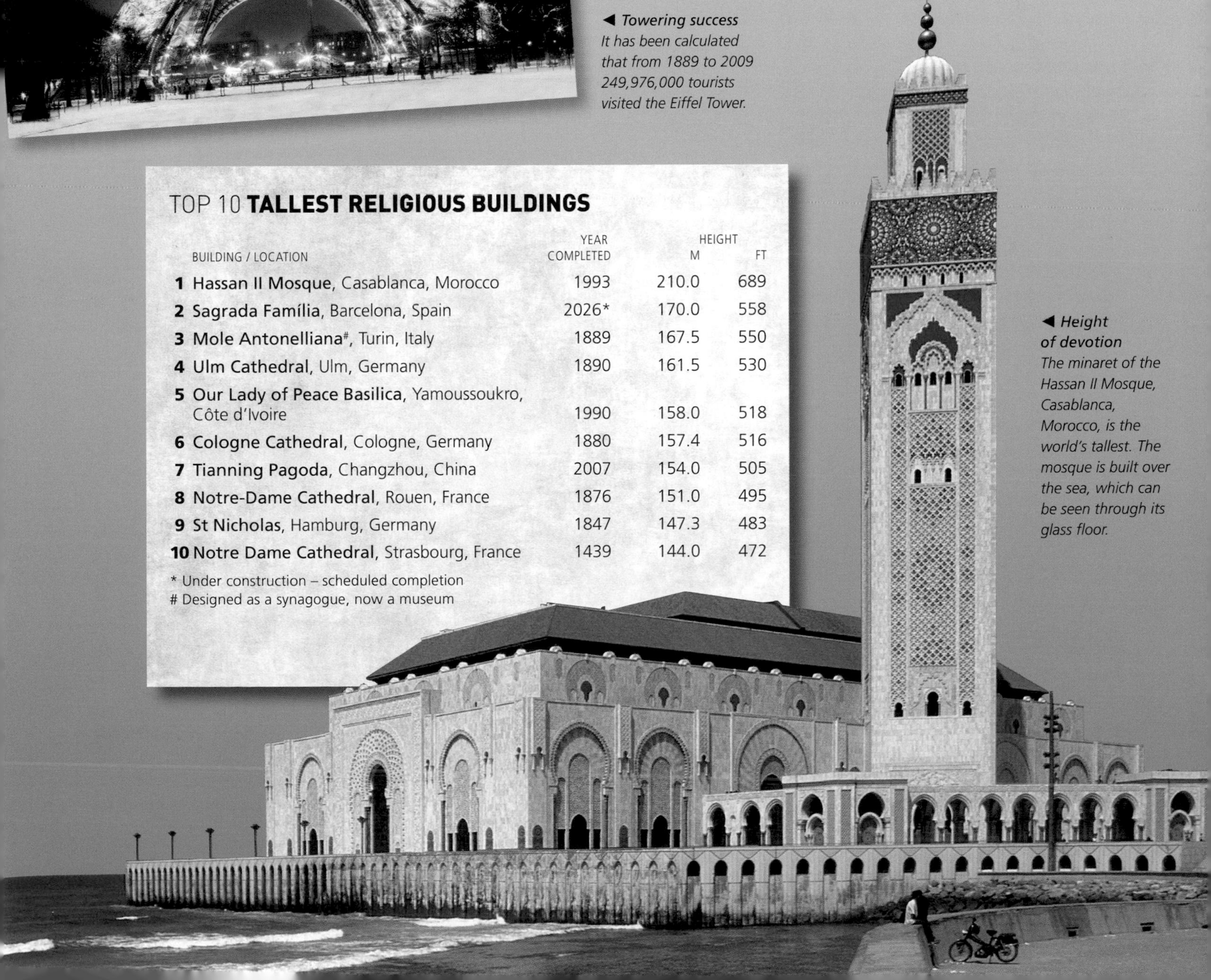

◀ ***Height of devotion***
The minaret of the Hassan II Mosque, Casablanca, Morocco, is the world's tallest. The mosque is built over the sea, which can be seen through its glass floor.

BRIDGES

► *Akashi-Kaikyo*
The central span of the road bridge is the world's longest, at almost 2 km (1.2 miles).

TOP 10 LONGEST SUSPENSION BRIDGES

	BRIDGE / LOCATION	YEAR COMPLETED	LENGTH OF MAIN SPAN M	FT
1	**Akashi-Kaikyō**, Kobe-Naruto, Japan	1998	1,991	6,532
2	**Xihoumen**, China	2007	1,650	5,413
3	**Great Belt**, Denmark	1997	1,624	5,328
4	**Ryungyang**, China	2005	1,490	4,888
5	**Nanjing Fourth Yangtse**, Jiangsu, China	2010	1,418	4,652
6	**Humber Estuary**, UK	1980	1,410	4,625
7	**Jiangyin**, China	1998	1,385	4,543
8	**Tsing Ma**, Hong Kong, China	1997	1,377	4,518
9	**Verrazano-Narrows**, New York, USA	1964	1,298	4,260
10	=**Golden Gate**, San Francisco, USA	1937	1,280	4,200
	=**Yangluo**, Wuhan, China	2007	1,280	4,200

The completion in 2013 of the 1,310-m (4,298-ft) Hardanger Bridge, Hardangerfjord, Norway, will eject the Golden Gate Bridge from the Top 10.

TOP 10 LONGEST SWING BRIDGES

	BRIDGE	YEAR COMPLETED	SWING SPAN M	FT
1	**El Ferdan**, Ismailia, Egypt	2001	340	1,115
2	**Fort Madison**, Mississippi River, Iowa, USA	1927	166	545
3	**George P. Coleman Memorial** (US-17), York River, Virginia, USA	1952	152	500
4	**Duluth**, St Louis Bay, Minnesota, USA*	1897	148	486
5	**S.W. Spokane Street**, Seattle, Washington, USA	1991	146	480
6	**C.M. & N. Railroad**, Chicago, Illinois, USA	1899	142	467
7	**Route 82**, East Haddam, Connecticut, USA	1913	142	465
8	**Coos Bay**, Oregon, USA	1914	140	458
9	**Rigolets Pass**, New Orleans, Louisiana, USA	1930	122	400
10	**Golden Horn Metro**, Istanbul, Turkey	2010	120	394

* Not operational since 21 December 1962

TOP 10 LONGEST BRIDGES IN THE UK

BRIDGE / TYPE* / LOCATION / YEAR COMPLETED / LENGTH OF MAIN SPAN (M/FT)

* S = Suspension; CT = Cantilever truss; CSG = Cable-stayed steel girder and truss; SA = Steel arch; PCG = Pre-stressed concrete girder

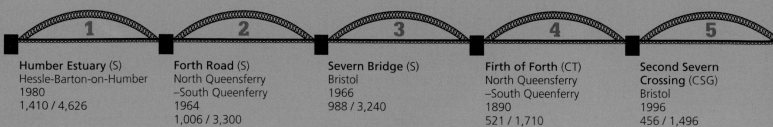

1. **Humber Estuary** (S)
Hessle-Barton-on-Humber
1980
1,410 / 4,626

2. **Forth Road** (S)
North Queensferry –South Queenferry
1964
1,006 / 3,300

3. **Severn Bridge** (S)
Bristol
1966
988 / 3,240

4. **Firth of Forth** (CT)
North Queensferry –South Queenferry
1890
521 / 1,710

5. **Second Severn Crossing** (CSG)
Bristol
1996
456 / 1,496

► *Millau Viaduct*
The French road bridge has the world's tallest bridge towers.

▲ *Rio Grande*
The bridge on Route 64 was voted America's 'Most Beautiful Long Span Steel Bridge'.

TOP 10 **TALLEST BRIDGES**

	BRIDGE / LOCATION	YEAR COMPLETED	HEIGHT* M	FT
1	**Siduhe** China	2009	472	1,550
2	**Balinghe River** China	2009	370	1,214
3	**Beipanjiang 2003** China	2003	366	1,200
4	**Beipanjiang 2009** China	2009	330	1,083
5	**Liuguanghe** China	2001	297	975
6	**Zhijinghe** China	2009	294	965
7	**Royal Gorge** Colorado, USA	1929	291	955
8	**Millau Viaduct** Millau, France	2004	277	909
9	**Beipanjiang#** China	2001	275	902
10	**Mike O'Callaghan-Pat Tilman Memorial**, Nevada, USA	2010	271	890

* Clearance above water; completed bridges only
\# Rail viaduct; all others road

TOP 10 **TALLEST BRIDGE TOWERS**

	BRIDGE / LOCATION	YEAR COMPLETED	HEIGHT M	FT
1	**Millau Viaduct** Millau, France	2004	336	1,102
2	**Sutong** Changsu, China	2008	306	1,004
3	**Akashi-Kaikyo** Akashi, Japan	1998	300	984
4	**Stonecutters** China	2009	298	978
5	**Gwangan** South Korea	2002	270	886
6	**Jingsha** China	2009	267	876
7	**East Bridge Great Belt Fixed Link** Sprogø, Denmark	1997	254	833
8	**Edong** China	2010	243	797
9	**Mezcala** Mexico	1993	242	794
10	**Golden Gate** San Francisco, USA	1937	227	754

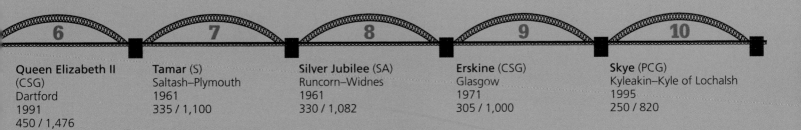

Queen Elizabeth II (CSG)
Dartford
1991
450 / 1,476

Tamar (S)
Saltash–Plymouth
1961
335 / 1,100

Silver Jubilee (SA)
Runcorn–Widnes
1961
330 / 1,082

Erskine (CSG)
Glasgow
1971
305 / 1,000

Skye (PCG)
Kyleakin–Kyle of Lochalsh
1995
250 / 820

TUNNELS

▲ *Boring event*
The world's longest rail tunnel, the Gotthard AlpTransit, Switzerland, was proposed as early as 1947 and given the go-ahead in 1998 after a referendum of the Swiss electorate. When completed, trains will travel through it at 250 km/h (155 mph).

TOP 10 **LONGEST RAIL TUNNELS**

TUNNEL / LOCATION / YEAR COMPLETED	LENGTH KM	MILES
1 Gotthard AlpTransit, Switzerland, 2017*	57.1	35.6
2 Seikan, Japan, 1988	53.9	33.6
3 Channel Tunnel, France/England, 1994	50.5	31.5
4 Moscow Metro (Serpukhovsko-Timiryazevskaya line), Russia, 2002	41.5	25.9
5 Moscow Metro (Kaluzhsko-Rizhskaya line), Russia, 1990	37.6	23.4
6 Lötschberg Base, Switzerland, 2007	34.6	21.6
7 Berlin U-Bahn (U7 line), 1984	31.8	19.8
8 Guadarrama, Spain, 2007	28.4	17.7
9 Taihang, China, 2008	27.9	17.4
10 London Underground (East Finchley/Morden, Northern Line), UK, 1939	27.8	17.3

* Under construction – scheduled completion date

TOP 10 **LONGEST TUNNELS IN THE UK***

TUNNEL / TYPE / LOCATION	YEAR COMPLETED	LENGTH M	FT
1 Stratford West, Rail (Channel Tunnel rail link)	2007	10,105	33,152
2 Stratford East, Rail (Channel Tunnel rail link)	2007	7,555	24,786
3 Severn, Rail Avon/Gwent	1886	7,008	22,992
4 Totley, Rail South Yorkshire	1893	5,596	18,359
5 Standedge, Canal Manchester / West Yorkshire	1811	5,210	17,093
6 Woodhead New#, Rail South Yorkshire	1953	4,888	16,036
7 Standedge, Rail Manchester / West Yorkshire	1949	4,886	16,030
8 Woodhead Old I#, Rail South Yorkshire	1845	4,848	15,905
9 Woodhead Old II#, Rail South Yorkshire	1852	4,840	15,879
10 Chipping Sodbury, Rail Avon	1902	4,063	13,330

* Excluding underground railways
# Disused

TOP 10 **LONGEST SUBSEA TUNNELS**

	TUNNEL / LOCATION	YEAR COMPLETED	LENGTH M	FT
1	**Seikan**, Japan	1988	53,850	176,673
2	**Channel Tunnel**, France/England	1994	50,450	165,518
3	**Shin-Kanmon**, Japan	1975	18,716	61,404
4	**Tokyo Bay Aqualine Expressway***, Japan	1997	9,583	31,440
5	**Great Belt Fixed Link** (Eastern Tunnel), Denmark	1997	8,024	26,325
6	**Bømlafjord***, Norway	2000	7,931	26,020
7	**Eiksund***, Norway	2008	7,797	25,581
8	**Karmöy**, Norway	2012	7,720	25,328
9	**Oslofjord***, Norway	2000	7,390	24,245
10	**Severn**, UK	1886	7,008	22,992

* Road; others rail

Japan has undertaken a wave of undersea tunnel building in recent years, with the Seikan the most ambitious project of all. Connecting Honshu and Hokkaido, 23.3 km (14.4 miles) of the tunnel is 100 m (328 ft) below the sea bed, bored through strata that presented considerable engineering problems, and took 24 years to complete.

▲ *Channel Tunnel*
The Channel Tunnel carries over 16 million passengers a year.

▼ *Laerdal Tunnel*
This road tunnel contains three caves in which drivers can rest.

TOP 10 **LONGEST ROAD TUNNELS**

TUNNEL / LOCATION / YEAR COMPLETED / LENGTH (M/FT)

1. **Lærdal**, Norway (2000) 24,510 / 80,413
2. **Zhongnanshan**, China (2007) 18,040 / 59,186
3. **St Gotthard**, Switzerland (1980) 16,918 / 55,505
4. **Arlberg**, Austria (1978) 13,972 / 45,850
5. **Hsuehshan**, Taiwan (2006) 12,900 / 42,323
6. **Fréjus**, France/Italy (1980) 12,895 / 42,306
7. **Mont-Blanc**, France/Italy (1965) 11,611 / 38,094
8. **Gudvangen**, Norway (1991) 11,428 / 37,493
9. **Folgefonn**, Norway (2001) 11,100 / 36,417
10. **Kan-Etsu II** (southbound), Japan (1991) 11,010 / 36,122

At one time, Nos. 1, 3, 4 and 7 each held the record as 'world's longest road tunnel'. Other previous, but since eclipsed, record-holders include the 5,854-m (19,206-ft) Grand San Bernardo (Italy-Switzerland; 1964); the 5,133-m (16,841-ft) Alfonso XIII or Viella (Spain; 1948); the 3,237-m (10,620-ft) Queensway (Mersey) Tunnel (connecting Liverpool and Birkenhead, UK; 1934); and the 3,186-m (10,453-ft) Col de Tende (France-Italy; 1882), originally built as a rail tunnel and converted for road use in 1928.

5

CULTURE & LEARNING

400TH ANNIVERSARY OF THE KING JAMES BIBLE

The Bible is the bestselling book of all time. Early versions of it were handwritten manuscripts, with the first printed version the Gutenberg Bible of around 1454. The Authorized, or King James Bible, so-called because it was produced under the direction of King James I of England, was a new English translation that has remained in print for 400 years. It remains protected by royal copyright, with only appointed printers permitted to issue it.

WORLD LANGUAGES

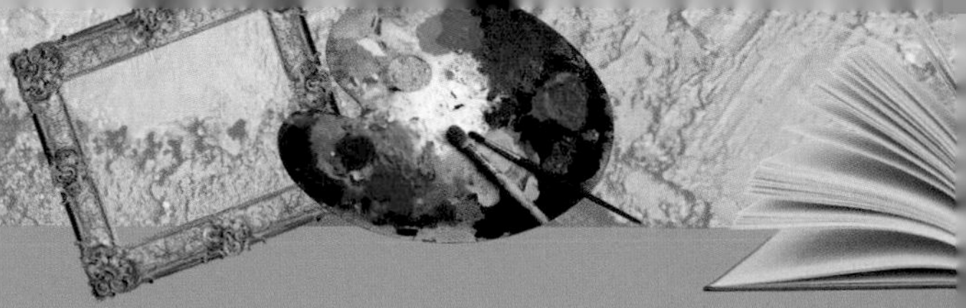

TOP 10 **COUNTRIES WITH THE MOST SPANISH LANGUAGE SPEAKERS**

	COUNTRY	SPEAKERS*
1	Mexico	106,770,268
2	USA	50,000,000
3	Spain	46,184,857
4	Colombia	44,937,600
5	Argentina	40,275,837
6	Venezuela	28,296,320
7	Peru	25,514,034
8	Chile	16,974,610
9	Ecuador	13,851,720
10	Brazil	12,445,005

* As first or second/foreign language

TOP 10 **COUNTRIES WITH THE MOST ENGLISH-LANGUAGE SPEAKERS**

	COUNTRY	APPROX. NO. OF ENGLISH SPEAKERS*
1	USA	215,423,557
2	UK	58,100,000
3	Canada	17,694,830
4	Australia	15,581,329
5	Ireland	4,122,100
6	Nigeria	4,000,000
7	New Zealand	3,673,679
8	South Africa	3,673,203
9	Philippines	3,427,000
10	Jamaica#	2,600,000

* People for whom English is their mother-tongue; latest available data

Includes English Creole

Source: Ethnologue

As a result of colonization in parts of Africa, the Americas and Asia, a total of 21 countries speak Spanish, making it the most spoken after Mandarin and the third most used language on the Internet.

TOP 10 **MOST-SPOKEN LANGUAGES***

	LANGUAGE	SPEAKERS
1	Chinese (Mandarin)	845,456,760
2	Spanish	328,518,810
3	English	328,008,138
4	Arabic	221,002,544
5	Hindi	181,676,620
6	Bengali	181,272,900
7	Portuguese	177,981,570
8	Russian	143,553,950
9	Japanese	122,080,100
10	German	90,294,110

* Primary speakers only

Source: Ethnologue

◀ ***Hindi speakers***
Estimates of the number speakers of Hindi as a first language vary, some sources claiming more than double the figure quoted by authoritative linguistic survey Ethnologue.

▲ *Voice of youth*
The number of young Arabic speakers and Internet users has accelerated rapidly in recent years.

TOP 10 **COUNTRIES WITH THE MOST ARABIC LANGUAGE SPEAKERS**

	COUNTRY	SPEAKERS
1	Egypt	67,367,000
2	Algeria	27,346,000
3	Saudi Arabia	22,809,000
4	Yemen	19,930,000
5	Morocco	19,390,000
6	Iraq	19,026,000
7	Sudan	18,818,000
8	Syria	15,829,000
9	Tunisia*	6,911,000
10	Libya	5,334,000

* A further 2,596,000 people speak Arabic-French

Arabic spread across Africa and the Middle East alongside the expansion of the Arabic Empire. Written or classical Arabic has changed little since the 7th century, but spoken Arabic, one of the official languages of the United Nations, varies from country to country.

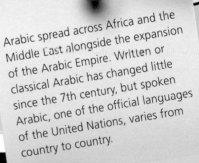

TOP 10 **ONLINE LANGUAGES**

	LANGUAGE	% OF ALL INTERNET USERS	INTERNET USERS*
1	English	27.5	495,843,462
2	Chinese (Mandarin)	22.6	407,650,713
3	Spanish	7.8	139,849,651
4	Japanese	5.3	95,979,000
5	Portuguese	4.3	77,569,900
6	German	4.0	71,782,234
7	Arabic	3.3	60,252,100
8	French	3.2	57,017,099
9	Russian	2.5	45,250,000
10	Korean	2.1	37,475,800
	Top 10 languages	*82.6*	*1,488,669,959*
	Rest of world languages	*17.4*	*313,660,498*
	World total	*100.0*	*1,802,330,457*

* As at 31 December 2009

Source: www.internetworldstats.com

EDUCATION

TOP 10 COUNTRIES WITH THE MOST PRIMARY SCHOOL PUPILS

	COUNTRY	PRIMARY SCHOOL PUPILS (2006)
1	India	139,170,000
2	China	108,925,000
3	Indonesia	28,983,000
4	USA	24,319,000
5	Nigeria	22,115,000
6	Brazil	18,661,000
7	Pakistan	17,979,000
8	Bangladesh	17,953,000
9	Mexico	14,595,000
10	Philippines	13,007,000
	UK	*4,518,000*
	Top 10 total	*405,707,000*
	World total	*688,608,000*

Source: UNESCO, *Global Education Digest 2008*

TOP 10 COUNTRIES WITH THE MOST UNIVERSITY STUDENTS

	COUNTRY	% FEMALE	STUDENTS IN TERTIARY EDUCATION (2006)
1	China	47	23,361,000
2	USA	57	17,487,000
3	India	40	12,853,000
4	Russia	57	9,167,000
5	Brazil	56	4,572,000
6	Japan	46	4,085,000
7	Indonesia	n/a	3,657,000
8	South Korea	37	3,204,000
9	Ukraine	54	2,819,000
10	Egypt	n/a	2,594,000
	UK	57	*2,336,000*
	Top 10 total		*83,799,000*
	World total		*143,889,000*

Source: UNESCO, *Global Education Digest 2008*

TOP 10 COUNTRIES WITH THE MOST SECONDARY SCHOOL PUPILS

	COUNTRY	SECONDARY SCHOOL PUPILS (2006)
1	China	101,195,000
2	India	91,529,000
3	Brazil	24,863,000
4	USA	24,552,000
5	Indonesia	16,798,000
6	Russia	11,548,000
7	Mexico	10,883,000
8	Bangladesh	10,355,000
9	Vietnam	9,975,000
10	Egypt	8,330,000
	UK	*5,358,000*
	Top 10 total	*310,028,000*
	World total	*513,766,000*

Source: UNESCO, *Global Education Digest 2008*

▲ *Graduation day*
Despite the economic downturn, university enrolment continues to rise in many countries.

▼ *Primary role*
The Indian education system has contributed to the country's economic progress.

TOP 10 **LARGEST UNIVERSITIES**

	UNIVERSITY / LOCATION	APPROX. ENROLMENT
1	**Allama Iqbal Open University**, Islamabad, Pakistan	1,806,214
2	**Indira Gandhi National Open University**, New Delhi, India	1,500,000
3	**Islamic Azad University**, Tehran, Iran	1,300,000
4	**Anadolu University**, Eskişehir, Turkey	884,081
5	**Bangladesh Open University**, Gazipur, Bangladesh	600,000
6	**Dr Babasaheb Ambedkar Open University**, Andhra Pradesh, India	450,000
7	**State University of New York**, New York, USA	418,000
8	**California State University**, California, USA	417,000
9	**Universitas Terbuka**, Jakarta, Indonesia	350,000
10	**Universidad de Buenos Aires**, Buenos Aires, Argentina	316,050

TOP 10 **OLDEST SCHOOLS IN THE UK**

	SCHOOL / LOCATION	FOUNDED
1	**The King's School**, Canterbury	AD 597
2	**The King's School**, Rochester	AD 604
3	**St Peter's School**, York	AD 627
4	**Beverley Grammar School**	AD 700
5	**Warwick School**	AD 914
6	**St Alban's School**	AD 948
7	**The King's School**, Ely	AD 970
8	**Salisbury Cathedral School**	1091
9	**Norwich School**	1096
10	**Thetford Grammar School**	1114

TOP 10 **COUNTRIES WITH MOST FOREIGN STUDENTS***

	COUNTRY / FOREIGN STUDENTS
1	USA 595,874
2	UK 351,470
3	France 246,612
4	Australia 211,526
5	Germany 206,875
6	Japan 125,877
7	Canada 68,520
8	South Africa 60,552
9	Russia 60,288
10	Italy 57,271

* In tertiary education

Source: UNESCO, *Global Education Digest 2009*

BESTSELLING BOOKS

◀ *Worldwide following*
J. K. Rowling's dominance of the global sales chart has seen her become the wealthiest author of all time.

TOP 10 BESTSELLING NOVELS

	BOOK / FIRST PUBLISHED	ESTIMATED SALES*
1	**J. K. Rowling**, Harry Potter and the Order of the Phoenix, 2003	210,000,000
2	**Charles Dickens**, A Tale of Two Cities, 1859	200,000,000
3	**J. K. Rowling**, Harry Potter and the Prisoner of Azkaban, 1999	180,000,000
4 =	**J. K. Rowling**, Harry Potter and the Chamber of Secrets, 1998	150,000,000
=	**J. R. R. Tolkien**, The Lord of the Rings, 1954–55	150,000,000
6	**J. K. Rowling**, Harry Potter and the Philosopher's Stone, 1997	120,000,000
7 =	**Agatha Christie**, And Then There Were None, 1939	100,000,000
=	**J. R. R. Tolkien**, The Hobbit, 1937	100,000,000
=	**Cao Xueqin**, Dream of the Red Chamber, 18th century	100,000,000
10	**H. Rider Haggard**, She, 1887	83,000,000

* Including translations

TOP 10 BESTSELLING NON-FICTION BOOKS

	BOOK / FIRST PUBLISHED	ESTIMATED SALES*
1	**The Bible**	6,000,000,000
2	**Quotations from the Works of Mao Tse-tung**, 1966	900,000,000
3	**Qur'an** (Koran)	800,000,000
4	**Xinhua Zidian** (Chinese dictionary), 1953	400,000,000
5	**Thomas Cranmer**, Book of Common Prayer, 1549	300,000,000
6	**John Bunyan**, The Pilgrim's Progress, 1678	250,000,000
7 =	**Robert Baden-Powell**, Scouting For Boys, 1908	150,000,000
=	**John Foxe**, Foxe's Book of Martyrs, 1563	150,000,000
9	**Noah Webster**, The American Spelling Book, 1783	100,000,000
10	**Benjamin Spock**, The Common Sense Book of Baby and Child Care, 1946	50,000,000

* Including translations, excluding annual publications, series and revised editions of dictionaries and encyclopedias

Although modern sales monitoring has made assessing book sales figures more accurate, it is often jokingly suggested that publishers' claims should be classified as 'fiction', while all-time cumulative sales and those of multiple editions of any book make such assessments round-figure estimates at best.

Religious and political texts and must-have manuals predominate among the world's biggest non-fiction bestsellers, with the Bible taking a commanding lead. Often, it was the only book a home would possess, acting also as a safe repository for preserving the handwritten family tree.

TOP 10 **BESTSELLING ENGLISH-LANGUAGE ADULT AUTHORS**

	AUTHOR / COUNTRY / DATES	ESTIMATED TOTAL SALES
1	= **Agatha Christie** (UK, 1890–1976)	4,000,000,000
	= **William Shakespeare** (England, 1564–1616)	4,000,000,000
3	**Barbara Cartland** (UK, 1901–2000)	1,000,000,000
4	**Harold Robbins** (USA, 1916–97)	750,000,000
5	**Danielle Steel** (USA, b. 1947)	570,000,000
6	= **Horatio Alger Jr** (USA, 1832–99)	400,000,000
	= **Jackie Collins** (UK, b. 1937)	400,000,000
	= **Sidney Sheldon** (USA, 1917–2007)	400,000,000
9	**Stephen King** (USA, b. 1947)	350,000,000
10	= **Dean Koontz** (USA, b. 1945)	325,000,000
	= **Erle Stanley Gardner** (USA, 1889–1970)	325,000,000

▲ ***Best Will in the world***
Shakespeare is rivalled only by Agatha Christie for his total sales.

TOP 10 **BESTSELLING NON-ENGLISH-LANGUAGE AUTHORS**

	AUTHOR / COUNTRY / DATES / ESTIMATED TOTAL SALES
1	**Georges Simenon** (Belgium, 1903–89) 700,000,000
2	**Leo Tolstoy** (Russia, 1828–1910) 413,000,000
3	**Corín Tellado** (Spain, 1927–2009) 400,000,000
4	**Alexander Ouskin** (Russia, 1799–1837) 357,000,000
5	= **Jirō Akagawa** (Japan, b. 1948) 300,000,000
	= **Jun Yong** (China, b. 1924) 300,000,000
7	**Frédéric Dard** (France, 1921–2000) 290,000,000
8	= **Karl May** (Germany, 1842–1912) 200,000,000
	= **Kyotaro Nishimura** (Japan, b. 1930) 200,000,000
	= **Ryōtarō Shiba** (Japan, 1923–1996) 200,000,000

TOP 10 **BESTSELLING ENGLISH-LANGUAGE CHILDREN'S AUTHORS**

	AUTHOR / COUNTRY / DATES	ESTIMATED TOTAL SALES
1	**J. K. Rowling** (UK, b. 1965)	800,000,000
2	**Enid Blyton** (UK, 1897–1968)	600,000,000
3	**Dr Seuss** (Theodor Seuss Geisel; USA, 1904–91)	500,000,000
4	**R. L. Stine** (USA, b. 1943)	400,000,000
5	**Stan and Jan Berenstain** (USA, 1923–2005; b. 1923)	260,000,000
6	**C. S. Lewis** (UK, 1898–1963)	200,000,000
7	**Ann M. Martin** (USA, b. 1955)	180,000,000
8	= **Beatrix Potter** (UK, 1866–1943)	150,000,000
	= **Richard Scarry** (USA, 1919–94)	150,000,000
10	**Norman Bridwell** (USA, b. 1928)	110,000,000

► ***Top cat***
Michelle Obama reads The Cat in The Hat, *one of Dr Seuss's multi-million bestsellers.*

BOOK AWARDS

◀ *Neil Gaiman*
British cult fantasy novelist Neil Gaiman's The Graveyard Book *gained him his second Hugo award,* Coraline *having won Best Novella in 2003.*

THE 10 LATEST WINNERS OF HUGO AWARDS FOR BEST SCIENCE FICTION NOVEL

YEAR	AUTHOR / TITLE
2009	Neil Gaiman, The Graveyard Book
2008	Michael Chabon, The Yiddish Policemen's Union
2007	Vernor Vinge, Rainbows End
2006	Robert Charles Wilson, Spin
2005	Susanna Clarke, Jonathan Strange & Mr Norrell
2004	Lois McMaster Bujold, Paladin of Souls
2003	Robert J. Sawyer, Hominids
2002	Neil Gaiman, American Gods
2001	J. K. Rowling, Harry Potter and the Goblet of Fire
2000	Vernor Vinge, A Deepness in the Sky

Hugo Awards for science-fiction novels, short stories and other fiction and non-fiction works are presented by the World Science Fiction Society. Named in honour of Hugo Gernsback, the 'father of magazine science fiction', they were established in 1953 as 'Science Fiction Achievement Awards for the best science fiction writing'. The prize in the Awards' inaugural year was presented to Alfred Bester for *The Demolished Man*.

THE 10 LATEST WINNERS OF THE GOLD DAGGER AWARD

YEAR	AUTHOR / TITLE
2009	William Brodrick, A Whispered Name
2008	Frances Fyfield, Blood From Stone
2007*	Peter Temple, The Broken Shore
2006*	Ann Cleeves, Raven Black
2005	Arnaldur Indriðason, Silence of the Grave
2004	Sara Paretsky, Blacklist
2003	Minette Walters, Fox Evil
2002	José Carlos Somoza, The Athenian Murders
2001	Henning Mankell, Sidetracked
2000	Jonathan Lethem, Motherless Brooklyn

* Award renamed Duncan Lawrie Dagger

THE 10 LATEST MAN BOOKER PRIZE WINNERS

YEAR	AUTHOR	COUNTRY	TITLE
2009	Hilary Mantell	UK	Wolf Hall
2008	Aravind Adiga	India	The White Tiger
2007	Anne Enright	Ireland	The Gathering
2006	Kiran Desai	India	The Inheritance of Loss
2005	John Banville	Ireland	The Sea
2004	Alan Hollinghurst	UK	The Line of Beauty
2003	D.B.C. Pierre	Australia	Vernon God Little
2002	Yann Martel	Canada	Life of Pi
2001	Peter Carey	Australia	True History of the Kelly Gang
2000	Margaret Atwood	Canada	The Blind Assassin

THE 10 **LATEST CARNEGIE MEDAL WINNERS**

YEAR*	AUTHOR / TITLE
2009	Siobhan Dowd, Bog Child
2008	Philip Reeve, Here Lies Arthur
2007	Meg Rosoff, Just in Case
2005	Mal Peet, Tamar
2004	Frank Cottrell Boyce, Millions
2003	Jennifer Donnelly, A Gathering Light
2002	Sharon Creech, Ruby Holler
2001	Terry Pratchett, Amazing Maurice and his Educated Rodents
2000	Beverley Naidoo, The Other Side of Truth
1999	Aidan Chambers, Postcards from No Man's Land

* Prior to 2007, publication year; since 2007, award year – hence there was no 2006 award

► *Herta Müller*
Romanian-born but writing in German, she received the 2009 Nobel Prize for Literature.

Established in 1937, the Carnegie Medal is awarded annually by the Library Association for an outstanding English-language children's book published during the previous year. It is named in honour of Scots-born millionaire Andrew Carnegie, who was a notable library benefactor. In its early years, winners included such distinguished authors as Arthur Ransome, Noel Streatfeild, Walter de la Mare and C. S. Lewis, while among notable post-war winners are books such as *Watership Down* by Richard Adams.

THE 10 **LATEST WINNERS OF THE NOBEL PRIZE FOR LITERATURE**

YEAR	WINNER / COUNTRY
2009	Herta Müller, Romania
2008	J.M.G. Le Clézio, France
2007	Doris Lessing, UK
2006	Orhan Pamuk, Turkey
2005	Harold Pinter, UK
2004	Elfriede Jelinek, Austria
2003	J. M. Coetzee, South Africa
2002	Imre Kertész, Hungary
2001	Sir V. S. Naipaul, UK
2000	Gao Xingjian, China

THE 10 **LATEST WINNERS OF THE COSTA* 'BOOK OF THE YEAR' AWARD**

YEAR	AUTHOR / TITLE
2009	Christopher Reid, A Scattering
2008	Sebasatian Barry, The Secret Scripture
2007	A. L. Kennedy, Day
2006	William Boyd, Restless: A Novel
2005	Hilary Spurling, Matisse The Master
2004	Andrea Levy, Small Island
2003	Mark Haddon, The Curious Incident of the Dog in the Night-Time
2002	Claire Tomalin, Samuel Pepys: The Unequalled Self
2001	Philip Pullman, The Amber Spyglass
2000	Matthew Kneale, English Passengers

* Whitbread until 2006

THE 10 OLDEST NATIONAL LIBRARIES

	LIBRARY / LOCATION	FOUNDED
1	**Národní Knihovna České Republiky National Library of the Czech Republic,** Prague, Czech Republic	1366
2	**Österreichische Nationalbibliothek National Library of Austria,** Vienna, Austria	1368
3	**Biblioteca Nazionale Marciana,** Venice, Italy	1468
4	**Bibliothèque Nationale de France National Library of France,** Paris, France	1480
5	**National Library of Malta,** Valetta, Malta	1555
6	**Bayericsche Staatsbibliothek,** Munich, Germany	1558
7	**Bibliothèque Royale Albert 1er National Library of Belgium,** Brussels, Belgium	1559
8	**Nacionalna i Sveučilišna Knjižnica Zagreb National and University Library,** Zagreb, Croatia	1606
9	**Helsingin Yliopisto Kirjasto National Library of Finland,** Helsinki, Finland	1640
10	**Det Kongeligie Bibliotek National Library of Denmark,** Copenhagen, Denmark	1653

▲ *Czech National Library*
The library's foundation dates from Charles IV's donation of a collection of codices in 1366.

THE 10 FIRST PUBLIC LIBRARIES IN THE UK

	LIBRARY	FOUNDED
1	Canterbury	1847
2	Warrington	1848
3	Salford	1849
4	Winchester	1851
5	Manchester Free	1852
6	Liverpool	1852
7	Bolton	1853
8	Ipswich	1853
9	Oxford	1854
10	Cambridge Kidderminster	1855 1855

TOP 10 **LARGEST REFERENCE LIBRARIES IN THE UK**

	LIBRARY / LOCATION	FOUNDED	BOOKS
1	**British Library**, London	1753	29,000,000
2	**National Library of Scotland**, Edinburgh	1682	14,000,000
3	**Bodleian Library**, Oxford	1602	11,000,000
4	**University of Cambridge Library**	c. 1400	7,000,000
5	**National Library of Wales**, Aberystwyth	1907	5,000,000
6	**British Library of Political and Economic Science**, London School of Economics	1896	4,000,000
7	**John Rylands University Library**, Manchester	1972*	3,500,000
8	**Leeds University Library**	1874	2,780,000
9	**Edinburgh University Library**	1580	2,739,000
10	**University of Birmingham Library**	1880	2,200,000

* In 1972 the John Rylands Library (founded in 1900) was amalgamated with Manchester University Library (founded 1851)

▲ *British Library*
The British Library moved from the British Museum to new premises in 1997, with the King's Library housed in the glass tower.

TOP 10 **LARGEST LIBRARIES**

	LIBRARY	LOCATION	FOUNDED	BOOKS
1	Library of Congress	Washington DC, USA	1800	32,124,001
2	British Library*	London, UK	1753	29,000,000
3	Library of the Russian Academy of Sciences	St Petersburg, Russia	1714	20,500,000
4	National Library of Canada	Ottawa, Canada	1953	19,500,000
5	Deutsche Bibliothek#	Frankfurt, Germany	1990	22,200,000
6	Russian State Library†	Moscow, Russia	1862	17,000,000
7	Harvard University Library	Cambridge, Massachusetts, USA	1638	15,826,570
8	Boston Public Library	Boston, Massachusetts, USA	1895	15,760,879
9	Vernadsky National Scientific Library of Ukraine	Kiev, Ukraine	1919	15,000,000
10	National Library of Russia	St Petersburg, Russia	1795	14,799,267

* Founded as part of the British Museum, 1753; became an independent body in 1973
# Formed in 1990 through the unification of the Deutsche Bibliothek, Frankfurt (founded 1947) and the Deutsche Bucherei, Leipzig
† Founded 1862 as Rumyantsev Library, formerly State V. I. Lenin Library

NEWSPAPERS & MAGAZINES

TOP 10 DAILY NEWSPAPERS

NEWSPAPER / COUNTRY / AVERAGE DAILY CIRCULATION* (2009)

1 Yomiuri Shimbun
Japan
10,021,000

2 Asahi Shimbun
Japan
8,054,000

3 Mainichi Shimbun
Japan
3,945,646

4 Bild
Germany
3,548,000

5 Canako Xiaoxi (Beijing)
China
3,183,000

6 The Times of India
India
3,146,000

7 Nihon Keizai Shimbun
Japan
3,034,481

8 The Sun
UK
3,026,556

9 People's Daily
China
2,808,000

10 Chunichi Shimbun
Japan
2,763,602

* Morning edition if published twice daily

Source: World Association of Newspapers 2008, or latest Audit Bureau of Circulations figure

► Newsreaders
Despite challenges from other media, the press has maintained its longstanding role in Japanese culture.

Yomiuri Shimbun was founded in Japan 1874. It became the country's and the world's bestselling daily newspaper when, in 1998, it achieved record average sales of 14,532,694 copies a day, including its morning and evening editions.

TOP 10 SUNDAY NEWSPAPERS IN THE UK

	NEWSPAPER	AVERAGE CIRCULATION*
1	News of the World	3,064,672
2	The Mail on Sunday	2,116,114
3	Sunday Mirror	1,207,051
4	The Sunday Times	1,192,464
5	Sunday Express	614,040
6	The Sunday Telegraph	588,469
7	The People	552,163
8	Sunday Mail (Scotland)	416,634
9	The Observer	366,918
10	Daily Star – Sunday	364,667

* October–November 2009

Source: Audit Bureau of Circulations Ltd

TOP 10 NEWSPAPER-READING COUNTRIES

	COUNTRY	DAILY COPIES PER 1,000 PEOPLE*
1	Iceland	551.62
2	Japan	551.23
3	Norway	516.00
4	Sweden	480.57
5	Finland	431.07
6	Switzerland	420.04
7	Singapore	360.78
8	Denmark	352.77
9	Netherlands	307.50
10	UK	289.75

* In latest year for which data available

Source: UNESCO

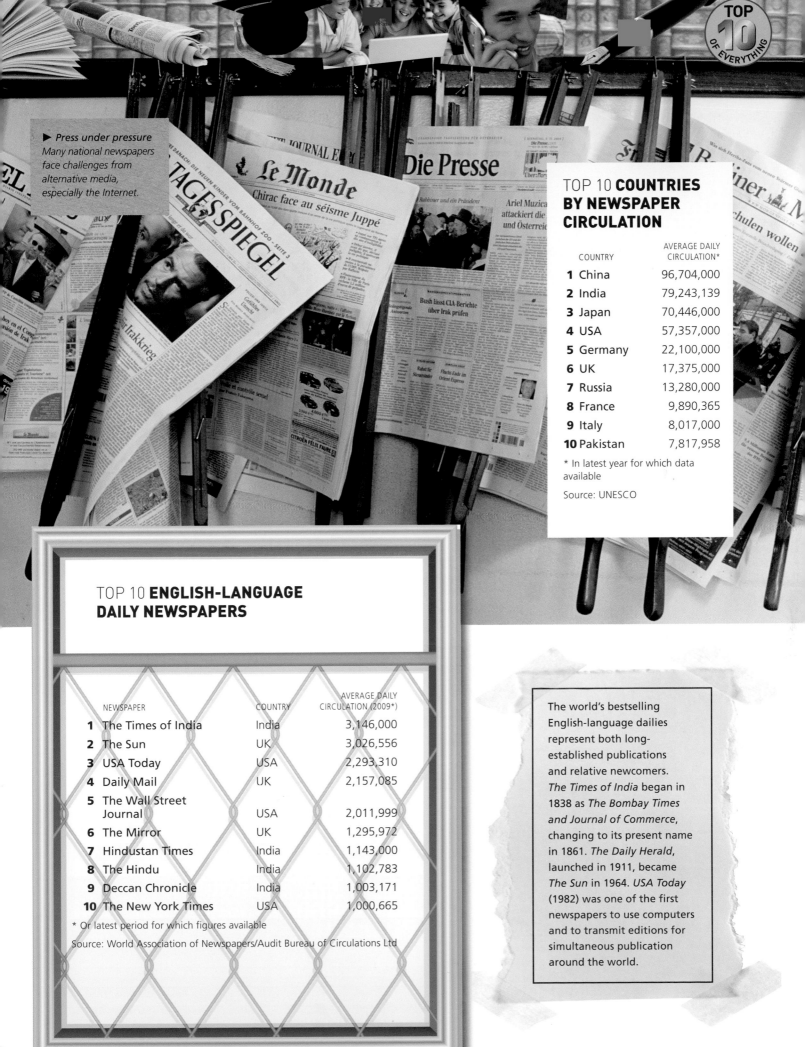

► *Press under pressure*
Many national newspapers face challenges from alternative media, especially the Internet.

TOP 10 **COUNTRIES BY NEWSPAPER CIRCULATION**

	COUNTRY	AVERAGE DAILY CIRCULATION*
1	China	96,704,000
2	India	79,243,139
3	Japan	70,446,000
4	USA	57,357,000
5	Germany	22,100,000
6	UK	17,375,000
7	Russia	13,280,000
8	France	9,890,365
9	Italy	8,017,000
10	Pakistan	7,817,958

* In latest year for which data available

Source: UNESCO

TOP 10 **ENGLISH-LANGUAGE DAILY NEWSPAPERS**

	NEWSPAPER	COUNTRY	AVERAGE DAILY CIRCULATION (2009*)
1	The Times of India	India	3,146,000
2	The Sun	UK	3,026,556
3	USA Today	USA	2,293,310
4	Daily Mail	UK	2,157,085
5	The Wall Street Journal	USA	2,011,999
6	The Mirror	UK	1,295,972
7	Hindustan Times	India	1,143,000
8	The Hindu	India	1,102,783
9	Deccan Chronicle	India	1,003,171
10	The New York Times	USA	1,000,665

* Or latest period for which figures available

Source: World Association of Newspapers/Audit Bureau of Circulations Ltd

The world's bestselling English-language dailies represent both long-established publications and relative newcomers. *The Times of India* began in 1838 as *The Bombay Times and Journal of Commerce*, changing to its present name in 1861. *The Daily Herald*, launched in 1911, became *The Sun* in 1964. *USA Today* (1982) was one of the first newspapers to use computers and to transmit editions for simultaneous publication around the world.

Most Expensive Paintings

TOP 10 **MOST EXPENSIVE PAINTINGS EVER SOLD AT AUCTION**

	PAINTING / ARTIST / NATIONALITY / DATES	SALE	PRICE (US$)
1	**Garçon à la pipe**, Pablo Picasso (Spanish; 1881–1973)	Sotheby's New York, 5 May 2004	104,168,000
2	**Dora Maar au chat**, Pablo Picasso	Sotheby's New York, 3 May 2006	95,216,000
3	**Portrait of Adele Bloch-Bauer II**, Gustav Klimt (Austrian; 1862–1918)	Christie's New York, 8 Nov 2006	87,936,000
4	**Triptych**, Francis Bacon (Irish; 1909–92)	Sotheby's New York, 14 May 2008	86,281,000
5	**Portrait du Dr Gachet**, Vincent van Gogh (Dutch; 1853–90)	Christie's New York, 15 May 1990	82,500,000
6	**Le Bassin aux Nymphéas**, Claude Monet (French; 1840–1926)	Christie's London, 24 Jun 2008	80,379,591 (£40,921,250)
7	**Bal au Moulin de la Galette, Montmartre**, Pierre-Auguste Renoir (French; 1841–1919)	Sotheby's New York, 17 May 1990	78,100,000
8	**The Massacre of the Innocents**, Sir Peter Paul Rubens (Flemish; 1577–1640)	Sotheby's London, 10 Jul 2002	75,930,440 (£49,506,648)
9	**White Center (Yellow, pink and lavender on rose)**, Mark Rothko (American; 1903–70)	Sotheby's New York, 15 May 2007	72,840,000
10	**Green Car Crash – Green Burning Car I**, Andy Warhol (American; 1928–87)	Christie's New York, 16 May 2007	71,720,000

The record prices paid for paintings at auction and in private sales have been successively broken for more than 20 years. However, in 2010, the most expensive work of art ceased to be a painting, when Swiss sculptor Alberto Giacometti's sculpture *L'homme qui marche I* was sold in London for £65 million.

▶ *Van Gogh's* Portrait du Dr Gachet
Since its $82.5-million sale set the 20th-century record, its ownership has remained a mystery.

Raphael rules
Works by Raphael (self-portrait below), such as his Sistine Madonna (right), have often held the title of 'world's most expensive painting'.

ROMAN NUMBERS

Russian oligarch Roman Abramovich was revealed as the buyer of Francis Bacon's *Triptych*. The total price, including buyer's premium, of $80,379,591 is a record for a post-war painting. The previous day, at Christie's New York, Abramovich had purchased Lucian Freud's *Benefits Supervisor Sleeping* for $33,641,000 – a record price for a work by a living artist.

MOST EXPENSIVE IN EACH CENTURY

The 17th-century record was set with Raphael's *La Perla Madonna*, owned by Charles I and sold for £2,600 after his execution in 1649. The same painter's *Sistine Madonna* established the 18th-century record when it was sold in 1759 for 17,000 ducats (£8,500). In 1885 the Duke of Marlborough sold Raphael's *Ansidei Madonna* to the National Gallery, London, for a 19th-century record of £70,000. After works by Van Gogh broke every record, his *Portrait du Dr Gachet* (see facing page), set the 20th-century high.

OOPS!

In October 2006, Pablo Picasso's 1932 painting *Le rêve* hit the headlines when its owner, Las Vegas casino owner Steve Wynn, agreed to sell it to billionaire Steven A. Cohen in a private transaction for $139 million. While showing it to a group of friends, Mr Wynn made a sweeping gesture and accidentally poked his elbow through the canvas, resulting in a 15-cm (6-in) tear – and the cancellation of the sale.

WOMAN ARTISTS

The highest price ever paid for a painting by a woman artist was the £5,529,250 ($10,860,832) at Christie's London, on 24 June 2008 for *Les Fleurs* by Russian Natalia Goncharova (1881–1962). The previous year her *Picking Apples* had set a new record of £4,948,000 ($9,778,656).

MOST EXPENSIVE PRIVATE SALE

By their nature, private sales of works of art are rarely publicized, but it is believed that in 2006 US music mogul David Geffen sold *No. 5, 1948* by Jackson Pollock (American, 1912–56) privately for an estimated $140 million.

ARTY FACTS

▲ *British Museum*
As well as attracting almost six million visitors a year, its exhibitions are among the UK's best-attended.

TOP 10 **MOST-VISITED GALLERIES AND MUSEUMS, 2009**

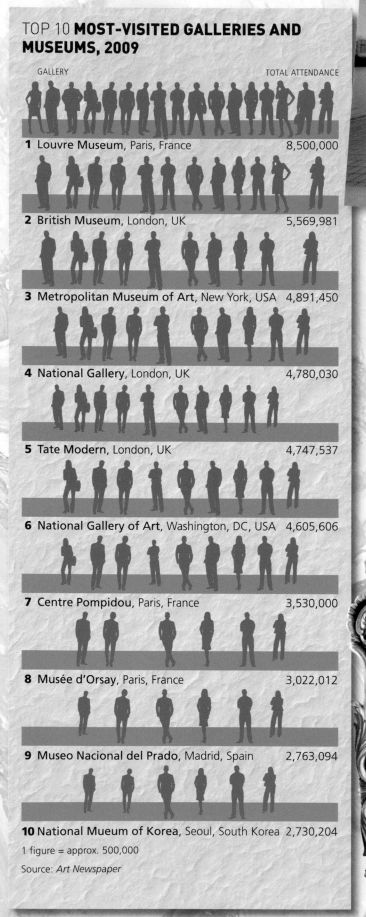

	GALLERY	TOTAL ATTENDANCE
1	**Louvre Museum**, Paris, France	8,500,000
2	**British Museum**, London, UK	5,569,981
3	**Metropolitan Museum of Art**, New York, USA	4,891,450
4	**National Gallery**, London, UK	4,780,030
5	**Tate Modern**, London, UK	4,747,537
6	**National Gallery of Art**, Washington, DC, USA	4,605,606
7	**Centre Pompidou**, Paris, France	3,530,000
8	**Musée d'Orsay**, Paris, France	3,022,012
9	**Museo Nacional del Prado**, Madrid, Spain	2,763,094
10	**National Mueum of Korea**, Seoul, South Korea	2,730,204

1 figure = approx. 500,000

Source: *Art Newspaper*

TOP 10 **BEST-ATTENDED EXHIBITIONS AT THE BRITISH MUSEUM, LONDON**

	EXHIBITION	YEAR	TOTAL ATTENDANCE
1	Treasures of Tutankhamun*	1972–73	1,694,117
2	Turner Watercolours	1975	585,046
3	The Vikings*	1980	465,000
4	Thracian Treasures from Bulgaria	1976	424,465
5	From Manet to Toulouse-Lautrec: French Lithographs 1860–1900	1978	355,354
6	The Ancient Olympic Games	1980	334,354
7	Treasures for the Nation*	1988–89	297,837
8	Excavating in Egypt	1982–83	285,736
9	Heraldry	1978	262,183
10 =	Drawings by Michelangelo	1975	250,000
=	Exploring the City: the Foster Studio	2001	250,000

* Admission charged, all others free

TOP 10 **BEST-ATTENDED EXHIBITIONS AT THE TATE MODERN, LONDON**

	EXHIBITION / YEAR(S)	TOTAL ATTENDANCE
1	Matisse/Picasso 2002	467,166
2	Edward Hopper 2004–05	429,909
3	Frida Kahlo 2005	369,249
4	Rothko 2008–09	327,244
5	Kandinsky: The Path to Abstraction 2006	282,439
6	Andy Warhol 2002	218,801
7	Between Cinema and a Hard Place 2000	200,937
8	Henri Rousseau: Jungles in Paris 2005–06	190,795
9	Surrealism: Desire Unbound 2001–02	168,825
10	Dalí and Film 2007	167,689

TOP 10 **TALLEST FREE-STANDING STATUES**

#	STATUE / LOCATION	HEIGHT M	FT
1	**Crazy Horse Memorial** Thunderhead Mountain, South Dakota, USA Started in 1948 by Polish-American sculptor Korczak Ziolkowski, and continued after his death in 1982 by his widow and eight of his children, this gigantic equestrian statue, even longer than it is high (195 m/641 ft), is not expected to be completed for several years.	172	563
2	**Foshan Jinfo** (Vairocana Buddha) Lushan, Henan, China Completed in 2002, the Buddha sits on a 20-m (66-ft) throne atop a 25-m (82-ft) pedestal.	128	420
3	**Ushiku Amida Buddha** Joodo Teien Garden, Japan This Japan-Taiwanese project, unveiled in 1995, took seven years to complete and weighs 1,000 tonnes.	120	394
4	**Laykyun Setkyar Buddha** Monywa, Myanmar Located in Khatakan Taung, this giant statue of Buddha, which took 12 years to complete, stands on a 13.5-m (44-ft) base.	116	380
5	**Nanshan Haishang Guanyin** (Avalokitesvara) Sanya, Hainan, China Depicting the bodhisattva Guan Yin, the statue was completed in 2005, after six years' construction.	108	354
6	**Emperors Yan and Huang** Zhengzhou, Henan, China Completed in 2007.	106	348
7	**The Indian Rope Trick** Riddersberg Säteri, Jönköping, Sweden Sculptor Calle Örnemark's 144-tonne wooden sculpture depicts a long strand of 'rope' held by a fakir, while another figure ascends.	103	337
8	**Peter the Great** Moscow, Russia Georgian sculptor Zurab Tsereteli's statue of the Russian ruler on a galleon was moved from St Petersburg in 1997.	96	315
9	=**Grand Buddha at Ling Shan** (Gautama Buddha) Wuxi, China This gigantic bronze statue was completed in 1996.	88	289
	=**Dai Kannon of Kita no Miyako Park** (Avalokitesvara) Ashibetsu, Hokkaidō, Japan Completed in 1989.	88	289

TOP 10 **BEST-ATTENDED EXHIBITIONS AT THE NATIONAL GALLERY, LONDON***

	EXHIBITION	YEAR(S)	TOTAL ATTENDANCE
1	Manet to Picasso	2006–07	1,110,044
2	Seeing Salvation: The Image of Christ	2000	355,175
3	Velázquez	2006–07	302,520
4	Vermeer and the Delft School	2001	276,164
5	Titian	2003	267,939
6	Raphael: From Urbino to Rome	2004–05	230,649
7	Picasso Prints: Challenging the Past	2009	227,831
8	El Greco	2004	219,000
9	Picasso: Challenging the Past	2009	204,862
10	Ron Mueck	2003	193,320

* 20th century

◄ *Standing Tall*
The colossal Monywa, Myanmar, buddha is sited near a 90 m (295-ft) long reclining buddha.

▼ *Thinking ahead*
The carving of the Crazy Horse Memorial statue has been in progress for over 60 years.

6
MUSIC

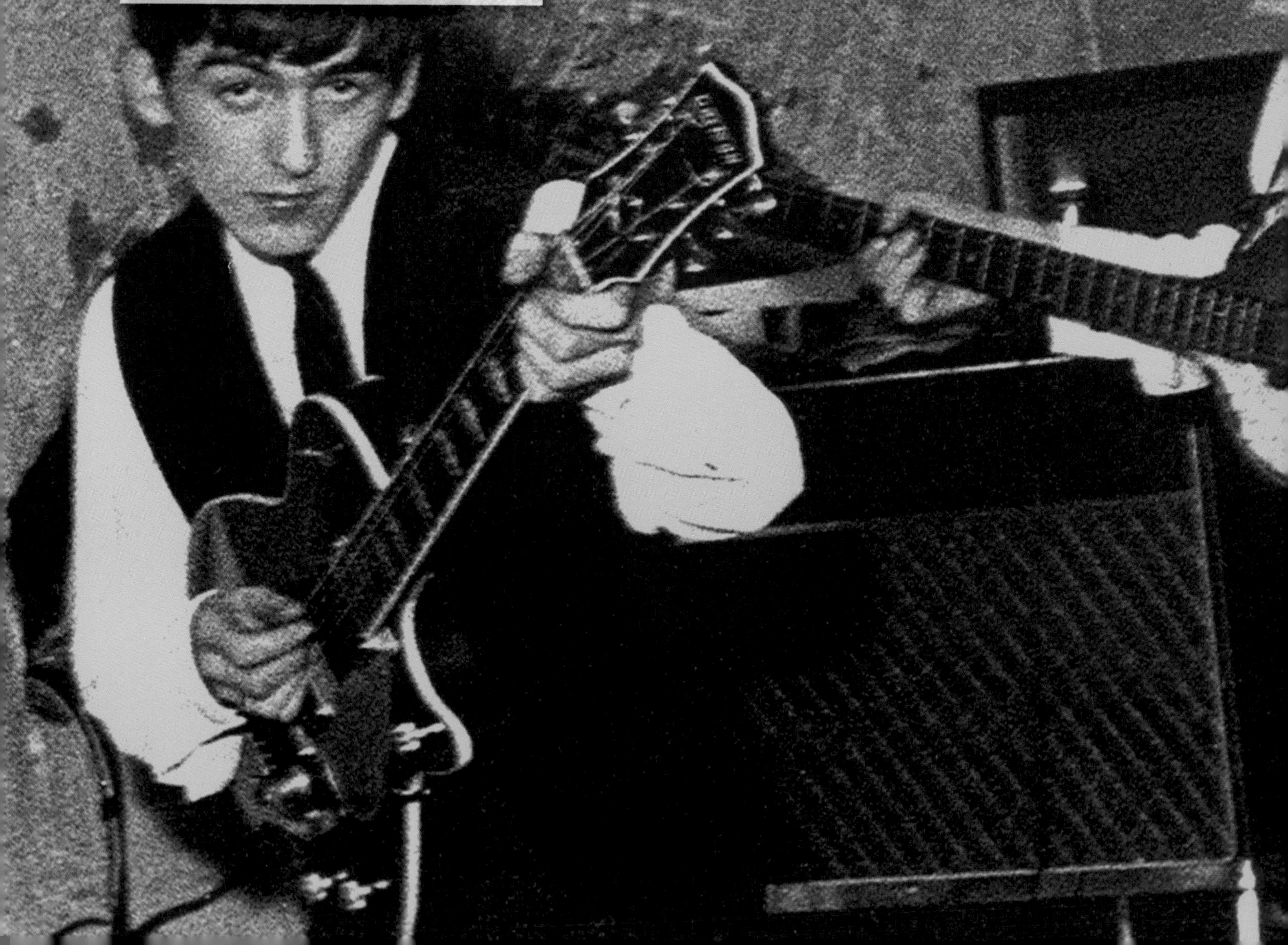

50TH ANNIVERSARY OF THE 'DISCOVERY' OF THE BEATLES
Having first performed as the Beatles in Hamburg, Germany, in 1960, the group made its debut appearance at the Cavern Club in their hometown of Liverpool at a lunchtime session on Tuesday 21 February 1961. Their further appearances later in the year were seen by Brian Epstein, who agreed to manage them and launched their rise to international stardom. From 1962 onwards the Beatles released a string of No. 1 singles and albums, becoming the world's most popular band for the rest of the decade. The last of their 274 Cavern appearances was on 3 August 1963.

HITS OF THE DECADES

▲ *Bill Haley*
'Rock Around the Clock' was the UK's bestselling single until overtaken by 'She Loves You'.

TOP 10 UK SINGLES OF THE 1950s

TITLE / ARTIST / YEAR

1. **(We're Gonna) Rock Around the Clock**
   Bill Haley & His Comets, 1955
2. **Diana**
   Paul Anka, 1957
3. **Mary's Boy Child**
   Harry Belafonte, 1957
4. **What Do You Want to Make Those Eyes at Me For?**
   Emile Ford & the Checkmates, 1959
5. **Jailhouse Rock**
   Elvis Presley, 1958
6. **What do You Want?**
   Adam Faith, 1959
7. **Living Doll**
   Cliff Richard, 1959
8. **All Shook Up**
   Elvis Presley, 1957
9. **Love Letters in the Sand**
   Pat Boone, 1957
10. **It Doesn't Matter Anymore**
    Buddy Holly, 1959

Source (all lists): Music Information Database

TOP 10 UK SINGLES OF THE 1960s

TITLE / ARTIST / YEAR

1. **She Loves You**
   The Beatles, 1963
2. **I Want to Hold Your Hand**
   The Beatles, 1963
3. **Tears**
   Ken Dodd, 1965
4. **Can't Buy Me Love**
   The Beatles, 1964
5. **I Feel Fine**
   The Beatles, 1964
6. **The Carnival is Over**
   The Seekers, 1965
7. **We Can Work It Out/ Day Tripper**
   The Beatles, 1965
8. **Release Me**
   Engelbert Humperdinck, 1967
9. **It's Now or Never**
   Elvis Presley, 1960
10. **Green Green Grass of Home**
    Tom Jones, 1966

TOP 10 UK SINGLES OF THE 1970s

TITLE / ARTIST / YEAR

1. **Bohemian Rhapsody**
   Queen, 1975
2. **Mull of Kintyre**
   Wings, 1977
3. **Rivers of Babylon/ Brown Girl in the Ring**
   Boney M, 1978
4. **You're the One That I Want**
   John Travolta & Olivia Newton-John, 1978
5. **Mary's Boy Child/ Oh My Lord**
   Boney M, 1978
6. **Summer Nights**
   John Travolta & Olivia Newton-John, 1978
7. **Imagine**
   John Lennon, 1975
8. **Y.M.C.A.**
   Village People, 1979
9. **Heart of Glass**
   Blondie, 1979
10. **Bright Eyes**
    Art Garfunkel, 1979

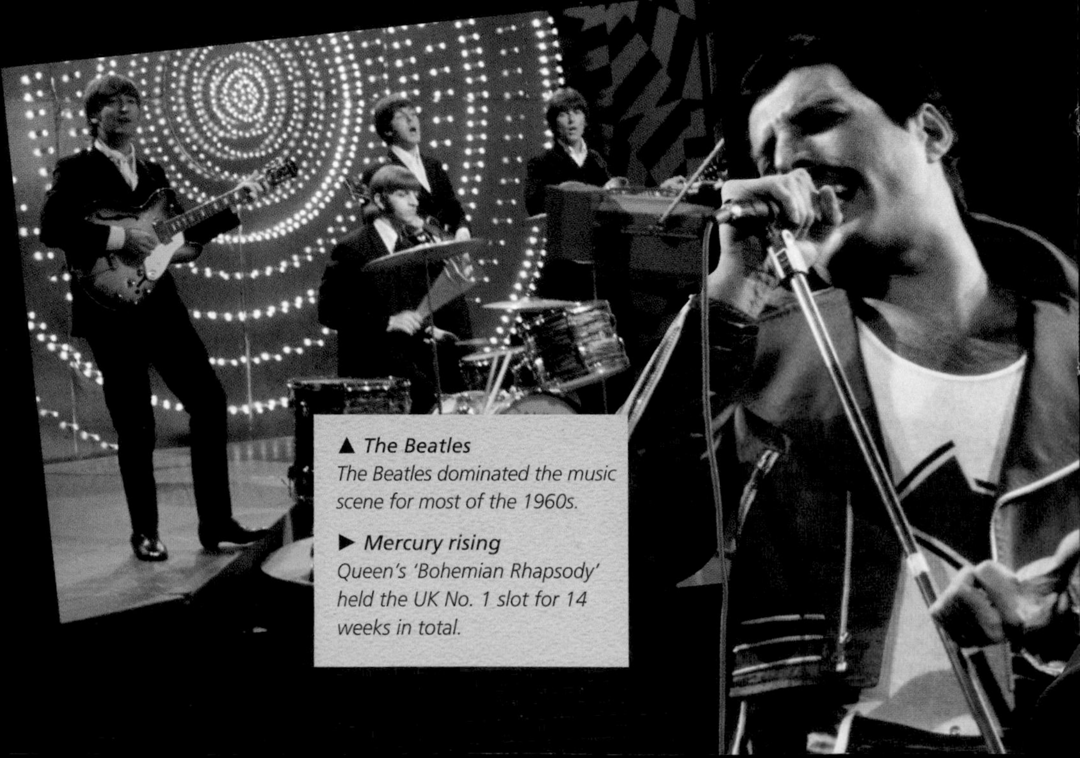

▲ *The Beatles*
The Beatles dominated the music scene for most of the 1960s.

► *Mercury rising*
Queen's 'Bohemian Rhapsody' held the UK No. 1 slot for 14 weeks in total.

TOP 10 **UK SINGLES OF THE 1980s**

TITLE / ARTIST / YEAR

1. **Do They Know It's Christmas?** Band Aid, 1984
2. **Relax** Frankie Goes to Hollywood, 1984
3. **I Just Called to Say I Love You** Stevie Wonder, 1984
4. **Two Tribes** Frankie Goes to Hollywood, 1984
5. **Don't You Want Me** Human League, 1981
6. **Last Christmas** Wham!, 1984
7. **Karma Chameleon** Culture Club, 1983
8. **Careless Whisper** George Michael, 1984
9. **The Power of Love** Jennifer Rush, 1985
10. **Come on Eileen** Dexy's Midnight Runners, 1982

▲ ***Houston takes off***
Houston's global hit 'I Will Always Love You' featured in her film debut The Bodyguard.

TOP 10 **UK SINGLES OF THE 1990s**

TITLE / ARTIST / YEAR

1. **Candle in the Wind/Something About the Way You Look Tonight** Elton John, 1997
2. **Unchained Melody/ The White Cliffs of Dover** Robson & Jerome, 1995
3. **Love is All Around** Wet Wet Wet, 1994
4. **Barbie Girl** Aqua, 1997
5. **Believe** Cher, 1998
6. **Perfect Day** Various Artists, 1997
7. **(Everything I Do) I Do it for You** Bryan Adams, 1991
8. **Baby One More Time** Britney Spears, 1999
9. **I'll Be Missing You** Puff Daddy & Faith Evans (feat. 112), 1997
10. **I Will Always Love You** Whitney Houston, 1992

◀ ***Record single***
Elton John's Princess Diana tribute has sold 37 million worldwide.

TOP 10 **UK SINGLES OF THE 2000s**

TITLE / ARTIST / YEAR

1. **Anything is Possible/Evergreen** Will Young, 2002
2. **Unchained Melody** Gareth Gates, 2002
3. **Is This the Way to Amarillo?** Tony Christie feat. Peter Kay, 2005
4. **It Wasn't Me** Shaggy feat. RikRok, 2001
5. **Do They Know It's Christmas?** Band Aid, 2004
6. **Pure and Simple** Hear'Say, 2001
7. **That's My Goal** Shayne Ward, 2005
8. **Can't Get You Out of My Head** Kylie Minogue, 2001
9. **Can We Fix It?** Bob the Builder, 2000
10. **Whole Again** Atomic Kitten, 2001

Record sales boomed in the 1950s with the advent of rock 'n' roll in 1955–56, and thus all of the Top 10 is from the latter half of the decade. The Beatles' domination of the 1960s is clear, with five of the decade's Top 10 singles by the group. Most of the biggest sellers of the 1970s in the UK occurred in an 18-month period between December 1977 and May 1979. Singles from the boom year of 1984 dominate the UK 1980s Top 10, two of them by newcomers Frankie Goes to Hollywood, and two by Wham!/ George Michael. In the 1990s, Elton John's 'Candle in the Wind' tribute sold close to five million copies and is unlikely to ever be surpassed. The early part of the 2000s showed a sharp decline, but with the advent of downloads they turned around, with sales of more than 100 million in both 2008 and 2009.

Bestselling Albums

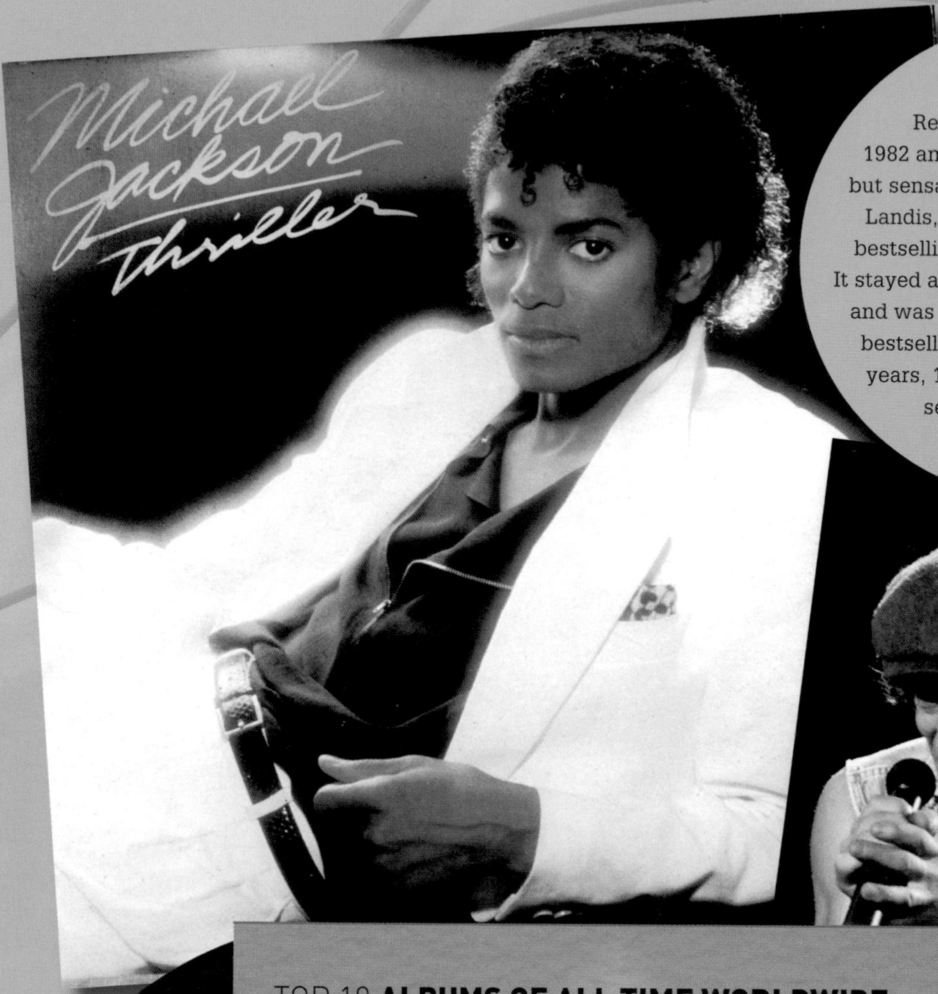

THRILLER

Released on 30 November 1982 and boosted by a controversial but sensational video directed by John Landis, *Thriller* became the world's bestselling album in little over a year. It stayed at No. 1 in the USA for 37 weeks and was the only album ever to be the bestselling there in two consecutive years, 1983–84, while Jackson won seven Grammy awards.

AC/DC

Australian band AC/DC's *Back in Black* reached No. 1 in the UK, but only No. 4 in the US, yet has gone on to be the all-time bestselling album by a group.

TOP 10 **ALBUMS OF ALL TIME WORLDWIDE**

	TITLE / ARTIST / YEAR OF ENTRY	ESTIMATED TOTAL SALES
1	**Thriller**, Michael Jackson (1982)	100,000,000
2	**Back in Black**, AC/DC (1980)	49,000,000
3	**Dark Side of the Moon**, Pink Floyd (1973)	45,000,000
4	**Bat Out of Hell**, Meat Loaf (1977)	43,000,000
5	=**Their Greatest Hits (1971–1975)**, Eagles (1976)	42,000,000
	=**Dirty Dancing**, Various Artists (1987)	42,000,000
	=**The Bodyguard**, Whitney Houston/Various Artists (1992)	42,000,000
8	=**Rumours**, Fleetwood Mac (1977)	40,000,000
	=**Saturday Night Fever**, Various Artists (1977)	40,000,000
	=**Millennium**, Backstreet Boys (1999)	40,000,000

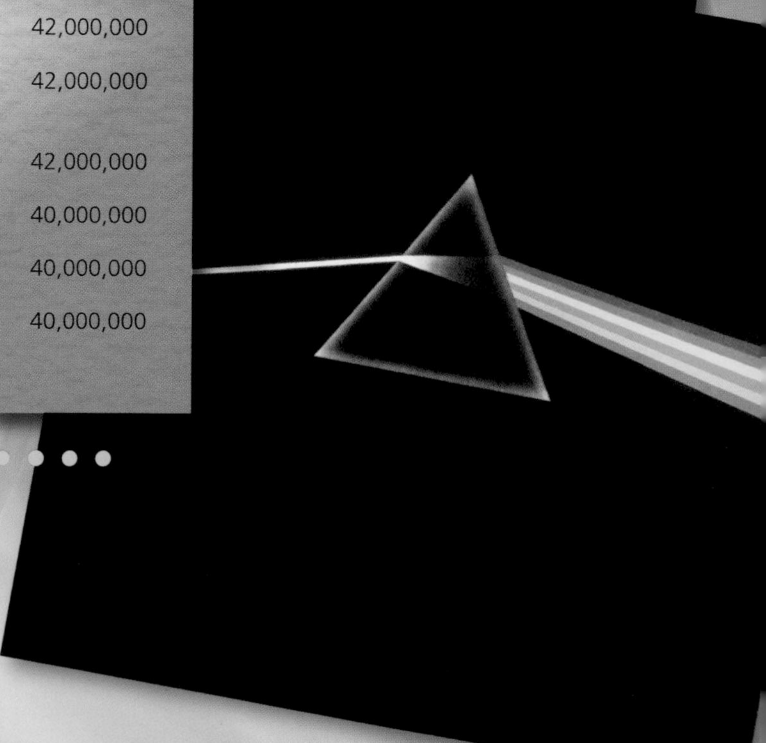

DARK SIDE OF THE MOON

Pink Floyd's 1973 album failed to reach No. 1 in the UK, but in the USA it not only hit No. 1, but remained in the album chart from 1973 to 1988, a record total of 742 weeks. Its estimated 45 million global sales includes 15 million in the USA and 3,956,177 in the UK (to 14 June 2009).

TOP 10 **ARTISTS OF ALL TIME WORLDWIDE**

ARTIST / ESTIMATED TOTAL SALES

1	The Beatles	346,000,000
2	Michael Jackson	235,000,000
3	Queen	200,000,000
4	Pink Floyd	194,000,000
5	Elvis Presley	187,000,000
6	Madonna	185,000,000
7	Celine Dion	183,000,000
8	Elton John	177,000,000
9	U2	170,000,000
10	The Rolling Stones	168,000,000

GREATEST ALBUM

A *Rolling Stone* poll ranked *Sgt. Pepper's Lonely Hearts Club Band* as the Greatest Album of All Time. It stayed at No. 1 in the USA for 15 weeks and for 23 weeks in the UK, where it remains the second bestselling. It won four Grammy awards, including Album of the Year, with its iconic cover, designed by pop artists Peter Blake and Jann Haworth, winning Best Album Cover.

TOP 10 **ARTISTS OF ALL TIME IN THE UK**

ARTIST / CERTIFIED SALES

1. **The Beatles** 28,000,000
2. **Queen** 17,200,000
3. **Robbie Williams** 16,400,000
4. **Madonna** 15,900,000
5. **Michael Jackson** 14,820,000
6. **Simply Red** 13,200,000
7. **Oasis** 12,600,000
8. **Phil Collins** 10,900,000
9. **Abba** 9,600,000
10. **Elton John** 8,940,000

Source: Music Information Database/BPI

TOP 10 **ALBUMS OF ALL TIME IN THE UK**

	TITLE / ARTIST / YEAR OF ENTRY	SALES
1	**Greatest Hits**, Queen (1981)	5,678,610
2	**Sgt. Pepper's Lonely Hearts Club Band**, The Beatles (1967)	4,908,288
3	**Abba Gold – Greatest Hits**, Abba (1990)	4,610,813
4	**(What's the Story) Morning Glory**, Oasis (1995)	4,421,505
5	**Brothers in Arms**, Dire Straits (1985)	4,069,764
6	**Dark Side of the Moon**, Pink Floyd (1973)	3,956,177
7	**Thriller**, Michael Jackson (1982)	3,825,857
8	**Greatest Hits II**, Queen (1991)	3,746,404
9	**Bad**, Michael Jackson (1987)	3,554,301
10	**The Immaculate Collection**, Madonna (1990)	3,402,160

Source: The Official Charts Company

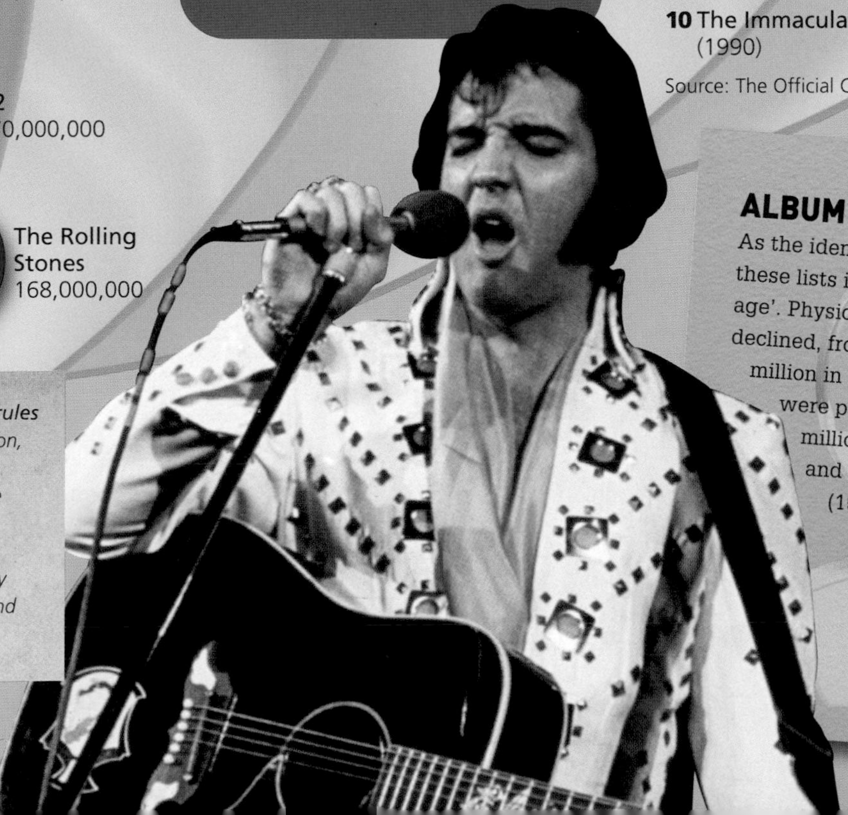

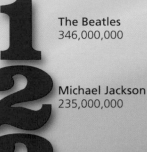

► ***The King still rules*** *Like Michael Jackson, Elvis Presley's cumulative lifetime album sales have been maintained since their untimely deaths, aged 50 and 42 respectively.*

ALBUM SALES OVER THE YEARS

As the identities of the albums and artists in these lists indicate, most date from a 'golden age'. Physical album sales in the US since declined, from 942.5 million in 2000 to 292.9 million in 2009 (128.9 million in the UK), but were partly offset by downloads of 76.4 million albums (16.1 million in the UK) and 1,138.3 million single tracks (152.7 million in the UK).

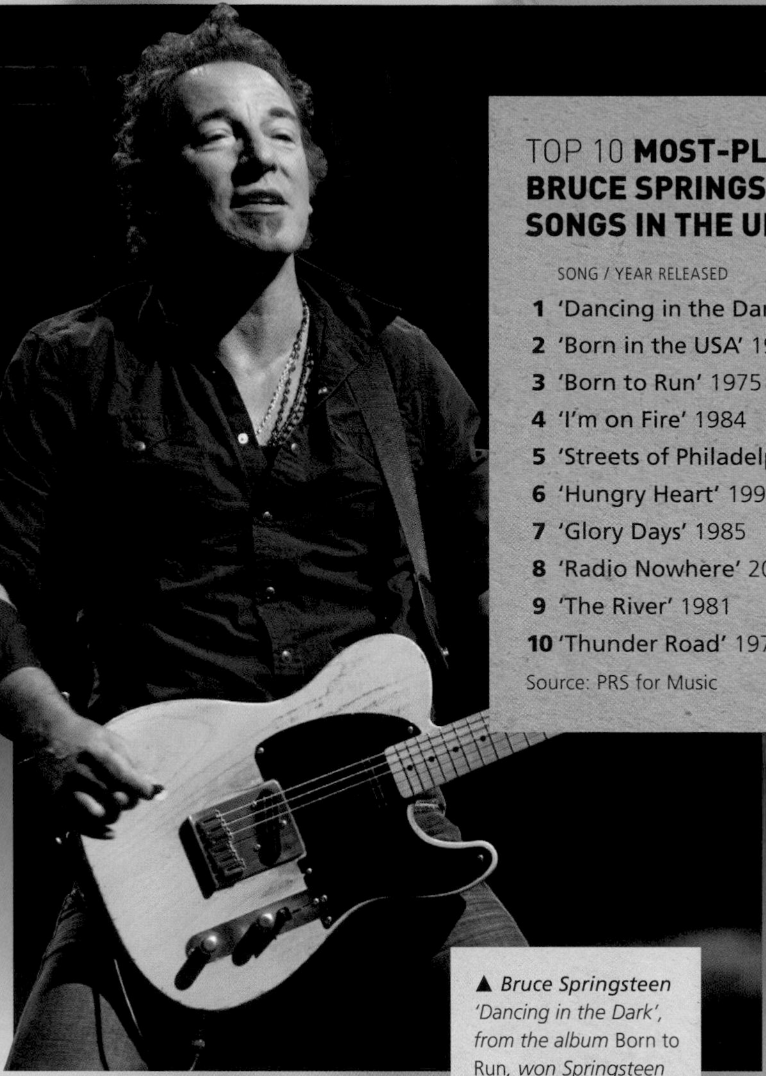

TOP 10 **MOST-PLAYED BRUCE SPRINGSTEEN SONGS IN THE UK**

SONG / YEAR RELEASED

1 'Dancing in the Dark' 1984
2 'Born in the USA' 1984
3 'Born to Run' 1975
4 'I'm on Fire' 1984
5 'Streets of Philadelphia' 1994
6 'Hungry Heart' 1995
7 'Glory Days' 1985
8 'Radio Nowhere' 2007
9 'The River' 1981
10 'Thunder Road' 1975

Source: PRS for Music

TOP 10 **MOST-PLAYED HEAVY METAL SONGS IN THE UK**

SONG / ARTIST / YEAR RELEASED

1 **'One'**, Metallica, 1989
2 **'Welcome to the Jungle'**, Guns N' Roses, 1987
3 **'Before I Forget'**, Slip Knot, 2005
4 **'Back in Black'**, AC/DC, 1980
5 **'Paranoid'**, Black Sabbath, 1970
6 **'Ace of Spades'**, Motörhead, 1980
7 **'Smoke on the Water'**, Deep Purple, 1973
8 **'The Number of the Beast'**, Iron Maiden, 1982
9 **'Twisted Transistor'**, Korn, 2005
10 **'When Love and Hate Collide'**, Def Leppard, 1995

Source: PRS for Music

▲ *Bruce Springsteen 'Dancing in the Dark', from the album* Born to Run, *won Springsteen his first Grammy Award.*

◀ *Michael Jackson Although only peaking at UK No. 10 on its release, 'Thriller' remains Michael Jackson's most-played song.*

TOP 10 **MOST-PLAYED MICHAEL JACKSON SONGS IN THE UK**

SONG / YEAR RELEASED

1 'Thriller' 1984
2 'Billie Jean' 1983
3 'Beat It' 1983
4 'You Rock My World' 2001
5 'Man in the Mirror' 1988
6 'The Way You Make Me Feel' 1988
7 'Smooth Criminal' 1988
8 'Bad' 1987
9 'Black or White' 1991
10 'Don't Stop Till You Get Enough' 1979

Source: PRS for Music

TOP 10 MOST-PLAYED CHRISTMAS SONGS IN THE UK

SONG / ARTIST / YEAR RELEASED

1. **Last Christmas**, Wham, 1984
2. **Do They Know It's Christmas?**, Band Aid, 1984
3. **Fairytale of New York**, Kirsty MacColl & The Pogues, 1987
4. **All I Want for Christmas is You**, Mariah Carey, 1994
5. **Santa Claus is Comin' to Town**, Bruce Springsteen, 1985
6. **Stop the Cavalry**, Jona Lewie, 1980
7. **I Wish it Could be Christmas Everyday**, Wizzard, 1973
8. **Merry Xmas Everybody**, Slade, 1973
9. **Lonely This Christmas**, Mud, 1974
10. **White Christmas**, Bing Crosby, 1942

Source: PRS for Music

TOP 10 MOST-PLAYED VALENTINE SONGS IN THE UK

	SONG / ARTIST	YEAR RELEASED
1	**'Sexual Healing'**, Marvin Gaye	1982
2	**'Let's Get it On'**, Marvin Gaye	1973
3	**'Three Times a Lady'**, Lionel Ritchie	1978
4	**'You're My First, My Last, My Everything'**, Barry White	1974
5	**'You're Beautiful'**, James Blunt	2005
6	**'Lady in Red'**, Chris de Burgh	1986
7	**'Don't Wanna Miss a Thing'**, Aerosmith	1998
8	**'Sex on Fire'**, Kings of Leon	2008
9	**'My Heart Will Go On'**, Celine Dion	1997
10	**'Can't Get Enough of Your Love, Babe'**, Barry White	1974

Source: PRS for Music

TOP 10 MOST-PLAYED DRIVING SONGS IN THE UK

SONG / ARTIST

1. **'Bat Out of Hell'**, Meatloaf
2. **'Bohemian Rhapsody'**, Queen
3. **'Don't Stop Me Now'**, Queen
4. **'Mr. Brightside'**, The Killers
5. **'Dancing Queen'**, ABBA
6. **'Sex on Fire'**, Kings of Leon
7. **'I Want to Break Free'**, Queen
8. **'Thriller'**, Michael Jackson
9. **'Sweet Child of Mine'**, Guns N' Roses
10. **'Freebird'**, Lynryd Skynrd

Source: PRS for Music

◄ *Bing Crosby*
The Irving Berlin-penned 'White Christmas', performed by Bing Crosby, is an enduring seasonal favourite in the UK.

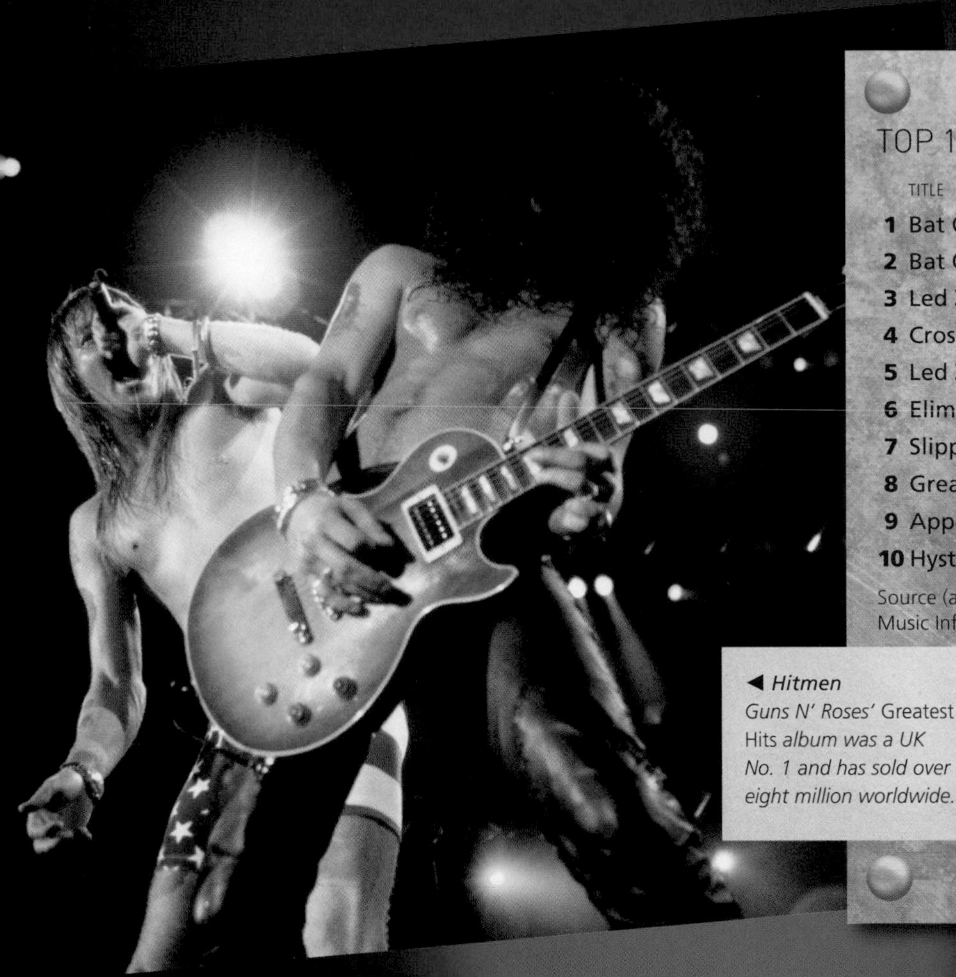

◀ *Hitmen*
Guns N' Roses' Greatest Hits *album was a UK No. 1 and has sold over eight million worldwide.*

TOP 10 **HEAVY METAL ALBUMS IN THE UK**

	TITLE	ARTIST	YEAR
1	Bat Out of Hell	Meat Loaf	1978
2	Bat Out of Hell II – Back to Hell	Meat Loaf	1993
3	Led Zeppelin IV	Led Zeppelin	1971
4	Cross Road – The Best of Bon Jovi	Bon Jovi	1994
5	Led Zeppelin II	Led Zeppelin	1969
6	Eliminator	ZZ Top	1983
7	Slippery When Wet	Bon Jovi	1986
8	Greatest Hits	Guns N' Roses	2004
9	Appetite for Destruction	Guns N' Roses	1987
10	Hysteria	Def Leppard	1987

Source (all lists): Music Information Database

Unlike its 1993 sequel, which made No. 1 in the UK, *Bat Out of Hell* only ever peaked at No. 9, but logged an impressive 470-plus weeks on the chart, an achievement split over three decades.

TOP 10 **RAP ALBUMS IN THE UK**

	TITLE / ARTIST	YEAR
1	The Marshall Mathers LP Eminem	2000
2	The Eminem Show Eminem	2002
3	Curtain Call – The Hits Eminem	2005
4	Encore Eminem	2004
5	The Slim Shady LP Eminem	2000
6	Big Willie Style Will Smith	1997
7	Get Rich or Die Tryin' 50 Cent	2003
8	Speakerboxxx/The Love Below Outkast	2003
9	Nellyville Nelly	2002
10	Greatest Hits 2Pac	1998

▶ *Eminem*
Five of Eminem's albums are among the UK's all-time Rap Top 10.

TOP 10 INSTRUMENTAL SINGLES IN THE UK

TITLE / ARTIST / YEAR

1. Stranger on the Shore
   Mr. Acker Bilk, 1961
2. Eye Level
   Simon Park Orchestra, 1973
3. Telstar
   The Tornados, 1962
4. The Harry Lime Theme (The Third Man)
   Anton Karas, 1950
5. Amazing Grace
   Royal Scots Dragoon Guards Band, 1972
6. Chi Mai
   Ennio Morricone, 1981
7. Wonderful Land
   The Shadows, 1962
8. Apache
   The Shadows, 1960
9. Albatross
   Fleetwood Mac, 1968
10. Mouldy Old Dough
    Lieutenant Pigeon, 1972

Acker Bilk's million-selling "Stranger on the Shore" was the first UK record to reach No. 1 in the USA, where it was so popular that in 1969 a cassette recording of the track was taken to the Moon by the *Apollo 10* crew.

TOP 10 DISCO/DANCE ALBUMS IN THE UK

TITLE / ARTIST / YEAR

1. Thriller
   Michael Jackson, 1982
2. Bad
   Michael Jackson, 1985
3. The Immaculate Collection
   Madonna, 1990
4. Whitney
   Whitney Houston, 1987
5. Dangerous
   Michael Jackson, 2003
6. True Blue
   Madonna, 1994
7. Can't Slow Down
   Lionel Richie, 1983
8. Born to Do It
   Craig David, 2000
9. Justified
   Justin Timberlake, 2002
10. Back to Front
    Lionel Richie, 1992

◀ ***Up Front***
Lionel Richie's Back to Front *album reached UK No. 1 in June 1982.*

TOP 10 COUNTRY ALBUMS IN THE UK

TITLE / ARTIST / YEAR

1. Come On Over
   Shania Twain, 1998
2. Up!
   Shania Twain, 2002
3. Greatest Hits
   Shania Twain, 2004
4. Johnny Cash at San Quentin
   Johnny Cash, 1969
5. Trampoline
   Mavericks, 1998
6. Images
   Don Williams, 1978
7. Ring of Fire – The Legend of Johnny Cash
   Johnny Cash, 2005
8. 20 Golden Greats
   Glen Campbell, 1976
9. 40 Golden Greats
   Jim Reeves, 1975
10. The Woman in Me
    Shania Twain, 2000

Shania Twain's 10-times-platinum *Come On Over* has probably sold more than the rest of this list combined. Of Johnny Cash's two celebrated live albums – recorded at two of America's most severe penal institutions – the San Quentin release holds the record for the longest-charting country album in UK chart history, with 115 weeks notched up between 1969 and 1971.

SOLO ARTISTS

▲ *Madonna*
Though trailing Elvis's overall UK album chart success by a considerable margin, Madonna equals his tally of 10 No. 1s.

TOP 10 **SINGLES BY SOLO SINGERS IN THE UK**

	TITLE / ARTIST	YEAR
1	**'Candle in the Wind (1997)'/'Something About the Way You Look Tonight'**, Elton John	1997
2	**'Anything is Possible'/'Evergreen'**, Will Young	2002
3	**'I Just Called to Say I Love You'**, Stevie Wonder	1984
4	**'Believe'**, Cher	1998
5	**'(Everything I Do) I Do It for You'**, Bryan Adams	1991
6	**'Tears'**, Ken Dodd	1965
7	**'Imagine'**, John Lennon	1975
8	**'...Baby One More Time'**, Britney Spears	1999
9	**'Careless Whisper'**, George Michael	1984
10	**'Release Me'**, Engelbert Humperdinck	1967

Source: Official Charts Company

This list represents a timeshaft through the history of British popular music, with singles from each decade reflecting the sometimes unpredictable taste of the British public. Four of the next six in this list are by female singers.

► *By George!*
His post-Wham! career has seen George Michael clock up a series of UK chart successes.

TOP 10 **SOLO ARTISTS WITH THE MOST NO. 1 ALBUMS IN THE UK**

	ARTIST* / NO. 1 ALBUMS
1	=Madonna (19) 10
	=Elvis Presley (113) 10
3	Michael Jackson (27) 9
4	=David Bowie (44) 8
	=Bruce Springsteen (22) 8
	=Robbie Williams (10) 8
7	=Bob Dylan (50) 7
	=Cliff Richard (61) 7
	=Rod Stewart (36) 7
10	=Elton John (40) 6
	=George Michael (7) 6

* Figures in brackets denote total chart hits

Source: Music Information Database

TOP 10 **SOLO ARTISTS WITH THE MOST NO. 1 SINGLES IN THE UK**

	ARTIST* / NO. 1 SINGLES
1	Elvis Presley (175) 22
2	Cliff Richard# (136) 15
3	Madonna (69) 13
4	=Kylie Minogue† (43) 7
	=George Michael§ (35) 7
	=Michael Jackson (58) 7
7	=Rod Stewart (57) 6
	=Robbie Williams∞ (29) 6
	=Eminem (24) 6
10	Britney Spears (26) 5

* Figures in brackets denote total chart hits
# 1 with the Young Ones
† 1 with Jason Donovan
§ 1 with Queen, 1 with Aretha Franklin and 1 with Elton John
∞ 1 with Nicole Kidman

Source: Music Information Database

TOP 10 **YOUNGEST SOLO SINGERS TO HAVE A NO. 1 SINGLE IN THE UK**

	ARTIST / TITLE	YEAR	AGE YRS	AGE MTHS	AGE DAYS
1	**Little Jimmy Osmond**, 'Long Haired Lover from Liverpool'	1972	9	8	7
2	**Donny Osmond**, 'Puppy Love'	1972	14	6	30
3	**Helen Shapiro**, 'You Don't Know'	1961	14	10	13
4	**Billie**, 'Because We Want To'	1998	15	9	20
5	**Paul Anka**, 'Diana'	1957	16	1	1
6	**Tiffany**, 'I Think We're Alone Now'	1988	16	3	28
7	**Nicole**, 'A Little Peace'	1982	17	0	0
8	**Britney Spears**, '...Baby One More Time'	1999	17	2	25
9	**Sean Kingston**, 'Beautiful Girls'	2007	17	7	5
10	**Sandie Shaw**, '(There's) Always Something There to Remind Me'	1964	17	7	26

Source: Music Information Database

If group members were eligible for the list, all three Hanson brothers would be in the Top 10. Isaac was 16 years and 6 months, Taylor 14 years, and 2 months and Zachary 11 years and 7 months when 'Mmmbop' topped the charts in 1997.

▲ *Overcome*
Shania Twain's hugely successful Come On Over *overcame the UK's supposed prejudice against country music.*

THE OLDEST SOLO SINGERS TO HAVE A NO. 1 SINGLE

Veteran American jazz trumpeter and singer Louis Armstrong (1901–71) is the oldest artist to have a No. 1 single in both the USA and UK. His US achievement was gained with 'Hello Dolly!', which reached No. 1 on 9 May 1964, when he was aged 63 years 9 months and 5 days – also ending the Beatles' consecutive run of three US No. 1s. Armstrong's UK record was set with 'What a Wonderful World', which hit No. 1 on 26 April 1968, when he was 66 years 9 months and 11 days old. This single failed to chart in the USA, but was the UK's biggest seller of 1968.

TOP 10 **ALBUMS BY SOLO ARTISTS IN THE UK**

	TITLE / ARTIST	YEAR
1	**Thriller**, Michael Jackson	1982
2	**Bad**, Michael Jackson	1987
3	**The Immaculate Collection**, Madonna	1990
4	**Come On Over**, Shania Twain	1998
5	**Back to Bedlam**, James Blunt	2006
6	**No Angel**, Dido	2000
7	**White Ladder**, David Gray	2000
8	**Bat Out of Hell**, Meat Loaf	1978
9	**Life for Rent**, Dido	2003
10	**But Seriously...**, Phil Collins	1989

Source: Official Charts Company

Michael Jackson's *Thriller* and *Bad* have both sold in excess of 3.5 million copies, meaning that approximately one in every six British households, or one in every 17 UK inhabitants, owns a copy of one or both of these mega-sellers.

GROUPS & DUOS

TOP 10 GROUPS AND DUOS WITH THE MOST NO. 1 SINGLES IN THE UK

	ARTIST	NO. 1 SINGLES
1	The Beatles	17
2	Westlife*	14
3	Take That#	11
4	=Abba	9
	=Spice Girls	9
6	=Oasis	8
	=Rolling Stones	8
8	=McFly	7
	=U2	7
10	=Blondie	6
	=Boyzone	6
	=Queen†	6
	=Slade	6
	=Sugababes	6

* Including one with Mariah Carey
# Including one with Lulu
† Including No. 1s with David Bowie, George Michael and Five

Source: Music Information Database

TOP 10 GROUPS AND DUOS WITH THE LONGEST SINGLES CHART CAREERS IN THE UK

	ARTIST	CHART SPAN	YRS	MTHS	DAYS
1	Spencer Davis Group	7 Nov 1964–12 Apr 2008	43	5	6
2	The Rolling Stones	27 Jul 1963–2 Sep 2006	43	1	6
3	Status Quo	24 Aug 1968–27 Dec 2008	40	4	3
4	The Kinks	15 Aug 1964–25 Sep 2004	40	1	10
5	Slade	19 Jun 1971–2 Jan 2010	39	6	14
6	Wizzard	8 Dec 1973–2 Jan 2010	37	0	25
7	Queen	9 Mar 1974–2 Jan 2010	35	9	23
8	Bee Gees	29 Apr 1967–5 May 2001	35	0	6
9	Abba	20 Apr 1974–23 Aug 2008	34	4	4
10	The Beatles	13 Oct 1962–27 Apr 1996	33	6	14

Source: Music Information Database

TOP 10 GROUPS AND DUOS WITH THE MOST NO. 1 ALBUMS IN THE UK

	ARTIST / NO. 1 ALBUMS
1	The Beatles 15
2	= Abba 10
	= Rolling Stones 10
	= U2 10
5	Queen 9
6	= Led Zeppelin 8
	= R.E.M. 8
8	Oasis 7
9	= Genesis 6
	= Police 6
	= Westlife 6

Source: Music Information Database

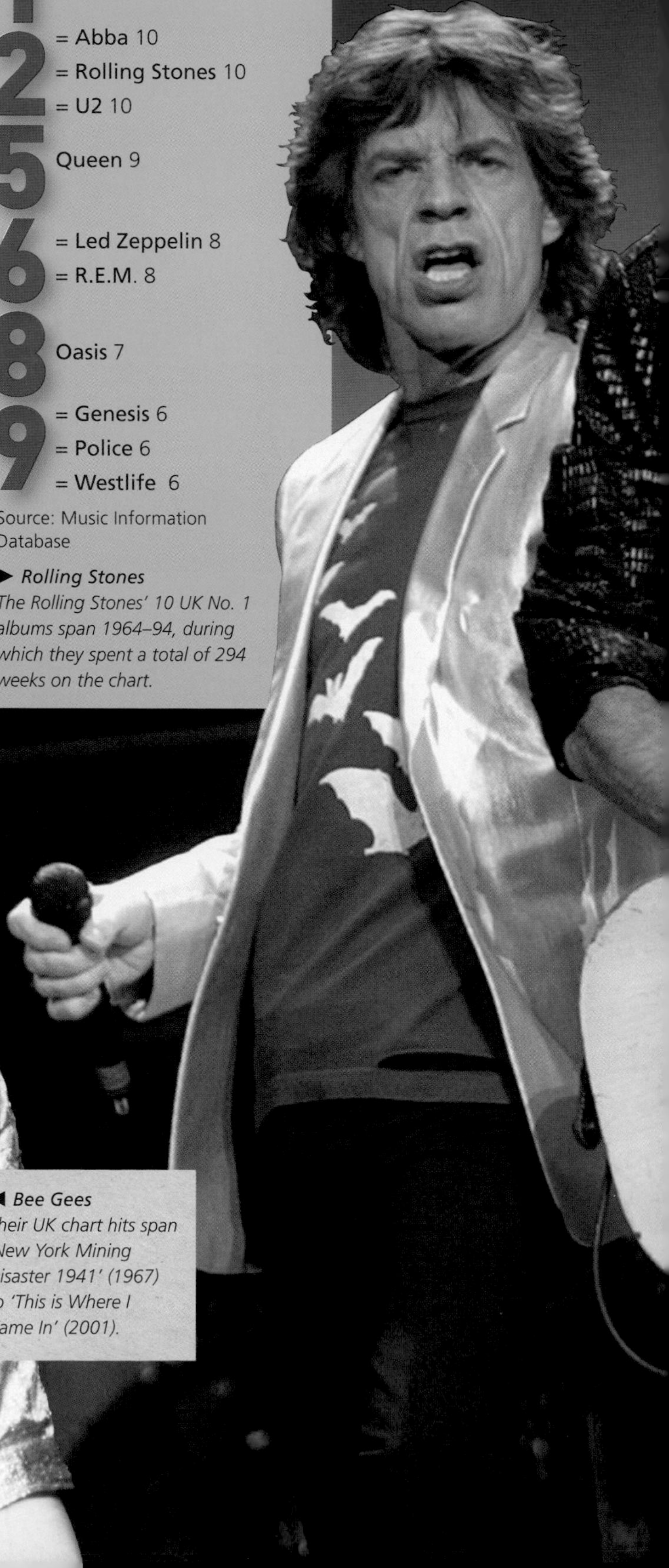

► *Rolling Stones*
The Rolling Stones' 10 UK No. 1 albums span 1964–94, during which they spent a total of 294 weeks on the chart.

◄ *Bee Gees*
Their UK chart hits span 'New York Mining Disaster 1941' (1967) to 'This is Where I Came In' (2001).

▲ *Strong* Rumours
Fleetwood Mac's 1977 album has sold over three million in the UK and 40 million globally.

TOP 10 **ALBUMS BY GROUPS AND DUOS IN THE UK**

	TITLE / ARTIST	YEAR
1	**Greatest Hits (Volume One)**, Queen	1981
2	**Sgt. Pepper's Lonely Hearts Club Band**, Beatles	1967
3	**(What's the Story) Morning Glory**, Oasis	1995
4	**Brothers in Arms**, Dire Straits	1985
5	**Abba Gold – Greatest Hits**, Abba	1992
6	**Dark Side of the Moon**, Pink Floyd	1973
7	**Greatest Hits Volume II**, Queen	1991
8	**Stars**, Simply Red	1991
9	**Rumours**, Fleetwood Mac	1977
10	**Hopes and Fears**, Keane	2004

Source: The Official Charts Company

TOP 10 **SINGLES OF ALL TIME BY GROUPS AND DUOS IN THE UK**

	TITLE / ARTIST	YEAR
1	**'Bohemian Rhapsody'**, Queen	1975
2	**'Mull of Kintyre'/'Girls' School'**, Wings	1977
3	**'Rivers of Babylon'/'Brown Girl in the Ring'**, Boney M	1978
4	**'You're the That I Want'**, John Travolta & Olivia Newton-John	1978
5	**'Relax'**, Frankie Goes To Hollywood	1984
6	**'She Loves You'**, The Beatles	1963
7	**'Unchained Melody'/'(There'll Be Bluebirds Over The) White Cliffs of Dover'**, Robson Green & Jerome Flynn	1995
8	**'Mary's Boy Child'/'Oh My Lord'**, Boney M	1978
9	**'Love is All Around'**, Wet Wet Wet	1994
10	**'I Want to Hold Your Hand'**, The Beatles	1963

Source: The Official Charts Company

Not only was Queen's 'Bohemian Rhapsody' the biggest-selling single by a group in the UK, but more than one poll has ranked it at the top of a list of '100 Greatest Singles' of all time. Its total sales in the UK alone are over 2.13 million. The list excludes informal groups or 'collectives', such as Band Aid's 'Do They Know It's Christmas?' (1984) and the 'various artists' hit 'Perfect Day' (1997).

GOLD & PLATINUM DISCS

GOLD AND PLATINUM AWARDS

Gold records have been awarded since 1 April 1973 in the UK. Based on sales certified by the British Phonographic Industry (BPI), they are presented for shipments of 400,000 singles or 100,000 albums, cassettes or CDs. Platinum albums are awarded to those that have achieved sales of 300,000. Multi-platinum awards have been presented since 1987.

◀ *Golden girl*
Almost all Mariah Carey's albums since 1991 have achieved UK gold or platinum status.

TOP 10 **MALE ARTISTS WITH THE MOST GOLD ALBUM AWARDS IN THE UK**

	ARTIST / GOLD ALBUM AWARDS
1	Rod Stewart 30
2	=Elton John 25
	=Cliff Richard 25
4	Neil Diamond 20
5	=David Bowie 18
	=Elvis Presley 18
7	=James Last 17
	=Mike Oldfield 17
9	Prince 16
10	Eric Clapton 14

Source (all lists): BPI

TOP 10 **ARTISTS WITH THE MOST GOLD SINGLES AWARDS IN THE UK**

	ARTIST / GOLD SINGLES AWARDS
1	Madonna 12
2	Abba 10
3	=Boyzone 7
	=Oasis 7
	=Take That 7
6	Blondie 6
7	=Michael Jackson 5
	=S Club 7 5
	=Shakin' Stevens 5
10	=Whitney Houston 4
	=Madness 4
	=Kylie Minogue 4
	=Queen 4
	=Cliff Richard 4
	=Shaggy 4
	=Steps 4
	=Vengaboys 4
	=Westlife 4
	=Robbie Williams 4

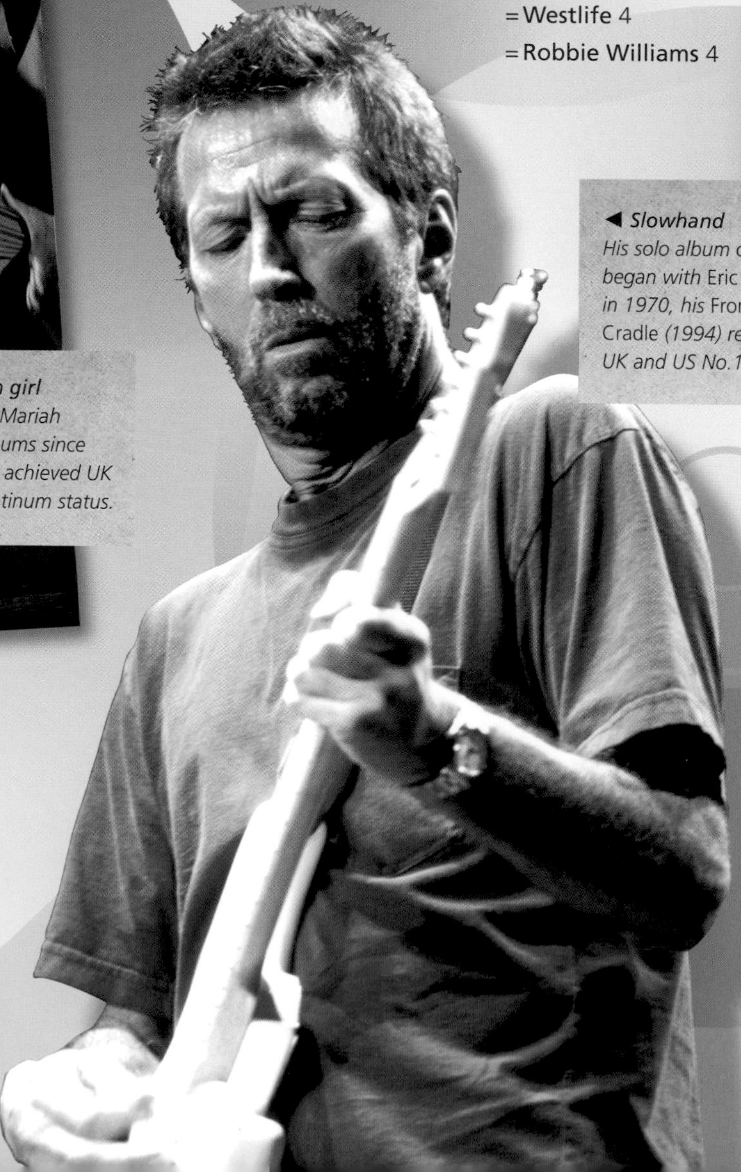

◀ *Slowhand*
His solo album career began with Eric Clapton *in 1970, his* From the Cradle *(1994) reaching UK and US No.1.*

TOP 10 **FEMALE ARTISTS WITH THE MOST GOLD ALBUM AWARDS IN THE UK**

	ARTIST / GOLD ALBUM AWARDS
1	Diana Ross 19
2	=Madonna 16
	=Barbra Streisand 16
4	Mariah Carey 12
5	Celine Dion 11
6	Donna Summer 10
7	=Cher 9
	=Tina Turner 9
9	=Kate Bush 8
	=Kylie Minogue 8

► *Golden boy*
As well as heading the UK list of Gold album awards, Rod Stewart has achieved world album sales of over 100 million.

TOP 10 **ARTISTS WITH THE MOST PLATINUM ALBUM AWARDS IN THE UK**

ARTIST / PLATINUM ALBUM AWARDS

1. Madonna 56
2. Robbie Williams 54
3. Michael Jackson 51
4. Simply Red 45
5. Oasis 44
6. U2 39
7. Queen 35
8. Phil Collins 34
9. Westlife 31
10. Elton John 29

Two notable omissions, Elvis Presley and The Beatles, are explained by the fact that certifications were not introduced by the BPI until 1973, as a result of which most of the albums by both acts were never certified.

TOP 10 **ARTISTS WITH THE MOST GOLD ALBUM AWARDS IN THE UK**

	ARTIST	GOLD ALBUM AWARDS
1	Rod Stewart	30
2	Queen	26
3	=Elton John	25
	=Cliff Richard	25
5	The Rolling Stones	22
6	=Neil Diamond	20
	=Status Quo	20
8	Diana Ross	19
9	=David Bowie	18
	=Elvis Presley	18

TOP 10 **GROUPS WITH THE MOST GOLD ALBUM AWARDS IN THE UK**

	GROUP	GOLD ALBUM AWARDS
1	Queen	26
2	The Rolling Stones	22
3	Status Quo	20
4	=The Beatles	17
	=U2	17
6	=Genesis	16
	=UB40	16
8	=Abba	15
	=Iron Maiden	15
10	Roxy Music	14

Having careers that began in the 1960s, several of the artists listed would have qualified for even more gold discs if they had been awarded prior to their introduction by the BPI (British Phonographic Industry) on 1 April 1973.

MUSIC AWARDS

THE 10 **LATEST BRIT RECORDS OF THE YEAR**

RECORD / ARTIST

2010
'Beat Again', JLS

2009
'The Promise', Girls Aloud

2008
'Shine', Take That

2007
'Patience', Take That

2006
'Speed of Sound', Coldplay

2005
'Your Game', Will Young

2004
'White Flag', Dido

2003
'Just a Little', Liberty X

2002
'Don't Stop Movin'', S Club 7

2001
'Rock DJ', Robbie Williams

Source: BRITS

▲ *Coldplay*
Coldplay won consecutive BRITs in 2001–02, two in 2003, and two in 2006.

THE 10 **ARTISTS WITH THE MOST BRIT AWARDS**

	ARTIST	AWARDS
1	Robbie Williams	12
2	Annie Lennox	8
3	= Take That	7
	= U2	7
5	= Coldplay	6
	= Michael Jackson	6
	= Oasis	6
8	= Phil Collins	5
	= Prince	5
	= Arctic Monkeys	5
	= Spice Girls	5

Source: BRITS

THE 10 **LONGEST-SPANNING BRIT WINNERS**

	ARTIST	YEARS	SPAN
1	Paul McCartney	1983–2008	25
2	Bob Geldof	1985–2005	20
3	= Take That	1993–2008	15
	= U2	1988–2003	15
5	Sting	1988–2002	14
6	= Elton John	1986–98	12
	= Annie Lennox	1984–96	12
	= Oasis	1995–2007	12
9	Prince	1985–96	11
10	= Trevor Horn	1983–92	9
	= George Michael	1988–97	9

Source: Music Information Database

Annie Lennox (as part of Eurythmics), U2, Oasis and the Spice Girls include the award for Outstanding Contribution to British Music. Lennox has won Best British Female Solo Artist six times. U2 won Best International Group three years in a row (1988–90).

► *Pro Bono*
U2 have received more BRITs than any other non-British act, as Best International Group and for Outstanding Contribution.

► R.E.M.
R.E.M. gained half their tally of 12 MTV awards in 1991 for Losing My Religion.

THE 10 **ARTISTS WITH MOST MTV AWARDS**

	ARTIST / AWARDS	
1	Madonna	20
2	Peter Gabriel	13
3	R.E.M.	12
4	Green Day	11
5	Aerosmith	10
6	=Beyoncé	9
	=Eminem	9
	=Fatboy Slim	9
	=Janet Jackson	9
10	Michael Jackson	8

Source: MTV

THE 10 **LATEST RECIPIENTS OF THE MERCURY MUSIC PRIZE**

YEAR	ARTIST / ALBUM
2009	Speech Debelle, Speech Therapy (65)
2008	Elbow, The Seldom Seen Kid (5 – 2 × Platinum)
2007	Klaxons, Myths of the Near Future (2 – Platinum)
2006	Arctic Monkeys, Whatever People Say I Am, That's What I'm Not (1 – 4 × Platinum)
2005	Antony & the Johnsons, I Am a Bird Now (16 – Gold)
2004	Franz Ferdinand, Franz Ferdinand (3 – 4 × Platinum)
2003	Dizzee Rascal, Boy In Da Corner (23 – Gold)
2002	Ms Dynamite, A Little Deeper (10 – Platinum)
2001	PJ Harvey, Stories from the City, Stories from the Sea (23 – Gold)
2000	Badly Drawn Boy, The Hour of Bewilderbeast (13 – Platinum)

Source: Barclaycard Mercury Prize

The figures in brackets denote the highest chart position and award certification. Between them, the 10 winners have managed only a combined 17 chart albums since their win.

TOP 10 **WINNERS OF THE MOST IVOR NOVELLO AWARDS FOR MUSIC WRITING**

	WINNER	AWARDS
1	Paul McCartney	20
2	=John Lennon	14
	=Andrew Lloyd Webber	14
4	Elton John	13
5	Tim Rice	12
6	=Barry Gibb	9
	=Robin Gibb	9
8	=Matt Aitken	8
	=Maurice Gibb	8
	=Tony MacAulay	8
	=Mike Stock	8
	=Bernie Taupin	8
	=Pete Waterman	8

Source: British Academy of Songwriters, Composers and Authors

The Ivor Novellos have been presented annually since 1955, mainly rewarding songwriting achievements by British writers and composers. McCartney and Lennon each received one award as members of the Beatles, the others either in partnership or individually.

TOP 10 BEST-ATTENDED BEATLES CONCERTS

	VENUE / DATE	ATTENDANCE
1	**Shea Stadium**, New York, USA 15 Aug 1965	55,600
2	**Rizal Memorial Football Stadium**, Manila, Philippines 4 Jul 1966	50,000
3	**Dodger Stadium**, Los Angeles, California, USA 28 Aug 1966	45,000
4	**Shea Stadium**, New York, USA 23 Aug 1966	44,600
5	**White Sox Park**, Chicago, Illinois, USA 20 Aug 1965	37,000
6	**DC Stadium**, Washington, DC, USA 15 Aug 1966	32,164
7	**Atlanta Stadium**, Atlanta, Georgia, USA 18 Aug 1965	30,000
8 =	**Candlestick Park**, San Francisco, California, USA 29 Aug 1966	25,000
=	**Metropolitan Stadium**, Bloomington, Minnesota, USA 21 Aug 1965	25,000
10	**Busch Stadium**, St Louis, Missouri, USA 21 Aug 1966	23,000

Source: Music Information Database

TOP 10 BEST-ATTENDED LED ZEPPELIN CONCERTS

	VENUE / DATE	ATTENDANCE
1	**Knebworth Festival**, Stevenage, UK 4 & 11 Aug 1979	200,000
2 =	**Madison Square Garden**, New York, USA 7–14 Jun 1977	120,000
=	**The Forum**, Inglewood, California, USA 21–27 Jun 1977	120,000
4 =	**Earls Court**, London, UK 17–25 May 1975	85,000
=	**The Forum**, Los Angeles, California, USA 24–27 Mar 1975	85,000
6	**Pontiac Silverdome**, Pontiac, Michigan, USA 30 Apr 1977	77,229
7	**Tampa Stadium**, Tampa, Florida, USA 3 Jun 1977	70,000
8	**Chicago Stadium**, Chicago, Illinois, USA 6–10 Apr 1977	69,268
9 =	**Madison Square Garden**, New York, USA 27–29 Jul 1973	60,000
=	**Madison Square Garden**, New York, USA 3–12 Feb 1975	60,000

Source: Music Information Database

On 5 May 1973, Led Zeppelin broke the Beatles attendance record of 55,600, when 56,800 people saw the band in concert at Tampa Stadium in Tampa, Florida.

◀ ***Out with a bang***
Led Zeppelin's record-breaking appearances at Knebworth were the band's last major concerts before their break-up a year later.

▲ *Spice Girls*
The Spice Girls reunion O_2 concerts were the UK's highest grossing.

TOP 10 **BEST-ATTENDED MADONNA CONCERTS**

	VENUE / DATE	ATTENDANCE
1	**Estadio River Plate**, Buenos Aires, Argentina 4–8 Dec 2008	263,693
2	**Estadio Nacional**, Santiago, Chile 10–11 Dec 2008	146,242
3	**Stade de France**, Paris, France 20–21 Sep 2008	138,163
4	**Ullevi Stadion**, Gothenburg, Sweden 8–9 Aug 2009	119,709
5	**Estádio do Marcanã**, Rio de Janeiro, Brazil 14–15 Dec 2008	107,000
6	**Foro Sol**, Mexico City, Mexico 29–30 Nov 2008	104,270
7	**Amsterdam Arena**, Amsterdam, Holland 3–4 Sep 2006	102,330
8	**Hayarkon Park**, Tel Aviv, Israel 1–2 Sep 2009	99,674
9	**Madison Square Garden**, New York, USA 28 Jun–19 Jul 2006	91,841
10	**Madison Square Garden**, New York, USA 16–24 Jun 2004	88,625

Source: Music Information Database

THE 10 **TOP-EARNING CONCERTS OF THE 2000s**

	ARTIST / VENUE	DATE	ATTENDANCE	GROSS (US$)
1	**Bruce Springsteen & the E Street Band** Giants Stadium, East Rutherford, New Jersey, USA	15 Jul–31 Aug 2003	566,560	38,684,050
2	**The Spice Girls** The O_2 Arena, London, UK	15 Dec 2006–22 Jan 2007	256,647	33,829,250
3	**U2** Croke Park, Dublin, Ireland	24–27 Jul 2009	243,198	28,815,352
4	**Celine Dion** Bell Centre, Montreal, Canada	15 Aug–1 Sep 2008	167,957	23,135,338
5	**Bruce Springsteen & the E Street Band** Giants Stadium, East Rutherford, New Jersey, USA	30 Sep–9 Oct 2009	260,668	22,570,336
6	**Madonna** Wembley Arena, London, UK	1–16 Aug 2006	86,061	22,090,582
7	**Prince** The O_2 Arena, London, UK	1 Aug–21 Sep 2007	351,527	22,052,026
8	**U2** Croke Park, Dublin, Ireland	24–27 Jun 2005	246,743	21,163,695
9	**U2** Stade de France, Paris, France	11–12 Jul 2009	186,544	20,902,760
10	**U2** Wembley Stadium, London, UK	14–15 Aug 2009	164,244	20,680,860

Source: *Billboard*

► ***Reigning Prince***
His 21-night Earth Tour O_2 concerts attracted a record UK attendance.

TOP 10 ORIGINAL SOUNDTRACK ALBUMS IN THE UK

	SOUNDTRACK	YEAR OF RELEASE
1	The Sound of Music	1965
2	Dirty Dancing	1998
3	Grease	1978
4	Saturday Night Fever	1977
5	The Bodyguard	1992
6	South Pacific	1958
7	Titanic	1997
8	Bridget Jones's Diary	2001
9	Trainspotting	1996
10	The Commitments	1991

Source: Music Information Database

► *Grease*
The soundtrack stayed at No.1 for 13 weeks and was a seven-times platinum album.

▼ *Success story*
West Side Story*'s UK popularity was matched in the USA, where the album stayed at No. 1 for a record 54 weeks.*

TOP 10 MUSICAL ALBUMS IN THE UK

ALBUM / YEAR OF RELEASE

1. The Sound of Music 1965
2. Grease 1978
3. South Pacific 1958
4. West Side Story 1962
5. Oklahoma 1955
6. The King and I 1956
7. Oliver 1968
8. Mary Poppins 1965
9. Evita 1996
10. My Fair Lady 1964

Source: Music Information Database

TOP 10 **FILM THEMES IN THE UK**

	THEME SONG / ARTIST / FILM	YEAR OF RELEASE
1	**(Everything I Do) I Do It For You**, Bryan Adams Robin Hood: Prince of Thieves	1991
2	**I Will Always Love You**, Whitney Houston The Bodyguard	1992
3	**My Heart Will Go On**, Celine Dion Titanic	1998
4	**Bright Eyes**, Art Garfunkel Watership Down	1979
5	**The Young Ones**, Cliff Richard & the Shadows The Young Ones	1962
6	**Eye of the Tiger**, Survivor Rocky III	1982
7	**Fame**, Irene Cara Fame	1982
8	**Ghostbusters**, Ray Parker Jr Ghostbusters	1984
9	**Jailhouse Rock**, Elvis Presley Jailhouse Rock	1958
10	**Help!**, The Beatles Help!	1965

Source: Music Information Database

▲ *On target*
Bryan Adams' track from Robin Hood: Prince of Thieves *spent 16 consecutive weeks at UK No. 1.*

► *Cashing in*
Joachim Phoenix as Johnny Cash in Walk the Line, *which made over $186 million worldwide.*

TOP 10 **MUSICIAN BIOPICS**

	FILM / SUBJECT	YEAR
1	Walk the Line Johnny Cash	2005
2	The Sound of Music von Trapp family	1965
3	Ray Ray Charles	2004
4	The Pianist Władysław Szpilman	2002
5	Shine David Helfgott	1996
6	La Vie en Rose Edith Piaf	2007
7	Coal Miner's Daughter Loretta Lynn	1980
8	La Bamba Ritchie Valens	1987
9	Amadeus Wolfgang Amadeus Mozart	1984
10	What's Love Got to Do with It Tina Turner	1993

Biopics (biographical pictures) on the often-dramatic lives of famous musicians have been a Hollywood staple for over 60 years. Those within and outside the Top 10 have encompassed both classical and popular musicians, including Tchaikovsky (*The Music Lovers*, 1970), Billie Holiday (*Lady Sings the Blues*, 1972) and John Lennon (*Imagine: John Lennon*, 1988 and *Nowhere Boy*, 2009).

CLASSICAL & OPERA

◄ *Bohemian tragedy*
Puccini's La Bohème *is the most-performed opera at the Royal Opera House.*

TOP 10 OPERAS MOST FREQUENTLY PERFORMED AT THE ROYAL OPERA HOUSE, COVENT GARDEN, 1833–2010

	OPERA / COMPOSER	FIRST PERFORMANCE	TOTAL*
1	La Bohème Giacomo Puccini	2 Oct 1897	580
2	Carmen Georges Bizet	27 May 1882	526
3	Aïda Giuseppi Verdi	22 Jun 1876	481
4	Rigoletto Giuseppi Verdi	14 May 1853	479
5	Faust Charles Gounod	18 Jul 1863	448
6	Tosca Giacomo Puccini	12 Jul 1900	447
7	Don Giovanni Wolfgang Amadeus Mozart	17 Apr 1834	434
8	La Traviata Giuseppi Verdi	25 May 1858	427
9	Madama Butterfly Giacomo Puccini	10 Jul 1905	387
10	Norma Vincenzo Bellini	12 Jul 1833	360

* To 31 January 2010

Most of the works listed were first performed at Covent Garden within a few years of their world premiers (in the case of *Tosca*, in the same year). Although some were considered controversial at the time, all of them are now regarded as important components of the classic opera repertoire.

TOP 10 BESTSELLING CLASSICAL ARTISTS IN THE UK

	ARTIST
1	Luciano Pavarotti
2	Placido Domingo
3	José Carreras
4	Andrea Bocelli
5	Russell Watson
6	Charlotte Church
7	Katherine Jenkins
8	Nigel Kennedy
9	Hayley Westenra
10	Aled Jones

Source: Music Information Database

► *Andrea Bocelli*
The crossover appeal of his albums has resulted in global sales topping 70 million.

THE 10 **LATEST BEST CLASSICAL ALBUM GRAMMY WINNERS**

YEAR*	COMPOSER / TITLE
2010	**Gustav Mahler,** Symphony No. 8; Adagio from Symphony No. 10
2009	**Kurt Weill,** Rise and Fall of the City of Mahagonny
2008	**Joan Tower** Made in America
2007	**Gustav Mahler** Symphony No. 7
2006	**William Bolcom** Songs of Innocence and of Experience
2005	**John Adams** On the Transmigration of Souls
2004	**Gustav Mahler** Symphony No. 3, Kindertotenlieder
2003	**Ralph Vaughan Williams,** A Sea Symphony (Symphony No. 1)
2002	**Hector Berlioz** Les Troyens
2001	**Dmitri Shostakovich** The String Quartets

* Of award, for albums released the previous year

Source: NARAS

TOP 10 **CLASSICAL ALBUMS IN THE UK**

	TITLE	PERFORMER/ORCHESTRA	YEAR
1	The Three Tenors In Concert	José Carreras, Placido Domingo, Luciano Pavarotti	1990
2	The Essential Pavarotti	Luciano Pavarotti	1990
3	Vivaldi: The Four Seasons	Nigel Kennedy/English Chamber Orchestra	1989
4	The Three Tenors – In Concert 1994	José Carreras, Placido Domingo, Luciano Pavarotti, Zubin Mehta	1994
5	The Voice	Russell Watson	2000
6	Voice of an Angel	Charlotte Church	1998
7	Pure	Hayley Westenra	2003
8	Encore	Russell Watson	2002
9	The Essential Pavarotti, 2	Luciano Pavarotti	1991
10	The Pavarotti Collection	Luciano Pavarotti	1986

Source: Music Information Database

Sales of classical music boomed at the end of the 1980s and early 1990s with recordings by an élite band of superstars, most notably tenors José Carreras, Placido Domingo and Luciano Pavarotti, the latter even achieving a No. 3 single with 'Nessun Dorma'.

▼ *Church music*
Her Voice of an Angel, recorded when she was 12, remains one of the bestselling classical albums ever.

7 ENTERTAINMENT

SPIDER-MAN'S 3D RETURN

The *Spider-Man* film franchise, *Spider-Man* (2002), *Spider-Man 2* (2004) and *Spider-Man 3* (2007), has earned a total of $2.5 billion at the world box office. In 2010, a planned sequel, *Spider-Man 4*, was cancelled, but, following the commercial success of *Avatar* and other 3D films, a new 3D version entered production with a release date of 2012. Music-video and rom-com director Marc Webb was appointed to direct the film, described as 'Spider-Man rebooted', which, it is rumoured, will be a prequel to the series, focusing on Peter Parker's high-school transformation into the eponymous hero.

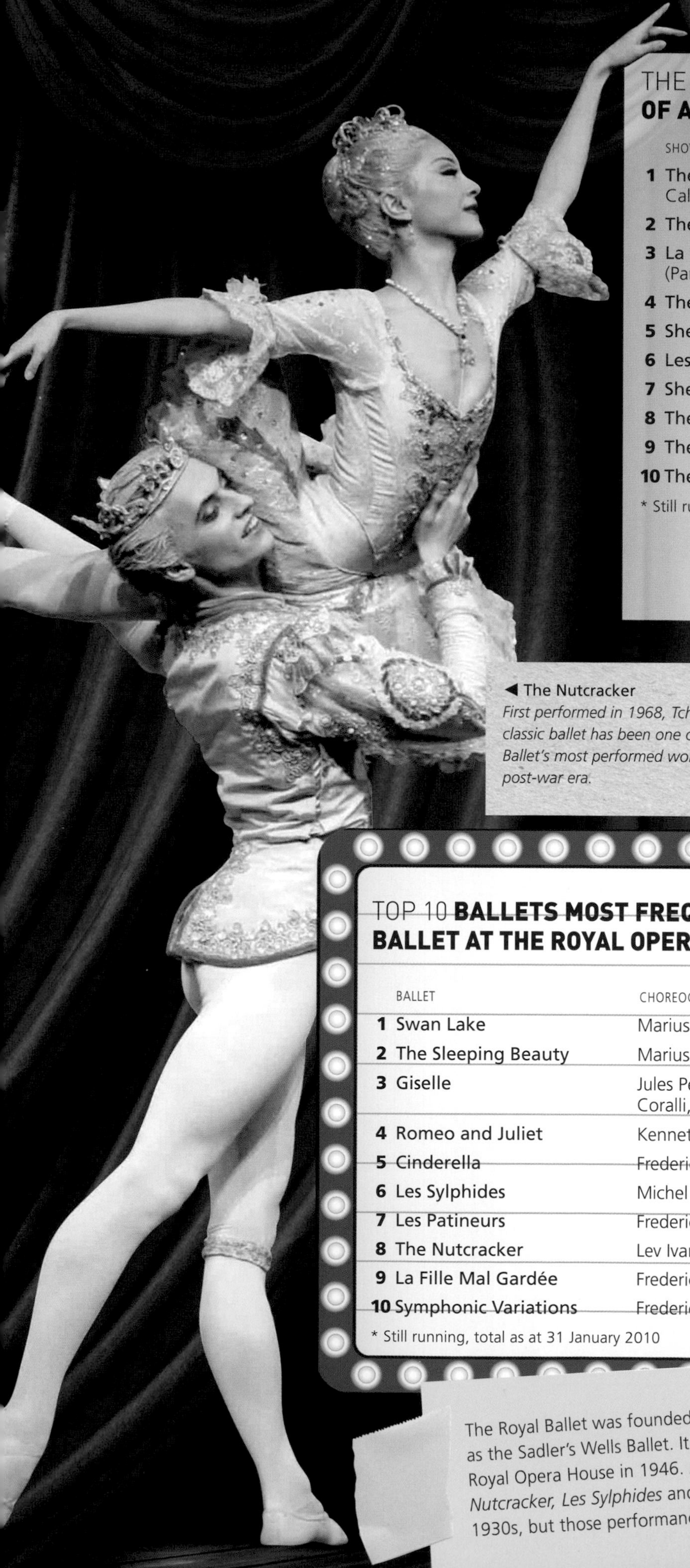

THE 10 LONGEST-RUNNING SHOWS OF ALL TIME

	SHOW / LOCATION / RUN	PERFORMANCES
1	**The Golden Horseshoe Revue** (Disneyland, California, 1955–86)	47,250
2	**The Mousetrap** (London, 1952–)	23,888*
3	**La Cantatrice Chauve** (The Bald Soprano) (Paris, 1957–)	17,527*
4	**The Fantasticks** (New York, 1960–2002)	17,162
5	**Shear Madness** (Boston, 1980–)	12,679*
6	**Les Misérables** (London, 1985–)	10,130*
7	**Shear Madness** (Washington, DC, 1987–)	9,826*
8	**The Phantom of the Opera** (London, 1986–)	9,795*
9	**The Mousetrap** (Toronto, 1977–2004)	9,648
10	**The Drunkard** (Los Angeles, 1933–59)	9,477

* Still running, total as at 31 March 2010

◄ **The Nutcracker**
First performed in 1968, Tchaikovsky's classic ballet has been one of the Royal Ballet's most performed works in the post-war era.

TOP 10 BALLETS MOST FREQUENTLY PERFORMED BY THE ROYAL BALLET AT THE ROYAL OPERA HOUSE, COVENT GARDEN, 1946–2010*

	BALLET	CHOREOGRAPHER	FIRST PERFORMANCE BY RB AT ROH	TOTAL
1	Swan Lake	Marius Petipa, Lev Ivanov	19 Dec 1946	944
2	The Sleeping Beauty	Marius Petipa	20 Feb 1946	840
3	Giselle	Jules Perrot, Jean, Coralli, Marius Petipa	12 Jun 1946	539
4	Romeo and Juliet	Kenneth MacMillan	9 Feb 1965	430
5	Cinderella	Frederick Ashton	23 Dec 1948	383
6	Les Sylphides	Michel Fokine	16 May 1946	373
7	Les Patineurs	Frederick Ashton	20 Mar 1946	335
8	The Nutcracker	Lev Ivanov	29 Feb 1968	326
9	La Fille Mal Gardée	Frederick Ashton	28 Jan 1960	323
10	Symphonic Variations	Frederick Ashton	24 Apr 1946	249

* Still running, total as at 31 January 2010

The Royal Ballet was founded in 1931 as the Vic-Wells Ballet, later known as the Sadler's Wells Ballet. It became the resident ballet company of the Royal Opera House in 1946. *Swan Lake*, *Giselle*, *The Sleeping Beauty*, *The Nutcracker*, *Les Sylphides* and *Les Patineurs* had been in its repertoire in the 1930s, but those performances do not figure in these statistics.

TOP 10 **OLDEST THEATRES IN THE UK**

THEATRE / OPENING SHOW / OPENED

1 **Theatre Royal,** Drury Lane, London
The Humorous Lieutenant
7 May 1663

2 **Sadler's Wells,** Rosebery Avenue, London
Musical performances
3 Jun 1683

3 **The Haymarket** (Theatre Royal), Haymarket, London
La Fille à la Mode
29 Dec 1720

4 **Royal Opera House,** Covent Garden, London
The Way of the World
7 Dec 1732

5 **York Theatre Royal** (founded as New Theatre; Royal from 1769)
Henry V
1744*

6 **Theatre Royal Bristol**
Concert of Music and a Specimen of Rhetorick
30 May 1764

7 **Grand Theatre,** Lancaster
10 Jun 1782#

8 **Theatre Royal,** Margate
She Stoops to Conquer
27 Jun 1787

9 **Theatre Royal,** Dumfries
Othello
29 Sep 1792

10 **Theatre Royal,** Bath
Richard III
12 Oct 1805

* Precise date unknown
\# Opening show unknown; *Hamlet* performed in August 1782

These are Britain's 10 oldest theatres still operating on their original sites – although most of them have been rebuilt, some several times.

TOP 10 **LONGEST-RUNNING NON-MUSICALS IN THE UK**

	SHOW / RUN	PERFORMANCES
1	**The Mousetrap** (25 Nov 1952–)	23,888*
2	**The Woman in Black** (7 Jun 1989–)	8,525*
3	**No Sex, Please – We're British** (1971–81; 1982–86; 1986–87)	6,761
4	**The Complete Works of William Shakespeare** (abridged) (1996–2005)	4,266
5	**Oh! Calcutta!** (1970–74; 28 Jan 1974–80)	3,918
6	**Run for Your Wife** (1983–91)	2,638
7	**There's a Girl in My Soup** (1966–69; 1969–72)	2,547
8	**Pyjama Tops** (1969–75)	2,498
9	**Sleuth** (1970; 1972; 1973–75)	2,359
10	**Worm's Eye View** (1945–51)	2,245

* Still running, total as at 31 March 2010

Oh! Calcutta! is included here as it is regarded as a revue with music.

◄ ***In the long run***
Agatha Christie's The Mousetrap *is British theatre's longest-running show of any kind.*

► ***The Bard on Broadway***
Katharine Hepburn and William Prince in Shakespeare's As You Like It *(1950), first performed on Broadway in 1786.*

TOP 10 **PRODUCTIONS OF SHAKEPEARE ON BROADWAY**

	TITLE (FIRST PRODUCTION OPENED/LATEST CLOSED)	PRODUCTIONS
1	**Hamlet** (26 Nov 1761–2009*)	66
2	**The Merchant of Venice** (28 Jan 1768–10 Mar 1990)	49
3	**Macbeth** (3 May 1768–24 May 2008)	46
4	**Romeo and Juliet** (28 Jan 1754–31 May 1987)	35
5	**Twelfth Night** (11 Jun 1804–30 Aug 1998)	30
6	**The Taming of the Shrew** (8 Jan 1768–10 Mar 1957)	24
7	**As You Like It** (14 Jul 1786–31 May 1987)	23
8	=**Richard III** (5 Mar 1750–15 Jul 1979)	20
	=**Othello** (23 Dec 1751–23 May 1982)	20
	=**Julius Caesar** (14 Mar 1794–12 Jun 2005)	20

* Running as at 5 October 2009

MOVIE BUSINESS

▲ *Supernatural*
The Blair Witch Project *was the most profitable film for 10 years until even cheaper* Paranormal Activity *became a surprise hit.*

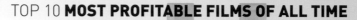

TOP 10 **MOST PROFITABLE FILMS OF ALL TIME**

	FILM / YEAR	BUDGET (US$)	TOTAL WORLD GROSS (US$)*	PROFIT RATIO
1	Paranormal Activity 2009	15,000	153,469,744	10,231.32
2	The Blair Witch Project 1999	35,000	248,662,839	7,104.65
3	Rocky 1976	1,100,000	225,000,000	204.55
4	American Graffiti 1973	750,000	115,000,000	153.33
5	Snow White and the Seven Dwarfs# 1937	1,488,000	187,670,866	126.12
6	The Rocky Horror Picture Show 1975	1,200,000	139,876,417	116.56
7	Gone With the Wind† 1939	3,900,000	390,525,192	100.13
8	Saw 2004	1,200,000	103,096,345	85.91
9	E.T.: The Extra-Terrestrial 1982	10,500,000	792,910,554	75.52
10	My Big Fat Greek Wedding 2002	5,000,000	368,744,044	73.75

* Minimum entry US$100 million world gross
\# Animated
† Won Best Picture Oscar

THE 10 **BIGGEST FILM FLOPS OF ALL TIME**

	FILM / YEAR	BUDGET (US$)*	WORLD BOX OFFICE RECEIPTS (US$)	TOTAL RECEIPTS AS % OF BUDGET
1	Eye See You (aka D-Tox) 2002	55,000,000	79,161	0.14
2	The Adventures of Pluto Nash 2002	100,000,000	7,103,972	7.10
3	Lolita 1997	62,000,000	5,173,783	8.34
4	Monkeybone 2001	75,000,000	7,622,365	10.16
5	Town & Country 2001	90,000,000	10,372,291	11.52
6	Cutthroat Island 1995	98,000,000	12,258,974	12.51
7	Gigli 2003	54,000,000	7,266,209	13.46
8	A Sound of Thunder 2005	80,000,000	11,665,465	14.58
9	Dudley Do-Right 1999	70,000,000	10,316,055	14.73
10	Stay 2005	50,000,000	8,342,132	16.68

* Films with estimated budgets of over US$50 million

▲ Monkeybone
Despite a cast including Whoopi Goldberg, Bridget Fonda and Brendan Fraser, 2001's Monkeybone *was a critical and box-office flop.*

After initial failure at the US box office, some films earn back their costs through overseas release, DVD sales and TV screenings – but in these cases extra earnings were insufficient to rescue them from 'flop' status. When British-made *Raise the Titanic* (1980) lost some US$33 million, its producer (Lord) Lew Grade commented, 'It would have been cheaper to lower the Atlantic!'

TOP 10 FILM-PRODUCING COUNTRIES

	COUNTRY	FEATURE FILMS PRODUCED (2008)
1	India	1,325
2	USA	520
3	Japan	418
4	China	406
5	France	240
6	Russia	220
7	Spain	173
8	Italy	154
9	Germany	125
10	South Korea	113
	UK	*111*

Source: *Screen Digest*

▲ *Bollywood*

The output of the Indian film industry overtook that of Hollywood in the 1970s, with Mumbai-produced Hindi-language 'Bollywood' its principal component.

TOP 10 COUNTRIES WITH MOST CINEMA ADMISSIONS PER CAPITA

COUNTRY / ADMISSIONS PER CAPITA (2008)

1 Iceland 5.4 **2=** Ireland 4.2 **2=** Singapore 4.2 **4 =** Australia 4.1 **4 =** USA 4.1 **6** New Zealand 3.6 **7** Canada 3.2 **8** South Korea 3.1 **9** France 3.0 **10** India 2.9 *UK* 2.8

Source: *Screen Digest*

TOP 10 BILLION-DOLLAR DIRECTORS

	DIRECTOR	FILMS	HIGHEST-EARNING FILM	TOTAL US GROSS ($)*
1	Steven Spielberg	25	E.T.: The Extra-Terrestrial	3,824,973,778
2	Robert Zemeckis	15	Forrest Gump	1,943,062,853
3	James Cameron	9	Avatar	1,896,600,269
4	Ron Howard	19	How the Grinch Stole Christmas	1,758,280,948
5	George Lucas	6	Star Wars	1,700,470,625
6	Chris Columbus	14	Harry Potter and the Philosopher's Stone	1,668,918,597
7	Tim Burton	15	Alice in Wonderland	1,593,628,562
8	Michael Bay	8	Transformers: Revenge of the Fallen	1,495,782,691
9	Peter Jackson	8	The Lord of the Rings: The Return of the King	1,315,538,479
10	Gore Verbinski	7	Pirates of the Caribbean: Dead Man's Chest	1,308,523,485

* Of all films

◀ ***Steven Spielberg***

E.T.: The Extra-Terrestrial *earned over $435 million in the USA and $793 worldwide.*

Most of this élite group of directors achieved their success with a high proportion, rather than sheer number, of high-earning films. Indeed, Andrew Adamson, just outside the Top 10, had US earnings of US$1.1 billion with just four films – but they were two *Chronicles of Narnia* and two *Shreks*.

Blockbusters

► Avatar
In 2010 Avatar *became the first film ever to earn more than $2 billion at the world box office.*

TOP 10 **FILMS OF ALL TIME**

FILM / YEAR	GROSS INCOME (US$) USA	OVERSEAS	WORLD TOTAL
1 Avatar 2009	740,684,275	1,944,000,000	2,684,684,275*
2 Titanic# 1997	600,788,188	1,248,025,607	1,848,813,795
3 The Lord of the Rings: The Return of the King# 2003	377,027,325	752,191,927	1,129,219,252
4 Pirates of the Caribbean: Dead Man's Chest 2006	423,315,812	642,863,913	1,066,179,725
5 The Dark Knight 2008	533,345,358	468,576,467	1,001,921,825
6 Harry Potter and the Philosopher's Stone 2001	317,575,550	668,242,109	985,817,659
7 Pirates of the Caribbean: At World's End 2007	309,420,425	651,582,238	961,002,663
8 Harry Potter and the Order of the Phoenix 2007	292,004,738	646,464,126	938,468,864
9 Harry Potter and the Half-Blood Prince 2009	301,959,197	632,000,000	933,959,000
10 The Lord of the Rings: The Two Towers 2002	341,786,758	584,500,642	926,287,400

* As at 1 April 2010
\# Won Best Picture Oscar

▼ *Blazing ahead*
The Dark Knight *is the fastest film ever to earn $200, $300 and $400 million in the USA.*

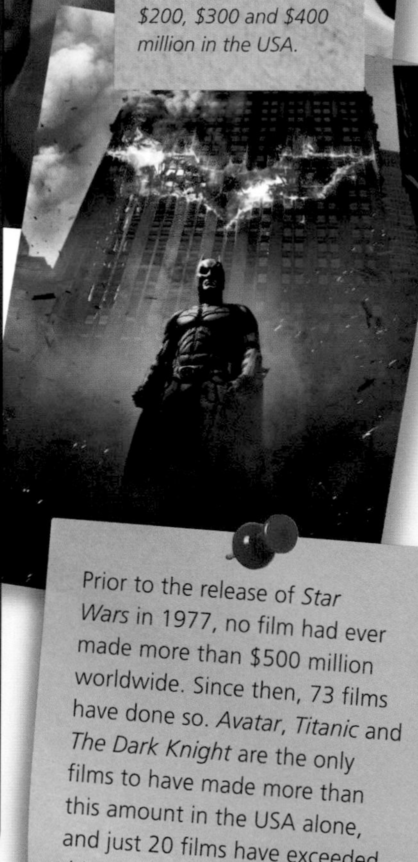

Prior to the release of *Star Wars* in 1977, no film had ever made more than $500 million worldwide. Since then, 73 films have done so. *Avatar*, *Titanic* and *The Dark Knight* are the only films to have made more than this amount in the USA alone, and just 20 films have exceeded this total in the rest of the world.

GONE WITH THE WIND

Taking inflation into account is fraught and generally avoided in *Top 10 of Everything* because few films achieved their total gross from a single year's release, but over a period of time, often with several re-releases, with variable ticket prices. Had the total for *Gone With the Wind* been earned in its 1939 release year, adjusting for inflation based on average ticket prices then (23 cents) compared with $7.18 in 2009, would produce an overall total of $2,921,288,151, making it the highest-earning film of all time. It is also the film with the greatest number of ticket sales, an estimated 202,044,600 in the USA alone.

THE TOP-EARNING FILM OF EACH DECADE

FILM / YEAR / ESTIMATED BUDGET (US$) / WORLD TOTAL GROSS (US$)

1910s
The Birth of a Nation (1915)
110,000 / 9,283,673

1920s
The Big Parade (1925)
245,000 / 5,120,791

1930s
Gone With the Wind* (1939)
3,900,000 / 400,180,470

1940s
Bambi (1942)
2,000,000 / 267,997,150

1950s
Lady and the Tramp (1955)
4,000,000 / 93,602,326

1960s
One Hundred and One Dalmatians (1961)
4,000,000 / 224,000,000

1970s
Star Wars (1977)
13,000,000 / 797,900,000

1980s
E.T.: The Extra-Terrestrial (1982)
0,500,000 / 792,910,554

1990s
Titanic* (1997)
200,000,000 / 1,848,813,795

2000s
Avatar (2009)
237,0000,0000 / 2,684,684,275#

* Won Best Picture Oscar
\# As at 1 April 2010

TOP FILM FRANCHISES OF ALL TIME

The total global earnings of all six *Harry Potter* films (2001–09) make the series the highest-earning of all time, a world gross of $5.4 billion. It is closely followed by the 22 official *James Bond* films (1963–2008) with $4.9 billion, six in the *Star Wars* series (1977–2005), which have earned $4.3 billion, and the *Lord of the Rings* trilogy (2001–03) with $2.9 billion. Each of the *Pirates of the Caribbean*, *Batman*, *Spider-Man* and *Shrek* franchises has made more than $2 billion, with *Indiana Jones* just under that amount.

▲ *Targeting the top*
Future Bond films may see the franchise move to top position after the completion of the final Harry Potter movie.

FASTEST DRAWS

Titanic (1997) took 98 days from its release to make $500 million at the US box office. *The Dark Knight* (2008) did so in 45 days, while *Avatar* (2009) achieved the feat in just 32 days.

BLOCKBUSTER OPENINGS

Driven in part by an attempt to resist piracy, simultaneous worldwide opening weekends have become a 21st-century phenomenon. *Harry Potter and the Half-Blood Prince*, for example, was released in more than 50 countries on 15–17 July 2009, earning a worldwide total of $394,022,354, the highest-ever cumulative global opening weekend, and 42 per cent of its eventual gross.

▲ *Box-office transformer*
Transformers: Revenge of the Fallen *is one of only six films to have opened with earnings of $300 million worldwide.*

SCI-FI & HORROR FIL S

▲ ***Biting back***
The three films in the Underworld *vampire series have earned a world total of $296 million.*

TOP 10 **VAMPIRE FILMS**

	FILM	YEAR	TOTAL WORLD GROSS (US$)
1	The Twilight Saga: New Moon	2009	707,186,022
2	Twilight	2008	384,997,808
3	Van Helsing	2004	300,257,475
4	Interview with the Vampire	1994	223,664,608
5	Bram Stoker's Dracula	1992	215,862,692
6	Blade II	2002	155,010,032
7	Blade	1998	131,237,688
8	Blade: Trinity	2004	128,905,366
9	Underworld: Evolution	2006	111,340,801
10	Underworld	2003	95,708,457

Vampires have figured in films since the silent era. The German film *Nächte des Grauens* (1916) was the first to tackle the theme, *The Great London Mystery* (1920) the first to do so in English, and the Hungarian film *Drakula halála* (1921), the first adaptation of Bram Stoker's *Dracula*. Since then there have been over 400 vampire films, with those in the Top 10 the highest-earning worldwide.

TOP 10 **SCI-FI FILMS BASED ON BOOKS**

	FILM	BOOK	YEAR	TOTAL WORLD GROSS (US$)
1	Jurassic Park	1990	1993	914,691,118
2	The Lost World: Jurassic Park	1995	1997	618,638,999
3	War of the Worlds	1898	2005	591,745,540
4	I, Robot	1950	2004	347,234,916
5	Jumper	1992	2008	222,231,186
6	Contact	1985	1997	171,120,329
7	Congo	1980	1995	152,022,101
8	The Time Machine	1895	2002	123,729,176
9	Starship Troopers	1959	1997	121,214,377
10	The Hitchhiker's Guide to the Galaxy	1979	2005	104,478,416

► ***Monster movie***
Michael Crichton's Jurassic Park *novel generated one of the most successful sci-fi film series.*

TOP 10 **WATER HORROR FILMS**

	FILM	YEAR	TOTAL WORLD GROSS (US$)
1	Jaws	1975	470,653,000
2	Jaws 2	1978	187,884,007
3	Deep Blue Sea	1999	164,648,142
4	Anaconda	1997	136,885,767
5	Jaws 3-D	1983	87,987,055
6	Anacondas: The Hunt for the Blood Orchid	2004	70,992,898
7	Lake Placid	1999	56,870,414
8	Open Water	2004	54,667,954
9	Jaws IV: The Revenge	1987	51,881,013
10	The Deep	1977	47,346,365

◄ *High water*
Although the earliest film in the Top 10, Jaws *remains the highest-earning in the genre.*

TOP 10 **HISTORICAL HORROR FILMS**

FILM / SET IN / YEAR / TOTAL WORLD GROSS (US$)

1. Van Helsing
1887
2004
300,257,475

2. The Village
1897
2004
256,697,520

3. Interview with the Vampire
1870
1994
223,664,608

4. Bram Stoker's Dracula
1897
1992
215,862,692

5. The Others
1940s
2001
209,947,037

6. Sleepy Hollow
1799
1999
206,071,502

7. Mary Shelley's Frankenstein
1816?
1994
112,006,296

8. Exorcist: The Beginning
1940s
2004
78,000,586

9. From Hell
1888
2001
74,558,115

10. The Ghost and the Darkness
1898
1996
38,619,405

▼ *Victorian horror*
Van Helsing *draws on the classic stories of* Dracula *and* Frankenstein.

TOP 10 FILMS BASED ON COMPUTER GAMES

	FILM	GAME*	YEAR
1	Lara Croft: Tomb Raider	1996	2001
2	AVP: Alien Vs. Predator	1999	2004
3	Lara Croft Tomb Raider: The Cradle of Life	1996	2003
4	Resident Evil: Extinction	1996	2007
5	Resident Evil: Apocalypse	1996	2004
6	Mortal Kombat	1992	1995
7	Resident Evil	1996	2002
8	Hitman	2000	2007
9	Street Fighter	1987	1994
10	Silent Hill	1999	2006

* Original if series

The video game *Ballistic: Ecks vs. Sever* was based on an early draft of the film, not the other way round. The *Pokémon* video games and films were based on a TV series, so have been disregarded.

▲ Game girl
Lara Croft: Tomb Raider *made $47.7 million in the USA on its opening weekend, the highest-earning ever with a heroine star.*

TOP 10 SUPERHERO FILMS

	FILM	YEAR
1	The Dark Knight	2008
2	Spider-Man 3	2007
3	Spider-Man	2002
4	Spider-Man 2	2004
5	The Incredibles*	2004
6	Hancock	2008
7	Iron Man	2008
8	X-Men: The Last Stand	2006
9	Batman	1989
10	X2: X-Men United	2003

* Animated

TOP 10 FILMS ABOUT FILMS AND FILM STARS

	FILM	YEAR
1	Notting Hill	1999
2	Who Framed Roger Rabbit?	1988
3	The Aviator	2004
4	Tropic Thunder	2008
5	Scream 3	2000
6	America's Sweethearts	2001
7	L.A. Confidential	1997
8	Get Shorty	1995
9	Bowfinger	1999
10	Be Cool	2005

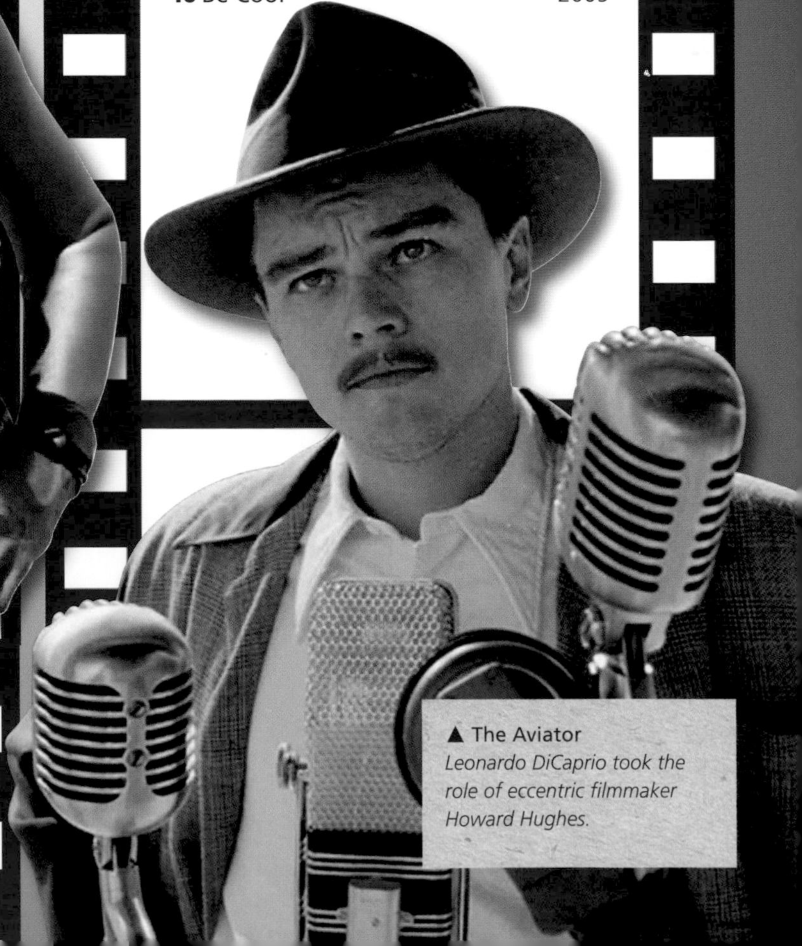

▲ The Aviator
Leonardo DiCaprio took the role of eccentric filmmaker Howard Hughes.

► *Close contest*
Dirty Dancing *made $213.9 worldwide, making it both the third highest-earning dance film of all time and the third highest-earning film of 1987.*

TOP 10 **DANCE FILMS**

	FILM	YEAR
1	Saturday Night Fever	1977
2	The Full Monty	1997
3	Dirty Dancing	1987
4	Save the Last Dance	2001
5	Step Up 2 the Streets	2008
6	Shall We Dance	2004
7	Staying Alive	1983
8	Step Up	2006
9	Coyote Ugly	2000
10	Billy Elliot	2000

TOP 10 **TIME-TRAVEL FILMS**

	FILM	YEAR
1	Harry Potter and the Prisoner of Azkaban	2004
2	Terminator II: Judgment Day	1991
3	Terminator 3: The Rise of the Machines	2003
4	Back to the Future	1985
5	Planet of the Apes	2001
6	Back to the Future Part II	1989
7	Austin Powers: The Spy Who Shagged Me	2000
8	Austin Powers in Goldmember	2002
9	Back to the Future Part III	1990
10	Click	2006

TOP 10 **WORLD WAR II FILMS**

	FILM	YEAR
1	Saving Private Ryan	1998
2	Pearl Harbor	2001
3	Schindler's List	1993
4	Inglourious Basterds	2009
5	The English Patient	1996
6	Life is Beautiful (La Vita è bella)	1997
7	Valkyrie	2008
8	U-571	2000
9	The Pianist	2002
10	The Thin Red Line	1998

▲ *War record*
Steven-Spielberg-directed Saving Private Ryan *made $481.8 million worldwide, a war-film total that has yet to be overtaken.*

ANIMATED HITS

TOP 10 ANIMATED FILMS

FILM / YEAR / TOTAL WORLD GROSS (US$)

1. Shrek 2* 2004 920,665,658
2. Ice Age: Dawn of the Dinosaurs# 2009 884,784,596
3. Finding Nemo† 2003 864,625,978
4. Shrek the Third* 2007 798,958,162
5. The Lion King† 1994 783,841,776
6. Up 2009 723,013,850
7. Ice Age: The Meltdown† 2006 655,388,158
8. Kung Fu Panda* 2008 631,908,951
9. The Incredibles† 2004 631,442,092
10. Ratatouille† 2007 623,707,397

* DreamWorks
# 20th Century Fox Animation
† Disney

► *Funny honey money*
Bee Movie *was one of a new wave of animated films commanding an estimated $150 million budget, but earned almost double that at the international box office.*

TOP 10 ANIMATED FILMS IN THE UK

	FILM	YEAR	TOTAL UK GROSS (£)
1	Shrek 2*	2004	48,243,628
2	Toy Story 2#	2000	44,306,070
3	The Simpsons Movie†	2007	38,312,694
4	Shrek the Third*	2007	38,079,462
5	Monsters, Inc.#	2002	37,907,451
6	Finding Nemo#	2003	37,364,251
7	Ice Age: Dawn of the Dinosaurs†	2009	34,872,218
8	Up	2009	34,284,193
9	The Incredibles#	2004	32,277,041
10	Wallace & Gromit: The Curse of the Were-Rabbit*	2005	32,007,310

* DreamWorks # Disney
† 20th Century Fox Animation

▲ *Greenback*
Sequel Shrek 2, *the top money-maker of 2004 and highest-earning animated film of all time.*

TOP 10 **ANIMATED FILM BUDGETS**

	FILM	YEAR	TOTAL WORLD GROSS (US$)	BUDGET (US$)
1	A Christmas Carol	2009	323,555,899	200,000,000
2	WALL-E	2008	534,767,889	180,000,000
3	Up	2009	723,013,850	175,000,000
4	The Polar Express	2004	303,200,434	170,000,000
5	Shrek the Third	2007	798,958,162	160,000,000
6	=Bee Movie	2007	287,594,577	150,000,000
	=Beowulf	2007	196,393,745	150,000,000
	=Bolt	2008	308,332,347	150,000,000
	=Madagascar: Escape 2 Africa	2008	603,899,043	150,000,000
	=Ratatouille	2007	623,707,397	150,000,000
	=Shrek 2	2004	920,665,658	150,000,000

Snow White and the Seven Dwarfs (1937) established a then-record animated film budget of $1.49 million. The $2.6 million budget for *Pinocchio* (1940) and $2.28 million for *Fantasia* (1940) were the two biggest of the 1940s, while *Sleeping Beauty* (1959) at $6 million was the highest of the 1950s. Since the 1990s, budgets of $50 million or more have become commonplace – *Tarzan* (1999) becoming the first to break through $100 million, *Shrek 2* (2004) the first to $150 million and *A Christmas Carol* (2009) $200 million.

THE 10 **LATEST WINNERS OF ANNIE AWARDS FOR BEST ANIMATED FEATURE**

YEAR*	FILM
2009	Up
2008	Kung Fu Panda
2007	Ratatouille
2006	Cars
2005	Wallace & Gromit: The Curse of the Were-Rabbit
2004	The Incredibles
2003	Finding Nemo
2002	Spirited Away
2001	Shrek
2000	Toy Story 2

* Of film – awards are made the following year

The Annie Awards have been presented by the International Animated Film Society since 1972. As well as individual and specialist category awards, it has honoured Best Animated Feature (originally Outstanding Achievement in an Animated Theatrical Feature) since 1992, when it was won by *Beauty and the Beast*.

▶ *Manmade monster*
King Kong was created with computer-generated imagery.

TOP 10 **FILMS WITH CGI STARS***

	FILM	YEAR	WORLDWIDE TOTAL GROSS (US$)
1	King Kong	2005	550,517,357
2	Godzilla	1998	379,014,294
3	Alvin and the Chipmunks	2007	359,656,974
4	Stuart Little	1999	300,235,367
5	Casper	1995	287,928,194
6	Scooby-Doo	2002	275,650,703
7	The Incredible Hulk	2008	263,427,064
8	Hulk	2003	245,360,480
9	Garfield: The Movie	2004	198,964,900
10	Scooby-Doo 2: Monsters Unleashed	2004	181,466,833

* Main or title-named character created by computer-generated imagery

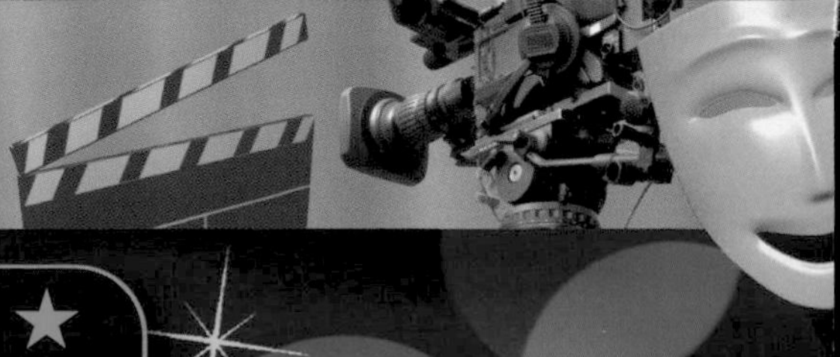

TOP 10 JACK BLACK FILMS

1. King Kong 2005
2. The Holiday 2006
3. Tropic Thunder 2008
4. Shallow Hal 2001
5. School of Rock 2003
6. Nacho Libre 2006
7. Year One 2009
8. High Fidelity 2000
9. Orange County 2002
10. Be Kind, Rewind 2008

◀ *Gorilla thriller*
Jack Black's highest-earning film, the latest remake of King Kong, *made a world total of $550.5 million.*

TOP 10 TOM CRUISE FILMS

1. War of the Worlds 2005
2. Mission: Impossible II 2000
3. The Last Samurai 2003
4. Mission: Impossible 1996
5. Rain Man 1988
6. Mission: Impossible III 2006
7. Minority Report 2002
8. Top Gun 1986
9. Jerry Maguire 1996
10. The Firm 1993

TOP 10 WILL SMITH FILMS

1. Independence Day 1996
2. Hancock 2008
3. Men in Black 1997
4. I Am Legend 2007
5. Men in Black II 2002
6. Hitch 2005
7. I, Robot 2004
8. The Pursuit of Happyness 2006
9. Bad Boys II 2003
10. Enemy of the State 1998

▼ *Back in black*
The two Men in Black *films, in which Will Smith starred as Agent Jay, earned more than $1 billion globally.*

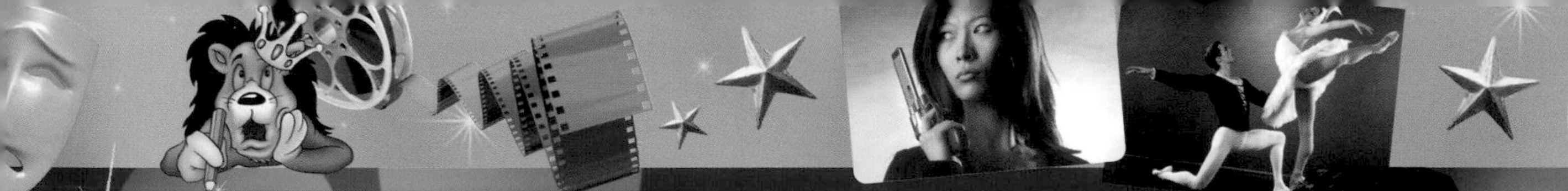

TOP 10 ERIC BANA FILMS

1. Troy
2004
2. Star Trek
2009
3. Hulk
2003
4. Black Hawk Down
2001
5. Munich
2005
6. The Other Boleyn Girl
2008
7. The Time Traveler's Wife
2009
8. Funny People
2009
9. Lucky You
2007
10. Romulus, My Father
2008

Eric Bana also provided the voice of Anchor in the animated blockbuster *Finding Nemo* (2003). If it were included in his Top 10, it would occupy the No. 1 slot.

► *Eric's epics*
Australian actor Eric Bana made his Hollywood debut in Black Hawk Down, *appearing as Hector in* Troy *and Prince Henry in* The Other Boleyn Girl.

TOP 10 AL PACINO FILMS

1. Oceans Thirteen
2007
2. The Godfather*
1972
3. Heat
1995
4. Dick Tracy
1990
5. The Devil's Advocate
1997
6. The Godfather: Part III
1990
7. Scent of a Woman#
1992
8. Donnie Brasco
1997
9. Insomnia
2002
10. Sea of Love
1989

* Won Best Picture Oscar
\# Won Best Actor Oscar

▲ The Last Samurai
This rare historical epic excursion for Tom Cruise made $456.8 million at the world box office

► The Godfather
Al Pacino was Oscar-nominated for his role.

ACTRESSES

TOP 10 PENELOPE CRUZ FILMS

1. Vanilla Sky
2001
2. Gothika
2003
3. Sahara
2005
4. Vicky Cristina Barcelona
2008
5. Volver
2006
6. Blow
2001
7. All About My Mother
1999
8. Captain Corelli's Mandolin
2001
9. Nine
2009
10. All the Pretty Horses
2000

► *Spanish success*
Spanish actress Penelope Cruz was nominated for an Oscar for her starring role in the Pedro Almodóvar-directed film Volver.

TOP 10 LIV TYLER FILMS

1. The Lord of the Rings: The Return of the King
2003
2. The Lord of the Rings: The Two Towers
2002
3. The Lord of the Rings: The Fellowship of the Ring
2001
4. Armageddon
1998
5. The Incredible Hulk
2008
6. The Strangers
2008
7. Jersey Girl
2004
8. That Thing You Do!
1996
9. Dr T and the Women
2001
10. Reign Over Me
2007

▲ *Tyler more*
Liv Tyler's Top 10 films have earned close to $4 billion worldwide.

TOP 10 GLENN CLOSE FILMS

1. 101 Dalmatians
1996
2. Fatal Attraction
1987
3. Air Force One
1997
4. Hook
1991
5. 102 Dalmatians
2000
6. The Stepford Wives
2004
7. Mars Attacks!
1996
8. The Big Chill
1983
9. The Paper
1994
10. The Natural
1984

► *Presidential p*
Air Force One *to*
box office, falling
the world's bigge

TOP 10 **KATE WINSLET FILMS**

1. Titanic 1997
2. The Holiday 2006
3. Sense and Sensibility 1995
4. Finding Neverland 2004
5. The Reader* 2008
6. Eternal Sunshine of the Spotless Mind 2004
7. Revolutionary Road 2008
8. The Life of David Gale 2003
9. Quills 2000
10. Iris 2001

* Won Best Actress Oscar

▲ *One for the road*
In 2009 Kate Winslet won a Best Actress Golden Globe Award for her role in Revolutionary Road, *followed by an Oscar for* The Reader.

► *Magic movie*
Susan Sarandon as Queen Narissa in the Disney fairytale Enchanted.

TOP 10 **SUSAN SARANDON FILMS**

1. Enchanted 2007
2. Shall We Dance 2004
3. Stepmom 1999
4. The Rocky Horror Picture Show 1975
5. The Client 1994
6. Speed Racer 2008
7. The Witches of Eastwick 1987
8. Little Women 1994
9. The Lovely Bones 2009
10. Elizabethtown 2005

409 at the global Fatal Attraction, *of 1987.*

OSCAR-WINNERS

TOP 10 FILMS TO WIN THE MOST OSCARS*

	FILM	YEAR#	NOMINATIONS	AWARDS
1	=Ben-Hur	1960	12	11
	=Titanic	1998	14	11
	=The Lord of the Rings: The Return of the King	2003	11	11
4	West Side Story	1961	11	10
5	=Gigi	1958	9	9
	=The Last Emperor	1987	9	9
	=The English Patient	1996	12	9
8	=Gone With the Wind	1939	13	8†
	=From Here to Eternity	1953	13	8
	=On the Waterfront	1954	12	8
	=My Fair Lady	1964	12	8
	=Cabaret§	1972	10	8
	=Gandhi	1982	11	8
	=Amadeus	1984	11	8
	=Slumdog Millionaire	2008	10	8

* Oscar® is a Registered Trade Mark
# Of win
† Plus two special awards
§ Did not win Best Picture Oscar

Ten other films have won seven Oscars each, including the award for Best Picture: *Going My Way* (1944), *The Best Years of Our Lives* (1946), *The Bridge on the River Kwai* (1957), *Lawrence of Arabia* (1962), *Patton* (1970), *The Sting* (1973), *Out of Africa* (1985), *Dances With Wolves* (1991), *Schindler's List* (1993) and *Shakespeare in Love* (1998).

◄ ***A night to remember***
It Happened One Night *was the first film with a clean sweep of Oscar wins.*

TOP 10 FILMS WITH THE HIGHEST RATIO OF OSCAR WINS TO NOMINATIONS*

	FILM	YEAR#	NOMS.	WINS	RATIO (%)
1	=It Happened One Night	1935	5	5	100.0
	=Gigi	1959	9	9	100.0
	=The Last Emperor	1988	9	9	100.0
	=The Lord of the Rings: The Return of the King	2004	11	11	100.0
5	Ben-Hur	1960	12	11	91.7
6	West Side Story	1962	11	10	90.9
7	=The Best Years of Our Lives	1947	8	7	87.5
	=The Bridge on the River Kwai	1958	8	7	87.5
9	The Bad and the Beautiful	1953	6	5	83.3
10	=Cabaret†	1973	10	8	80.0
	=The Departed	2007	5	4	80.0
	=Slumdog Millionaire	2009	10	8	80.0

* Minimum qualification 5 wins
# Of Award
† Did not win Best Picture – awarded to *The Godfather*

Based on the nomination-win ratio, blockbusters *Titanic* (1997), with 14 nominations and 11 wins (78.6 per cent), and *Gone with the Wind* (1939), with 13 nominations and 10 wins, including two special awards (76.9 per cent), fall short of the Top 10.

THE 10 LATEST ACTORS AND ACTRESSES TO RECEIVE THREE OR MORE CONSECUTIVE OSCAR NOMINATIONS

	ACTOR	NOMINATIONS	WINS*	YEARS#
1	Renée Zellweger	3	1	2002–04
2	Russell Crowe	3	1	2000–02
3	William Hurt	3	1	1986–88
4	Glenn Close	3	0	1983–85
5	Meryl Streep	3	1	1982–84
6	Jane Fonda	3	1	1978–80
7	Al Pacino	4	0	1973–76
8	Jack Nicholson	3	1	1974–76
9	Richard Burton	3	0	1965–67
10	Elizabeth Taylor	4	1	1958–61

* During consecutive period; some also won before or after
\# Of nominations (for films of previous year)

◀ ***Russell's victory***
Russell Crowe's Best Actor Academy Award for Gladiator *was sandwiched between nominations in the same category for* The Insider *and* A Beautiful Mind.

Two actresses, (Bette Davis, 1939–43 and Greer Garson, 1942–46), were nominated in five consecutive years. Jennifer Jones (1944–47), Thelma Ritter (1951–54) and Marlon Brando (1952–55) were all nominated four times.

TOP 10 HIGHEST-EARNING BEST PICTURE OSCAR WINNERS

	FILM	YEAR*	WORLD BOX OFFICE (US$)
1	Titanic	1997	1,848,813,795
2	The Lord of the Rings: The Return of the King	2003	1,129,219,252
3	Forrest Gump	1994	677,386,686
4	Gladiator	2000	457,640,427
5	Dances With Wolves	1990	424,208,842
6	Rain Man	1988	416,011,462
7	Gone With the Wind	1939	400,176,459
8	Slumdog Millionaire	2008	377,417,293
9	American Beauty	1999	356,296,601
10	Schindler's List	1993	321,267,179

* Of release; Oscars are awarded the following year

◀ **Forrest Gump**
The film won six Oscars and achieved box-office success.

Egyptian dishes
300,000 new satellite dishes are installed in Egypt every month, providing users with over 500 channels.

TOP 10 TV PROGRAMMES OF THE 2000s IN THE UK

	PROGRAMME / CHANNEL / DATE	AUDIENCE
1	Only Fools and Horses BBC One, 25 Dec 2001	21,344,000
2	EastEnders BBC One, 5 Apr 2001	20,047,000
3	Coronation Street ITV1, 24 Feb 2003	19,428,000
4	Britain's Got Talent ITV1, 30 May 2009	18,294,000
5	Wallace & Gromit: A Matter of Loaf and Death BBC One, 25 Dec 2008	16,152,000
6	Millionaire Tonight Special ITV1, 21 Apr 2003	16,103,000
7	Who Wants to be a Millionaire ITV1, 19 Jan 2000	15,875,000
8	The X Factor ITV1,13 Dec 2009	15,495,000
9	Heartbeat ITV1, 6 Feb 2000	15,159,000
10	I'm a Celebrity... Get Me Out of Here! ITV1, 9 Feb 2004	14,993,000

Source: BARB/Ratings Analyser for 2000 data and BARB/Infosys thereafter

TOP 10 TV COUNTRIES

	COUNTRY / TV HOUSEHOLDS*
1	China 384,288,600
2	USA 120,233,800
3	India 87,514,100
4	Indonesia 63,287,100
5	Brazil 54,853,200
6	Russia 51,323,500
7	Japan 50,578,900
8	Germany 39,326,500
9	Mexico 27,971,900
10	UK 27,409,500

* Households with colour TVs, 2010 forecast

Source: Euromonitor International

TOP 10 SATELLITE TV COUNTRIES

	COUNTRY	SATELLITE TV HOUSEHOLDS*
1	USA	40,281,100
2	Japan	20,730,500
3	Germany	16,750,100
4	Egypt	13,014,800
5	India	11,235,900
6	UK	10,330,100
7	Turkey	8,311,100
8	Italy	8,030,400
9	France	7,487,600
10	Algeria	5,642,200

* 2011 forecast

Source: Euromonitor International

TOP 10 **BBC iPLAYER RADIO PROGRAMMES, 2009***

	PROGRAMME / STATION	AUDIENCE
1	**Test Match Special** (21 Aug) 5 Live	183,300
2	**I'm Sorry I Haven't A Clue** (Series 51 Episode 1) Radio 4	167,000
3	**5 Live Sport: Premier League 2009–10** (14 Mar) 5 Live	162,700
4	**The Chris Moyles Show** (6 Jul) Radio 1	129,700
5	**Stephen Nolan** (7 Nov) 5 Live	115,800
6	**Jo Whiley** (18 Sep) Radio 1	90,700
7	**Fry's English Delight** (Series 2, Episode 1) Radio 4	86,800
8	**Classic Serial: The Complete Smiley** (Episode 1) Radio 4	82,200
9	**The News Quiz** Radio 4	80,700
10	**Desert Island Discs** (Morrissey, 29 Nov) Radio 4	79,900

* 1 January to 13 December

TOP 10 **LONGEST-RUNNING PROGRAMMES ON BRITISH TELEVISION**

	PROGRAMME	FIRST BROADCAST
1	Panorama	11 Nov 1953
2	What the Papers Say	5 Nov 1956
3	The Sky at Night	24 Apr 1957
4	Blue Peter	16 Oct 1958
5	Coronation Street	9 Dec 1960
6	Songs of Praise	1 Oct 1961
7	Horizon	2 May 1964
8	Match of the Day	22 Aug 1964
9	The Money Programme	5 Apr 1966
10	Gardeners' World	5 Jan 1968

Only programmes appearing every year since their first screenings are listed. *The Queen's Christmas Message* began broadcasting in sound only in 1952 and in vision from 1957, but as it was not broadcast in 1969 it has not had a continuous run. All those in the Top 10 are BBC programmes except *Coronation Street*. The first nine programmes pre-date the colour era.

TOP 10 **LONGEST-RUNNING PROGRAMMES ON BBC RADIO**

	PROGRAMME	FIRST BROADCAST
1	The Week's Good Cause	24 Jan 1926
2	The Shipping Forecast	26 Jan 1926
3	Choral Evensong	7 Oct 1926
4	Daily Service	2 Jan 1928*
5	The Week in Westminster	6 Nov 1929
6	Sunday Half Hour	14 Jul 1940
7	Desert Island Discs	29 Jan 1942
8	Saturday Night Theatre	3 Apr 1943
9	Composer of the Week#	2 Aug 1943
10	From Our Own Correspondent	4 Oct 1946

* Experimental broadcast; national transmission began December 1929
# Formerly *This Week's Composer*

8 THE COMMERCIAL WORLD

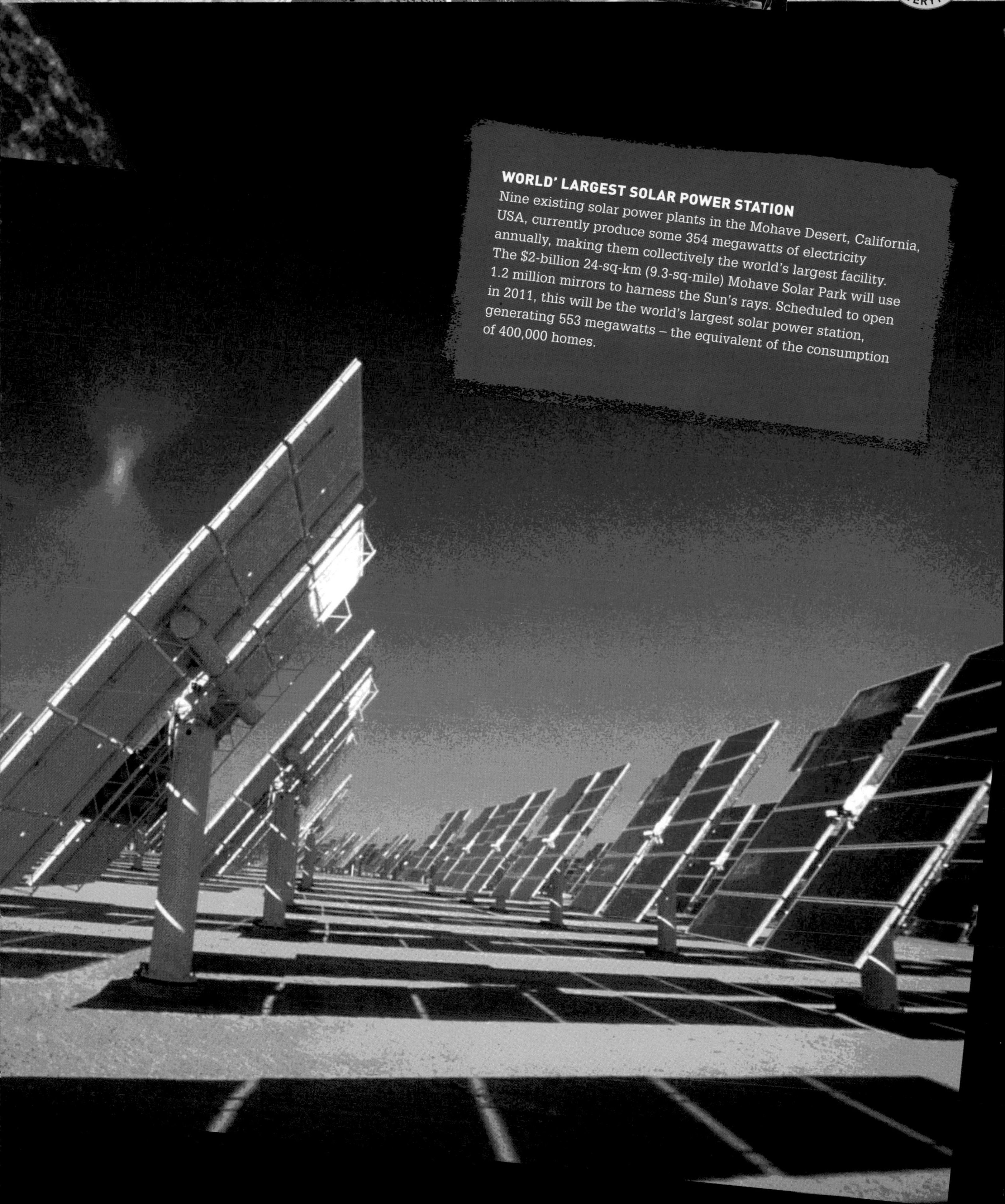

WORLD' LARGEST SOLAR POWER STATION

Nine existing solar power plants in the Mohave Desert, California, USA, currently produce some 354 megawatts of electricity annually, making them collectively the world's largest facility. The $2-billion 24-sq-km (9.3-sq-mile) Mohave Solar Park will use 1.2 million mirrors to harness the Sun's rays. Scheduled to open in 2011, this will be the world's largest solar power station, generating 553 megawatts – the equivalent of the consumption of 400,000 homes.

WORKERS OF THE WORLD

TOP 10 COMPANIES WITH THE MOST EMPLOYEES

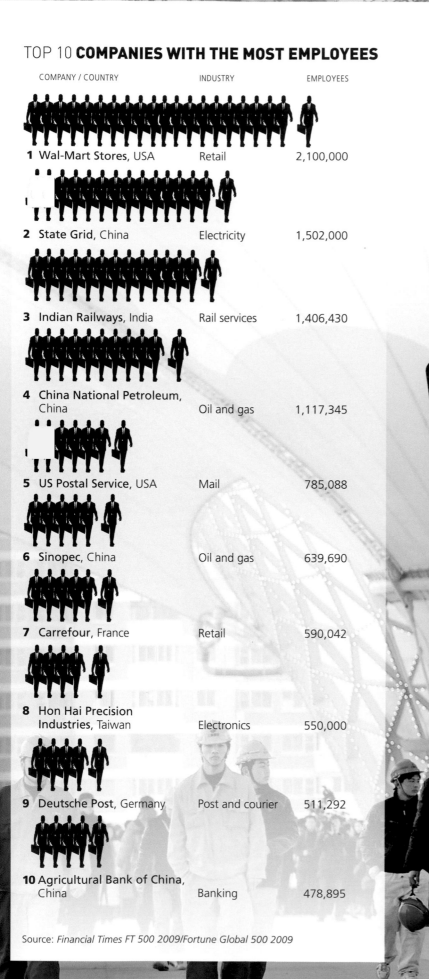

COMPANY / COUNTRY	INDUSTRY	EMPLOYEES
1 Wal-Mart Stores, USA	Retail	2,100,000
2 State Grid, China	Electricity	1,502,000
3 Indian Railways, India	Rail services	1,406,430
4 China National Petroleum, China	Oil and gas	1,117,345
5 US Postal Service, USA	Mail	785,088
6 Sinopec, China	Oil and gas	639,690
7 Carrefour, France	Retail	590,042
8 Hon Hai Precision Industries, Taiwan	Electronics	550,000
9 Deutsche Post, Germany	Post and courier	511,292
10 Agricultural Bank of China, China	Banking	478,895

Source: *Financial Times FT 500 2009/Fortune Global 500 2009*

TOP 10 BRITISH COMPANIES WITH THE MOST EMPLOYEES

COMPANY	EMPLOYEES (2008)
1 Compass Group	388,181
2 Tesco	364,015
3 HSBC Holdings	331,458
4 Royal Bank of Scotland	199,500
5 Royal Mail Holdings	162,310
6 Barclays	151,500
7 British Telecommunications	107,000
8 Anglo American	105,000
9 GlaxoSmithKline	99,003
10 J. Sainsbury	97,300

Source: *Fortune Global 500 2009*

This list includes only publicly quoted companies (companies whose shares are on the stock exchange), and is led by the Compass Group, a catering business that supplies food to many public institutions. As well as these, there are government and other organizations that are major employers – the National Health Service, for example, employs about 1.3 million people, making it the largest employer in Europe and the 5th in the world (after the Chinese Army, Indian Railways, WalMart and the US Department of Defense).

TOP 10 COUNTRIES WITH THE HIGHEST PROPORTION OF FEMALE WORKERS

	COUNTRY	LABOUR FORCE %*
1	Mozambique	53.4
2	= Burundi	51.4
	= Rwanda	51.4
4	Cambodia	50.7
5	Malawi	50.0
6	Tanzania	49.7
7	Kazakhstan	49.4
8	Mali	49.2
9	Belarus	49.1
10	Lithuania	49.0
	UK	*45.4*
	World average	*39.9*

* Aged 15–64 who are currently employed; unpaid groups are not included

Source: World Bank, *World Development Indicators 2008*

THE 10 COUNTRIES WITH THE HIGHEST UNEMPLOYMENT

	COUNTRY	ESTIMATED % LABOUR FORCE UNEMPLOYED*
1	Nauru	90.0
2	Liberia	85.0
3	Zimbabwe	80.0
4	Burkina Faso	77.0
5	Turkmenistan	60.0
6	Djibouti	59.0
7	Zambia	50.0
8	Senegal	48.0
9	Nepal	46.0
10	Lesotho	45.0
	UK	*5.5*
	World average	*30.0*

* 2008 or latest year for which data available

Source: CIA, *The World Factbook 2010*

▲ ***Liberia***
The Liberian Civil War (1989–96) severely damaged the country's economy, resulting in a high level of unemployment.

▼ ***Labour force***
Half the Top 10 largest world employers are based in China, with 4.3 million employees between them.

COMPANIES, RETAILERS, ADVERTISERS

TOP 10 **GLOBAL RETAILERS**

COMPANY / COUNTRY / ESTIMATED RETAIL SALES 2009 (US$)

1. Wal-Mart Stores Inc, USA
   397,858,300,000
2. Carrefour SA, France
   121,017,100,000
3. Tesco Plc, UK
   82,298,500,000
4. Seven & I Holdings Co. Ltd, Japan
   81,265,000,000
5. Kroger Co., USA
   66,112,500,000
6. Target Corp, USA
   65,178,700,000
7. Schwarz Beteiligungs GmbH, Germany
   64,467,200,000
8. Aldi Group, Germany
   61,953,500,000
9. Costco Wholesale Corp, USA
   60,711,700,000
10. Walgreen Co., USA
    59,870,300,000

Source: Euromonitor International

TOP 10 **MOST VALUABLE GLOBAL BRANDS**

	BRAND NAME*	INDUSTRY	BRAND VALUE 2009 (US$)
1	Coca-Cola	Beverages	68,734,000,000
2	IBM	Technology	60,211,000,000
3	Microsoft	Technology	56,647,000,000
4	General Electric	Diversified	47,777,000,000
5	Nokia (Finland)	Technology	34,864,000,000
6	McDonald's	Food retail	32,275,000,000
7	Google	Internet	31,980,000,000
8	Toyota (Japan)	Automotive	31,330,000,000
9	Intel	Technology	30,636,000,000
10	Disney	Leisure	28,000,000,000

* All US-owned unless otherwise stated

Source: Interbrand

Brand consultants Interbrand use a method of estimating value that takes account of the profitability of individual brands within a business (rather than the companies that own them), as well as such factors as their potential for growth.

TOP 10 **GLOBAL COMPANIES BY VALUE**

	COMPANY	COUNTRY	SECTOR	MARKET VALUE 2009 (US$)
1	Exxon Mobil	USA	Oil and gas	336,524,900,000
2	Petrochina	China	Oil and gas	287,185,200,000
3	Wal-Mart	USA	Retail	204,364,800,000
4	Industrial and Commercial Bank of China	China	Banking	187,885,400,000
5	China Mobile	China	Telecommunications	174,672,900,000
6	Microsoft	USA	Software	163,319,500,000
7	AT&T	USA	Telecommunications	148,511,300,000
8	Johnson & Johnson	USA	Health care	145,481,200,000
9	Royal Dutch Shell	UK	Oil and gas	138,999,200,000
10	Procter & Gamble	USA	Consumer goods	138,012,600,000

Source: *Financial Times Global 500 2009*

TOP 10 **COUNTRIES SPENDING THE MOST ON ADVERTISING**

	COUNTRY	TOTAL AD SPEND 2008 (US$)
1	USA	172,454,000,000
2	Japan	42,267,200,000
3	Germany	25,000,100,000
4	UK	23,231,200,000
5	China	20,074,800,000
6	France	17,453,100,000
7	Italy	13,020,300,000
8	Brazil	12,535,300,000
9	Russia	10,964,500,000
10	Spain	10,425,600,000
	Top 10 total	*347,426,100,000*
	World total	*495,336,700,000*

Source: Euromonitor International

▲ ***Global brand***
In the past 100 years, Coca-Cola has become the most widespread, recognizable and most highly valued brand in the world.

TOP 10 COUNTRIES WITH THE MOST SHOPS

	COUNTRY	RETAIL OUTLETS (2009)
1	India	13,873,854
2	China	4,817,367
3	Indonesia	2,799,231
4	Egypt	1,463,762
5	Brazil	1,266,198
6	Mexico	1,193,084
7	Thailand	1,190,518
8	Iran	1,115,144
9	USA	921,110
10	Philippines	875,313
	UK	*283,134*
	World total	*43,557,900*

Source: Euromonitor International

SALE

TOP 10 WORLD INTERNET RETAILERS

	COMPANY / COUNTRY	ESTIMATED RETAIL SALES 2009 (US$)*
1	Amazon.com Inc, USA	20,807,800,000
2	Apple Inc, USA	10,329,900,000
3	Dell Inc, USA	7,683,800,000
4	CVS Caremark Inc, USA	3,944,600,000
5	Tesco Plc, UK	3,454,800,000
6	Wal-Mart Stores Inc, USA	3,399,800,000
7	Otto GmbH & Co KG, Germany	3,350,300,000
8	Arcandor AG, Germany	2,624,000,000
9	PPR SA, France	2,617,700,000
10	Sears Holdings Corp, USA	2,371,800,000

* Retail value excluding sales taxes

Source: Euromonitor International

▼ ***Online store***
Founded in Seattle, Washington, USA, in 1994 as an online book shop, Amazon has expanded its product range and established itself as the leading global Internet retailer.

RESOURCES & RESERVES

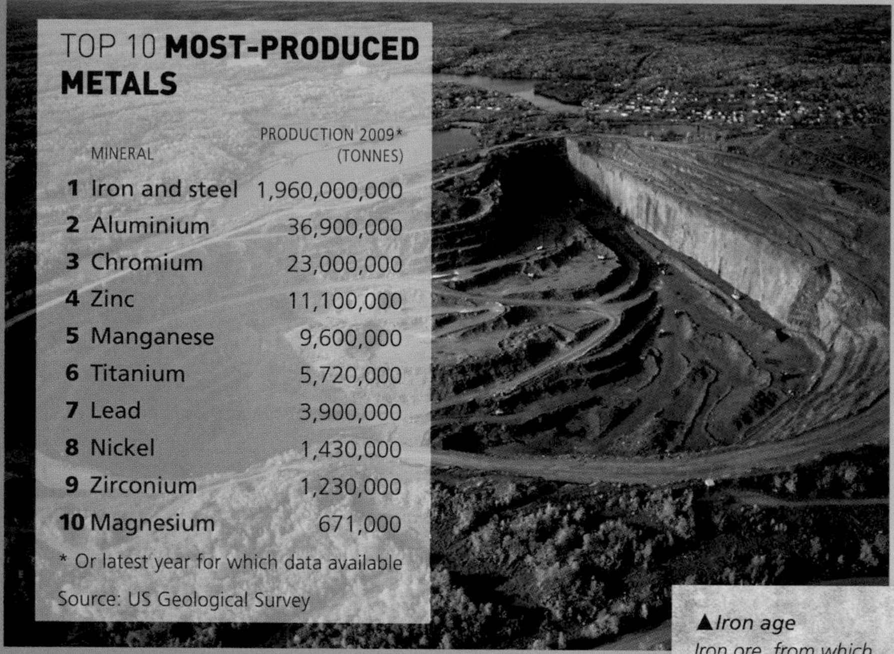

TOP 10 MOST-PRODUCED METALS

	MINERAL	PRODUCTION 2009* (TONNES)
1	Iron and steel	1,960,000,000
2	Aluminium	36,900,000
3	Chromium	23,000,000
4	Zinc	11,100,000
5	Manganese	9,600,000
6	Titanium	5,720,000
7	Lead	3,900,000
8	Nickel	1,430,000
9	Zirconium	1,230,000
10	Magnesium	671,000

* Or latest year for which data available

Source: US Geological Survey

▲*Iron age*
Iron ore, from which iron and steel are made, is the world's most-mined metallic element.

TOP 10 METALLIC ELEMENTS WITH THE GREATEST RESERVES

	ELEMENT	ESTIMATED GLOBAL RESERVES (TONNES)
1	Iron	110,000,000,000
2	Magnesium	20,000,000,000
3	Potassium	10,000,000,000
4	Aluminium	6,000,000,000
5	Manganese	3,600,000,000
6	Zirconium	>1,000,000,000
7	Chromium	1,000,000,000
8	Barium	450,000,000
9	Titanium	440,000,000
10	Copper	310,000,000

This list includes accessible reserves of commercially mined metallic elements, excluding calcium and sodium, which exist in such vast quantities that their reserves are considered 'unlimited' and unquantifiable. In contrast, there are relatively small amounts of certain precious metals: the world's silver reserves are put at 1,000,000 tonnes, mercury at 590,000 tonnes and gold at 15,000 tonnes, and there are even rarer metals, with global reserves of rhenium estimated at only 3,500 tonnes.

TOP 10 GOLD-PRODUCING COUNTRIES

	COUNTRY / PRODUCTION 2009 (TONNES)	
1	China	324.0
2	Australia	222.8
3	South Africa	219.8
4	USA	219.2
5	Russia	205.2
6	Peru	182.4
7	Indonesia	157.5
8	Canada	96.0
9	Ghana	90.3
10	Uzbekistan	74.5
	World total	2,571.8

Source: Gold Fields Mineral Services Ltd, *Gold Survey 2010*

South Africa's former place at the head of this list has declined since its 1993 production high of 619.5 tonnes. With gold hitting a record $1,212.50 per Troy ounce on 3 December 2009, the world's mine production for the year was valued at more than $100 billion.

TOP 10 SILVER PRODUCERS

	COUNTRY	2008 PRODUCTION (TONNES)
1	Peru	3,679
2	Mexico	3,241
3	China	2,557
4	Australia	1,925
5	Chile	1,397
6	Poland	1,210
7	Russia	1,123
8	USA	1,120
9	Bolivia	1,113
10	Canada	669
	World total	*21,178*

Source: The Silver Institute/GFMS, *World Silver Survey 2009*

◀ *Salt pan*
Salt for domestic and industrial use is produced worldwide by evaporation from seawater and by mining.

TOP 10 **SALT PRODUCERS**

	COUNTRY	PRODUCTION 2009 (TONNES)
1	China	60,000,000
2	USA	46,000,000
3	Germany	16,500,000
4	India	15,800,000
5	Canada	14,000,000
6	Australia	11,500,000
7	Mexico	8,800,000
8	Brazil	7,000,000
9	France	6,000,000
10	UK	5,800,000
	World	*260,000,000*

Source: US Geological Survey

TOP 10 **CEMENT PRODUCERS**

	COUNTRY	PRODUCTION 2009 (TONNES)
1	China	1,400,000,000
2	India	180,000,000
3	USA*	72,800,000
4	Japan	60,000,000
5	Russia	55,000,000
6	South Korea	53,000,000
7	Turkey	51,000,000
8	Mexico	45,000,000
9	Italy	43,000,000
10	Spain	42,000,000
	UK	*11,900,000*
	World	*2,800,000,000*

* Including Puerto Rico

Source: US Geological Survey

TOP 10 **RUBBER-PRODUCING COUNTRIES**

	COUNTRY	PRODUCTION 2008 (TONNES)
1	Thailand	3,193,213
2	Indonesia	2,921,872
3	Malaysia	1,072,400
4	India	819,000
5	Vietnam	659,600
6	China	565,000
7	Philippines	411,044
8	Côte d'Ivoire	188,532
9	Nigeria	143,000
10	Sri Lanka	129,240

World total 10,605,618

Source: Food and Agriculture Organization of the United Nations

Richest of All Time

THE 10 **RICHEST MEN OF ALL TIME***

NAME / DATES / PEAK WEALTH / AS % OF GDP / 2008 VALUE

* Based on peak wealth at death, or in case of Bill Gates, as at 5 April 1999; all US unless otherwise stated

1
John D. Rockefeller
(1839–1937)
$1,400,000,000
1.54%
$222,397,560,000

Rockefeller's rags-to-riches life, from humble childhood home to America's first billionaire, was based on his ownership of Standard Oil. 'As rich as Rockefeller' became a byword for vast wealth.

2
Cornelius Vanderbilt
(1794–1877)
$105,000,000
1.15%
$166,076,100,000

3
John Jacob Astor
(1763–1848)
$20,000,000
0.93%
$134,305,020,000

America's first multi-millionaire, Astor began amassing his fortune trading furs, later diversifying into land ownership in New York.

4
Bill Gates
(b. 1955)
$101,000,000,000
0.92%
$132,860,880,000

Microsoft co-founder Bill Gates's assets peaked at $101 billion in 1999. He has since become the world's most generous philanthropist.

6
Andrew Carnegie
(1835–1919)
$475,000,000
0.60%
$86,648,400,000

Scots-born Carnegie's wealth came from steel. He donated vast sums to educational institutions, libraries and other charitable projects.

7
Alexander Turney Stewart
(1803–76)
$50,000,000
0.56%
$80,871,840,000

Department stores and mail order to serve a burgeoning US market established the fortune of Irish-born entrepreneur Stewart.

8
Frederick Weyerhäuser
(1834–1914)
$200,000,000
0.55%
$79,427,700,000

German-born Weyerhäuser acquired forests and developed the world's largest logging business during the 19th-century construction boom.

9
Jay Gould
(1836–1892)
$77,000,000
0.54%
$77,983,560,000

The son of a farmer, Gould was a ruthless businessman who amassed a fortune speculating in the expansion of America's railroads.

RICHEST OF THE PAST

Estimating the wealth of often long-dead individuals is fraught with difficulty, not least because allowance has to be made for inflation and fluctuating currency values, as well as the secrecy surrounding their finances. One method is to compare the value of their assets at the peak in their lifetime as a percentage of US Gross Domestic Product at the time, with that in the latest available year ($1,441.4 billion in 2008).

Once America's richest man, Vanderbilt was a steamship and railroad owner who capitalized on the growth in US transport and trade.

WEALTHY RULERS

The hereditary rulers of many countries are often discounted from rich rankings, as their wealth is usually considered to be national and held in trust rather than personal assets, but King Bhumibol Adulyadej of Thailand is claimed to be the world's richest, with assets estimated at $30 billion.

5

Stephen Girard
(1750–1831)
$7,500,000
0.67%
$96,757,380,000

At the time of his death, French-born Philadelphia banker and philanthropist Girard was the wealthiest man in America.

10

Stephen Van Rensselaer
(1764–1839)
$10,000,000
0.52%
$75,095,280,000

One of America's biggest landowners, Van Rensselaer inherited a Dutch colonial estate of some million acres of New York State.

TODAY'S RICHEST MEN

Mexican telecoms magnate Carlos Slim Helu has recently become the world's richest man, a place long occupied by Bill Gates. He has moved into second place, with Warren Buffet in third, as both have contributed the largest ever charitable donations to the Bill & Melinda Gates Foundation.

NAME / COUNTRY / SOURCE / NET WORTH (US$)

Carlos Slim Helu, Mexico Communications	1	53,500,000,000
William H. Gates III, USA Microsoft (software)	2	53,000,000,000
Warren Edward Buffett, USA Berkshire Hathaway (investments)	3	47,000,000,000
Mukesh Ambani, India Reliance Industries (petrochemicals)	4	29,000,000,000
Lakshmi Mittal, India/UK Mittal Steel	5	28,700,000,000

Source: Forbes magazine, *The World's Billionaires 2010*

ENERGY

TOP 10 COUNTRIES WITH THE GREATEST OIL RESERVES

	COUNTRY	PROVED RESERVES (2008) TONNES	% OF WORLD TOTAL
1	Saudi Arabia	36,300,000,000	21.0
2	Iran	18,900,000,000	10.9
3	Iraq	15,500,000,000	9.1
4	Kuwait	14,000,000,000	8.1
5	Venezuela	13,600,000,000	7.9
6	United Arab Emirates	13,000,000,000	7.8
7	Russia	10,800,000,000	6.3
8	Libya	5,700,000,000	3/5
9	Kazakhstan	5,300,000,000	3.2
10	Nigeria	4,900,000,000	2.9
	UK	*500,000,000*	*0.3*
	World total	*170,800,000,000*	*100.00*

Source (all lists): *BP Statistical Review of World Energy 2009*

▲ *Leading the field*
World's leading oil producer Saudi Arabia supplies over 500 million tonnes of oil a year and holds one-fifth of the world's reserves.

TOP 10 COUNTRIES WITH THE GREATEST COAL RESERVES

	COUNTRY	PROVED RESERVES (2008) TONNES	% OF WORLD TOTAL
1	USA	238,308,000,000	28.9
2	Russia	157,010,000,000	19.0
3	China	114,500,000,000	13.9
4	Australia	76,200,000,000	9.2
5	India	58,600,000,000	7.1
6	Ukraine	33,873,000,000	4.1
7	Kazakhstan	31,300,000,000	3.8
8	South Africa	30,408,000,000	3.7
9	Poland	7,502,000,000	0.9
10	Brazil	7,059,000,000	0.9
	UK	*155,000,000*	*0.02*
	World total	*826,001,000,000*	*100.0*

Coal reserves are estimates based on current engineering and economic conditions. Over time these may change, as technological advances and world demand make it feasible and viable to extract previously unexploited seams.

TOP 10 COUNTRIES WITH THE GREATEST NATURAL-GAS RESERVES

		PROVED RESERVES (2008)		
	COUNTRY	TRILLION CU M	TRILLION CU FT	% OF WORLD TOTAL
1	Russia	43.30	1,529.2	23.4
2	Iran	29.61	1,045.7	16.0
3	Qatar	25.46	899.3	13.8
4	Turkmenistan	7.94	280.6	4.3
5	Saudi Arabia	7.57	267.3	4.1
6	USA	6.73	237.7	3.6
7	United Arab Emirates	6.43	227.1	3.5
8	Nigeria	5.22	184.2	2.8
9	Venezuela	4.84	170.9	2.6
10	Algeria	4.50	159.1	2.4
	UK	*0.34*	*12.1*	*0.2*
	World total	*185.0*	*6,534.0*	*100.0*

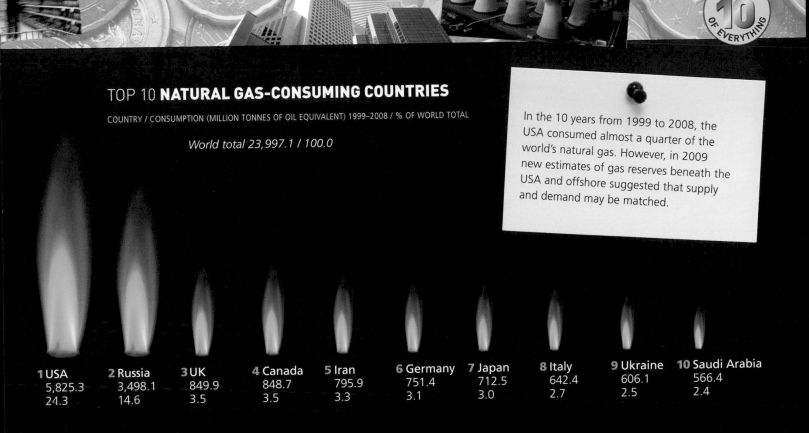

TOP 10 **NATURAL GAS-CONSUMING COUNTRIES**

COUNTRY / CONSUMPTION (MILLION TONNES OF OIL EQUIVALENT) 1999–2008 / % OF WORLD TOTAL

World total 23,997.1 / 100.0

In the 10 years from 1999 to 2008, the USA consumed almost a quarter of the world's natural gas. However, in 2009 new estimates of gas reserves beneath the USA and offshore suggested that supply and demand may be matched.

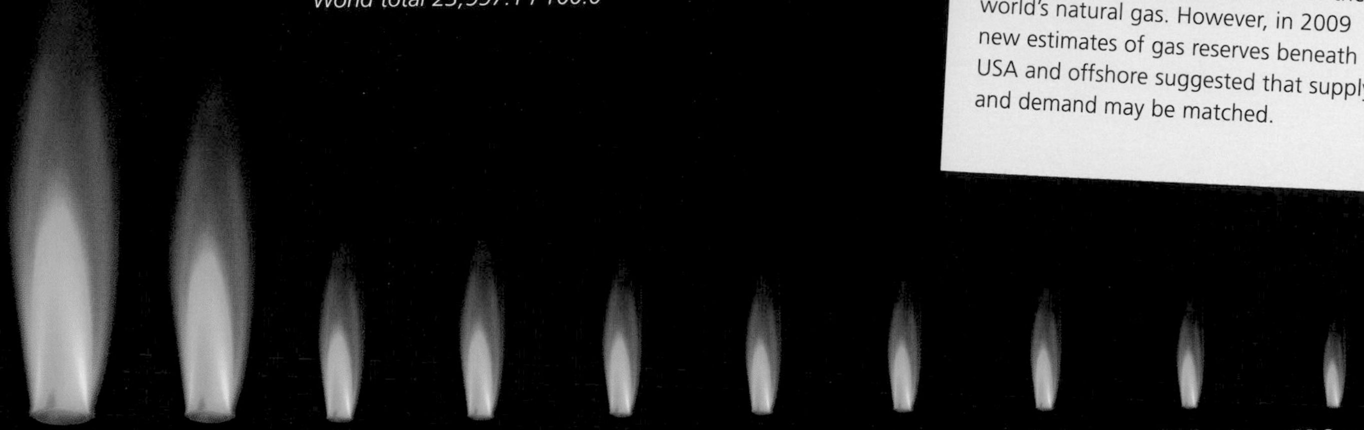

1 USA
5,825.3
24.3

2 Russia
3,498.1
14.6

3 UK
849.9
3.5

4 Canada
848.7
3.5

5 Iran
795.9
3.3

6 Germany
751.4
3.1

7 Japan
712.5
3.0

8 Italy
642.4
2.7

9 Ukraine
606.1
2.5

10 Saudi Arabia
566.4
2.4

TOP 10 **OIL-CONSUMING COUNTRIES**

COUNTRY / CONSUMPTION (MILLION TONNES OF OIL EQUIVALENT) 1999–2008 / % OF WORLD TOTAL

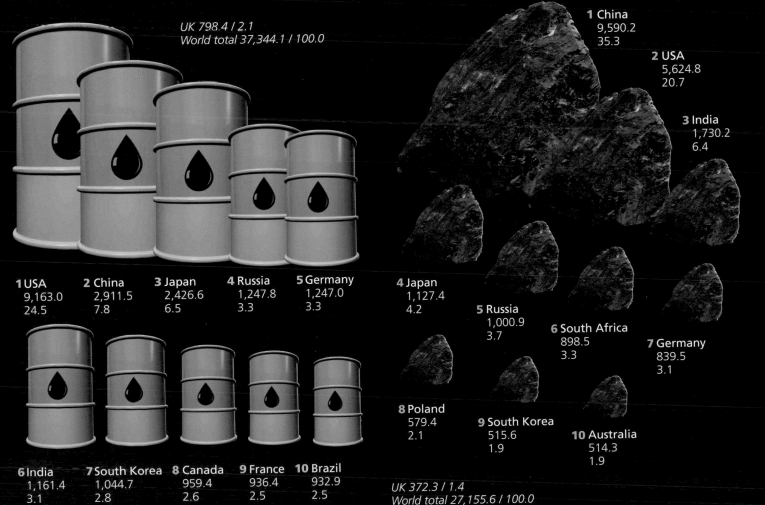

UK 798.4 / 2.1
World total 37,344.1 / 100.0

1 USA
9,163.0
24.5

2 China
2,911.5
7.8

3 Japan
2,426.6
6.5

4 Russia
1,247.8
3.3

5 Germany
1,247.0
3.3

6 India
1,161.4
3.1

7 South Korea
1,044.7
2.8

8 Canada
959.4
2.6

9 France
936.4
2.5

10 Brazil
932.9
2.5

TOP 10 **COAL-CONSUMING COUNTRIES**

COUNTRY / CONSUMPTION (MILLION TONNES OF OIL EQUIVALENT) 1999–2008 / % OF WORLD TOTAL

1 China
9,590.2
35.3

2 USA
5,624.8
20.7

3 India
1,730.2
6.4

4 Japan
1,127.4
4.2

5 Russia
1,000.9
3.7

6 South Africa
898.5
3.3

7 Germany
839.5
3.1

8 Poland
579.4
2.1

9 South Korea
515.6
1.9

10 Australia
514.3
1.9

UK 372.3 / 1.4
World total 27,155.6 / 100.0

THE 10 **WORST ENVIRONMENTAL PERFORMANCE INDEX COUNTRIES**

	COUNTRY	EPI SCORE*
1	Sierra Leone	32.1
2	Central African Republic	33.3
3	Mauritania	33.7
4	Angola	36.3
5	Togo	36.4
6	Niger	37.6
7	Turkmenistan	38.4
8	Mali	39.4
9	Haiti	39.5
10	Benin	39.6

* Environmental Performance Index score out of 100

Source: Environmental Performance Index 2010

TOP 10 **CARBON DIOXIDE-EMITTING COUNTRIES (PER CAPITA)**

	COUNTRY	% CHANGE 1990–2007	CO_2 EMISSIONS PER CAPITA 2007 (TONNES)
1	Qatar	+87.3	58.01
2	United Arab Emirates	+2.8	29.91
3	Bahrain	+19.0	28.23
4	Kuwait	+119.0	25.09
5	Luxembourg	-18.4	22.35
6	Trinidad and Tobago	+135.2	21.85
7	USA	-1.8	19.10
8	Australia	+23.9	18.75
9	Canada	+11.3	17.37
10	Saudi Arabia	+50.1	14.79
	UK	*-10.9*	*8.60*
	World average	*+9.8*	*4.38*

Source: International Energy Agency, CO_2 Emissions from Fuel Consumption, 2009

▲ *Environmental disaster*
The Environmental Performance Index places Sierra Leone in unenviable worst place.

TOP 10 **RUBBISH PRODUCERS***

DOMESTIC WASTE PER CAPITA 2006#

1 = Ireland 800 KG 1,764 LB
= Norway 800 KG 1,764 LB

3 USA 760 KG 1,676 LB

4 Denmark 740 KG 1,631 LB

5 Switzerland 700 KG 1,543 LB

6 Australia 689 KG 1,518 LB

7 Luxembourg 680 KG 1,499 LB

8 Netherlands 625 KG 1,379 LB

9 Spain 600 KG 1,323 LB

10 = Austria 585 KG 1,290 LB
= UK 585 KG 1,290 LB

* OECD countries only
\# Or latest year for which data available

Source: Organisation for Economic Co-operation and Development

TOP 10 **ENVIRONMENTAL PERFORMANCE INDEX COUNTRIES**

	COUNTRY	EPI SCORE*
1	Iceland	93.5
2	Switzerland	89.1
3	Costa Rica	86.4
4	Sweden	86.0
5	Norway	81.1
6	Mauritius	80.6
7	France	78.2
8	= Austria	78.1
	= Cuba	78.1
10	Colombia	76.8
	UK	*74.2*

* Environmental Performance Index score out of 100

Source: Environmental Performance Index 2010

The Environmental Performance Index (formerly Environmental Sustainability Index) is a measure of environmental health and ecosystem vitality based on an assessment of 16 indicators in each country. These include air quality, water resources, biodiversity and habitat, productive natural resources and sustainable energy.

▲ ***High performance***
Switzerland was ironically relegated from its former No. 1 EPI ranking by Iceland just prior to the environmental impact of the eruption of the latter's Eyjafjallajökull volcano.

TOP 10 **ENVIRONMENTAL QUALITY CITIES IN THE UK***

	CITY	AIR QUALITY	BIODIVERSITY	WASTE COLLECTED PER CAPITA	ECOLOGICAL FOOTPRINT	TOTAL
1	Newcastle	14	20	9	13	56
2	Nottingham	5	18	17	12	52
3	= Bradford	19	4	12	16	51
	= Leicester	2	13	18	18	51
5	= Birmingham	4	17	8	20	49
	= Coventry	8	16	10	15	49
7	Sheffield	17	11.5	11	8.5	48
8	= Glasgow	16	19	4	7	46
	= Leeds	13	15	13	5	46
10	Bristol	10	11.5	20	4	45.5

* Based on an annual survey of Britain's 20 largest cities

Source: Forum for the Future, Sustainable Cities Index

THE 10 FIRST CITIES AND COUNTRIES TO ISSUE POSTAGE STAMPS

	CITY/COUNTRY	STAMPS ISSUED
1	Great Britain	1 May 1840
2	New York City, USA	1 Feb 1842
3	Zurich, Switzerland	1 Mar 1843
4	Brazil	1 Aug 1843
5	Geneva, Switzerland	30 Sep 1843
6	Basle, Switzerland	1 Jul 1845
7	USA	1 Jul 1847
8	Mauritius	21 Sep 1847
9	Bermuda	1848
10	France	1 Jan 1849

THE 10 FIRST COUNTRIES TO SEND PICTURE POSTCARDS

	COUNTRY	EARLIEST KNOWN CARD
1	Germany	4 Jul 1883
2	Belgium	23 Nov 1887
3	Switzerland	9 Aug 1888
4	France	24 Aug 1889
5	Italy	15 Mar 1888
6	Norway	11 Aug 1890
7	Hawaii	15 Dec 1890
8	Netherlands	23 Jul 1891
9	Sweden	30 Sep 1891
10	Egypt	28 Dec 1891
	UK	19 Dec 1894

TOP 10 COUNTRIES SENDING AND RECEIVING THE MOST LETTERS

	COUNTRY	ITEMS OF MAIL HANDLED (2007)
1	USA	200,311,000,000
2	Japan	21,994,621,000
3	Germany	20,857,000,000
4	UK	19,903,000,000
5	France	17,202,000,000
6	Brazil	8,538,594,199
7	China	6,904,013,451
8	Italy	6,270,201,242
9	India	5,901,300,000
10	Spain	5,406,100,000
	Top 10 total	*313,287,829,892*
	World total	*433,344,087,517*

Source: Universal Postal Union

▲ ***Post by punt***
As some homes lack road access, mail is delivered by water in Luebbenau, Germany.

TOP 10 **COUNTRIES WITH THE MOST TELEPHONES**

	COUNTRY	SUBSCRIBERS PER 100	TOTAL (2007)
1	China	68.71	912,943,000
2	USA	136.86	418,566,000
3	India	23.36	273,033,000
4	Russia	145.62	207,500,000
5	Brazil	83.62	160,379,700
6	Japan	123.92	158,571,000
7	Germany	182.69	150,901,000
8	UK	173.90	105,674,600
9	Italy	181.39	105,461,300
10	Indonesia	43.03	99,662,500
	Top 10	–	*2,682,850,700*
	World	*68.89*	*4,600,578,600*

Source: International Telecommunication Union

▲ ***Remote access***
Mobile phones have revolutionized the lives of lives of rural dwellers, such as these Mongolian herdsmen.

TOP 10 **MOBILE-PHONE COUNTRIES**

	COUNTRY	% OF POPULATION	TOTAL SUBSCRIBERS (2010*)
1	China	57.36	765,970,000
2	India	47.91	563,794,992
3	USA	89.66	276,610,580
4	Russia	146.79	208,330,000
5	Brazil	92.28	176,700,000
6	Indonesia	60.60	140,200,000
7	Japan	84.29	107,490,000
8	Germany	130.68	107,000,000
9	Pakistan	57.91	97,579,940
10	Italy	147.41	88,580,000
	UK	*122.95*	*75,750,000*

* Or latest year for which data available

The anomaly of countries with more mobile phones than people is partly explained by the fact that many people open up new accounts without cancelling their old one, or have two phones, for work and private use.

TOP 10 **iPHONE APPS**

	PAID	FREE	TOP-GROSSING
1	Crash Bandicoot Nitro Kart 3D	Facebook	TomTom UK & Ireland
2	Moto Chaser	iPint	Call of Duty: World at War: Zombies
3	Virtual Pool Online	Google Earth	TomTom Western Europe
4	Cro-Mag Rally	Pac-Man Lite	Where's Wally? The Fantastic Journey
5	Flick Fishing	Touch Hockey: FS5	Need for Speed Shift
6	Koi Pond	Labyrinth Lite Edition	The Sims 3
7	Monopoly Here & Now: The World Edition	Lightsaber Unleashed	Who Wants to Be a Millionaire?
8	Super Monkey Ball	Tap Tap Revenge	The Simpsons Arcade
9	Pocket Guitar	Flashlight	CoPilot Live UK & Ireland
10	iCopter	Shazam	Bejeweled 2

TOP 10 **BROADBAND COUNTRIES**

	COUNTRY	BROADBAND SUBSCRIBERS (2009)
1	China	103,641,000
2	USA	85,287,100
3	Japan	31,428,500
4	Germany	25,103,450
5	France	19,028,200
6	UK	18,356,000
7	South Korea	16,334,969
8	Italy	13,232,890
9	Brazil	11,006,400
10	Russia	10,870,000
	World total	*466,952,606*

Source: Point Topic, *World Broadband Statistics*

TOP 10 **INTERNET COUNTRIES**

	COUNTRY	% OF POPULATION	% OF WORLD TOTAL	INTERNET USERS (2009)
1	China	26.9	20.8	360,000,000
2	USA	74.1	13.1	227,719,000
3	Japan	75.5	5.5	95,979,000
4	India	7.0	4.7	81,000,000
5	Brazil	34.0	3.9	67,510,400
6	Germany	65.9	3.1	54,229,325
7	UK	76.4	2.7	46,683,900
8	Russia	32.3	2.6	45,250,000
9	France	69.3	2.5	43,100,134
10	South Korea	77.3	2.2	37,475,800
	World total	*25.6*	*100.0*	*1,733,993,741*

Source: Internet World Stats

TOP 10 **MOST-VISITED WEBSITES***

1 Google – google.com
2 Facebook – facebook.com
3 YouTube – youtube.com
4 Yahoo! – yahoo.com
5 Windows Live – live.com
6 Wikipedia – wikipedia.org
7 Blogger.com
8 Baidu.com
9 Microsoft Network (MSN) – msn.com
10 Yahoo! Japan – yahoo.co.jp

* Based on Alexa traffic rankings

▲ *Café society*
Social networking has been a major cultural development of the 21st century.

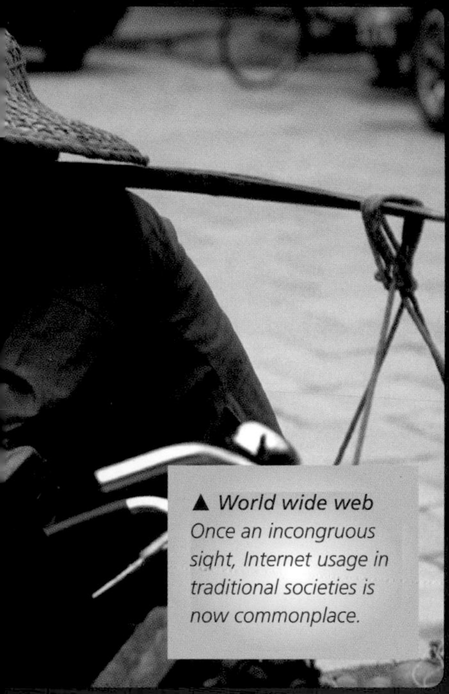

▲ ***World wide web***
Once an incongruous sight, Internet usage in traditional societies is now commonplace.

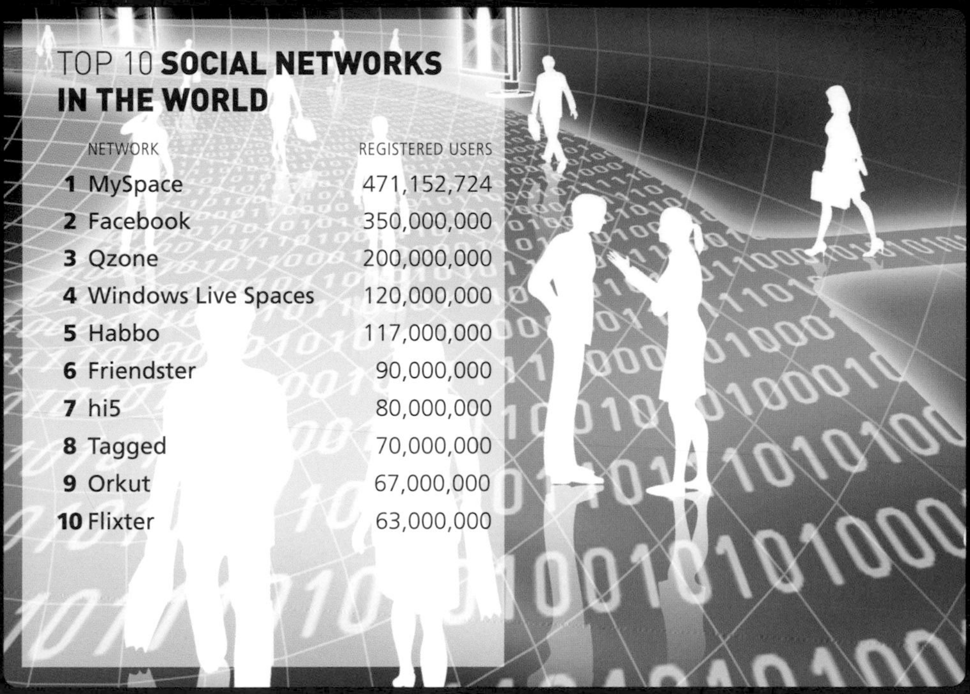

TOP 10 **SOCIAL NETWORKS IN THE WORLD**

	NETWORK	REGISTERED USERS
1	MySpace	471,152,724
2	Facebook	350,000,000
3	Qzone	200,000,000
4	Windows Live Spaces	120,000,000
5	Habbo	117,000,000
6	Friendster	90,000,000
7	hi5	80,000,000
8	Tagged	70,000,000
9	Orkut	67,000,000
10	Flixter	63,000,000

▲ ***Dominant domain***
Google.com has become acknowledged as the world's foremost Internet search engine.

TOP 10 **MOST-FOLLOWED PEOPLE ON TWITTER**

	NAME / SCREEN NAME	FOLLOWERS*
1	Ashton Kutcher (aplusk)	4,778,407
2	Britney Spears (britneyspears)	4,738,817
3	Ellen DeGeneres (TheEllenShow)	4,506,024
4	Barack Obama (BarackObama)	3,699,530
5	Lady Gaga (ladygaga)	3,653,680
6	Oprah Winfrey (Oprah)	3,413,294
7	Kim Kardashian (KimKardashian)	3,397,769
8	John Mayer (johncmayer)	3,218,360
9	Twitter (twitter)	3,110,426
10	Ryan Seacrest (RyanSeacrest)	3,087,883

* As at 19 April 2010

Source: twitterholic.com

▲ ***Ashton Kutcher***
In 2009 Kutcher won the race to be the first Twitter user with over one million followers.

WORLD TOURISM

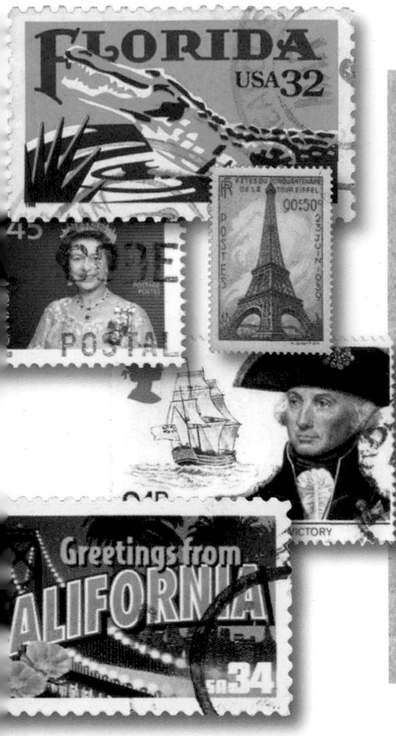

TOP 10 **WORLD TOURIST ATTRACTIONS**

	TOURIST ATTRACTION	LOCATION	COUNTRY	ESTIMATED ANNUAL VISITORS
1	Times Square	New York City	USA	35,000,000
2	National Mall and Memorial Parks	Washington, DC	USA	25,000,000
3	Magic Kingdom	Lake Buena Vista, Orlando	USA	16,600,000
4	Trafalgar Square	London	UK	15,000,000
5	Disneyland Park	Anaheim, California	USA	14,700,000
6	Niagara Falls	Ontario/New York	Canada/USA	14,000,000
7	Fisherman's Wharf & Golden Gate	San Francisco, California	USA	13,000,000
8	Tokyo Disneyland & Tokyo DisneySea	Urayasu	Japan	12,900,000
9	Notre Dame de Paris	Paris	France	12,000,000
10	Disneyland Paris	Paris	France	10,600,000

Source: *Forbes Traveler*, 2008

TOP 10 **COUNTRIES SPENDING THE MOST ON TOURISM**

	COUNTRY	TOURISM SPENDING PER CAPITA 2008 (£)
1	Austria	2,848.30
2	Sweden	2,017.50
3	Finland	1,633.70
4	Australia	1,513.20
5	USA	1,362.00
6	Singapore	1,354.40
7	France	1,310.40
8	Norway	1,306.10
9	Greece	1,293.80
10	Denmark	1,189.00
	UK	*644.00*
	World average	*212.20*

Source: Euromonitor International

TOP 10 **TOURIST DESTINATIONS**

	COUNTRY	INTERNATIONAL VISITORS (2008)
1	France	79,300,000
2	USA	58,030,000
3	Spain	57,316,000
4	China	53,049,000
5	Italy	42,734,000
6	UK	30,182,000
7	Ukraine	25,392,000
8	Turkey	24,994,000
9	Germany	24,886,000
10	Mexico	22,637,000
	Top 10 total	*418,520,000*
	World total	*922,000,000*

▼ *Sign of the Times*
Named after the New York Times that was once based there, Times Square has become the world's most visited tourist location.

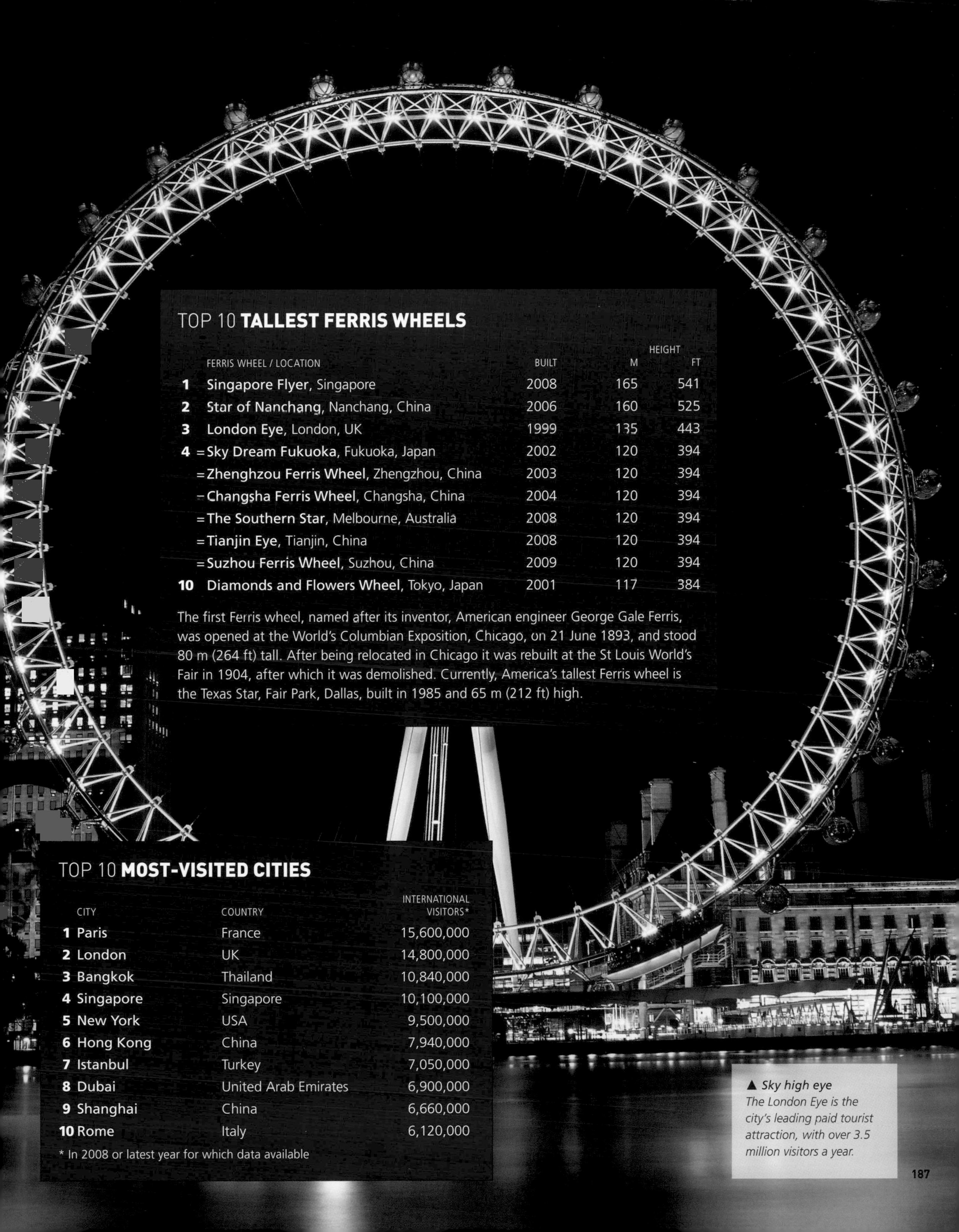

TOP 10 **TALLEST FERRIS WHEELS**

	FERRIS WHEEL / LOCATION	BUILT	HEIGHT M	HEIGHT FT
1	**Singapore Flyer**, Singapore	2008	165	541
2	**Star of Nanchang**, Nanchang, China	2006	160	525
3	**London Eye**, London, UK	1999	135	443
4	=**Sky Dream Fukuoka**, Fukuoka, Japan	2002	120	394
	=**Zhenghzou Ferris Wheel**, Zhengzhou, China	2003	120	394
	=**Changsha Ferris Wheel**, Changsha, China	2004	120	394
	=**The Southern Star**, Melbourne, Australia	2008	120	394
	=**Tianjin Eye**, Tianjin, China	2008	120	394
	=**Suzhou Ferris Wheel**, Suzhou, China	2009	120	394
10	**Diamonds and Flowers Wheel**, Tokyo, Japan	2001	117	384

The first Ferris wheel, named after its inventor, American engineer George Gale Ferris, was opened at the World's Columbian Exposition, Chicago, on 21 June 1893, and stood 80 m (264 ft) tall. After being relocated in Chicago it was rebuilt at the St Louis World's Fair in 1904, after which it was demolished. Currently, America's tallest Ferris wheel is the Texas Star, Fair Park, Dallas, built in 1985 and 65 m (212 ft) high.

TOP 10 **MOST-VISITED CITIES**

	CITY	COUNTRY	INTERNATIONAL VISITORS*
1	**Paris**	France	15,600,000
2	**London**	UK	14,800,000
3	**Bangkok**	Thailand	10,840,000
4	**Singapore**	Singapore	10,100,000
5	**New York**	USA	9,500,000
6	**Hong Kong**	China	7,940,000
7	**Istanbul**	Turkey	7,050,000
8	**Dubai**	United Arab Emirates	6,900,000
9	**Shanghai**	China	6,660,000
10	**Rome**	Italy	6,120,000

* In 2008 or latest year for which data available

▲ ***Sky high eye***
The London Eye is the city's leading paid tourist attraction, with over 3.5 million visitors a year.

9

ON THE MOVE

BERLIN-BRANDENBURG INTERNATIONAL AIRPORT
German capital Berlin's new international airport replaces three – Tempelhof, Tegel and Schönefeld – which have outgrown their capacity. The airport will be able to handle up to 45 million passengers and 600,000 tonnes of airfreight a year. Built with concern for minimizing environmental damage and noise pollution, the airport's construction has involved relocating the entire population of a village on the site, and the building of an autobahn and a six-track underground railway, providing a 20-minute link to the city centre.

LAND TRANSPORT

TOP 10 BESTSELLING CARS OF ALL TIME

	MANUFACTURER/MODEL	YEARS IN PRODUCTION	APPROX. SALES*
1	Toyota Corolla	1966–	37,000,000
2	Volkswagen Golf	1974–	26,000,000
3	Volkswagen Beetle	1937–2003#	21,529,464
4	Ford Escort/Orion	1968–2003	20,000,000
5	Ford Model T	1908–27	16,536,075
6	Honda Civic	1972–	16,500,000
7	Nissan Sunny/Sentra/Pulsar	1966–	16,000,000
8	Volkswagen Passat	1973–	15,000,000
9	Lada Riva	1980–†	13,500,000
10	Chevrolet Impala/Caprice	1958–	13,000,000

* To 2009 unless otherwise indicated
\# Produced in Mexico 1978–2003
† Still manufactured in Ukraine and Egypt

[car symbol] = 1,000,000 cars

THE 10 COUNTRIES WITH MOST PEOPLE PER CAR

	COUNTRY	CARS	PEOPLE PER CAR (2007)
1	Myanmar	8,200	5,777.3
2	Bangladesh	37,750	4,027.4
3	Central African Republic	1,950	2,244.6
4	Tanzania	23,000	1,712.3
5	Mali	9,500	1,262.6
6	Afghanistan	29,000	1,099.7
7	Ethiopia	73,100	1,093.5
8	Malawi	12,650	1,075.3
9	Sudan	39,500	996.9
10	Côte d'Ivoire	21,500	918.5
	UK	*31,225,329*	*1.9*
	World average	*645,286,033*	*9.9*

Source: *Ward's Motor Vehicle Facts & Figures 2009*

TOP 10 COUNTRIES WITH THE LONGEST ROAD NETWORKS

	COUNTRY	TOTAL ROAD NETWORK KM	MILES
1	USA	6,465,799	4,017,661
2	India	3,316,452	2,060,747
3	China	1,930,544	1,199,584
4	Brazil	1,751,868	1,088,560
5	Japan	1,196,999	743,781
6	Canada	1,042,300	647,655
7	France	951,500	591,235
8	Russia	933,000	579,739
9	Australia	812,972	505,157
10	Spain	681,224	423,293
	UK	*398,366*	*247,533*
	World total	*31,320,688*	*19,461,770*

Source: CIA, *The World Factbook 2010*

The CIA's assessment of road lengths includes both paved (mostly tarmac-surfaced) and unpaved highways (gravel and earth-surfaced).

▼ *Taking the crown*
Although the Toyota Corolla (from the Latin for 'small crown') has undergone a series of design changes since its launch in October 1966, the model is the world's bestselling.

◀ *First railway*
The inaugural run of the Stockton & Darlington Railway in 1825.

TOP 10 **FASTEST RAIL JOURNEYS**

	JOURNEY*	TRAIN	DISTANCE KM	DISTANCE MILES	SPEED KM/H	SPEED MPH
1	LORRAINE–CHAMPAGNE, FRANCE	TGV 5422	167.6	104.1	279.3	173.6
2	OKAYAMA–HIROSHIMA, JAPAN	NOZOMI 1	144.9	90.0	255.7	158.9
3	TAICHUNG–ZUOYING, TAIWAN	7 TRAINS	179.5	111.5	244.7	152.0
4	BRUSSELS, BELGIUM–VALENCE, FRANCE	THALYS SOLEIL	831.7	516.8	244.6	152.0
5	FRANKFURT–SIEGBURG/BONN, GERMANY	ICE 10	143.3	89.04	232.4	144.4
6	MADRID–ZARAGOZA, SPAIN	7 AVE TRAINS	307.2	190.9	227.6	141.4
7	SHENYANG–QINHUANGDAO, CHINA	D24 & D28	404.0	251.0	197.1	122.5
8	SEOUL–SEODAEJEON, SOUTH KOREA	KTX 410 & 411	161.0	100.0	193.2	120.0
9	LONDON–YORK, UK	1 IC255	303.2	188.4	173.3	107.7
10	ALVESTA–HÄSSLEHOLM, SWEDEN	X2000 543	98.0	60.9	172.9	107.4

* Fastest journey for each country; all those in the Top 10 have other equally or similarly fast services

Source: Railway Gazette International, *2007 World Speed Survey*

THE 10 **FIRST COUNTRIES WITH RAILWAYS**

	COUNTRY	FIRST RAILWAY ESTABLISHED
1	UK	27 Sep 1825
2	France	7 Nov 1829
3	USA	24 May 1830
4	Ireland	17 Dec 1834
5	Belgium	5 May 1835
6	Germany	7 Dec 1835
7	Canada	21 Jul 1836
8	Russia	30 Oct 1837
9	Austria	6 Jan 1838
10	Netherlands	24 Sep 1839

Although some offered limited services, these dates mark the beginning of each country's steam railway system. By 1850, railways had also begun operating in other countries, including Italy (1839), Hungary (1846), Denmark (1847) and Spain (1848).

▼ *Rail records*
France's TGV (Train à Grande Vitesse) holds the record for the fastest scheduled service and fastest train, with 574.8 km/h (357.2 mph) in a test run.

Land Speed

► *ThrustSSC*
Set in 1997, RAF pilot Andy Green's Land Speed Record remains unbroken.

▼ *Green Monster*
Art Arfons set three Land Speed Records in 1964–65 in his jet-propelled car.

► *Blue Flame*
Gary Gabelich's rocket-powered car broke the record in 1970.

THE 10 **LATEST HOLDERS OF THE LAND SPEED RECORD**

		SPEED	
DRIVER / COUNTRY / CAR	DATE	KM/H	MPH
1 Andy Green (UK), ThrustSSC*	15 Oct 1997	1,227.99	763.04
2 Richard Noble (UK), Thrust2*	4 Oct 1983	1,013.47	633.47
3 Gary Gabelich (USA), The Blue Flame	23 Oct 1970	995.85	622.41
4 Craig Breedlove (USA), Spirit of America – Sonic 1	15 Nov 1965	960.96	600.60
5 Art Arfons (USA), Green Monster	7 Nov 1965	922.48	576.55
6 Craig Breedlove (USA), Spirit of America – Sonic 1	2 Nov 1965	888.76	555.48
7 Art Arfons (USA), Green Monster	27 Oct 1964	858.73	536.71
8 Craig Breedlove (USA), Spirit of America	15 Oct 1964	842.04	526.28
9 Craig Breedlove (USA), Spirit of America	13 Oct 1964	749.95	468.72
10 Art Arfons (USA), Green Monster	5 Oct 1964	694.43	434.02

* Location, Black Rock Desert, Nevada, USA; all other speeds were achieved at Bonneville Salt Flats, Utah, USA; speed averaged over a measured mile in two directions

RACING ON ICE

In 1904, Henry Ford, the founder of the Ford Motor Company, set a new Land Speed Record – but not on land: he drove his Ford Arrow 999 across the frozen surface of Lake St Clair, Michigan, on 12 January 1904 at a speed of 147.68 km/h (91.37 mph). It was the first Land Speed Record set outside Europe, but was not recognized by the Automobile Club de France, the then record-governing body.

▼ *Record run*
ThrustSSC breaks the sound barrier as it sets the world record.

THE FIRST HOLDERS OF THE LAND SPEED RECORD

The official Land Speed Record was set and broken five times within a year. The first six holders were rival racers Comte Gaston de Chasseloup-Laubat (France) and Camille Jenatzy (Belgium). The trial, held under the aegis of the Automobile Club de France over a 2-km (1.2-mile) course at Achères, near Paris, was open to any vehicle, but both the *Jeantaud* and the *Jenatzy* (nicknamed *La Jamais Contente* – 'Never Satisfied') were electrically powered. Leon Serpollet, the first driver to beat them, drove a steam-powered car. American millionaire William Vanderbilt was the first to hold the record driving a petrol-engined vehicle.

▲ ***Never content***
Camille Jenatzy (1868–1913) held the Land Speed Record three times in 1899 in La Jamais Contente.

DIED TRYING

J. G. Parry-Thomas (Land Speed Record in 1926), was killed in 1927, while record-holders Henry Segrave (1927), John Cobb (1938–47) and Donald Campbell (1964) all died in later attempts on the Water Speed Record.

BREAKING THE BARRIERS

In the history of the Land Speed Record several drivers have not only set new marks but also broken through 'milestone' speeds – the escalation from 600 to 700 mph the longest at 34 years.

FIRST OVER
DRIVER / COUNTRY
LOCATION
DATE
SPEED (KM/H / MPH)

100 mph (161 km/h)
Louis Rigolly (France)
Ostend, Belgium
13 Nov 1904
175.31 / 103.55

200 mph (322 km/h)
Henry Segrave (UK)
Daytona Bach, USA
22 Apr 1927
327.97 / 203.79

300 mph (483 km/h)
Malcolm Campbell (UK)
Bonneville Salt Flats, USA
3 Sep 1935
484.62 / 301.13

400 mph (644 km/h)
Craig Breedlove (USA)
Bonneville Salt Flats, USA
5 Sep 1963
655.72 / 407.45

500 mph (805 km/h)
Art Arfons (USA)
Bonneville Salt Flats, USA
27 Oct 1964
863.79 / 536.71

600 mph (918 km/h)
Craig Breedlove
Bonneville Salt Flats, USA
5 Sep 1963
966.57 / 600.60

700 mph (1,127 km/h)
Andy Green (UK)
Black Rock Desert, USA
25 Sep 1997
1,149.30 / 714.14

MEASURING SPEED

Under the rules of governing body Féderation Internationale de l'Automobile, the Land Speed Record takes the fastest speed over one kilometre or one mile with a flying start, averaged over two runs. A distinction is made between wheel-driven and jet- and rocket-propelled cars. Since 1963 all record-holders have been in the latter category, their speeds measured to 1/1,000th of a second using electronic timing equipment.

TOP 10 METROS WITH THE MOST STATIONS

METRO / STATIONS	
1 **New York**, USA	468
2 **Paris**, France	380
3 **Seoul**, South Korea	348
4 **Tokyo**, Japan	290
5 **Madrid**, Spain	281
6 **London**, UK	268
7 **Berlin**, Germany	192
8 **Moscow**, Russia	177
9 **Mexico City**, Mexico	175
10 **Shanghai**, China	162
World total	8,264

TOP 10 LONGEST UNDERGROUND RAILWAY NETWORKS

CITY	OPENED	STATIONS	TOTAL TRACK LENGTH KM	MILES
1 **London**, UK	1863	268	408	254
2 **New York**, USA	1904	468	368	229
3 **Shanghai**, China	1995	230	334	208
4 **Tokyo**, Japan	1927	290	305	190
5 **Moscow**, Russia	1935	180	299	186
6 **Seoul**, South Korea	1974	348	287	178
7 **Madrid**, Spain	1919	281	284	176
8 **Beijing**, China	1969	147	228	142
9 **Paris**, France	1900	380	213	132
10 **Mexico City**, Mexico	1969	175	202	126

Source: World Metro Database

TOP 10 BUSIEST UNDERGROUND RAILWAY NETWORKS

CITY / PASSENGERS PER ANNUM (2008)*	
1 **Tokyo**, Japan	3,174,000,000
2 **Moscow**, Russia	2,573,000,000
3 **Seoul**, South Korea	2,047,000,000
4 **New York**, USA	1,624,000,000
5 **Mexico City**, Mexico	1,460,000,000
6 **Paris**, France	1,388,000,000
7 **Hong Kong**, China	1,309,000,000
8 **Beijing**, China	1,200,000,000
9 **London**, UK	1,197,000,000
10 **Shanghai**, China	1,122,000,000

* Or latest year for which figures available

TOP 10 BUSIEST LONDON UNDERGROUND STATIONS

STATION / ANNUAL PASSENGERS (2008)*	
1 **Victoria**	78,410,000
2 **Waterloo**	77,200,000
3 **Oxford Circus**	72,910,000
4 **King's Cross St Pancras**	67,070,000
5 **Liverpool Street**	64,160,000
6 **London Bridge**	60,550,000
7 **Canary Wharf**	43,510,000
8 **Bank and Monument**	42,820,000
9 **Paddington**	40,700,000
10 **Piccadilly Circus**	38,850,000

* Estimated total number of passengers entering and exiting the station

Source: Transport for London

▲ ***Spanish station***
The Nuevos Ministerios station on the Madrid metro, one of the world's most extensive systems.

THE 10 **FIRST UNDERGROUND RAILWAY SYSTEMS**

	CITY	FIRST LINE ESTABLISHED*
1	**London**, UK	10 Jan 1863
2	**Budapest**, Hungary	2 May 1896
3	**Glasgow**, UK	14 Dec 1896
4	**Boston**, USA	1 Sep 1897
5	**Paris**, France	19 Jul 1900
6	**Berlin**, Germany	15 Feb 1902
7	**New York**, USA	27 Oct 1904
8	**Philadelphia**, USA	4 Mar 1907
9	**Hamburg**, Germany	15 Feb 1912
10	**Buenos Aires**, Argentina	1 Dec 1913

* Excluding those where overground part preceded underground, such as the Chicago 'L', 6 June 1892

▶ ***Surreal station***
Zbigniew Peter Pininski's design for the Bockenheimer Warte station on the Frankfurt metro was influenced by surrealist painter René Magritte.

TOP 10 **COUNTRIES WITH MOST CITIES WITH METROS**

	COUNTRY / CITIES WITH METROS
1	=Germany 19
	=USA 19
3	Japan 15
4	China 11
5	Russia 8
6	=France 7
	=Italy 7
8	=Brazil 6
	=South Korea 6
	=Spain 6
	UK 3

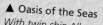

▲ **Oasis of the Seas**
With twin ship Allure of the Seas (2010), the largest passenger vessels ever built can carry over 6,000 passengers and 2,000 crew.

◀ **Zheng He**
Named after the 15th-century Chinese mariner, this is a replica of one of his celebrated treasure ships.

TOP 10 LARGEST WOODEN SHIPS*

	SHIP / COUNTRY BUILT	LAUNCHED	LENGTH M	LENGTH FT
1	**Eureka**, USA	1890	91.3	299.5
2	**Al Hashemi II**, Kuwait	2000	83.8	274.8
3	**Zheng He**, China	2008	71.1	233.3
4	**Jylland**, Denmark	1860	71.0	233.0
5	**Vasa**, Sweden	1627#	69.0	226.3
6	**SV Tenacious**†, UK	2000	65.0	213.3
7	**Cutty Sark**, UK	1869	64.8	212.5
8	**Neptune**, Italy	1985	61.9	203.0
9	**Zinat Al Bihaar**, Oman	1988	61.0	200.0
10	**HMS Victory**, UK	1765	56.7	186.0

* Surviving vessels only
# Sunk, recovered 1959
† Renamed *SV Carrick*

TOP 10 LARGEST PASSENGER SHIPS

	SHIP	ENTERED SERVICE	LENGTH M	LENGTH FT	TONNAGE
1	Oasis of the Seas	2009	360	1,181	225,282
2	Allure of the Seas	2010*	360	1,181	220,000
3	=Freedom of the Seas	2006	339	1,112	154,407
	=Liberty of the Seas	2007	339	1,112	154,407
	=Independence of the Seas	2008	339	1,112	154,407
6	Norwegian Epic#	2010*	330	1,080	153,000
7	Queen Mary 2#	2004	345	1,132	148,528
8	=Adventure of the Seas	2001	311	1,020	138,000
	=Navigator of the Seas	2003	311	1,020	138,000
	=Mariner of the Seas	2004	311	1,020	138,000

* Under construction – scheduled completion
# Built in France, all other built in Finland

TOP 10 LARGEST SAILING VESSELS*

#	SHIP / COUNTRY BUILT	YEAR	LENGTH M	LENGTH FT	GROSS TONNAGE
1	Wind Surf France	1990	187	617	14,745
2	Wind Star France	1986	134	440	5,350
3	Royal Clipper Poland	2000	134	439	5,000
4	Kruzenshtern Germany	1926	114	376	3,545
5	Moshulu UK	1904	121	396	3,200
6	Gorch Fock Germany	1958	89	293	3,181
7	Peking Germany	1911	115	378	3,100
8	Juan Sebastián Elcano Spain	1927	113	370	2,983
9	Amerigo Vespucci Italy	1930	101	331	2,686
10	Sea Cloud II Spain	2001	117	384	2,532

* Currently afloat

► **Kruzenshtern**
The German-built barque is used as a training vessel.

TOP 10 LONGEST SHIPS*

SHIP / TYPE / LAUNCHED / LENGTH (M/FT)

1. Emma Mærsk#, Container ship, 2006, 397 / 1,300
2. TI Oceania#, Supertanker, 2002, 379 / 1,245
3. Queen Mary 2, Cruise ship, 2004, 345 / 1,132
4. Al Ghuwairiya, LNG carrier, 2008, 345 / 1,131
5. Berge Stahl, Bulk cargo ship, 1986, 343 / 1,125
6. USS Enterprise, Aircraft carrier, 1961, 342 / 1,123
7. Brasil Maru, Ore carrier, 2007, 340 / 1,115
8. USS Iowa#, Battleship, 1942, 270 / 887
9. Wind Surf, Sailing ship, 1990, 187 / 617
10. Eclipse, Motor yacht, 2009, 170 / 560

* Longest example of each type
\# More than one vessel of same length in class

Knock Nevis (formerly *Seawise Giant*, *Happy Giant* and *Jahre Viking*), built in 1979, was the longest ship ever built, at 458 m (1,504 ft).

AIR TRAVEL

TOP 10 AIRLINES WITH THE MOST AIRCRAFT

AIRLINE / COUNTRY* / MAIN FLEET SIZE#

1 Delta Air Lines
675

2 America Airlines
614

3 Southwest Airlines
544

4 Air France-KLM
362

5 United Airlines
359

6 US Airways
345

7 Air Canada
Canada 339

8 Continental Airlines
338

9 China Southern Airlines
China 328

10 SkyWest Airlines
289

British Airways, UK 223

* USA unless otherwise stated
# 2009 or latest available year

▼ ***Delta Air Lines***
Delta's 2008 acquisition of Northwest Airlines has made it the world's largest in fleet size.

TOP 10 AIRLINES WITH THE MOST PASSENGERS

AIRLINE / COUNTRY / SCHEDULED PASSENGERS CARRIED (2009)*

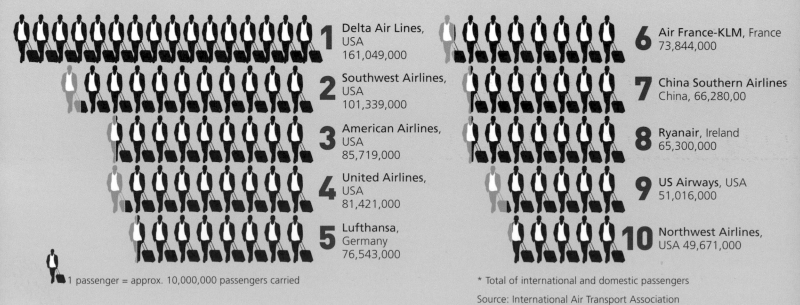

1 Delta Air Lines, USA
161,049,000

2 Southwest Airlines, USA
101,339,000

3 American Airlines, USA
85,719,000

4 United Airlines, USA
81,421,000

5 Lufthansa, Germany
76,543,000

6 **Air France-KLM**, France
73,844,000

7 **China Southern Airlines**
China, 66,280,00

8 **Ryanair**, Ireland
65,300,000

9 **US Airways**, USA
51,016,000

10 **Northwest Airlines**,
USA 49,671,000

1 passenger = approx. 10,000,000 passengers carried

* Total of international and domestic passengers

Source: International Air Transport Association

TOP 10 BUSIEST AIRPORTS

AIRPORT / COUNTRY / PASSENGERS (2008)

1	Atlanta	USA	90,039,280
2	Chicago	USA	69,353,876
3	London Heathrow	UK	67,056,379
4	Tokyo	Japan	66,754,829
5	Paris	France	60,874,681
6	Los Angeles	USA	59,497,539
7	Dallas/Fort Worth	USA	57,093,187
8	Beijing	China	55,937,289
9	Frankfurt	Germany	53,467,450
10	Denver	USA	51,245,334

Source: Airports Council International

◀ *Heathrow*
Opened in 1946, London Heathrow now handles more international passengers than any airport in the world.

TOP 10 FREIGHT CARRIERS

AIRLINE / COUNTRY	FREIGHT TONNES/KM*
1 Federal Express, USA	15,122,000,000
2 UPS Airlines, USA	10,977,000,000
3 Korean Air, South Korea	8,890,000,000
4 Cathay Pacific Airways, Hong Kong, China	8,245,000,000
5 Lufthansa, Germany	8,206,000,000
6 Singapore Airlines, Singapore	7,486,000,000
7 Emirates, United Arab Emirates	6,013,000,000
8 Air France, France	5,820,000,000
9 Cargolux, Luxembourg	5,334,000,000
10 China Airlines, Taiwan	5,261,000,000

* Total weight of cargo multiplied by distance carried, 2008

World's largest air carrier Federal Express operates a fleet of 299 aircraft, including 59 McDonnell Douglas MD-11s, the plane that Chuck Noland, the FedEx employee played by Tom Hanks in *Cast Away* (2000), was flying when he crashed on a Pacific island.

TOP 10 COUNTRIES WITH THE MOST AIRPORTS

COUNTRY	AIRPORTS (2009 EST.)
1 USA	15,095
2 Brazil	4,000
3 Mexico	1,744
4 Canada	1,388
5 Russia	1,216
6 Argentina	1,130
7 Colombia	992
8 Bolivia	952
9 Paraguay	798
10 Indonesia	683
UK	*506*
World total	*43,867*

Source: CIA, *The World Factbook 2010*

◀ **Moment of impact**
Pilot Antoly Kvochur successfully ejects from his MiG-29 seconds before it crashes in flames at the 1989 Paris Air Show. Military aircraft account for almost 13 per cent of all aviation accidents in a ranking that is headed by scheduled flights.

▼ **Fatal flight**
Lt Selfridge, 26, prepares for the flight in the Wright Flyer that resulted in his becoming the first victim of a plane crash.

THE 10 MOST COMMON AIR ACCIDENTS BY FLIGHT TYPE

	FLIGHT TYPE	% OF ALL ACCIDENTS*
1	Scheduled	35.41
2	Military	12.79
3	Cargo	11.99
4	Private	7.75
5	Training	7.63
6	Charter	5.10
7	Executive	4.02
8	Survey	3.28
9	Postal	2.39
10	Positioning	1.85

* 1918–2000

Source: Aircraft Crashes Record Office

This analysis of aircraft accidents also reveals that 50.39 per cent of all accidents occurred during take-off, 27.73 per cent during flight and 20.96 during landing.

THE 10 FIRST POWERED AIRCRAFT FATALITIES

	VICTIM / NATIONALITY / LOCATION	DATE
1	**Lt Thomas Etholen Selfridge** American, Fort Myer, USA	17 Sep 1908
2	**Eugène Lefèbvre** French, Juvisy, France	7 Sep 1909
3	**Ferdinand Ferber** French, Boulogne, France	22 Sep 1909
4	**Ena Rossi** Italian, Rome, Italy	22 Sep 1909
5	**Antonio Fernandez** Spanish, Nice, France	6 Dec 1909
6	**Léon Delagrange** French, Croix d'Hins, France	4 Jan 1910
7	**Hubert Le Blon** French, San Sebastián, Spain	2 Apr 1910
8	**Hauvette Michelin** French, Lyons, France	13 May 1910
9	**Aindan de Zoseley** Hungarian, Budapest, Hungary	2 Jun 1910
10	**Thaddeus Robl** German, Stettin, Germany	18 Jun 1910

THE 10 WORST YEARS FOR AIR ACCIDENTS*

	YEAR	FATALITIES
1	1972	3,210
2	1985	2,886
3	1996	2,758
4	1973	2,739
5	1974	2,586
6	1979	2,508
7	1989	2,469
8	1976	2,445
9	1977	2,398
10	1992	2,266
	2008	*879*

* 1918–2008

Source: Aircraft Crashes Record Office

From 1918 to 9 May 2009, a total of 121,870 people were killed in aviation accidents, an average of 1,339 a year.

THE 10 WORST AIR DISASTERS

LOCATION / DATE / INCIDENT — NO. KILLED

1. **New York, USA, Sep 11, 2001** — *c.* 1,622
Following a hijacking by terrorists, an American Airlines Boeing 767 was deliberately flown into the North Tower of the World Trade Center, killing all 81 passengers (including five hijackers), 11 crew on board, and an estimated 1,530 on the ground.

2. **New York, USA, Sep 11, 2001** — *c.* 677
As part of the coordinated attack, hijackers commandeered a second Boeing 767 and crashed it into the South Tower of the World Trade Center, killing all 56 passengers and nine crew on board, and approximately 612 on the ground.

3. **Tenerife, Canary Islands, Mar 27, 1977** — 583
Two Boeing 747s (PanAm and KLM, carrying 380 passengers and 16 crew, and 234 passengers and 14 crew respectively) collided and caught fire on the runway.

4. **Mt. Ogura, Japan, Aug 12, 1985** — 520
A JAL Boeing 747 on an internal flight from Tokyo to Osaka crashed, killing all but four of the 509 passengers and all 15 crew on board.

5. **Charkhi Dadri, India, Nov 12, 1996** — 349
A Saudi Arabian Airlines Boeing 747 collided with a Kazakh Airlines Ilyushin IL 76 cargo aircraft and exploded, killing all 312 on the Boeing and all 37 on the Ilyushin.

6. **Paris, France, Mar 3, 1974** — 346
Immediately after takeoff for London, a Turkish Airlines DC-10 suffered an explosive decompression when a door burst open, and crashed killing all on board.

7. **Off the Irish coast, Jun 23, 1985** — 329
An Air India Boeing 747 on a flight from Vancouver to Delhi exploded in midair, probably as a result of a terrorist bomb, killing all 307 passengers and 22 crew.

8. **Riyadh, Saudi Arabia, Aug 19, 1980** — 301
Following an emergency landing, a Saudia (Saudi Arabian) Airlines Lockheed TriStar caught fire. The crew were unable to open the doors and all on board died from smoke inhalation.

9. **Off the Iranian coast, Jul 3, 1988** — 290
An Iran Air A300 airbus was shot down in error by a missile fired by the USS *Vincennes*, resulting in the deaths of all 274 passengers and 16 crew.

10. **Sirach Mountain, Iran, Feb 19, 2003** — 275
An Ilyushin 76 carrying 257 Revolutionary Guards and a crew of 18 crashed in poor weather.

THE 10 WORST AIRSHIP DISASTERS

LOCATION / DATE / INCIDENT — NO. KILLED

1. **Coast off New Jersey, USA, Apr 4, 1933** — 73
US Navy airship *Akron* crashed into the sea in a storm, leaving only three survivors.

2. **Over the Mediterranean, Dec 21, 1923** — 52
French airship *Dixmude* is assumed to have been struck by lightning, broke up, and crashed into the sea.

3. **Near Beauvais, France, Oct 5, 1930** — 50
British airship *R101* crashed into a hillside leaving 48 dead, with two dying later, and six survivors.

4. **Coast off Hull, UK, Aug 24, 1921** — 44
Airship *R38* broke in two on a training and test flight.

5. **Lakehurst, New Jersey, USA, May 6, 1937** — 36
German Zeppelin *Hindenburg* caught fire when mooring. Remarkably, 62 survived the blaze.

6. **Hampton Roads, Virginia, USA, Feb 21, 1922** — 34
Roma, an Italian airship bought by the US Army, hit power lines and crashed, killing all but 11 men on board.

7. **Berlin, Germany, Oct 17, 1913** — 28
The first air disaster with more than 20 fatalities, German airship *LZ18* crashed after engine failure and an explosion during a test flight at Berlin-Johannisthal.

8. **Baltic Sea, Mar 30, 1917** — 23
German airship *SL9* was struck by lightning on a flight from Seerappen to Seddin and crashed into the sea.

9. **Mouth of the River Elbe, Germany, Sep 3, 1915** — 19
German airship *L10* was struck by lightning and plunged into the sea.

10. **Coast off Barnegat City, New Jersey, USA, Jul 6, 1960** — 18
Largest-ever nonrigid airship US Navy *Goodyear ZPG-3W* crashed into the sea. There were three survivors.

◄ **Hindenburg**
The Hindenburg's dramatic fate effectively marked the end of the airship era.

10

SPORT

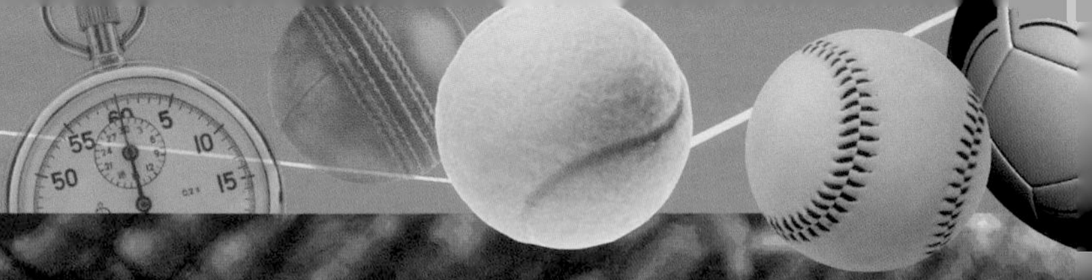

INDIANAPOLIS 500 CENTENARY

The first Indianapolis 500, a 500-mile race consisting of 200 laps of the Indianapolis Motor Speedway was held on Memorial Day, 30 May 1911, when it was won by Ray Harroun driving a Marmon Wasp at a speed of 120.06 km/h (74.60 mph) – compared with Dutch driver Arie Luyendyk's 1990 record-winning speed of 299.31 km/h (185.98 mph). The 2011 event is the 95th, as the race was not run in 1917–18 or 1942–44 because of the World Wars. With seating for 250,000 and a total capacity of some 400,000, the 'Indy 500' is claimed to be the best-attended one-day sporting event in the world.

OLYMPIC COUNTRIES

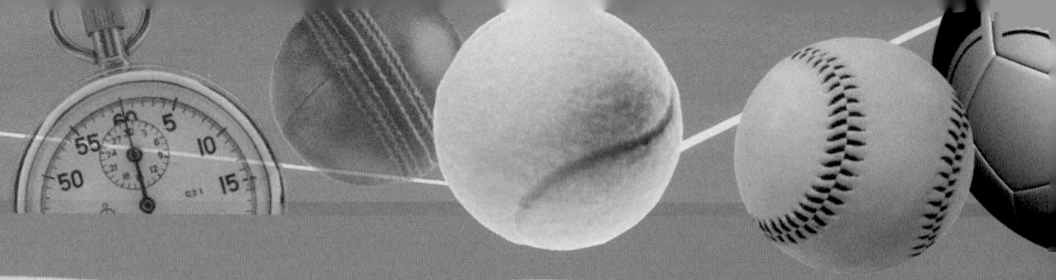

TOP 10 **COUNTRIES WINNING THE MOST MEDALS AT ONE SUMMER OLYMPICS***

	COUNTRY / VENUE	YEAR	GOLD	SILVER	BRONZE	TOTAL
1	USA# St Louis	1904	78	82	79	239
2	USSR# Moscow	1980	80	69	46	195
3	USA# Los Angeles	1984	83	60	30	173
4	Great Britain# London	1908	56	51	38	145
5	USSR Seoul	1988	55	31	46	132
6	East Germany Moscow	1980	47	37	42	126
7	USSR Montreal	1976	49	41	35	125
8	Unified Team Barcelona	1992	45	38	29	112
9	USA Beijing	2008	36	38	36	110
10	USA Barcelona	1992	37	34	37	108

* All Summer Olympic Games 1896–2008
# Host nation

TOP 10 **HOST NATIONS AT THE SUMMER OLYMPICS***

	HOST	YEAR	GOLD	SILVER	BRONZE	TOTAL
1	USA	1904	78	82	79	239
2	Soviet Union	1980	80	69	46	195
3	USA	1984	83	60	30	173
4	Great Britain	1908	56	51	38	145
5	USA	1932	41	32	30	103
6	=France	1900	26	41	34	101
	=USA	1996	44	32	25	101
8	China	2008	51	21	28	100
9	Germany	1936	33	26	30	89
10	Sweden	1912	24	24	17	65

* Based on total medals won

Source: International Olympic Committee

Canada in 1976 is the only host nation not to have won a gold medal – they won five silver and six bronze medals. In 1968, Mexico won a record low number of medals by a host nation with just three gold, three silver and three bronze medals, for a total of nine.

◀ ***Chinese divers***
Lin Yue and Huo Liang win the men's synchronized 10-metre platform event at Beijing 2008.

▼ ***Greek gold***
Kelly Holmes after capturing the 1,500-metres gold at Athens 2004, adding it to the 800-metres gold she had previously won.

TOP 10 SUMMER OLYMPICS WITH THE MOST COUNTRIES WINNING GOLD MEDALS

YEAR / HOST CITY / COUNTRY / COMPETING COUNTRIES / COUNTRIES WINNING GOLD

1	2004	Athens, Greece	201 / 56
2	2008	Beijing, China	204 / 55
3	1996	Atlanta, USA	197 / 53
4	2000	Sydney, Australia	199 / 51
5	1992	Barcelona, Spain	169 / 37
6	1988	Seoul, South Korea	159 / 31
7	1968	Mexico City, Mexico	112 / 30
8	1928	Amsterdam, Netherlands	46 / 28
9	1952	Helsinki, Finland	69 / 27
10	= 1964	Tokyo, Japan	93 / 26
	= 1976	Montreal, Canada	92 / 26

Source: International Olympic Committee

TOP 10 COUNTRIES WITH THE MOST SUMMER OLYMPIC MEDALS WITHOUT WINNING A GOLD MEDAL

	COUNTRY	GOLD	SILVER	BRONZE	TOTAL
1	Philippines	0	2	7	9
2	Puerto Rico	0	1	5	6
3	Moldova	0	2	3	5
4	=Bohemia	0	1	3	4
	=Ghana	0	1	3	4
	=Iceland	0	2	2	4
	=Lebanon	0	2	2	4
	=Malaysia	0	2	2	4
	=Namibia	0	4	0	4
10	=Kyrgyzstan	0	1	2	3
	=Serbia	0	1	2	3

Forty-two countries have won Olympic medals but not gold. At the 1992 Games, athletes from Macedonia and the Federal Republic of Yugoslavia competed as Independent Participants. Between them they won one silver and two bronze medals.

TOP 10 SUMMER PARALYMPICS WITH THE MOST COUNTRIES WINNING GOLD MEDALS

	YEAR	HOST / COUNTRY	COMPETING COUNTRIES	COUNTRIES WINNING GOLD
1	2004	Athens, Greece	136	60
2	2008	Beijing, China	148	52
3	=1996	Atlanta, USA	104	51
	=2000	Sydney, Australia	127	51
5	1992	Barcelona, Spain	82	41
6	1988	Seoul, South Korea	61	38
7	=1980	Arnhem, Netherlands	42	34
	=1984	Stoke Mandeville, England and New York, USA	45	34
9	1976	Toronto, Canada	32	29
10	1972	Heidelberg, Germany	41	26

Source: International Paralympic Committee

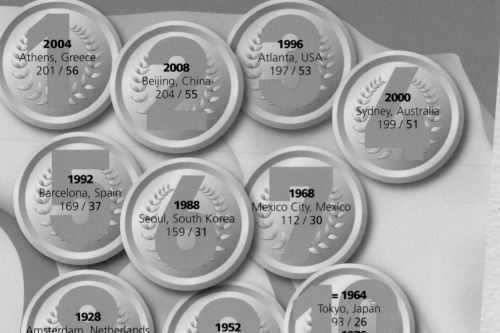

◀ *Blade runner*
South Africa's Oscar Pistorius won gold at Athens in 2004 and three more at Beijing in 2008.

GREAT OLYMPIANS

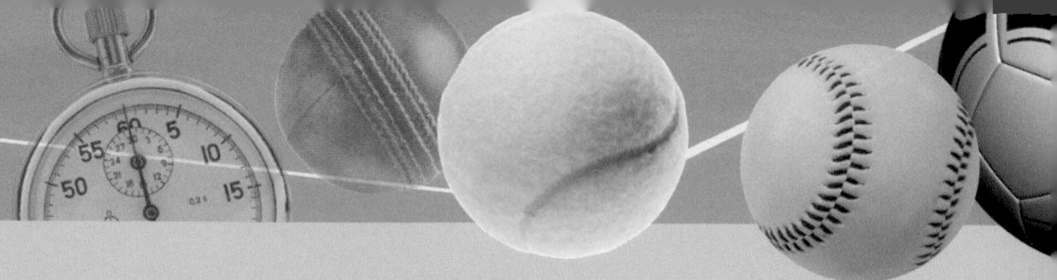

▲ *Michael Phelps*
Michael Phelps' eight gold medals at Beijing in 2008 beat Mark Spitz's old record of seven.

TOP 10 **MOST OLYMPIC SWIMMING MEDALS***

	SWIMMER / COUNTRY	YEARS	GOLD	SILVER	BRONZE	TOTAL
1	Michael Phelps, USA	2004–08	14	0	2	16
2	=Dara Torres, USA	1984–2008	4	4	4	12
	=Jenny Thompson, USA	1992–2004	8	3	1	12
4	=Mark Spitz, USA	1968–72	9	1	1	11
	=Matt Biondi, USA	1984–92	8	2	1	11
	=Natalie Coughlin, USA	2004–08	3	4	4	11
7	=Franziska Van Almsick, Germany	1992–2004	0	4	6	10
	=Gary Hall Jr, USA	1996–2004	5	3	2	10
9	=Alexsandr Popov, Unified Team/Russia	1992–2000	4	5	0	9
	=Ian Thorpe, Australia	2000–04	5	3	1	9

* Up to and including the 2008 Beijing Olympics

Source: International Olympic Committee

UNBROKEN RECORD
Bob Beamon's Olympic long-jump record has stood for over 40 years – perhaps unsurprisingly, since when he leapt to a massive 8.90 m at Mexico City in 1968, he shattered Ralph Boston's old Olympic record by a clear 78 cm and was 71 cm ahead of Klaus Beer of East Germany, who won silver with a jump of 8.19 m.

TOP 10 **OLDEST OLYMPIC TRACK AND FIELD RECORDS***

	EVENT / ATHLETE / COUNTRY	TIME/DISTANCE/POINTS	DATE SET
1	Men's long jump Bob Beamon, USA	8.90 m	18 Oct 1968
2	Women's shot put Ilona Slupianek, East Germany	22.41 m	24 Jul 1980
3	Women's 800 metres Nadezhda Olizarenko, USSR	1 min 53.43 sec	27 Jul 1980
4	Women's 4 × 100 metres East Germany	41.60 sec	1 Aug 1980
5	Men's shot Ulf Timmermann, East Germany	22.47 m	23 Sep 1988
6	=(Women's) Heptathlon Jackie Joyner-Kersee, USA	7,291 points	24 Sep 1988
	=Women's 100 metres Florence Griffith Joyner, USA	10.62 sec	24 Sep 1988
8	Men's hammer Sergey Litvinov, USSR	84.80 m	26 Sep 1988
9	=Women's 200 metres Florence Griffith Joyner, USA	21.34 sec	29 Sep 1988
	=Women's long jump Jackie Joyner-Kersee, USA	7.40 m	29 Sep 1988
	=Women's discus Martina Hellmann, East Germany	72.30 m	29 Sep 1988

* Up to and including the 2008 Beijing Olympics

Source: International Olympic Committee

Joyner-Kersee
Between 1984 and 1996 Jackie Joyner-Kersee won six Olympic medals in the heptathlon and long jump.

▼ *Alexei Nemov*
Russian gymnast Alexei Nemov won four golds, two silvers and six bronze medals in 1996 and 2000.

► *Al Oerter*
Al Oerter was only 20 when he won his first gold.

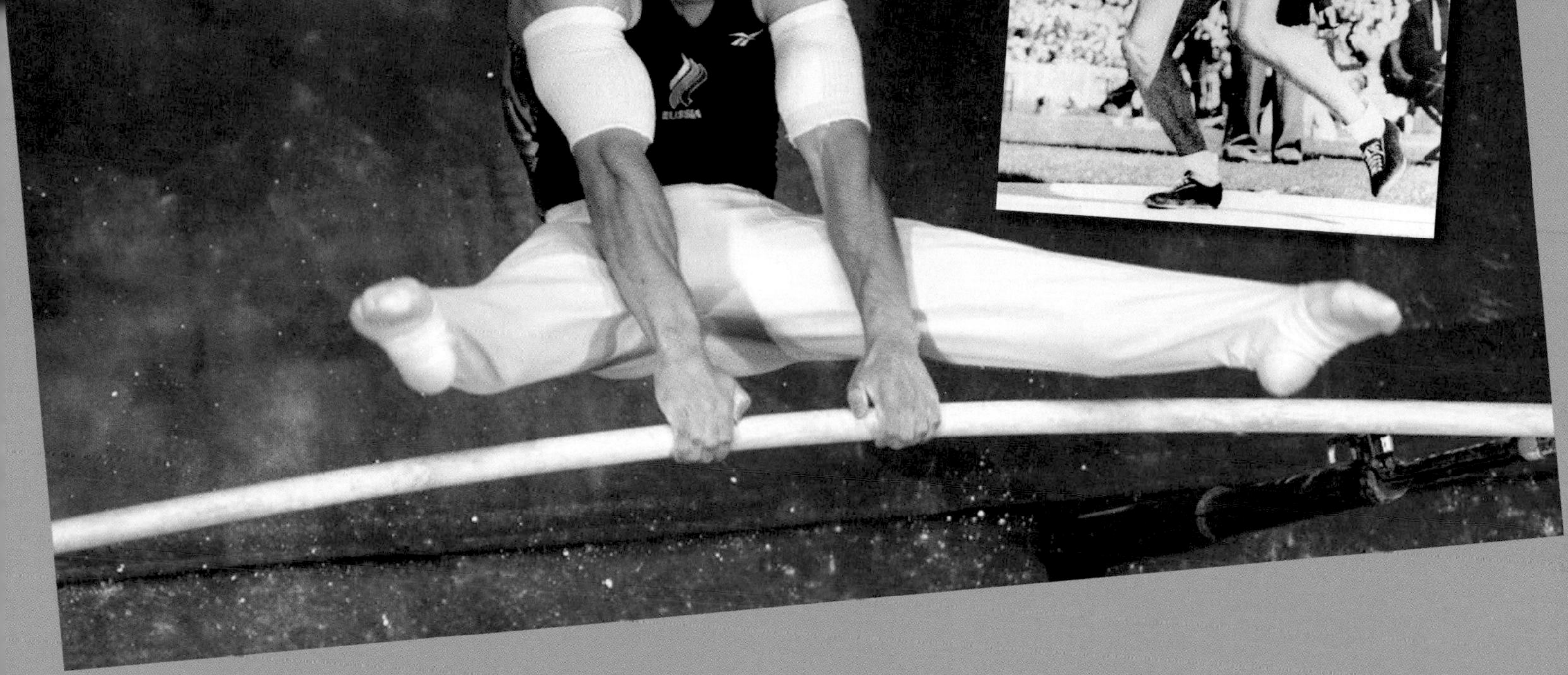

THE 10 **FIRST ATHLETES TO WIN GOLD IN THE SAME EVENT AT FOUR SUMMER OLYMPICS**

	ATHLETE / COUNTRY / SPORT	EVENT	YEARS
1	=Aladár Gerevich* Hungary, Fencing	Team sabre	1932–52
	=Pál Kovács Hungary, Fencing	Team sabre	1932–52
3	Paul Elvstrøm Denmark, Sailing	Finn	1948–60
4	Edoardo Mangiarotti Italy, Fencing	Team épée	1936–60
5	Rudolf Kárpáti Hungary, Fencing	Team sabre	1948–60
6	Al Oerter USA, Athletics	Discus	1956–68
7	Hans-Günther Winkler, Germany/West Germany, Show jumping	Team	1956–72
8	Reiner Klimke# Germany/West Germany, Dressage	Team	1964–84
9	Carl Lewis USA, Athletics	Long jump	1984–96
10	Teresa Edwards USA, Basketball	Team	1984–2000

* Also won gold in the same event in 1956 and 1960
# Also won gold in the same event in 1988

THE 10 **LATEST LEADING MEDAL-WINNERS AT THE SUMMER OLYMPICS**

YEAR	HOST CITY / ATHLETE / COUNTRY	SPORT	GOLD	SILVER	BRONZE	TOTAL
2008	Beijing Michael Phelps, USA	Swimming	8	0	0	8
2004	Athens Michael Phelps, USA	Swimming	6	0	2	8
2000	Sydney Alexei Nemov, Russia	Gymnastics	2	1	3	6
1996	Atlanta Alexei Nemov, Russia	Gymnastics	2	1	3	6
1992	Barcelona Vitaliy Scherbo, Unified Team	Gymnastics	6	0	0	6
1988	Seoul Matt Biondi, USA	Swimming	5	1	1	7
1984	Los Angeles Li Ning, China	Gymnastics	3	2	1	6
1980	Moscow Alexsandr Ditiyatin, USSR	Gymnastics	3	4	1	8
1976	Montreal Nikolai Andrianov, USSR	Gymnastics	4	2	1	7
1972	Munich Mark Spitz, USA	Swimming	7	0	0	7

The last woman to be the Games' leading medallist was Larissa Latynina (USSR), with two gold, two silver and two bronze medals in the gymnastics events in 1964.

The World's Fastest

TOP 10 **FASTEST MEN OVER 100 METRES***

	ATHLETE / COUNTRY	VENUE	DATE	TIME (SECS)
1	**Usain Bolt**, Jamaica	Berlin, Germany	16 Aug 2009	9.58
2	**Tyson Gay**, USA	Shanghai, China	20 Sep 2009	9.69
3	**Asafa Powell**, Jamaica	Lausanne, Switzerland	2 Sep 2008	9.72
4	**Maurice Greene**, USA	Athens, Greece	16 Jun 1999	9.79
5	=**Donovan Bailey**, Canada	Atlanta, Georgia, USA	27 Jul 1996	9.84
	=**Bruny Surin**, Canada	Seville, Spain	22 Aug 1999	9.84
7	=**Justin Gatlin**, USA	Athens, Greece	22 Aug 2004	9.85
	=**Olusoji A. Fasuba**, Nigeria	Doha, Qatar	12 May 2006	9.85
	=**Leroy Burrell**, USA	Lausanne, Switzerland	6 Jul 1994	9.85
10	=**Carl Lewis**, USA	Tokyo, Japan	25 Aug 1991	9.86
	=**Frank Fredericks**, Namibia	Lausanne, Switzerland	3 Jul 1996	9.86
	=**Ato Boldon**#, Trinidad	Walnut, California, USA	19 Apr 1998	9.86
	=**Francis Obikwelu**, Portugal	Athens, Greece	22 Aug 2004	9.86

* Based on the fastest official time achieved by each athlete
# Boldon equalled his personal best mark of 9.86 seconds on three more occasions

Source: IAAF

When Usain Bolt set a new world record in the 100-m final at the 2009 World Championships, he broke his own world record of 9.69 seconds, which he had set at the Beijing Olympics exactly one year earlier.

TOP 10 **FASTEST TIMES FOR THE 100 METRES**

TIME	RUN BY
9.58	Usain Bolt (Jamaica)
9.69	Usain Bolt Tyson Gay (USA)
9.71	Tyson Gay
9.72	Usain Bolt Asafa Powell (Jamaica)
9.74	Asafa Powell
9.76	Usain Bolt
9.77	Asafa Powell Tyson Gay Usain Bolt
9.78	Asafa Powell
9.79	Usain Bolt Maurice Greene (USA)
9.80	Maurice Greene

Source: IAAF

▼ *Usain Bolt*
Jamaica's Usain Bolt (No. 7) in his 100-m semi-final at Beijing, which he won with a time of 9.85 seconds.

◄ *Justin Gatin*
Justin Gatlin (USA) on his way to winning the Olympic 100 metres in 2004.

► *Jim Hines*
Jim Hines, the first man under 10 seconds for the 100 metres.

USAIN BOLT

Jamaican-born Usain Bolt first hit the headlines with his record-breaking run in the 2008 Olympic final, when he lowered the world record by 3/100ths of a second. But that was nothing compared to his remarkable run exactly one year later, when he lowered it by a further 11/100ths of a second. Bolt emulated Carl Lewis in winning three sprint gold medals at one Olympics – the 100 m, 200 m and 4 × 100-m relay – all of them in world record times, the first occasion on which this had been achieved. Bolt also became the first man simultaneously to hold the world 100-m and 200-m record when he shattered the 200-m record at the 2009 World Championships in Berlin.

THE WORLD 100-METRE RECORD

The first 100-m record to be recognized by the IAAF was the 10.6 seconds run by Don Lippincott of the USA, in winning his first-round heat at the 1912 Stockholm Olympic Games. Although he collected only bronze in the final, his world record stood until broken by fellow countryman Charlie Paddock in 1921. Jim Hines was the first man to officially break the 10-second barrier when he ran 9.9 seconds (manually timed) in the US National Championships at Sacramento on 20 June 1968. Ben Johnson (Canada) ran 9.83 seconds for a new world record on 30 August 1987, and 9.79 seconds on 24 September 1988. The latter was never ratified because Johnson tested positive for steroid use, and his 1987 world record was subsequently rescinded by the IAAF.

THE FASTEST WOMEN OVER 100 METRES

	ATHLETE / COUNTRY / VENUE / DATE	TIME (SECS)
1	**Florence Griffith Joyner**, USA Indianapolis, 16 Jul 1988	10.49
2	**Carmelita Jeter**, USA Shanghai, 28 Sep 2009	10.64
3	= **Christine Arron**, France Budapest, 9 Aug 1998	10.73
	= **Shelly-Ann Fraser**, Jamaica Berlin, 17 Aug 2009	10.73
5	**Marion Jones**, USA Johannesburg, 12 Sep 1998	10.65

► *Florence Griffith Joyner*
America's Florence Griffith Joyner tragically died in 1998 aged 38.

▼ *Kerron Stewart*
Beijing 100-m Olympic silver medallist Kerron Stewart of Jamaica.

CRICKET

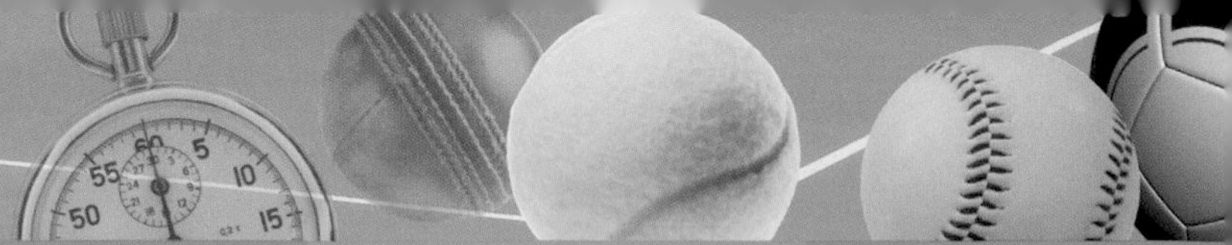

TOP 10 **HIGHEST INDIVIDUAL INNINGS IN THE ICC WORLD TWENTY20**

	BATSMAN	COUNTRY	OPPONENTS	VENUE	DATE	RUNS
1	Chris Gayle	West Indies	South Africa	Johannesburg	11 Sep 2007	117
2	Tillakaratne Dilshan	Sri Lanka	West Indies	The Oval	19 Jun 2009	96*
3	Herschelle Gibbs	South Africa	West Indies	Johannesburg	11 Sep 2007	90*
4	Justin Kemp	South Africa	New Zealand	Durban	19 Sep 2007	89*
5	=Sanath Jayasuriya	Sri Lanka	Kenya	Johannesburg	14 Sep 2007	88
	=Chris Gayle	West Indies	Australia	The Oval	6 Jun 2009	88
7	Sanath Jayasuriya	Sri Lanka	West Indies	Trent Bridge	10 Jun 2009	81
8	=Kevin Pietersen	England	Zimbabwe	Cape Town	13 Sep 2007	79
	=AB de Villiers	South Africa	Scotland	The Oval	7 Jun 2009	79*
10	Mahela Jayawardene	Sri Lanka	Ireland	Lord's	14 Jun 2009	78

* In the two ICC World Twenty20 competitions held in South Africa in 2007 and England in 2009

TOP 10 **MOST WICKETS IN TEST CRICKET***

	PLAYER / COUNTRY	YEARS	MATCHES	WICKETS
1	**Muttiah Muralitharan,** Sri Lanka#	1992–2009	129	783
2	**Shane Warne,** Australia	1992–2007	145	708
3	**Anil Kumble,** India	1990–2008	132	619
4	**Glenn McGrath,** Australia	1993–2007	124	563
5	**Courtney Walsh,** West Indies	1984–2001	132	519
6	**Kapil Dev,** India	1978–94	131	434
7	**Richard Hadlee,** New Zealand	1973–90	86	431
8	**Shaun Pollock,** South Africa	1995–2008	108	421
9	**Wasim Akram,** Pakistan	1985–2002	104	414
10	**Curtly Ambrose,** West Indies	1988–2000	98	405

* As at 1 January 2010
# Also played for the ICC World XI

The best total by an Englishman is 383 by Ian Botham, 1977–92.

► *Wicket-taker*
Sri Lankan Muttiah Muralitharan is the most prolific wicket-taker in both Test Match cricket and in One-Day Internationals.

TOP 10 **MOST DISMISSALS BY A WICKETKEEPER IN TEST CRICKET***

	PLAYER / COUNTRY	YEARS	MATCHES	CAUGHT	STUMPED	TOTAL DISMISSALS
1	**Mark Boucher**, South Africa#	1997–2009	126	453	22	475
2	**Adam Gilchrist**, Australia	1999–2008	96	379	37	416
3	**Ian Healy**, Australia	1988–99	119	366	29	395
4	**Rodney Marsh**, Australia	1970–84	96	343	12	355
5	**Jeff Dujon**, West Indies	1981–91	81	265	5	270
6	**Alan Knott**, England	1967–81	95	250	19	269
7	**Alec Stewart**, England	1990–2003	133	227	14	241
8	**Wasim Bari**, Pakistan	1967–84	81	201	27	228
9	=**Godfrey Evans**, England	1946–59	91	173	46	219
	=**Ridley Jacobs**, West Indies	1998–2004	65	207	12	219

* As at 1 January 2010
# Boucher also played for the ICC World XI

◀ ***Gayle force***
Gayle is the only cricketer to score centuries in the three forms of International cricket.

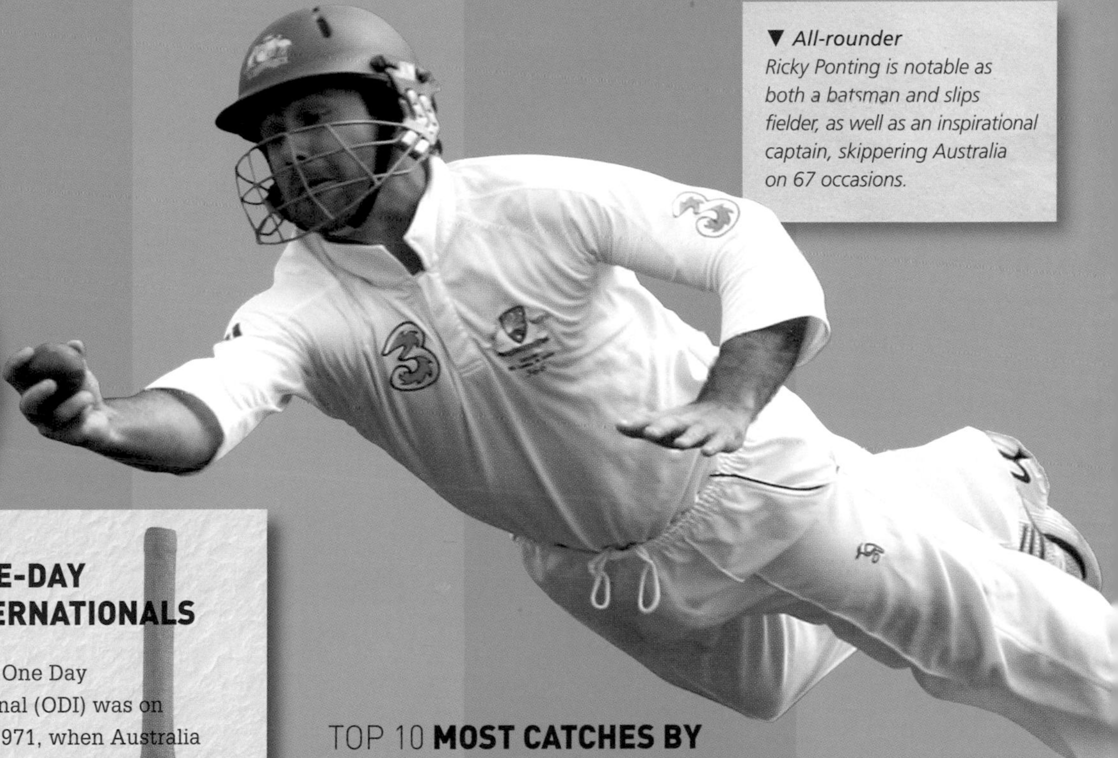

▼ ***All-rounder***
Ricky Ponting is notable as both a batsman and slips fielder, as well as an inspirational captain, skippering Australia on 67 occasions.

ONE-DAY INTERNATIONALS

The first One Day International (ODI) was on 5 January 1971, when Australia beat England by five wickets at the Melbourne Cricket Ground. The match was played after the first three days of the third Test were washed out, and officials decided to abandon the Test and play a one-day match instead. The match consisted of 40 overs of eight balls each. Now, ODIs consist of 50 overs (six balls) per side. The ODIs brought night-time cricket to the game and also introduced colourful playing strips. There are currently 10 Test-playing nations with full ODI status.

TOP 10 **MOST CATCHES BY AN OUTFIELDER IN TEST CRICKET***

	PLAYER / COUNTRY	YEARS	MATCHES	CATCHES
1	**Rahul Dravid**, India#	1996–2009	134	184
2	**Mark Waugh**, Australia	1991–2002	128	181
3	**Stephen Fleming**, New Zealand	1994–2008	111	171
4	**Brian Lara**, West Indies#	1990–2006	131	164
5	**Ricky Ponting**, Australia	1995–2009	136	159
6	**Mark Taylor**, Australia	1989–99	104	157
7	**Allan Border**, Australia	1978–94	156	156
8	**Mahela Jayawardene**, Sri Lanka	1997–2009	107	151
9	**Jacques Kallis**, South Africa#	1995–2009	131	147
10	**Matthew Hayden**, Australia	1994–2009	103	128

* As at 1 January 2010
# Also played for the ICC World XI

BASEBALL

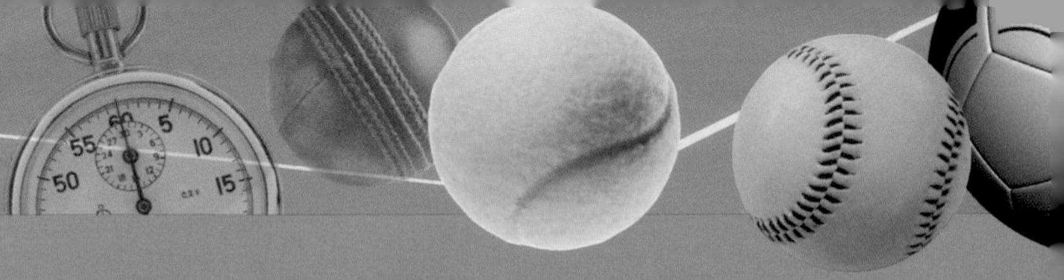

TOP 10 **MOST WORLD SERIES APPEARANCES***

	PLAYER	TEAM(S)	YEARS	APPEARANCES
1	Yogi Berra	New York Yankees	1947–63	75
2	Mickey Mantle	New York Yankees	1951–64	65
3	Elston Howard	New York Yankees, Boston Red Sox	1955–67	54
4	=Hank Bauer	New York Yankees	1949–58	53
	=Gil McDougald	New York Yankees	1951–60	53
6	Phil Rizzuto	New York Yankees	1941–55	52
7	Joe DiMaggio	New York Yankees	1936–51	51
8	Frankie Frisch	New York Giants, St Louis Cardinals	1921–34	50
9	Pee Wee Reese	Brooklyn Dodgers	1941–56	44
10	=Roger Maris	New York Yankees, St Louis Cardinals	1960–68	41
	=Babe Ruth	Boston Red Sox, New York Yankees	1915–32	41

* Individual game appearances, up to and including the 2009 World Series

▲ *World class*
Yogi Berra won the World Series 13 times, 10 times as a player with the Yankees and three times as a coach.

► *Barry Bonds*
Barry Bonds is the all-time leader in career home runs and the most homers in one season, racking up 73 in 2001.

TOP 10 **MOST HOME RUNS IN A CAREER***

	PLAYER	YEARS	HOMERS
1	Barry Bonds	1986–2007	762
2	Hank Aaron	1954–76	755
3	Babe Ruth	1914–36	714
4	Willie Mays	1951–73	660
5	Ken Griffey, Jr	1989–2009	630
6	Sammy Sosa	1989–2007	609
7	Frank Robinson	1956–76	586
8	=Mark McGwire	1986–2001	583
	=Alex Rodriguez	1994–2009	583
10	Harmon Killebrew	1954–75	573

* In a regular season, up to and including 2009

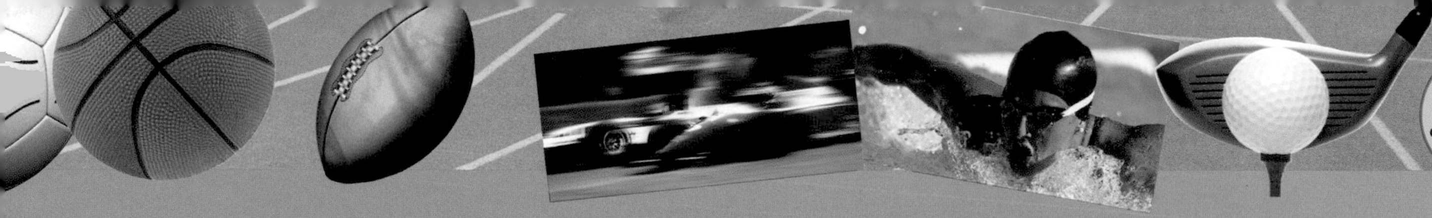

TOP 10 **MOST LITTLE LEAGUE WORLD SERIES WINS***

	TEAM	YEARS	WINS
1	Chinese Taipei (Taiwan)	1969, 1971–74, 1977–81 1986–88, 1990–91, 1995–96	17
2	=Japan	1967–68, 1976, 1999, 2001, 2003	6
	=California, USA	1961–63, 1992–93, 2009	6
4	=Pennsylvania, USA	1947–48, 1955, 1960	4
	=New Jersey, USA	1949, 1970, 1975, 1988	4
	=Connecticut, USA	1951–52, 1965, 1989	4
7	=Mexico	1957–58, 1997	3
	=Georgia, USA	1983, 2006–07	3
9	=New York, USA	1954, 1964	2
	=Texas, USA	1950, 1966	2
	=South Korea	1984–85	2
	=Venezuela	1994, 2000	2
	=Hawaii, USA	2005, 2008	2

* Up to and including 2009

An annual tournament for baseball players between the ages of 11 and 13, the Little League World Series was first contested in 1947. The biggest winning margin was in 1987 when Hua Lien, representing Taiwan, beat Irvine of California 21–1.

TOP 10 **BIGGEST SINGLE GAME WINS IN THE WORLD SERIES***

	TEAMS (WINNERS FIRST) / GAME / DATE	SCORE
1	New York Yankees vs. New York Giants (Game 2) 2 Oct 1936	18–4
2	=New York Yankees vs. Pittsburgh Pirates (Game 2) 6 Oct 1960	16–3
	=Arizona Diamondbacks vs. New York Yankees (Game 6) 3 Nov 2001	15–2
4	=New York Yankees vs. New York Giants (Game 5) 9 Oct 1951	13–1
	=New York Yankees vs. Pittsburgh Pirates (Game 6) 12 Oct 1960	12–0
	=Detroit Tigers vs. St Louis Cardinals (Game 6) 9 Oct 1968	13–1
	=New York Yankees vs. Milwaukee Brewers (Game 6) 19 Oct 1982	13–1
	=San Francisco Giants vs. Anaheim Angels (Game 5) 24 Oct 2002	16–4
	=Boston Red Sox vs. Colorado Rockies (Game 1) 24 Oct 2007	13–1
10	=New York Yankees vs. Philadelphia Athletics (Game 6) 26 Oct 1911	13–2
	=St Louis Cardinals vs. Detroit Tigers (Game 7) 9 Oct 1934	11–0
	=Chicago White Sox vs. Los Angeles Dodgers (Game 1) 1 Oct 1959	11–0
	=Kansas City Royals vs. St Louis Cardinals (Game 7) 27 Oct 1985	11–0
	=Atlanta Braves vs. New York Yankees (Game 1) 20 Oct 1996	12–1

* Based on winning margin

Source: Major League Baseball

◀ *Randy Johnson*
Johnson retired in 2010 after a 22-year career which saw him play for six Major League teams.

TOP 10 **PITCHERS WITH THE MOST MLB CAREER STRIKEOUTS***

	PITCHER	YEARS	STRIKEOUTS
1	Nolan Ryan	1966–93	5,714
2	Randy Johnson	1988–2009	4,875
3	Roger Clemens	1984–2007	4,672
4	Steve Carlton	1965–88	4,136
5	Bert Blyleven	1970–92	3,701
6	Tom Seaver	1967–86	3,640
7	Don Sutton	1966–88	3,574
8	Gaylord Perry	1962–83	3,534
9	Walter Johnson	1907–25	3,509
10	Greg Maddux	1986–2008	3,371

* In a regular season, up to and including 2009

BASKETBALL

TOP 10 **HIGHEST-PAID PLAYERS IN THE NBA IN 2009–10**

	PLAYER	TEAM	SALARY (US$)
1	Tracy McGrady	Houston Rockets	23,239,561
2	Kobe Bryant	LA Lakers	23,034,375
3	Jermaine O'Neal	Miami Heat	22,995,000
4	Tim Duncan	San Antonio Spurs	22,183,218
5	Shaquille O'Neal	Cleveland Cavaliers	20,000,000
6	= Dirk Nowitzki	Dallas Mavericks	19,795,714
	= Paul Pierce	Boston Celtics	19,795,712
8	Ray Allen	Boston Celtics	19,766,860
9	Rashard Lewis	Orlando Magic	18,876,000
10	Michael Redd	Milwaukee Bucks	17,040,000

TOP 10 **MOST POINTS PER GAME IN AN NBA CAREER***

	PLAYER / YEARS	POINTS PER GAME
1	Michael Jordan 1984–2003	30.12
2	Wilt Chamberlain 1959–73	30.07
3	LeBron James 2003–09	27.53
4	Elgin Baylor 1958–72	27.36
5	Allen Iverson 1996–2009	27.07
6	Jerry West 1960–74	27.03
7	Bob Pettit 1954–65	26.36
8	George Gervin 1976–86	26.18
9	Oscar Robertson 1960–74	25.68
10	Kobe Bryant 1996–2009	25.13

* Up to and including the 2008–09 season; regular season games only

► *Allen Iverson*
Allen Inverson was the No. 1 Draft pick by the 76ers in 1996.

◄ *Kobe Bryant*
Lakers guard Kobe Bryant was the NBA's Most Valuable Player in 2008 and the NBA Final's MVP in 2009.

TOP 10 **MOST GAMES PLAYED IN AN NBA CAREER***

	PLAYER	SEASONS PLAYED	GAMES PLAYED
1	Robert Parish	21	1,611
2	Kareem Abdul-Jabbar	20	1,560
3	John Stockton	19	1,504
4	Karl Malone	19	1,476
5	Kevin Willis	21	1,424
6	Reggie Miller	18	1,389
7	Clifford Robinson	18	1,380
8	Gary Payton	17	1,335
9	Moses Malone	19	1,329
10	Buck Williams	17	1,307

* Up to and including the 2008–09 season; regular season games only

If games played in the ABA (American Basketball Association) are included, Moses Malone's total would be 1,455, putting him in 5th place, and there would be a new No. 10 with the addition of Artis Gilmore on 1,329.

TOP 10 **MOST POINTS IN AN NBA CAREER***

	PLAYER / YEARS	POINTS
1	Kareem Abdul-Jabbar 1969–89	38,387
2	Karl Malone 1985–2004	36,928
3	Michael Jordan 1984–2003	32,292
4	Wilt Chamberlain 1959–73	31,419
5	Shaquille O'Neal 1993–2009	27,619
6	Moses Malone 1976–95	27,409
7	Elvin Hayes 1968–84	27,313
8	Hakeem Olajuwon 1984–2002	26,946
9	Oscar Robertson 1960–74	26,710
10	Dominique Wilkins 1982–99	26,668

* Up to and including the 2008–09 season

Source: NBA

TOP 10 **BIGGEST NBA ARENAS***

	TEAM / ARENA / LOCATION / OPENED	CAPACITY
1	**Detroit Pistons,** The Palace of Auburn Hills Auburn Hills, MI 1988	22,076
2	**Philadelphia 76ers,** Wachovia Center Philadelphia, PA 1996	21,600
3	**Chicago Bulls,** United Center Chicago, IL 1994	20,917
4	**Cleveland Cavaliers,** Quicken Loans Arena Cleveland, OH 1994	20,562
5	**Minnesota Timberwolves,** Target Center Minneapolis, MN 1990	20,500
6	**Washington Wizards,** Verizon Center Washington, DC 1997	20,173
7	**New Jersey Nets,** Izod Center East Rutherford, NJ 1981	20,049
8	**Utah Jazz,** EnergySolutions Arena Salt Lake City, UT 1991	19,991
9	**Portland Trail Blazers,** Rose Garden Arena Portland, OR 1995	19,980
10	**Toronto Raptors,** Air Canada Center Toronto, Ontario 1999	19,800

* By 2009 capacity

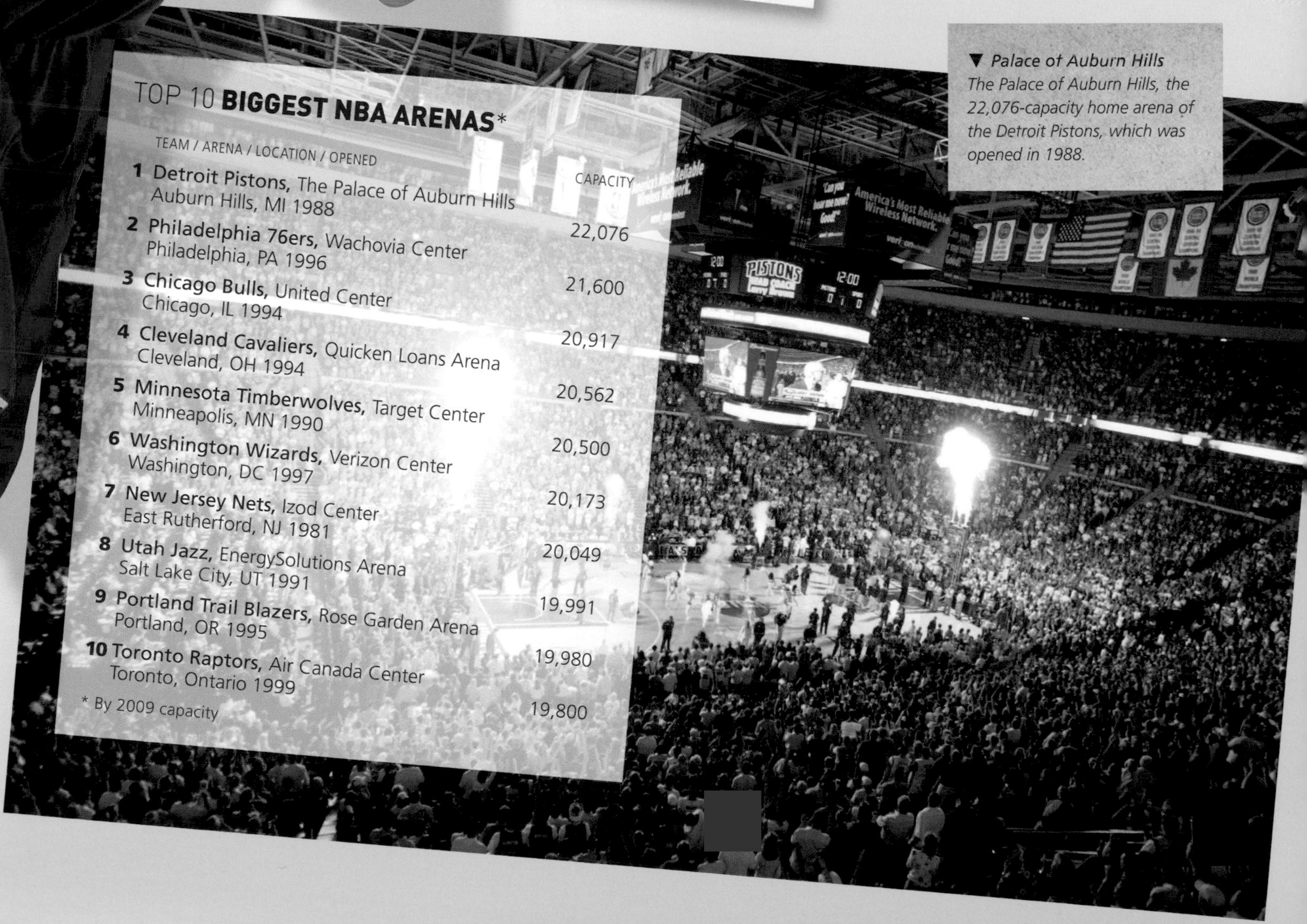

▼ *Palace of Auburn Hills*
The Palace of Auburn Hills, the 22,076-capacity home arena of the Detroit Pistons, which was opened in 1988.

COMBAT SPORTS

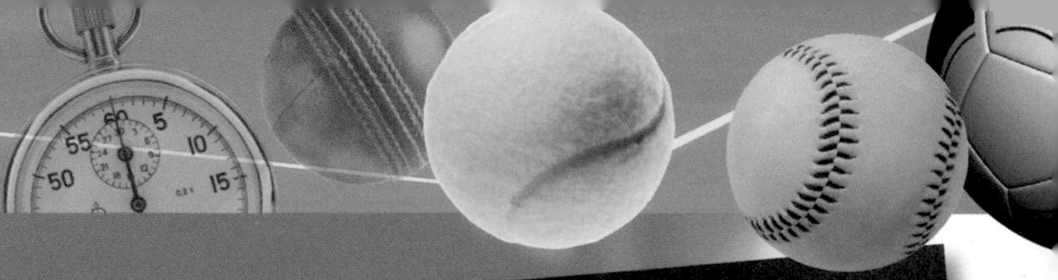

TOP 10 OLYMPIC WRESTLING COUNTRIES*

	COUNTRY	GOLD	SILVER	BRONZE	TOTAL
1	USA	49	42	31	122
2	USSR	62	31	23	116
3	Finland	26	29	29	84
4	Sweden	28	27	27	82
5	Bulgaria	16	31	20	67
6	Turkey	28	16	13	57
7	Japan	24	17	15	56
8	Hungary	19	15	17	51
9	Russia	21	11	8	40
10	South Korea	10	11	13	34

* Based on total medals won at all Olympics 1896–2008 (Greco-Roman) and 1904–2008 (Freestyle), including women's freestyle events 2004–08

◀ ***Undisputed victory***
Mike Tyson beats Tony Tucker (USA) on points in 1987 at Las Vegas to become the undisputed World Heavyweight Champion.

◀ ***Fighting freestyle***
Turk Ramazan Sahin takes out Ukraine's Andriy Stadnik at the 2008 Olympics.

THE 10 LATEST WINNERS OF THE 'ROYAL RUMBLE'

YEAR / WINNER / POSITION ENTERING RING

2010 Edge 29
2009 Randy Orton 8
2008 Joe Cena 30
2007 The Undertaker 30
2006 Rey Mesterio 2
2005 Batista 28
2004 Chris Benoit 1
2003 Brock Lesnar 29
2002 Triple H 22
2001 Steve Austin 27

Source: WWE (World Wrestling Entertainment)

The Royal Rumble is an annual 'last man standing' event with 30 wrestlers taking part. They draw lots, and numbers one and two enter the ring first. Then, at various intervals, the remaining fighters enter the ring according to their lot number. The idea is to eliminate all other wrestlers until there is just one man remaining. The first Royal Rumble was at Hamilton Ontario in January 1988 and won by Jim Duggan. 'Stone Cold' Steve Austin has won the Royal Rumble a record three times. The first woman to take part was Chyna in 1999. Beth Phoenix was the second, in 2010.

THE 10 LAST UNDISPUTED WORLD HEAVYWEIGHT BOXING CHAMPIONS

	BOXER	REIGN BEGAN	REIGN ENDED
1	Mike Tyson	1 Aug 1987	6 May 1989*
2	Leon Spinks	15 Feb 1978	18 Mar 1978#
3	Muhammad Ali	30 Oct 1974	15 Feb 1978
4	George Foreman	22 Jan 1973	30 Oct 1974
5	Joe Frazier	16 Feb 1970	22 Jan 1973
6	Muhammad Ali	6 Feb 1967	29 Apr 1967†
7	Cassius Clay (later Muhammad Ali)	25 Feb 1964	19 Jun 1964§
8	Sonny Liston	25 Sep 1962	25 Feb 1964
9	Floyd Patterson	20 Jun 1960	25 Sep 1962
10	Ingemar Johansson (Sweden)	26 Jun 1959	20 Jun 1960

* Tyson held the WBC, WBA and IBF titles from 1 August 1987 to 11 February 1990 and was generally acknowledged as the universal champion despite the fact that a new body, the WBO, came into being in 1988 and had its first heavyweight champion (Francesco Damiani of Italy) on 6 May 1989

Spinks was stripped of his title by the WBC for refusing to fight their No. 1 contender Ken Norton

† Ali was stripped of his title by the WBA and then WBC for failing to be drafted into the US Army

§ The WBA withdrew recognition of Ali after refusing a re-match with Sonny Liston

All boxers are from the USA unless otherwise stated.

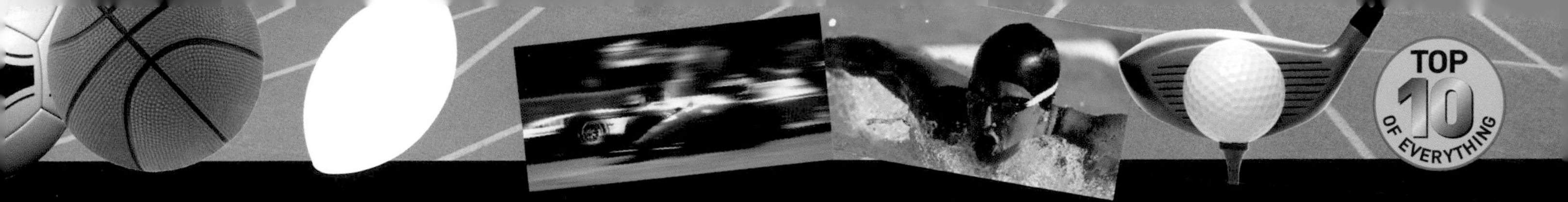

THE 10 **FIRST BOXERS TO WIN WORLD TITLES IN THREE DIFFERENT WEIGHT DIVISIONS***

	BOXER / COUNTRY / WEIGHT DIVISION	DATE OF 3RD TITLE
1	**Bob Fitzsimmons**, UK Middleweight, Heavyweight, Light-heavyweight	25 Nov 1903
2	**Tony Canzoneri**, USA Featherweight, Lightweight, Light-welterweight	23 Apr 1931
3	**Barney Ross**, USA Lightweight, Light-welterweight, Welterweight	28 May 1934
4	**Henry Armstrong**, USA Featherweight, Welterweight, Lightweight	17 Aug 1938
5	**Wilfred Benitez**#, Puerto Rico Light-welterweight, Welterweight, Light-middleweight	23 May 1981
6	**Alexis Argüello**, Nicaragua Featherweight, Super-featherweight, Lightweight	20 Jun 1981
7	**Roberto Durán**, Panama Lightweight, Welterweight, Light-middleweight	16 Jun 1983
8	**Wilfredo Gómez**, Puerto Rico Light featherweight, Featherweight, Super-featherweight	19 May 1985
9	**Thomas Hearns**, USA Welterweight, Light-middleweight, Light-heavyweight	7 Mar 1987
10	**'Sugar' Ray Leonard**, USA Welterweight, Light-middleweight, Middleweight	6 Apr 1987

* As recognized by the four leading bodies: WBA, WBC, IBF, WBO
# Formerly known as Wilfredo Benitez

THE 10 **HEAVIEST MEN TO TAKE PART IN A WORLD HEAVYWEIGHT BOXING TITLE FIGHT***

	BOXER (COUNTRY) / OPPONENT (COUNTRY)	YEAR	WEIGHT (LB)
1	**Nikolay Valuev**#, Russia Monte Barrett, USA	2006	328
2	**Shannon Briggs**, USA Sultan Ibragimov#, Russia	2007	273
3	=**Primo Carnera**#, Italy Tommy Loughran, USA	1934	270
	=**Jameel McCline**, USA Chris Byrd#, USA	2004	270
	=**Danny Williams**, UK Vitali Klitschko#, Ukraine	2004	270
6	**Derrick Jefferson**, USA Wladimir Klitschko#, Ukraine	2001	260
7	**Lennox Lewis**#, UK Vitali Klitschko, Ukraine	2003	256½
8	**Matt Skelton**, UK Rusian Chagaev#, Uzbekistan	2008	254¾
9	**Peter Okhello**, Uganda Oleg Maskaev#, Kazakhstan	2006	254½
10	=**Samuel Peter**, USA Vitali Klitschko#, Ukraine	2008	253½
	=**Hashim Rahman**, USA Wladimir Klitschko#, Ukraine	2009	253½

* As recognized by the WBA, WBC, IBF and WBO
# Winner

Where a boxer would appear on the list on more than one occasion, only his heaviest weight is taken into consideration. Valuev would occupy the first seven places if this criterion were not used.

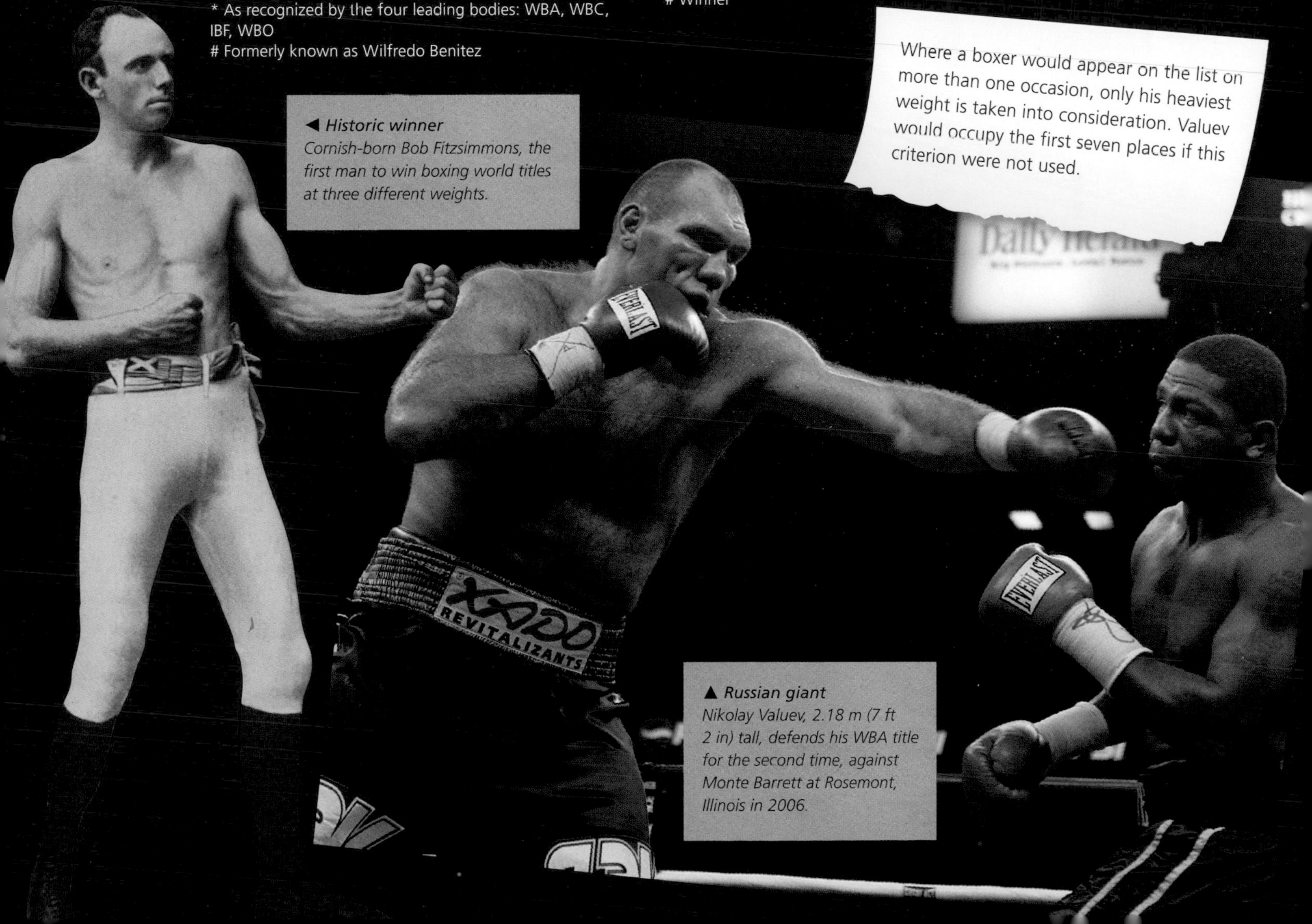

◀ *Historic winner*
Cornish-born Bob Fitzsimmons, the first man to win boxing world titles at three different weights.

▲ *Russian giant*
Nikolay Valuev, 2.18 m (7 ft 2 in) tall, defends his WBA title for the second time, against Monte Barrett at Rosemont, Illinois in 2006.

ON TWO WHEELS

THE 10 **OLDEST MEN TO WIN TOUR DE FRANCE***

	RIDER / COUNTRY	YEAR	AGE YEARS	MONTHS	DAYS
1	**Firmin Lambot**, Belgium	1922	36	4	9
2	**Henri Pélissier**, France	1923	34	6	0
3	**Gino Bartali**, Italy	1948	34	0	7
4	**Lance Armstrong**, USA	2005	33	10	6
5	**Joop Zoetemelk**, Netherlands	1980	33	7	18
6	**Léon Scieur**, France	1921	33	4	5
7	**Carlos Sastre**, Spain	2008	33	3	5
8	**Fausto Coppi**, Italy	1952	32	10	4
9	**Maurice De Waele**, Belgium	1929	32	7	1
10	**Maurice Garin**, France	1903	32	4	17

* As at the time of winning their last Tour in the case of multiple winners; as at the end of the 2009 Tour

► Carlos Sastre
Carlos Sastre won the 2008 Tour de France from Australia's Cadel Evans by just 58 seconds.

No. 10 on the list, Maurice Garin, was the very first winner of the Tour de France in 1903. The youngest winner of the race is Henri Cornet of France, who was 10 days short of his 20th birthday when he won the 1904 race.

TOP 10 **OLYMPIC CYCLING COUNTRIES***

		MEDALS GOLD	SILVER	BRONZE	TOTAL
1	France	40	25	22	87
2	UK	18	26	21	65
3	Italy	33	17	8	58
4	USA	14	15	20	49
5	Australia	13	16	13	42
6	Netherlands	15	16	9	40
7	Germany	12	10	13	35
8	=Belgium	6	8	10	24
	=USSR	11	4	9	24
10	Denmark	6	8	8	22

* Based on total medals won 1896–2008

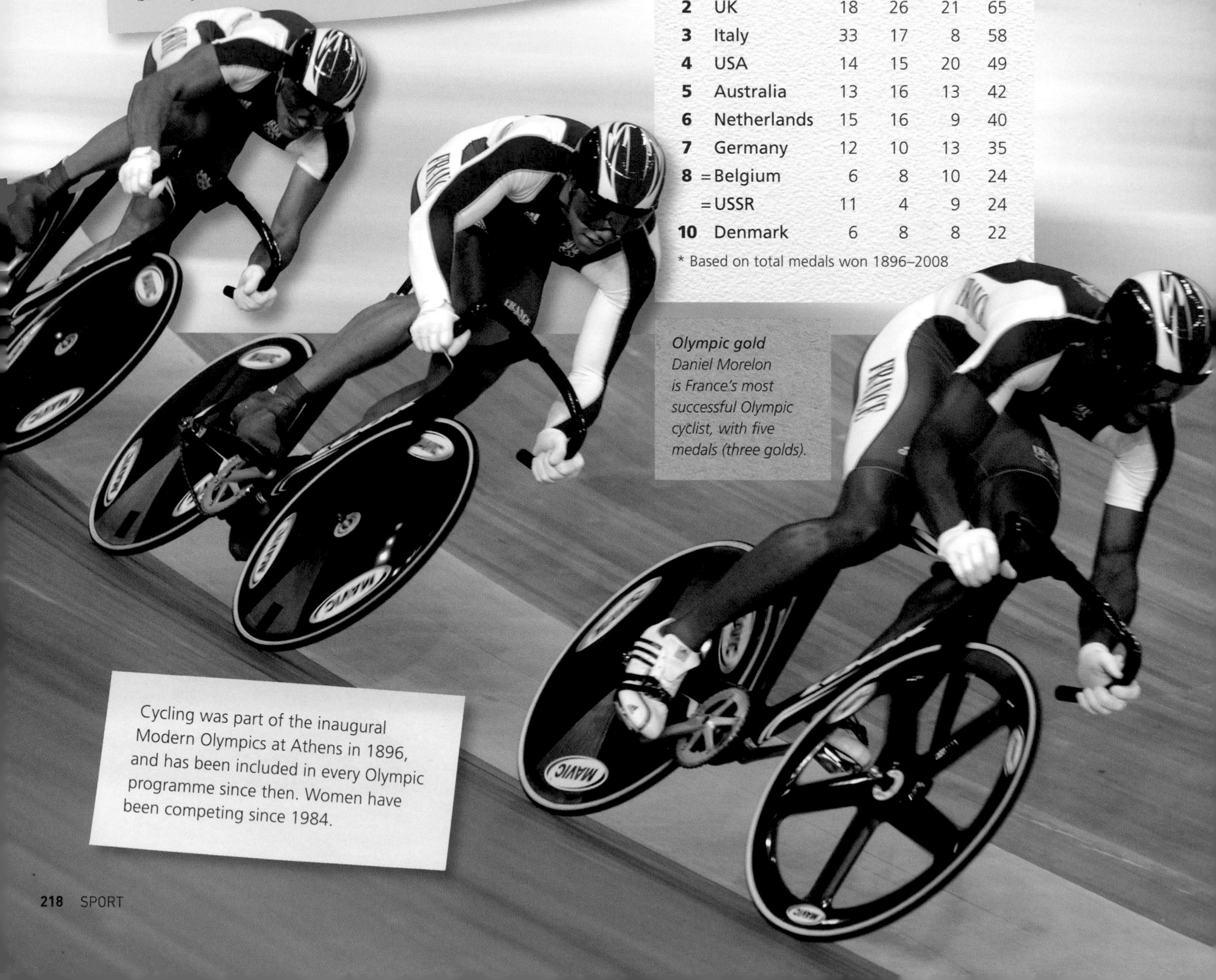

Olympic gold
Daniel Morelon is France's most successful Olympic cyclist, with five medals (three golds).

Cycling was part of the inaugural Modern Olympics at Athens in 1896, and has been included in every Olympic programme since then. Women have been competing since 1984.

TOP 10 **RIDERS WITH THE MOST MOTOGP RACE WINS***

	Rider	Country / Years	Wins
1	Valentino Rossi	Italy, 2000–09	77
2	Giacomo Agostini	Italy, 1965–76	68
3	Mick Doohan	Australia, 1990–98	54
4	Mike Hailwood	UK, 1961–67	37
5	Eddie Lawson	USA, 1984–92	31
6	Kevin Schwantz	USA, 1988–94	25
7	Wayne Rainey	USA, 1988–93	24
8	= Geoff Duke	UK, 1950–59	22
	= John Surtees	UK, 1956–60	22
	= Kenny Roberts	USA, 1978–83	22

* Moto GP 2002–09, 500cc 1949–2001

TOP 10 **MOST INDIVIDUAL WORLD SPEEDWAY TITLES***

	RIDER / COUNTRY	YEARS	WINS
1	=**Ivan Mauger**, New Zealand	1968–70, 1972, 1977, 1979	6
	=**Tony Rickardsson**, Sweden	1994, 1998–99, 2001–02, 2005	6
3	=**Barry Briggs**, New Zealand	1957–58, 1964–66	5
	=**Ove Fundin**, Sweden	1956, 1960–61, 1963, 1967	5
5	**Hans Nielsen**, Denmark	1986–87, 1989, 1995	4
6	=**Ole Olsen**, Denmark	1971, 1975, 1978	3
	=**Erik Gundersen**, Denmark	1984–85, 1988	3
	=**Nicki Pedersen**, Denmark	2003, 2007–08	3
9	=**Jack Young**, Australia	1951–52	2
	=**Freddie Williams**, UK	1950, 1953	2
	=**Ronnie Moore**, New Zealand	1954, 1959	2
	=**Peter Craven**, UK	1955, 1962	2
	=**Bruce Penhall**, USA	1981–82	2
	=**Jason Crump**, Australia	2004, 2006	2

* Up to and including 2009

The first World Championship was at Wembley Stadium in 1936 and won by Australia's Lionel Van Praag. From 1936 to 1994 the champion was decided after a single night's racing. Since 1995 the championship consists of a season-long series of Grand Prix events, with the world champion the rider to accrue the most points.

► *Nicki Pedersen*
Nicki Pedersen was a member of the Denmark team that finished runners-up in the 2002 World Cup. His brother Ronni was also in the team.

TOP 10 HIGHEST-PAID PLAYERS IN THE MLS*

	PLAYER / COUNTRY	CLUB	ANNUAL SALARY (US$)
1	**David Beckham**, England	LA Galaxy	6,500,000
2	**Cuauhtémoc Blanco**, Mexico	Chicago Fire	2,943,702
3	**Juan Pablo Angel**, Colombia	NY Red Bulls	1,798,000
4	**Freddie Ljungberg**, Sweden	Seattle Sounders	1,314,000
5	**Landon Donovan**, USA	LA Galaxy	900,000
6	**Guillermo Barros Schelleto**, Argentina	Columbus Crew	775,000
7	**Luciano Emilio**, Brazil	DC United	758,857
8	**Shalrie Joseph**, Grenada	New England Revolution	450,000
9	**Dwayne DeRosario**, Canada	Toronto FC	425,750
10	**Taylor Twellman**, USA	New England Revolution	420,000

* As at the start of the 2009 season

Source: Major League Soccer Players Union

TOP 10 WORLD CUP GOALSCORERS*

	PLAYER / COUNTRY	YEARS	GOALS
1	**Ronaldo**, Brazil	1998–2006	15
2	**Gerd Müller**, West Germany	1970–74	14
3	**Just Fontaine**, France	1958	13
4	**Pelé**, Brazil	1958–70	12
5	=**Sándor Kocsis**, Hungary	1954	11
	=**Jürgen Klinsmann**, Germany	1990–98	11
7	=**Helmut Rahn**, West Germany	1954–58	10
	=**Teófilio Cubillas**, Peru	1970–78	10
	=**Grzegorz Lato**, Poland	1974–82	10
	=**Gary Lineker**, England	1986–90	10
	=**Gabriel Batistuta**, Argentina	1994–2002	10
	=**Miroslav Klose**, Germany	2002–06	10

* In the final stages of the FIFA World Cup, 1930–2006

Fontaine's 13 goals in the 1958 finals is a record for one tournament.

◀ ***Shear brilliance***
Alan Shearer is the first – and so far the only – player to score over 200 goals in the Barclays Premier League.

▼ ***Golden boots***
David Beckham divides his time between LA Galaxy and AC Milan.

TOP 10 GOALSCORERS IN THE BARCLAYS PREMIER LEAGUE

PLAYER / GOALS* / CLUB(S)

1. **Alan Shearer** 260
   Blackburn Rovers, Newcastle United
2. **Andy Cole** 187
   Newcastle United, Manchester United, Blackburn Rovers, Fulham, Manchester City, Portsmouth
3. **Thierry Henry** 174
   Arsenal
4. **Robbie Fowler** 163
   Liverpool, Leeds United, Manchester City
5. **Les Ferdinand** 149
   Queens Park Rangers, Newcastle United, Tottenham Hotspur, West Ham United, Leicester City, Bolton Wanderers
6. **Teddy Sheringham** 147
   Nottingham Forest, Tottenham Hotspur, Manchester United, Portsmouth, West Ham United
7. **Michael Owen** 146
   Liverpool, Newcastle United, Manchester United
8. **Jimmy Floyd Hasselbaink** 127
   Leeds United, Chelsea, Middlesbrough, Charlton Athletic
9. **Dwight Yorke** 123
   Aston Villa, Manchester United, Blackburn Rovers, Birmingham City, Sunderland
10. **Robbie Keane** 121
    Coventry City, Leeds United, Tottenham Hotspur, Liverpool

* As at 26 January 2010

Source: FA Premier League

TOP 10 **TRANSFERS WORLDWIDE***

	PLAYER / COUNTRY	FROM	TO	YEAR	FEE (£)
1	**Cristiano Ronaldo**, Portugal	Manchester United	Real Madrid	2009	80,000,000
2	**Zlatan Ibrahimovic**, Sweden	Inter Milan	Barcelona	2009	60,700,000
3	**Kaká**, Brazil	AC Milan	Real Madrid	2009	56,000,000
4	**Zinedine Zidane**, France	Juventus	Real Madrid	2001	47,700,000
5	**Carlos Tévez**, Argentina	#	Manchester City	2009	47,000,000
6	**Luis Figo**, Portugal	Barcelona	Real Madrid	2000	37,400,000
7	**Hernán Crespo**, Argentina	Parma	Lazio	2000	35,700,000
8	**Gianluigi Buffon**, Italy	Parma	Juventus	2001	33,000,000
9	**Robinho**, Brazil	Real Madrid	Manchester City	2008	32,500,000
10	**Christian Vieri**, Italy	Lazio	Inter Milan	1999	31,000,000

* As at 26 January 2010
# Carlos Tevéz moved from Manchester United to Manchester City but United did not hold his contract, which was owned by Media Sports Investment, hence they received the transfer fee from Manchester City

In June 2009, Kaká held the world transfer record for just over two weeks. The record transfer fee paid for a goalkeeper is the £33,000,000 paid by Juventus for Gianluigi Buffon (No. 8). The world's first £1,000,000 footballer was Giuseppe Savoldi, when he moved from Bologna to Napoli in 1975 for £1.2 million.

THE 10 **COUNTRIES WITH THE MOST 100-CAPPED FOOTBALLERS**

	COUNTRY	PLAYERS WITH 100 CAPS*
1	USA	11
2	=Egypt	7
	=South Korea	7
	=Mexico	7
5	=Estonia	6
	=France	6
	=Saudi Arabia	6
	=Sweden	6
9	=Costa Rica	5
	=Denmark	5
	=England	5
	=Germany/West Germany	5
	=Latvia	5
	=United Arab Emirates	5

* As at 1 January 2010

▶ ***Double victory***
Ronaldo was twice a World Cup winner, in both the 1994 and 2002 tournaments.

▶ ***Most-capped***
Cobi Jones is the most-capped American, with 164 caps. He made his debut in a 2–0 win over Canada at Greensboro on 3 September 1992.

AMERICAN FOOTBALL

TOP 10 POINTS IN AN NFL CAREER*

	PLAYER / YEARS	POINTS
1	Morten Andersen 1982–2007	2,544
2	Gary Anderson 1982–2004	2,434
3	John Carney 1988–2009	2,044
4	Matt Stover 1991–2009	2,004
5	George Blanda 1949–75	2,002
6	Jason Elam 1993–2009	1,983
7	Jason Hanson 1992–2009	1,835
8	Norm Johnson 1982–99	1,736
9	John Kasay 1991–2009	1,731
10	Nick Lowery 1980–96	1,711

* In a regular season up to and including 2009

Source: NFL

TOP 10 MOST SUPER BOWL WINS*

	TEAM / YEARS	WINS
1	Pittsburgh Steelers 1975–76, 1979–80, 2006, 2009	6
2	=Dallas Cowboys 1972, 1978, 1993–94, 1996	5
	=San Francisco 49ers 1982, 1985, 1989–90, 1995	5
4	=Green Bay Packers 1967–68, 1997	3
	=Oakland/Los Angeles Raiders 1977, 1981, 1984	3
	=Washington Redskins 1983, 1988, 1992	3
	=New York Giants 1987, 1991, 2008	3
	=New England Patriots 2002, 2004–05	3
9	=Baltimore/ Indianapolis Colts 1971, 2007	2
	=Miami Dolphins 1973–74	2
	=Denver Broncos 1998–99	2

* Up to and including 2010

▲ *Pittsburgh Steelers*
The Steelers beat the Cardinals in 2009 to win their record 6th Super Bowl.

► *Matt Stover*
At 42, Matt Stover is the oldest man to play in the Super Bowl.

TOP 10 MOST YARDS GAINED PASSING IN A CAREER*

	PLAYER	YEARS	YARDS
1	Brett Favre	1991–2009	69,329
2	Dan Marino	1983–99	61,361
3	John Elway	1983–98	51,475
4	Peyton Manning	1998–2009	50,128
5	Warren Moon	1984–2000	49,325
6	Fran Tarkenton	1961–78	47,003
7	Vinny Testaverde	1987–2007	46,233
8	Drew Bledsoe	1993–2006	44,611
9	Dan Fouts	1973–87	43,040
10	Joe Montana	1979–94	40,551

* Up to and including the 2009 regular season

Source: NFL

BIGGEST NFL STADIUMS

The NFL is the most-watched sporting league in the world, with average attendances in excess of 65,000. Dallas Cowboys, who moved to their new 111,000-capacity Cowboys Stadium in September 2009, had an average attendance of 89,756 for the 2009 regular season, 5,000 more than Washington Redskins' FedEx Field.

▲ *LaDainian Tomlinson*
LaDainian Tomlinson's 31 touchdowns in 2006 is an all-time NFL record for a single season.

TOP 10 NFL COACHES WITH THE MOST WINS*

	COACH	YEARS	GAMES	WINS
1	Don Shula	1963–95	490	328
2	George Halas	1920–67	497	318
3	Tom Landry	1960–88	418	250
4	Curly Lambeau	1921–53	380	226
5	Paul Brown	1946–75	326	213
6	Marty Schottenheimer	1984–2006	327	200
7	Chuck Noll	1969–91	342	193
8	Dan Reeves	1981–2003	357	190
9	Chuck Knox	1973–94	334	186
10	Bill Parcells	1983–2006	303	172

* Up to and including the 2009 regular season

TOP 10 MOST TOUCHDOWNS IN A CAREER*

	PLAYER	YEARS	TOUCHDOWNS
1	Jerry Rice	1984–2004	207
2	Emmitt Smith	1990–2004	175
3	LaDainian Tomlinson	2001–09	153
4	Randy Moss	1998–2009	149
5	Terrell Owens	1996–2009	147
6	Marcus Allen	1982–97	144
7	Marshall Faulk	1994–2006	136
8	Cris Carter	1987–2002	130
9	Marvin Harrison	1996–2008	128
10	Jim Brown	1957–65	126

* Up to and including the 2009 regular season

Source: NFL

Don Shula took the Colts to the Super Bowl, losing to the Jets in 1968. But his greatest success came after taking over at Miami in 1970. He spent 25 years at the Dolphins and guided them to five Super Bowls, winning back-to-back in 1973 and 1974.

ICE HOCKEY

The most wins in a season by a goalie is 48 by Martin Brodeur of New Jersey Devils in 2006–07. In his 19 years with the Devils, Brodeur helped them to the play-offs 18 times.

TOP 10 **GOALTENDERS IN AN NHL CAREER***

	PLAYER	YEARS	GAMES PLAYED	GAMES WON
1	Martin Brodeur	1991–2009	999	557
2	Patrick Roy	1984–2003	1,029	551
3	Ed Belfour	1988–2007	963	484
4	Curtis Joseph	1989–2009	943	454
5	Terry Sawchuk	1949–70	971	447
6	Jacques Plante	1952–73	837	437
7	Tony Esposito	1968–84	886	423
8	Glenn Hall	1952–71	906	407
9	Grant Fuhr	1981–2000	868	403
10	=Dominik Hasek	1990–2008	735	389
	=Chris Osgood	1993–2009	710	389

* Based on games won in regular season up to and including 2008–09

► ***Brodeur froideur***
Canadian-born Brodeur has spent his entire NHL career with the New Jersey Devils.

▲ ***Record-breaker***
In 2008–09, Detroit Red Wings' Chris Chelios was the oldest active player in the NHL and had played more games than any other active player.

TOP 10 **MOST GAMES IN AN NFL CAREER***

	PLAYER	YEARS	GAMES
1	Gordie Howe	1946–80	1,767
2	Mark Messier	1979–2004	1,756
3	Ron Francis	1981–2004	1,731
4	Chris Chelios	1983–2009	1,644
5	Dave Andreychuk	1982–2006	1,639
6	Scott Stevens	1982–2004	1,635
7	Larry Murphy	1980–2001	1,615
8	Raymond Bourque	1979–2001	1,612
9	=Alex Delvecchio	1950–74	1,549
	=John Bucyk	1955–78	1,549

* In regular season games up to and including the 2008–09 season

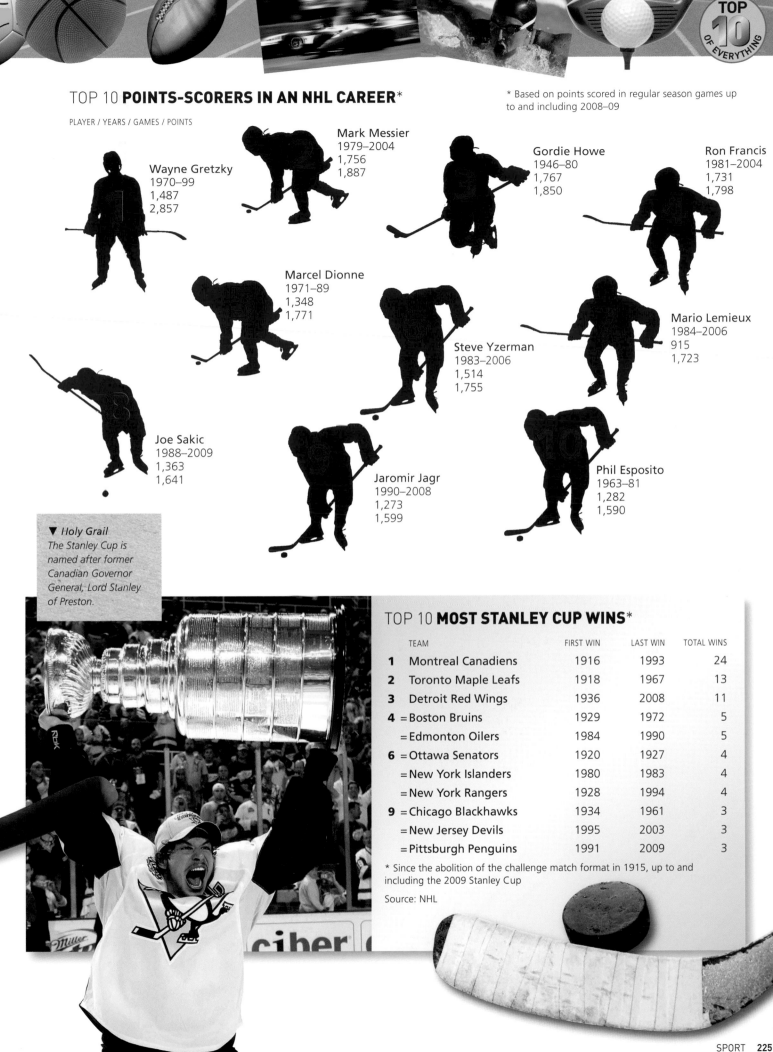

TOP 10 **POINTS-SCORERS IN AN NHL CAREER***

* Based on points scored in regular season games up to and including 2008–09

PLAYER / YEARS / GAMES / POINTS

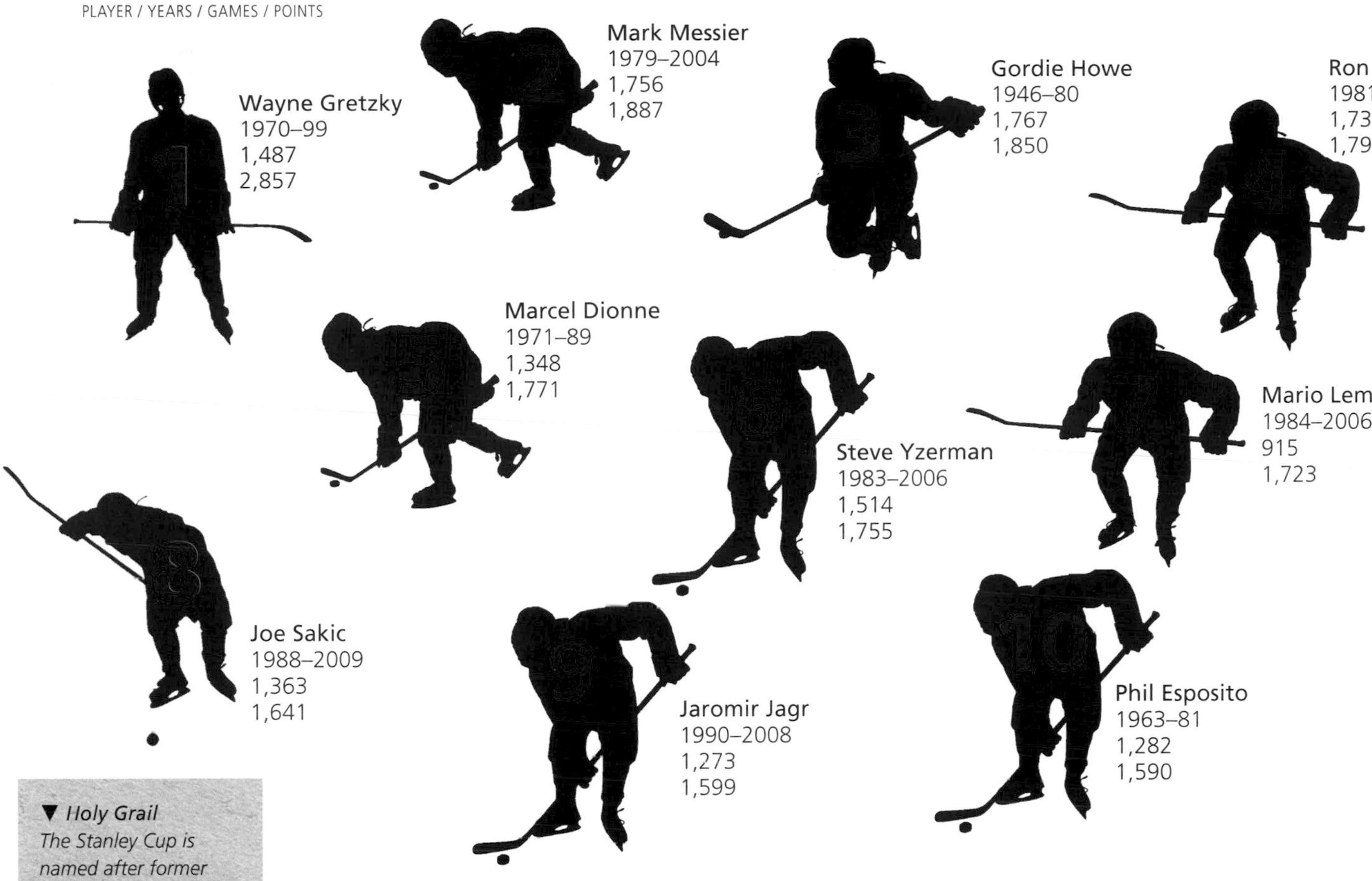

Wayne Gretzky
1970–99
1,487
2,857

Mark Messier
1979–2004
1,756
1,887

Gordie Howe
1946–80
1,767
1,850

Ron Francis
1981–2004
1,731
1,798

Marcel Dionne
1971–89
1,348
1,771

Steve Yzerman
1983–2006
1,514
1,755

Mario Lemieux
1984–2006
915
1,723

Joe Sakic
1988–2009
1,363
1,641

Jaromir Jagr
1990–2008
1,273
1,599

Phil Esposito
1963–81
1,282
1,590

▼ Holy Grail
The Stanley Cup is named after former Canadian Governor General, Lord Stanley of Preston.

TOP 10 **MOST STANLEY CUP WINS***

	TEAM	FIRST WIN	LAST WIN	TOTAL WINS
1	Montreal Canadiens	1916	1993	24
2	Toronto Maple Leafs	1918	1967	13
3	Detroit Red Wings	1936	2008	11
4	=Boston Bruins	1929	1972	5
	=Edmonton Oilers	1984	1990	5
6	=Ottawa Senators	1920	1927	4
	=New York Islanders	1980	1983	4
	=New York Rangers	1928	1994	4
9	=Chicago Blackhawks	1934	1961	3
	=New Jersey Devils	1995	2003	3
	=Pittsburgh Penguins	1991	2009	3

* Since the abolition of the challenge match format in 1915, up to and including the 2009 Stanley Cup

Source: NHL

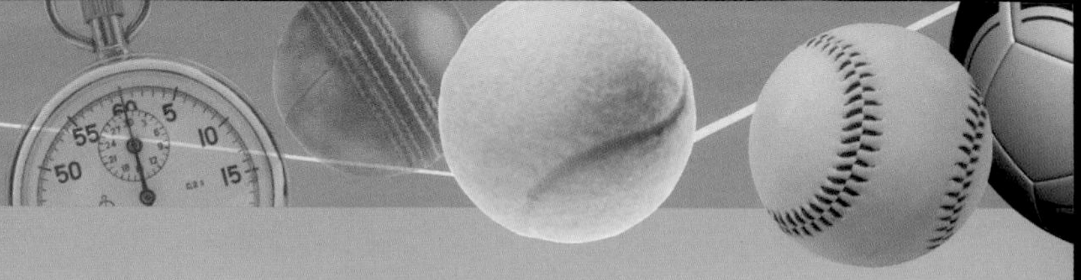

GOLF

TOP 10 MOST WOMEN'S MAJORS*

	GOLFER#	YEARS	A	B	C	D	E	F	G	TOTALS
1	Patty Berg	1937–58	–	–	1	–	–	7	7	15
2	Mickey Wright	1958–66	–	4	4	–	–	2	3	13
3	Louise Suggs	1946–59	–	1	2	–	–	4	4	11
4	=Babe Zaharias	1940–54	–	–	3	–	–	3	4	10
	=Annika Sörenstam, Sweden	1995–2006	3	3	3	1	–	–	–	10
6	Betsy Rawls	1951–69	–	2	4	–	–	–	2	8
7	=Juli Inkster	1984–2002	2	2	2	–	1	–	–	7
	=Karrie Webb, Australia	1999–2006	2	1	2	1	1	–	–	7
9	=Kathy Whitworth	1965–75	–	3	–	–	–	2	1	6
	=Pat Bradley	1980–86	1	1	1	–	3	–	–	6
	=Patty Sheehan	1983–96	1	3	2	–	–	–	–	6
	=Betsy King	1987–97	3	1	2	–	–	–	–	6

* As recognized by the Ladies Professional Golf Association (LPGA), up to and including 2009
# All golfers from the USA unless otherwise stated
A = Kraft Nabisco Championship (previously Nabisco Dinah Shore, Nabisco Championship) 1983–2009; B = LPGA Championship 1955–2009; C = US Women's Open 1946–2009; D = Women's British Open 2001–09; E = du Maurier Classic 1979–2000; F = Titleholders Championship 1937–42, 1946–66, 1972; G = Western Open 1930–67

▼ *Annika Sörenstam*
In 2003, Sörenstam played in a men's PGA Tour event – the Bank of America Colonial Golf Tournament.

Although the Ladies Professional Golf Association (LPGA) was not founded until 1950, the Western Open, Titleholders and US Women's Open winners prior to that date are regarded by the LPGA as Major winners.

TOP 10 MOST MEN'S MAJORS*

	GOLFER#	YEARS	US MASTERS	US OPEN	BRITISH OPEN	US PGA	TOTAL
1	Jack Nicklaus	1962–86	6	4	3	5	18
2	Tiger Woods	1997–2008	4	3	3	4	14
3	Walter Hagen	1914–29	–	2	4	5	11
4	=Ben Hogan	1946–53	2	4	1	2	9
	=Gary Player, South Africa	1959–78	3	1	3	2	9
6	Tom Watson	1975–83	2	1	5	–	8
7	=Harry Vardon, Jersey	1896–1914	–	1	6	–	7
	=Gene Sarazen	1922–35	1	2	1	3	7
	=Bobby Jones	1923–30	–	4	3	–	7
	=Sam Snead	1942–54	3	–	1	3	7
	=Arnold Palmer	1958–64	4	1	2	–	7

* Professional Majors only, up to and including 2009
# All golfers from the USA unless otherwise stated

In 1930, Bobby Jones achieved an unprecedented Grand Slam when he won the US and British Open titles, as well as the Amateur titles of both countries. Nicklaus, Woods, Hogan, Player and Sarazen are the only golfers to have won all four Majors at least once.

TOP 10 **MOST WINS ON THE CHAMPIONS TOUR**

	GOLFER*	YEARS	WINS#
1	Hale Irwin	1995–2007	45
2	Lee Trevino	1990–2000	29
3	Gil Morgan	1996–2007	25
4	Miller Barber	1981–89	24
5	Bob Charles, New Zealand	1987–96	23
6	= Don January	1980–87	22
	= Chi-Chi Rodriguez, Puerto Rico	1986–93	22
8	= Bruce Crampton, Australia	1986–97	20
	= Jim Colbert	1991–2001	20
10	= Gary Player, South Africa	1985–98	19
	= George Archer	1989–2000	19
	= Larry Nelson	1998–2004	19

* All golfers from the USA unless otherwise stated
\# As at 14 March 2010

Source: PGA Tour

Organized by the PGA Tour, the Champions Tour is a season-long series of events for golfers over the age of 50. Originally called the Senior PGA Tour, it was inaugurated in 1980 and changed its name to the Champions Tour in 2002.

▲ *Vijay Singh*
Vijay Singh of Fiji is the highest-earning non-American golfer in the world.

◀ *Tiger economy*
Tiger Woods has topped the PGA annual money list a record nine times.

TOP 10 **CAREER MONEY-WINNERS ON THE PGA TOUR**

	GOLFER*	TOTAL WON (US$)#
1	Tiger Woods	92,862,539
2	Vijay Singh, Fiji	62,443,635
3	Phil Mickelson	56,286,361
4	Jim Furyk	43,007,329
5	Davis Love III	39,148,701
6	Ernie Els, South Africa	37,761,663
7	David Toms	31,890,013
8	Kenny Perry	30,965,035
9	Justin Leonard	29,468,849
10	Stewart Cink	28,443,445

* All golfers from the USA unless otherwise stated
\# As at 14 March 2010

Source: PGA Tour

MONEY-WINNERS ON THE EUROPEAN TOUR

South Africa's Ernie Els, who is No. 6 on the US PGA Tour list, is the top money-winner on the PGA European Tour, with over €24 million. As at 14 March 2010, he was just €500,000 ahead of Scotland's Colin Montgomerie, with Ireland's Pádraig Harrington in third place. Montgomerie topped the annual money list a record eight times between 1993 and 2005.

► *Mike Smith*
Mike Smith wins his second Breeders' Cup Classic in 2009 aboard five-year-old Zenyatta.

TOP 10 JOCKEYS IN THE BREEDERS' CUP*

	JOCKEY	YEARS	WINS
1	Jerry Bailey	1991–2005	15
2	Mike Smith	1992–2009	13
3	Pat Day	1984–2001	12
4	=Chris McCarron	1985–2001	9
	=Frankie Dettori	1994–2009	9
	=Garrett Gomez	2005–09	9
7	Gary Stevens	1990–2000	8
8	=Eddie Delahoussaye	1984–93	7
	=Laffit Pincay Jr.	1985–93	7
	=Jose Santos	1986–2002	7
	=Pat Valenzuela	1986–2003	7
	=Corey Nakatani	1996–2006	7
	=John Velazquez	1998–2006	7

* Up to and including 2009

Source: The Breeders' Cup

The 14 Breeders' Cup races in 2009 were worth $25.5 million in prize money, with the Breeders' Cup Classic offering $5 million.

THE 10 MONEY-WINNING HORSES

	HORSE* / STARTS / WINS / LAST WIN	PRIZEMONEY (US$)#
1	Curlin 16 / 11 / 2008	10,501,800
2	Cigar 33 / 19 / 1996	9,999,815
3	Skip Away 38 / 18 / 1998	9,616,360
4	Fantastic Light 25 / 12 / 2001	8,486,957
5	Invasor 12 / 11 / 2007	7,804,070
6	Pleasantly Perfect 18 / 9 / 2004	7,789,880
7	Smarty Jones 9 / 8 / 2004	7,613,555
8	Silver Charm 24 / 12 / 1999	6,944,369
9	Captain Steve 25 / 9 / 2001	6,828,356
10	Alysheba 26 / 11 / 1988	6,679,242

* All horses from the USA except Invasor, who was Argentinian-bred

\# As at 1 January 2010

TOP 10 FASTEST WINNING TIMES OF THE AINTREE GRAND NATIONAL*

	HORSE / YEAR	TIME: MIN	SEC
1	Mr Frisk 1990	8	47.8
2	Rough Quest 1996	9	00.8
3	Red Rum 1973	9	01.9
4	Royal Athlete 1995	9	04.6
5	Silver Birch 2007	9	13.6
6	Don't Push It 2010	9	04.7
7	Party Politics 1992	9	06.3
8	Bindaree 2002	9	09.0
9	Papillon 2000	9	09.7
10	Grittar 1982	9	12.6

* Up to and including 2010

The times of the substitute races held at Gatwick in the years 1916–18 are not included.

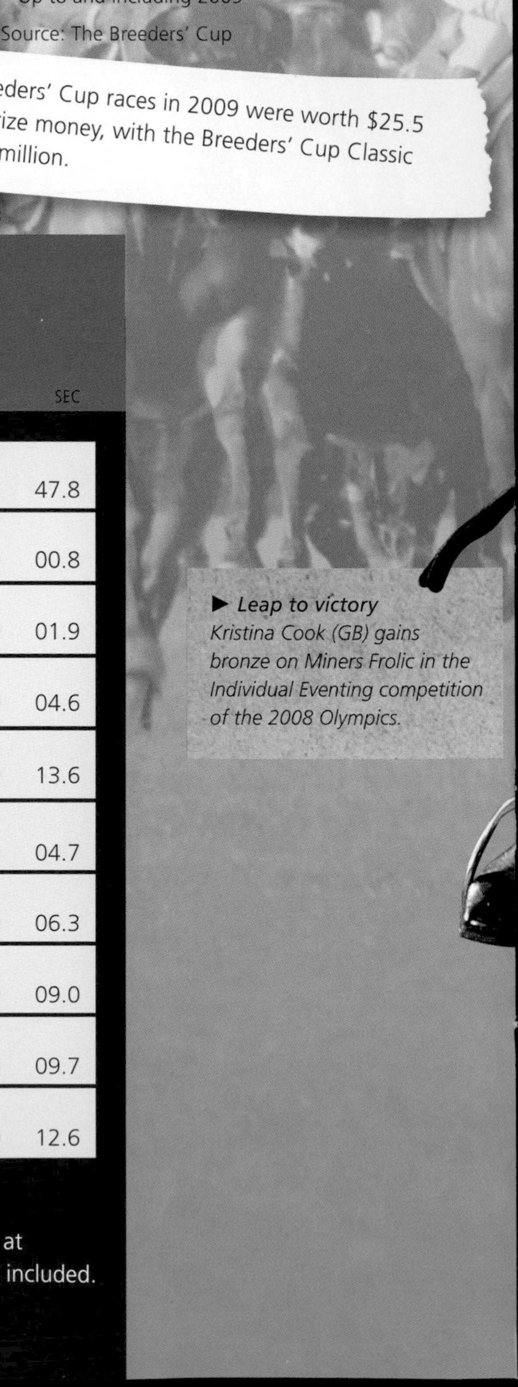

► *Leap to victory*
Kristina Cook (GB) gains bronze on Miners Frolic in the Individual Eventing competition of the 2008 Olympics.

TOP 10 **OLYMPIC EQUESTRIAN COUNTRIES***

	COUNTRY	DRESSAGE	EVENTING	JUMPING	TOTAL
1	Germany	11	4	6	21
2	Sweden	7	7	3	17
3	France	3	3	6	12
4	=USA	0	6	5	11
	=West Germany	7	1	3	11
6	Netherlands	3	5	2	10
7	Italy	0	3	4	7
8	=Australia	0	6	0	6
	=Great Britain	0	5	1	6
	=Soviet Union	4	1	1	6

* Up to and including 2008; based on gold medals won in the three main disciplines: dressage, three-day eventing and show jumping

► Anky van Grunsven
Anky Van Grunsven won her third dressage gold medal at Beijing in 2008.

TOP 10 **MOST OLYMPIC EQUESTRIAN GOLD MEDALS***

	RIDER / COUNTRY / YEARS	DISCIPLINE	GOLDS
1	Reiner Klimke Germany/ West Germany, 1964–88	Dressage	6
2	=Hans-Günther Winkler Germany/West Germany, 1956–76	Show jumping	5
	=Isabell Werth Germany, 1992–2008	Dressage	5
4	=Charles Pahud de Mortanges Netherlands, 1924–36	Eventing	4
	=Henri Saint Cyr Sweden, 1952–56	Dressage	4
	=Nicole Uphoff West Germany/Germany, 1988–92	Dressage	4
	=Ludger Beerbaum West Germany/ Germany, 1988–2000	Show jumping	4
8	=Adolph van der Voort van Zijp, Netherlands, 1924–1928	Eventing	3
	=Andrew Hoy Australia, 1992–2000	Eventing	3
	=Matthew Ryan Australia, 1992–2000	Eventing	3
	=Anky van Grunsven Netherlands, 1992–2008	Dressage	3

* Up to and including 2008 Olympics

TOP 10 **MOST FORMULA ONE RACES IN A CAREER**

	DRIVER / COUNTRY	YEARS	RACES*
1	**Rubens Barrichello**, Brazil	1993–2009	288
2	**Riccardo Patrese**, Italy	1977–93	257
3	**Michael Schumacher**, Germany	1991–2006	250
4	**David Coulthard**, UK	1994–2008	247
5	**Giancarlo Fisichella**, Italy	1996–2009	231
6	**Jarno Trulli**, Italy	1997–2009	219
7	**Michele Alboreto**, Italy	1981–94	215
8	**Andrea de Cesaris**, Italy	1980–94	214
9	**Gerhard Berger**, Austria	1984–97	210
10	**Nelson Piquet**, Brazil	1978–91	207

* Up to and including the 2009 season

▲ *Rubens Barrichello*
Despite nearly 300 Formula One races, Barrichello has just 11 wins to his credit.

TOP 10 **FASTEST WINNING SPEEDS OF THE INDIANAPOLIS 500***

	DRIVER#	CAR	YEAR	SPEED KM/H	SPEED MPH
1	**Arie Luyendyk**, Netherlands	Lola-Chevrolet	1990	299.307	185.981
2	**Rick Mears**	Chevrolet-Lumina	1991	283.980	176.457
3	**Bobby Rahal**	March-Cosworth	1986	274.750	170.722
4	**Juan Montoya**, Colombia	G Force-Aurora	2000	269.730	167.607
5	**Emerson Fittipaldi**, Brazil	Penske-Chevrolet	1989	269.695	167.581
6	**Hélio Castroneves**, Brazil	Dallara-Chevrolet	2002	267.954	166.499
7	**Rick Mears**	March-Cosworth	1984	263.308	163.612
8	**Mark Donohue**	McLaren-Offenhauser	1972	262.619	162.962
9	**Al Unser**	March-Cosworth	1987	260.995	162.175
10	**Tom Sneva**	March-Cosworth	1983	260.902	162.117

* Up to and including the 2009 race
# All drivers from the USA unless otherwise stated

MOST INDIANAPOLIS 500 RACE WINS

Three men have won the Indianapolis 500 a record four times. A.J. Foyt was the first to do so when he won for the fourth time in 1977. Al User emulated Foyt in 1987, and in 1991 Rick Mears became the third man to win the race a fourth time. The 2009 winner, Hélio Castroneves, of Brazil has won the race three times.

▲ *Castroneves*
Eventual winner Hélio Castroneves leads the field during the 2009 Indianapolis 500.

TOP 10 **MOST-USED CIRCUITS FOR FORMULA ONE CHAMPIONSHIP RACES**

	CIRCUIT / GRAND PRIX(S)	FIRST RACE	LAST RACE	TOTAL
1	Monza Italian GP	1950	2009*	59
2	Circuit de Monaco Monaco GP	1950	2009*	56
3	Silverstone British GP	1950	2009*	43
4	Spa-Francorchamps Belgian GP	1950	2009*	42
5	Nürburgring German GP, European GP Luxembourg GP	1951	2009	38
6	Hockenheimring German GP	1970	2009*	31
7	=Zandvoort Dutch GP	1952	1985	30
	=Circuit Gilles Villeneuve Canadian GP	1978	2008*	30
9	=Interlagos (Autódromo José Carlos Pace) Brazilian GP	1973	2009*	27
	=Imola San Marino GP, Italian GP	1980	2006	27

* Scheduled for 2010 Formula One calendar

TOP 10 **CONSTRUCTORS WITH THE MOST WORLD RALLY CHAMPIONSHIP TITLES**

	CONSTRUCTOR	COUNTRY	YEARS	TITLES*
1	Lancia	Italy	1974–76, 1983, 1987–92	10
2	=Peugeot	France	1985–86, 2000–02	5
	=Citroën	France	2003–05, 2008–09	5
4	=Fiat	Italy	1977–78, 1980	3
	=Ford	USA	1979, 2006–07	3
	=Toyota	Japan	1993–94, 1999	3
	=Subaru	Japan	1995–97	3
8	Audi	Germany	1982, 1984	2
9	=Alpine-Renault	France	1973	1
	=Talbot	UK	1981	1
	=Mitsubishi	Japan	1998	1

* Up to and including 2009

The inaugural World Championship in 1973 was a championship for manufacturers only. The drivers' World Championship was first held in 1979, when it was won by Björn Waldegård (Sweden).

▲ *Citroen*
The Citroën C4 driven by Frenchman Sébastien Loeb, the 2009 World Champion.

RUGBY

TOP 10 **MOST WINS IN THE ENGAGE SUPER LEAGUE 1996–2009**

	TEAM	WINS
1	St Helens	273
2	Bradford Bulls	258
3	Leeds Rhinos	254
4	Wigan Warriors	245
5	Warrington Wolves	167
6	Hull FC	147
7	Castleford Tigers	132
8	London Broncos	116
9	Wakefield Trinity Wildcats	111
10	Huddersfield Giants/ Huddersfield-Sheffield Giants	104

The first season of the Super League was in 1996 and was called the Stones Bitter Super League I. Twelve teams took part, and the first Champions were St Helens who beat Wigan Warriors by one point. Workington Town was the first team to be relegated from the Super League.

TOP 10 **POINTS SCORERS IN THE IRB WORLD CUP***

	PLAYER / COUNTRY	MATCHES	POINTS
1	**Jonny Wilkinson**, England	15	249
2	**Gavin Hastings**, Scotland	13	227
3	**Michael Lynagh**, Australia	15	195
4	**Grant Fox**, New Zealand	10	170
5	**Andrew Mehrtens**, New Zealand	10	163
6	**Gonzalo Quesada**, Argentina	8	135
7	=**Matt Burke**, Australia	13	125
	=**Nicky Little**, Fiji	11	125
9	**Thierry Lacroix**, France	9	124
10	**Gareth Rees**, Canada	13	120

* Up to and including the 2007 tournament

Source: IRB

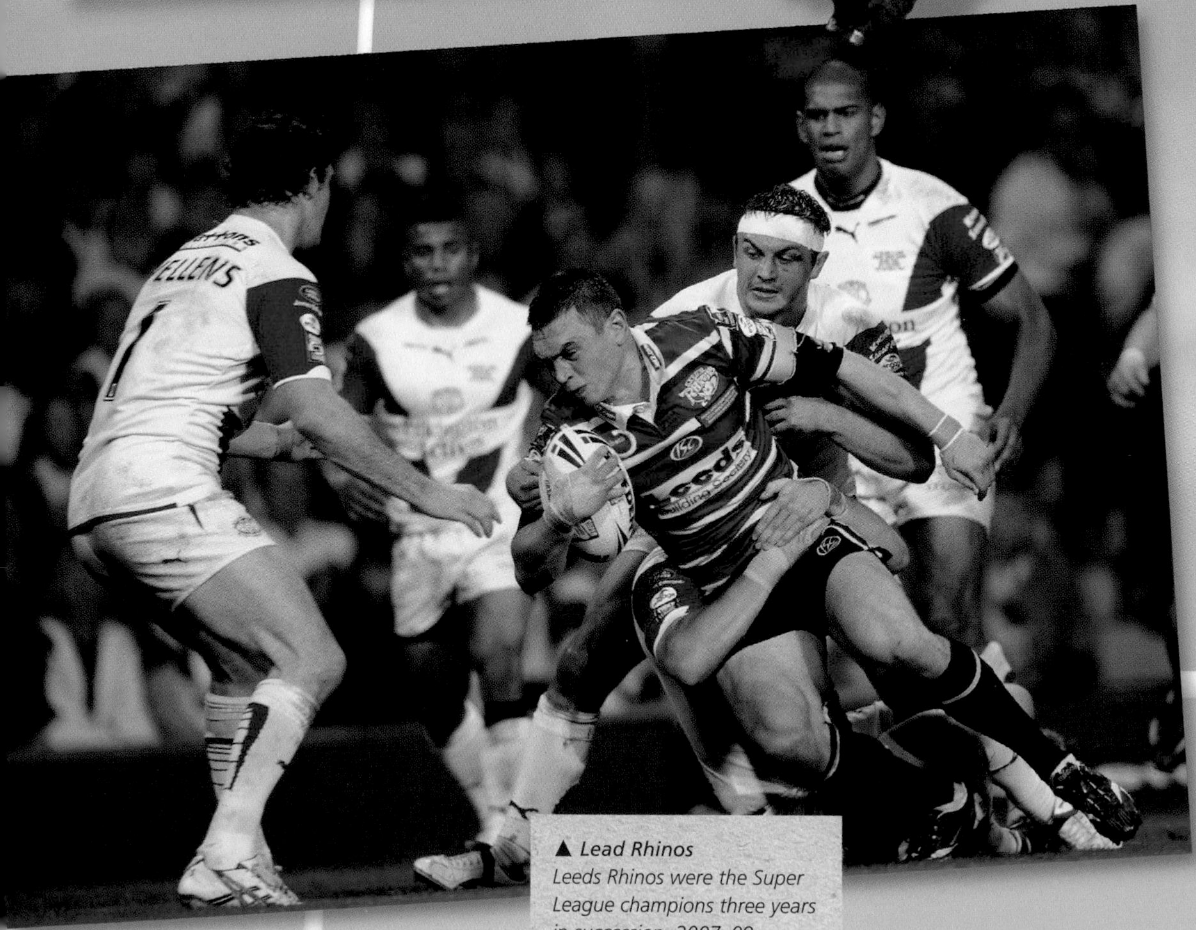

▲ *Lead Rhinos*
Leeds Rhinos were the Super League champions three years in succession, 2007–09.

◀ *Brian O'Driscoll*
Against Wales in 2010 Brian O'Driscoll became the second Irishman to win 100 International caps.

TOP 10 **MOST-CAPPED PLAYERS IN INTERNATIONAL RUGBY***

	PLAYER	COUNTRY	YEARS	TOTAL CAPS
1	George Gregan	Australia	1994–2007	139
2	Jason Leonard	England/Lions	1990–2004	119(5)
3	Fabien Pelous	France	1995–2007	118
4	Philippe Sella	France	1982–95	111
5	George Smith	Australia	2000–09	109
6	Brian O'Driscoll	Ireland/Lions	1999–2010	107(6)
7	John Hayes	Ireland/Lions	2000–10	104(2)
8	Gareth Thomas	Wales/Lions	1995–2007	103(3)
9	=Stephen Larkham	Australia	1996–2007	102
	=Percy Montgomery	South Africa	1997–2008	102

* As at 28 April 2010 among the 'Big 10' nations: Australia, Argentina, England, France, Italy, Ireland, New Zealand, Scotland, South Africa and Wales

Figures in brackets indicate the number of appearances for the British and Irish Lions

TOP 10 **MOST RUGBY LEAGUE CHALLENGE CUP WINS**

	CLUB / FIRST WIN / LAST WIN	TOTAL WINS
1	Wigan/Wigan Warriors 1924 / 2002	17
2	St Helens 1956 / 2008	12
3	Leeds/Leeds Rhinos 1910 / 1999	11
4	Widnes 1930 / 1984	7
5	=Warrington/Warrington Wolves 1905 / 2009	6
	=Huddersfield 1913 / 1953	6
7	=Halifax 1903 / 1987	5
	=Wakefield Trinity 1908 / 1963	5
	=Bradford/Bradford Bulls 1944 / 2003	5
10	Castleford 1935 / 1986	4

▼ *Leicester Tigers*
Leicester Tigers have won the Guinness Premiership a record eight times between 1988 and 2009.

THE 10 **LATEST WINNERS OF THE GUINNESS PREMIERSHIP**

YEAR	CHAMPIONS
2009	Leicester Tigers
2008	London Wasps
2007	Leicester Tigers
2006	Sale Sharks
2005	London Wasps
2004	London Wasps
2003	London Wasps
2002	Gloucester
2001	Leicester Tigers
2000	Leicester Tigers*

* Decided by League standing only – no play-offs

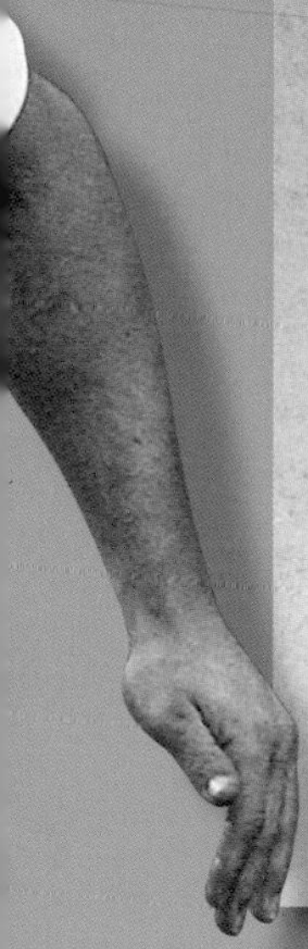

◀ *Jonny Wilkinson*
Jonny Wilkinson is the top points scorer in international rugby and also in the World Cup.

The English Premiership, currently sponsored by Guinness, is the top division in English club rugby. First contested in 1987–88, the inaugural champions were Leicester Tigers. Currently there are 12 teams in the Premiership, who play each other twice throughout the season, with the top four meeting in end-of-season play-offs. The eventual winners are declared the champions.

LAWN TENNIS

TOP 10 MOST ATP CAREER TITLES*

	PLAYER / COUNTRY	YEARS	TITLES
1	**Jimmy Connors**, USA	1972–89	109
2	**Ivan Lendl**, Czechoslovakia/USA	1980–93	94
3	**John McEnroe**, USA	1978–91	77
4	**Pete Sampras**, USA	1990–2002	64
5	**Björn Borg**, Sweden	1974–81	63
6	**Guillermo Vilas**, Argentina	1973–83	62
7	**Roger Federer**, Switzerland	2001–09	61
8	**Andre Agassi**, USA	1987–2005	60
9	**Ilie Nastase**, Romania	1969–78	57
10	**Boris Becker**, Germany	1985–96	49

* In the Open era 1968–2009 as recognized by the ATP; as at 1 January 2010

► Connors bows out
Jimmy Connors' final title was at Tel Aviv, Israel, in 1989, when he beat local player Gilad Bloom.

TOP 10 CAREER MONEY-WINNERS (WOMEN)

	PLAYER / COUNTRY	WINNINGS (US$)*
1	**Serena Williams**, USA	28,506,993
2	**Venus Williams**, USA	25,066,990
3	**Lindsay Davenport**, USA	22,144,735
4	**Steffi Graf**, USA	21,895,277
5	**Martina Navratilova**, Czechoslovakia/USA	21,626,089
6	**Martina Hingis**, Switzerland	20,130,657
7	**Justine Henin**, Belgium	19,461,375
8	**Arantxa Sánchez Vicario**, Spain	16,942,640
9	**Kim Clijsters**, Belgium	16,396,856
10	**Amelie Mauresmo**, France	15,022,476

* As at 1 January 2010

Source: WTA

► Serena Williams
Although keen rivals, Venus and Serena Williams have teamed up to win 11 Grand Slam doubles titles between 1999–2010.

TOP 10 MOST WTA CAREER TITLES*

	PLAYER / COUNTRY	YEARS	TITLES
1	**Martina Navratilova**, Czechoslovakia/USA	1974–94	167
2	**Chris Evert**, USA	1971–88	154
3	**Steffi Graf**, Germany	1986–99	107
4	**Margaret Court** (née Smith), Australia	1968–76	92
5	**Evonne Cawley** (née Goolagong), Australia	1970–80	68
6	**Billie Jean King**, USA	1968–83	67
7	=**Lindsay Davenport**, USA	1993–2008	55
	=**Virginia Wade**, UK	1968–78	55
9	**Monica Seles**, Yugoslavia/USA	1989–2002	53
10	**Martina Hingis**, Switzerland	1996–2007	43

* In the Open era 1968–2009 as recognized by the WTA; as at 1 January 2010

TOP 10 MOST YEARS ENDING YEAR AS NO. 1 ON THE ATP RANKINGS*

	PLAYER / COUNTRY	YEARS	TIMES
1	**Pete Sampras**, USA	1993–98	6
2	=**Jimmy Connors**, USA	1974–78	5
	=**Roger Federer**, Switzerland	2004–07, 2009	5
4	=**John McEnroe**, USA	1981–84	4
	=**Ivan Lendl**, Czechoslovakia	1985–87, 1989	4
6	=**Björn Borg**, Sweden	1979–80	2
	=**Stefan Edberg**, Sweden	1990–91	2
	=**Lleyton Hewitt**, Australia	2001–02	2
9	=**Ilie Nastase**, Romania	1973	1
	=**Mats Wilander**, Sweden	1988	1
	=**Jim Courier**, USA	1992	1
	=**Andre Agassi**, USA	1999	1
	=**Gustavo Kuerten**, Brazil	2000	1
	=**Andy Roddick**, USA	2003	1
	=**Rafael Nadal**, Spain	2008	1

Source: ATP

* Between the launch of the ATP rankings in 1973 and 2009

TOP 10 CAREER MONEY WINNERS (MEN)

	PLAYER / COUNTRY	WINNINGS (US$)*
1	**Roger Federer**, Switzerland	53,362,068
2	**Pete Sampras**, USA	43,280,489
3	**Andre Agassi**, USA	31,152,975
4	**Rafael Nadal**, Spain	27,224,163
5	**Boris Becker**, Germany	25,080,956
6	**Yevgeny Kafelnikov**, Russia	23,883,797
7	**Ivan Lendl**, Czechoslovakia/USA	21,262,417
8	**Stefan Edberg**, Sweden	20,630,941
9	**Goran Ivanisevic**, Croatia	19,876,579
10	**Michael Chang**, USA	19,145,632

* As at 1 January 2010

Source: ATP

► *Roger Federer*
Roger Federer has ended the year as No. 1 in five of the last six years.

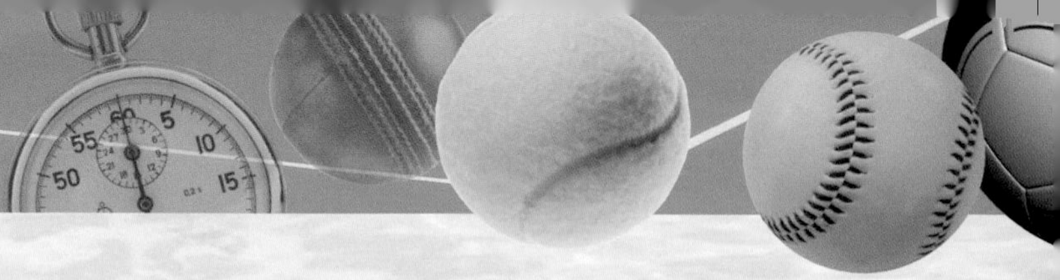

WATER SPORTS

◀ *Hungarian victors*
Hungary won its third consecutive men's water polo title at the 2008 Beijing Olympics.

TOP 10 **OLYMPIC WATER POLO COUNTRIES***

	COUNTRY	GOLD	SILVER	BRONZE	TOTAL
		MEDALS			
1	Hungary	9	3	3	15
2	USA	1	6	5	12
3	=Italy	4	1	2	7
	=USSR	2	2	3	7
	=Yugoslavia	3	4	0	7
6	Belgium	0	4	2	6
7	Great Britain	4	0	0	4
8	=France	1	0	2	3
	=Germany	1	2	0	3
	=Netherlands	1	0	2	3
	=Russia	0	1	2	3
	=Sweden	0	1	2	3

* Based on total medals won between 1900–2008 for men, and 2000–08 for women

◀ *World Championship*
Action during the 2009 World Aquatics Championships in Rome.

THE 10 **COUNTRIES HOLDING THE MOST SWIMMING WORLD RECORDS***

	COUNTRY	MEN	WOMEN	TOTAL
1	USA	9	3	12
2	Australia	3	3	6
3	Germany	2	2	4
4	=China	1	2	3
	=Great Britain	1	2	3
6	=Italy	0	2	2
	=Sweden	0	2	2
8	=Brazil	1	0	1
	=Canada	0	1	1
	=France	1	0	1
	=Netherlands	0	1	1
	=Russia	0	1	1
	=South Africa	1	0	1
	=Spain	1	0	1
	=Zimbabwe	0	1	1

* FINA Long Course world records as at 1 January 2010, excluding records awaiting ratification

Source: FINA

TOP 10 **OLYMPIC SWIMMING COUNTRIES***

	COUNTRY	GOLD	SILVER	BRONZE	TOTAL
		MEDALS			
1	USA	214	155	120	4896
2	Australia	56	54	58	168
3	East Germany	38	32	22	92
4	Great Britain	15	21	28	64
5	Hungary	23	23	17	63
6	Japan	20	21	21	62
7	=Germany	13	18	28	59
	=USSR	12	21	26	59
9	Netherlands	17	17	18	52
10	Canada	7	13	20	40

* Based on total medals won in swimming events only, excluding diving and synchronized swimming; men's events 1896–2008; women's events 1912–2000

The total for Germany does not include the one gold, five silver and six bronze medals won by the United Germany team between 1956–64.

THE 10 **LATEST WINNERS OF THE AMERICA'S CUP**

YEAR / VENUE / WINNER / COUNTRY / SKIPPER(S)

2010
Valencia, Spain
USA 17,
USA
Russell Coutts

2007
Valencia, Spain
Alinghi, Switzerland
Brad Butterworth

2003
Auckland, New Zealand
Alinghi, Switzerland
Russell Coutts

2000
Auckland, New Zealand
Team New Zealand,
New Zealand
Russell Coutts/Dan Barker

1995
San Diego, USA
Black Magic, New Zealand
Russell Coutts

1992
San Diego, USA
America3, USA
Bill Koch/Buddy Melges

1988
San Diego, USA
Stars & Stripes, USA
Dennis Conner

1987
Fremantle, Australia
Stars & Stripes, USA
Dennis Conner

1983
Newport, USA
Australia II, Australia
John Bertrand

1980
Newport, USA
Freedom, USA
Dennis Conner

After much wrangling and legal issues, it was eventually announced in December 2009 that the 33rd America's Cup would take place at Valencia, Spain in February 2010.

▼ *Underwater hockey*
The 2006 women's World Underwater Hockey Championship at Sheffield, 2006, was won by Australia.

TOP 10 **COUNTRIES IN THE UNDERWATER HOCKEY WORLD CHAMPIONSHIPS***

	COUNTRY	MEDALS GOLD	SILVER	BRONZE	TOTAL
1	Australia	17	5	4	26
2	New Zealand	3	8	3	14
3	South Africa	3	5	4	12
4	France	4	1	5	10
5	Canada	1	3	4	8
6	=Netherlands	2	3	1	6
	=USA	0	1	5	6
8	Great Britain	0	2	2	4
9	Turkey	0	2	0	2
10	=Slovenia	0	0	1	1
	=Spain	0	0	1	1

* CMAS (Confédération Mondiale des Activités Subaquatiques) World Championships 1980–2006; CMAS World Games 2007; WAA (World Aquachallenge Association) World Championship 2008

Underwater Polo, or Octopush as it was then known, was first played at the Southsea (England) Sub-Aqua Club in 1954. The first men's world championship was held at Vancouver, Canada, in 1980 and won by the Netherlands. The first women's championship was in Chicago, USA, in 1984 and won by Australia.

WINTER SPORTS

◀ *Austria 2006*
Felix Gottwald of Austria, winner of the 7.5-km sprint and 4 x 5-km relay gold medals at the 2006 Turin Winter Olympics.

◀ *Nordic winner*
Kjersti Bauss, one of Norway's record-breaking Olympic medallists, wins bronze in the halfpipe event at Turin, 2006.

TOP 10 NORDIC SKIING OLYMPIC COUNTRIES*

	COUNTRY	GOLD	SILVER	BRONZE	TOTAL
1	Norway	50	51	40	141
2	Finland	33	38	36	107
3	USSR#	26	23	23	72
4	Sweden	24	17	19	60
5	Austria	8	11	16	35
6	Italy	9	11	13	33
7	Russia#	12	6	7	25
8	Germany†	5	10	5	20
9	East Germany	7	4	7	18
10	=Japan	5	5	2	12
	=Czechoslovakia§	1	3	8	12

* At all Winter Olympics 1924–2006.
# USSR totals are for the period 1956–88, Russia totals from 1994; totals for the Unified Team in 1992 are not included
† Germany totals are for the periods 1928–32, 1952 and 1992–2006
§ Competed as Czechoslovakia from 1920–92 and Czech Republic from 1994–2006

Nordic Skiing events at the Winter Olympics consist of cross-country skiing, ski jumping, biathlon (which combines cross-country skiing and shooting), and Nordic combined, which is a combination of cross-country skiing and ski jumping.

THE 10 WINTER OLYMPIC HOST NATIONS

COUNTRY / TIMES HOSTED / YEAR / VENUES

1. USA (4)
1932, 1980 Lake Placid, 1960 Squaw Valley, 2002 Salt Lake City

2. France (3)
1924 Chamonix, 1968 Grenoble, 1992 Albertville

3. =Switzerland (2)
1928, 1948 St Moritz

=Austria (2)
1964, 1976 Innsbruck

=Japan (2)
1972 Sapporo, 1998 Nagano

=Norway (2)
1952 Oslo, 1994 Lillehammer

=Italy (2)
1956 Cortina d'Ampezzo, 2006 Turin

=Canada (2)
1988 Calgary, 2010 Vancouver

4. =Germany (1)
1936 Garmisch-Partenkirchen

=Yugoslavia (1)
1984 Sarajevo

TOP 10 MEDAL-WINNING COUNTRIES AT THE WINTER OLYMPICS*

	COUNTRY	GOLD	SILVER	BRONZE	TOTAL
1	Norway	98	98	84	280
2	USA	78	80	58	216
3	USSR#	78	57	59	194
4	Austria	51	64	70	185
5	Germany†	60	59	41	160
6	Finland	41	57	52	150
7	Canada	38	38	43	119
8	Sweden	43	31	44	118
9	Switzerland	37	37	43	117
10	East Germany	39	36	35	110

* Up to and including the 2006 Turin Games, including medals won at figure skating and ice hockey included in the Summer Olympics prior to the inauguration of the Winter Games in 1924
# USSR totals are for the period 1956–88
† Germany totals are for the periods 1928–32, 1952 and 1992–2006

TOP 10 **WINTER PARALYMPIC COUNTRIES**

	COUNTRY	GOLD	SILVER	BRONZE	TOTAL
1	Norway	133	98	78	309
2	Austria	99	104	100	303
3	USA	92	92	64	248
4	Germany	76	61	60	197
5	Finland	76	46	58	180
6	Switzerland	48	53	48	149
7	France	46	40	47	133
8	Russia	42	44	29	115
9	West Germany	32	42	35	109
10	Canada	26	36	38	100

Source: IPC (International Paralympic Committee)

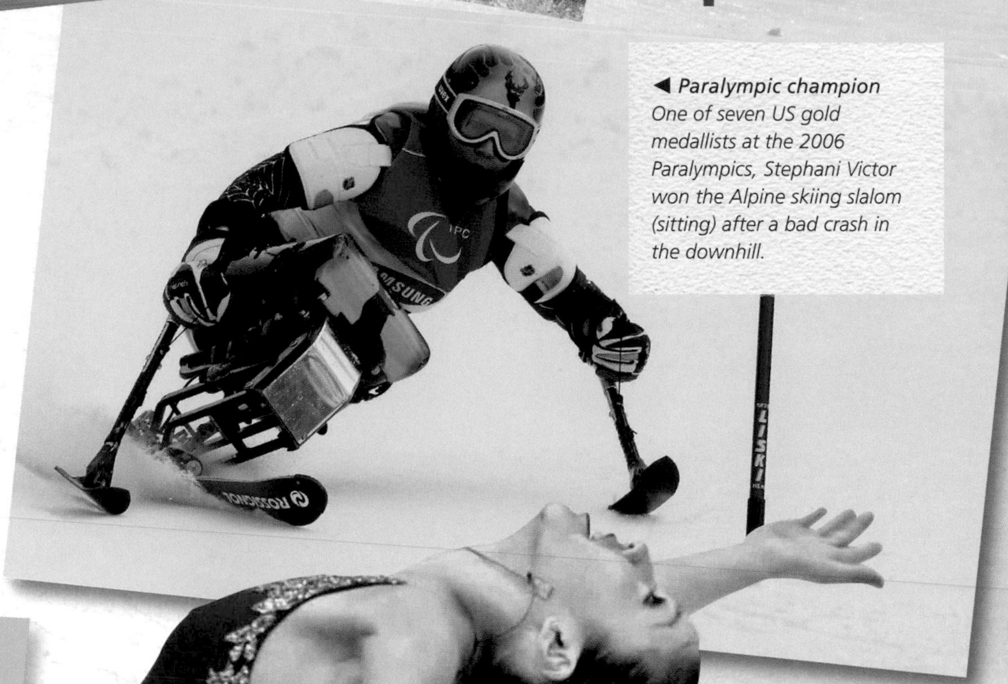

◀ *Paralympic champion*
One of seven US gold medallists at the 2006 Paralympics, Stephani Victor won the Alpine skiing slalom (sitting) after a bad crash in the downhill.

The first Winter Paralympics were held at Örnsköldsvik, Sweden, from 21–28 February 1976. More than 250 athletes from 17 countries took part. Austria led the medal table with five gold, 16 silver and 14 bronze medals for a total of 35. West Germany and Switzerland won the most golds, with 10 each.

Olympic Events
Prior to the launch of the Winter Olympics at Chamonix, France in 1924, figure skating and ice hockey had been part of the Olympic programme. Figure skating was included in the 1908 and 1920 Summer Games, while ice hockey made its debut in 1920.

▲ *Fine figure*
Nine times US champion and five times world figure-skating champion, Michelle Kwan gained Olympic silver in 1998 and bronze in 2002, but never won gold.

TOP 10 **MOST WORLD AND OLYMPIC FIGURE-SKATING TITLES***

	SKATER / COUNTRY	MALE/ FEMALE	WORLD TITLES	OLYMPIC TITLES	TOTAL TITLES
1	**Sonja Henie**, Norway	F	10	3	13
2	**Ulrich Salchow**, Sweden	M	10	1	11
3	**Karl Schäfer**, Austria	M	7	2	9
4	**Richard Button**, USA	M	5	2	7
5	=**Gillis Grafström**, Sweden	M	3	3	6
	=**Carol Heiss**, USA	F	5	1	6
	=**Herma Planck-Szabo**, Austria	F	5	1	6
	=**Katarina Witt**, East Germany	F	4	2	6
9	=**Scott Hamilton**, USA	M	4	1	5
	=**Hayes Alan Jenkins**, USA	M	4	1	5
	=**Michelle Kwan**, USA	F	5	0	5

* Individual men's and women's titles at all World Championships 1896–2009 (1906–2009 for women) and Olympic Games 1908–2006

▲ *Michellie Jones*
Michellie Jones won the Ironman World Championship in Hawaii in 2006 at the age of 37.

TOP 10 **MOST WORLD TRIATHLON CHAMPIONSHIP MEDALS***

	TRIATHLETE / COUNTRY	YEARS	GOLD	SILVER	BRONZE	TOTAL
1	**Michellie Jones**, Australia	1991–2003	2	2	4	8
2	**Simon Lessing**, UK	1992–99	4	2	1	7
3	**Peter Robertson**, Australia	2000–05	3	2	0	5
4	=**Emma Carney**, Australia	1994–99	2	1	1	4
	=**Jackie Gallagher**, Australia	1995–99	1	3	0	4
	=**Laura Bennett** (née Reback), USA	2003–07	0	1	3	4
	=**Emma Snowsill**, Australia	2003–07	3	1	0	4
8	=**Brad Beven**, Australia	1990–95	0	3	0	3
	=**Karen Smyers**, USA	1990–95	2	1	0	3
	=**Carol Montgomery**, Canada	1990–2000	0	2	1	3
	=**Joanne Ritchie**, Canada	1991–93	1	1	1	3
	=**Miles Stewart**, Australia	1991–99	1	0	2	3
	=**Hamish Carter**, New Zealand	1993–2006	0	2	1	3
	=**Iván Raña**, Spain	2002–04	1	2	0	3
	=**Javier Gómez**, Spain	2007–09	1	2	0	3

* Senior men and women's medals up to and including 2009

TOP 10 **GOLD MEDALLISTS AT THE SUMMER X GAMES***

	ATHLETE / COUNTRY	SPORT	YEARS	GOLDS
1	**Dave Mirra**, USA	BMX	1996–2005	13
2	**Tony Hawk**, USA	Skateboarding	1995–2003	9
3	=**Travis Pastrana**, USA	Moto X/Rally car racing	1999–2008	8
	=**Andy Macdonald**, USA	Skateboarding	1996–2002	8
5	**Fabiola da Silva**, Brazil	In-line skating	1996–2007	7
6	**Bucky Lasek**, USA	Skateboarding	1999–2006	6
7	=**Bob Burnquist**, Brazil	Skateboarding	2001–08	5
	=**Jamie Bestwick**, England	BMX	2000–09	5
	=**Pierre-Luc Gagnon**, Canada	Skateboarding	2002–09	5
	=**Biker Sherlock**, USA	Street luge	1996–98	5

* Up to and including X Games XV in 2009

THE X GAMES

The first ESPN Extreme Games (now X Games) for 'alternative' sports were held in June/July 1995 at Rhode Island, USA. The sports contested at X Games XV in 2009 were: BMX, Moto X, skateboarding, surfing and rallying. Since 1997 there has also been an annual Winter X Games, the first one held at Big Bear Lake, California, USA. At the Winter X Games 14 at Aspen, Colorado, USA – which has been the permanent home of the Winter X Games since 2001 – competitors took part in three sports: skiing, snowmobile and snowboarding.

► *Andy MacDonald*
Andy Macdonald holds the record for winning the most X Games medals – 15 in total. He has also won the World Cup Skateboarding title eight times.

TOP 10 **NATIONS AT THE WORLD HOT-AIR BALLOON CHAMPIONSHIPS***

	COUNTRY	GOLD	SILVER	BRONZE	TOTAL
1	USA	12	9	7	28
2	Germany	1	3	2	6
3	Sweden	0	2	3	5
4	France	1	1	2	4
5	=Australia	1	0	2	3
	=UK	1	2	0	3
7	Austria	0	1	1	2
8	=Lithuania	0	0	1	1
	=Russia	0	1	0	1
	=West Germany	1	0	0	1

* Up to and including 2009

▲ *Ironman*
Competitors set off on the 2.4-mile open-water swim in Kailua-Kona Bay during the 2007 Ironman World Championship in Hawaii.

Ballooning might not be everyone's idea of an 'extreme sport', but competitive ballooning includes all the elements that define such activities, such as the fact that there are few rules and competitors use their skill to control the risks.

THE 10 **LATEST WINNERS OF THE WORLD'S STRONGEST MAN TITLE**

YEAR	CHAMPION / COUNTRY
2009	Zydrunas Savickas, Lithuania
2008	Mariusz Pudzianowski, Poland
2007	Mariusz Pudzianowski, Poland
2006	Phil Pfister, USA
2005	Mariusz Pudzianowski, Poland
2004	Vasyl Virastyuk, Ukraine
2003	Mariusz Pudzianowski, Poland
2002	Mariusz Pudzianowski, Poland
2001	Svend Karlsen, Norway
2000	Janne Virtanen, Finland

TOP 10 **FASTEST TIMES IN THE IRONMAN WORLD CHAMPIONSHIP**

	TRIATHLETE / COUNTRY	YEAR	TIME HR:MIN:SEC
1	**Luc Van Lierde**, Belgium	1996	8:04:08
2	**Mark Allen**, USA	1993	8:07:45
3	**Mark Allen**, USA	1992	8:09:08
4	**Mark Allen**, USA	1989	8:09:15
5	**Normann Stadler**, Germany	2006	8:11:56
6	**Faris Al-Sultan**, Germany	2005	8:14:17
7	**Chris McCormack**, Australia	2007	8:15:34
8	**Luc Van Lierde**, Belgium	1999	8:17:17
9	**Craig Alexander**, Australia	2008	8:17:45
10	**Mark Allen**, USA	1991	8:18:32

The first Ironman world championship was held in 1978, when Gordon Haller (USA) won the title with a time of 11 hours 46 minutes 58 seconds for the 2.4-mile swim, 112-mile cycle ride and full marathon of 26 miles 385 yards.

OTHER SPORTS

TOP 10 **MOST SNOOKER RANKING EVENT TITLES**

	PLAYER / COUNTRY	FIRST WIN	LAST WIN	TOTAL*
1	**Stephen Hendry**, Scotland	1987	2005	36
2	**Steve Davis**, England	1981	1995	28
3	**Ronnie O'Sullivan**, England	1993	2009	22
4	**John Higgins**, Scotland	1994	2010	21
5	**Mark Williams**, Wales	1996	2006	16
6	**Jimmy White**, England	1986	2004	10
7	**John Parrott**, England	1989	1996	9
8	**Peter Ebdon**, England	1993	2009	8
9	**Ken Doherty**, Ireland	1993	2006	6
10	**Ray Reardon**, Wales	1974	1982	5

* As at 14 March 2010

The World Professional Billiards and Snooker Association (WPBSA) introduced its ranking system in 1976. In the 2009–10 season, six tournaments were classed as ranking events.

▲ *John Higgins*
Scotland's John Higgins, also known as 'The Wizard of Wishaw', has won three world titles.

TOP 10 **MOST MOSCONI CUP APPEARANCES**

PLAYER / COUNTRY / APPEARANCES

1 Ralf Souquet, Germany 15

2 = Johnny Archer*, USA 13
= Mika Immonen*, Finland 13
= Earl Strickland, USA 13

3 Steve Davis, England 11

15 = Jeremy Jones, USA 7
= Nick Varner*†, USA 7

6 Oliver Ortmann#, Germany 9

9 = Niels Feijen*, Netherlands 6
= Corey Deuel*, USA 6
= Marcus Chamat, Sweden 6
= Rodney Morris, USA 6

* Played in 2009 event
\# Total includes one appearance as non-playing captain
† Total includes three appearances as non-playing captain, including 2009

The Mosconi Cup tournament is named after Willie Mosconi, the former American pool champion and technical adviser for the film *The Hustler*. An annual 9-ball pool event between teams from Europe and the USA, it was first held in 1994.

TOP 10 **OLYMPIC FIELD HOCKEY COUNTRIES***

	COUNTRY	GOLD	SILVER	BRONZE	TOTAL
1	Netherlands	4	4	6	14
2	=Australia	4	3	4	11
	=India	8	1	2	11
4	Great Britain	3	2	5	10
5	Pakistan	3	3	2	8
6	Germany	3	2	2	7
7	Spain	1	3	1	5
8	West Germany	1	3	0	4
9	=Argentina	0	1	2	3
	=South Korea	0	3	0	3

* At all Olympics 1908–2008 for men and 1980–2008 for women, except in 1912 and 1924, when hockey was excluded

▼ *Field hockey*
Spain and Germany competing in the 2008 men's Olympic hockey final.

▼ *Volleyball*
The Swiss pair of Kuhn and Zumkehr in action during the 2009 FIVB world championships.

▲ *Softball*
Australia batting (against New Zealand) in the Oceania qualifiers for the 2008 World Softball Championships.

TOP 10 **MOST SOFTBALL WORLD CHAMPIONSHIP MEDALS***

	COUNTRY	GOLD	SILVER	BRONZE	TOTAL
1	USA	13	3	3	19
2	New Zealand	6	4	4	14
3	Canada	3	6	2	11
4	=Australia	2	1	5	8
	=Japan	1	4	3	8
6	China	0	2	1	3
7	=Mexico	0	1	1	2
	=Taiwan	0	1	1	2
9	=Bahamas	0	0	1	1
	=Philippines	0	0	1	1

* Men's and Women's championships up to and including 2009

TOP 10 **MOST BEACH VOLLEYBALL WORLD CHAMPIONSHIP MEDALS***

	COUNTRY	GOLD	SILVER	BRONZE	TOTAL
1	Brazil	7	6	6	19
2	USA	5	4	4	13
3	=Australia	0	0	2	2
	=China	0	1	1	2
	=Germany	1	0	1	2
	=Switzerland	0	2	0	2
7	=Argentina	1	0	0	1
	=Czech Republic	0	0	1	1
	=Norway	0	0	1	1
	=Russia	0	1	0	1

* Men's and Women's medals won at all championships up to and including 2009

The first official World Beach Volleyball Championship organized by the Fédération Internationale de Volleyball (FIVB) was at Los Angeles, California, in 1997 and is now held every two years. Prior to that, an unofficial championship was held annually at Rio de Janeiro from 1987–96.

TOP 10 **MOST PROFESSIONAL BOWLERS ASSOCIATION (PBA) TITLES**

	BOWLER*	FIRST/ LAST WIN	TOTAL WINS#
1	Walter Ray Williams Jr	1986–2010	47
2	Earl Anthony	1970–1984	43
3	=Mark Roth	1975–1995	34
	=Pete Weber	1982–2007	34
5	Norm Duke	1983–2009	33
6	Parker Bohn III	1987–2008	32
7	Dick Weber	1959–1977	30
8	Mike Aulby	1979–2001	29
9	Don Johnson	1964–1977	26
10	Brian Voss	1983–2006	24

* All bowlers from the USA
\# As at 14 March 2010
Source: PBA

SPORTS & GAMES MISCELLANY

THE 10 **LARGEST*** ATHLETES' HEARTS

1 Tour de France cyclists
2 Marathon runners
3 Rowers
4 Boxers
5 Sprint cyclists
6 Middle-distance runners
7 Weightlifters
8 Swimmers
9 Sprinters
10 Decathletes

* Based on average medical measurements

TOP 10 **HIGHEST-EARNING SPORTSMEN**

Source: *Forbes Magazine*

	SPORTSMAN* / SPORT	EARNINGS# (US$)
1	Tiger Woods Golf	110,000,000
2 =	Kobe Bryant Basketball	45,000,000
=	Michael Jordan Basketball	45,000,000
=	Kimi Räikkönen Finland, Formula One	45,000,000
5	David Beckham UK, Soccer	42,000,000
6 =	LeBron James Basketball	40,000,000
=	Phil Mickelson Golf	40,000,000
=	Manny Pacquiao Philippines, Boxing	40,000,000
9	Valentino Rossi Italy, Motor cycling	35,000,000
10	Dale Earnhardt, Jr Auto racing	34,000,000

* All from the USA unless otherwise stated
# Earnings for the period June 2008–June 2009

◀ *Tour de France*
Tour de France riders give their hearts a pounding, covering over 3,500 km (2,175 ml) in three weeks.

▲ ***Winning formula***
Formula One champion Kimi Räikkönen is the highest earning non-American sportsman.

TOP 10 **COUNTRIES SPENDING THE MOST ON TOYS & GAMES**

COUNTRY / SPEND PER CAPITA 2009 (£)

In 2009, the world market for toys and games of all kinds (traditional and video) was estimated to be £97,949,600,000 ($138,644,700,000).

1	UK	113.20
2	USA	107.90
3	Netherlands	100.20
4	France	97.70
5	Australia	97.00

TOP 10 **VIDEO GAME-BUYING COUNTRIES**

COUNTRY / VIDEO GAME SALES PER CAPITA 2009 (£)

1 UK 75.30
2 Australia 67.30
3 USA 55.40
4 France 54.80
5 Netherlands 52.50
6 Belgium 41.10
7 Canada 40.30
8 Sweden 40.00
9 Spain 27.60
10 Italy 23.80

World average 6.90

Source: Euromonitor

▲ The Blind Side
The Blind Side *is the 21st century's highest-earning live-action sport film.*

TOP 10 **SPORT FILMS**

FILM / YEAR / SUBJECT	WORLD BOX OFFICE (US$)
1 Cars* (2006) Car racing	461,981,604
2 Rocky IV (1985) Boxing	300,473,716
3 The Blind Side (2009) American football	298,502,119
4 Million Dollar Baby (2004) Boxing	216,763,646
5 Space Jam (1996) Basketball	230,418,342
6 The Longest Yard (2005) American football	190,320,568
7 The Waterboy (1998) American football	190,191,646
8 Dodgeball: A True Underdog Story (2004) Dodgeball	167,722,310
9 Days of Thunder (1990) Stock car racing	165,870,733
10 Talladega Nights: The Ballad of Ricky Bobby (2006) NASCAR racing	162,967,452

* Animated

World average 14.40

Source: Euromonitor International

6 Belgium 74.90
7 Sweden 69.60
8 Canada 65.90
9 Italy 58.20
10 Japan 53.80

FURTHER INFORMATION

THE UNIVERSE & THE EARTH

Caves
caverbob.com
Lists of long and deep caves

Disasters
emdat.be
Emergency Events Database covering major disasters since 1900

Encyclopedia Astronautica
astronautix.com
Spaceflight news and reference

Islands
worldislandinfo.com
Information on the world's islands

Mountains
peaklist.org
Lists of the world's tallest mountains

NASA
nasa.gov
The main website for the US space programme

Oceans
oceansatlas.org
The UN's resource on oceanographic issues

Planets
nineplanets.org
A multimedia tour of the Solar System

Rivers
rev.net/~aloe/river
The River Systems of the World website

Space exploration
spacefacts.de
Manned spaceflight data

LIFE ON EARTH

Animals
animaldiversity.ummz.umich.edu
A wealth of animal data

Birds
avibase.bsc-eoc.org
A database on the world's birds

Conservation
iucn.org
The leading nature-conservation site

Endangered
cites.org
Lists of endangered species of flora and fauna

Extinct
nhm.ac.uk/nature-online/life/dinosaurs-other-extinct-creatures
Dinosaurs and other extinct animals

Fish
www.fishbase.org
Global information on fish

Food and Agriculture Organization
fao.org
Statistics from the UN's FAO website

Forests
www.fao.org/forestry
FAO's forestry website

Insects
entnemdept.ufl.edu/walker/ufbir
The University of Florida Book of Insect Records

Sharks
flmnh.ufl.edu/fish/sharks
The Florida Museum of Natural History's shark data files

THE HUMAN WORLD

Crime (UK)
homeoffice.gov.uk
Home Office crime and prison population figures

Leaders
terra.es/personal2/monolith
Facts about world leaders since 1945

Military
globalfirepower.com
World military statistics and rankings

Nobel Prizes
nobelprize.org
The official website of the Nobel Foundation

Population (UK)
statistics.gov.uk/hub/population
UK population figures

Religion
worldchristiandatabase.org
World religion data (subscription required)

Royalty
royal.gov.uk
The official site of the British monarchy

Rulers
rulers.org
A database of the world's rulers and political leaders

Supercentenarians
grg.org/calment.html
A world listing of those who have reached 110 or older

World Health Organization
who.int/en
World health information and advice

TOWN & COUNTRY

Bridges and tunnels
en.structurae.de
Facts and figures on the world's buildings, tunnels and other structures

Bridges (highest)
highestbridges.com
Detailed facts and stats on the world's highest bridges

Buildings
emporis.com/en
The Emporis database of high-rise and other buildings

Country and city populations
citypopulation.de
A searchable guide to the world's countries and major cities

Country data
cia.gov/library/publications/the-world-factbook
The CIA's acclaimed *World Factbook*

Country populations
un.org/esa/population/unpop
The UN's worldwide data on population issues

Development
worldbank.org
Development and other statistics from around the world

Population
census.gov/ipc
International population statistics

Skyscrapers
skyscraperpage.com
Data and images of the world's skyscrapers

Tunnels
lotsberg.net
A database of the longest rail, road and canal tunnels

CULTURE & LEARNING

Art
artnet.com
World art info, with price database available to subscribers

The Art Newspaper
theartnewspaper.com
News and views on the art world

The British Library
bl.uk
Catalogues and exhibitions in the national library

Education
dfes.gov.uk/statistics
Official statistics relating to education in the UK

Languages of the world
ethnologue.com
Online reference work on the world's 6,912 living languages

The Man Booker Prize
themanbookerprize.com
Britain's most prestigious literary prize

Museums and galleries
culture24.org.uk
Exhibitions and cultural events in the UK

Newspapers
wan-press.org
The World Association of Newspapers' website

Oxford English Dictionary
oed.com
Accessible online to most UK public library subscribers

UNESCO
unesco.org
Comparative international statistics on education and culture

MUSIC

All Music Guide
allmusic.com
A comprehensive guide to all genres of music

Billboard
billboard.com
US music news and charts data

BRIT Awards
brits.co.uk
The official website for the popular music awards

The British Phonographic Industry Ltd
bpi.co.uk
Searchable database of gold discs and other certified awards

Grammy Awards
naras.org
The official site for the famous US music awards

MTV
mtv.co.uk
The online site for the MTV UK music channel

New Musical Express
nme.com
The online version of the popular music magazine

Official UK Charts
theofficialcharts.com
Weekly and historical music charts

PRS for Music
The organization that collects performance royalties for musicians

VH1
vh1.com
Online UK music news

ENTERTAINMENT

Academy Awards
oscars.org
The official 'Oscars' website

BAFTAs
bafta.org
The home of the BAFTA Awards

BBC
bbc.co.uk
Gateway to BBC TV and radio, with a powerful Internet search engine

Film Distributors' Association
launchingfilms.com
Trade site for UK film releases and statistics

Golden Globe Awards
hfpa.org
Hollywood Foreign Press Association's Golden Globes site

Internet Movie Database
imdb.com
The best of the publicly accessible film websites; IMDbPro is available to subscribers

London Theatre Guide
londontheatre.co.uk
A comprehensive guide to West End theatre productions

Screen Daily
screendaily.com
Daily news from the film world at the website of UK weekly *Screen International*

Variety
variety.com
Extensive entertainment information (extra features available to subscribers)

Yahoo! Movies
uk.movies.yahoo.com
Charts plus features, trailers and links to the latest film UK releases

THE COMMERCIAL WORLD

The Economist
economist.com
Global economic and political news

Energy
bp.com
Online access to the *BP Statistical Review of World Energy*

Environment
epi.yale.edu
The latest Environmental Performance Index rankings

Internet
internetworldstats.com
Internet World Stats

Organization for Economic Co-operation and Development
oecd.org
World economic and social statistics

Rich lists
forbes.com
Forbes magazine's celebrated lists of the world's wealthiest people

Telecommunications
itu.int
Worldwide telecommunications statistics

UK tourist attractions
alva.org.uk
Information and visitor statistics on the UK's top tourist attractions

The World Bank
worldbank.org
World development, trade and labour statistics, now freely accessible

World Tourism Organization
world-tourism.org
The world's principal travel and tourism organization

ON THE MOVE

Aircraft crashes
baaa-acro.com
The Aircraft Crashes Record Office database

Airlines
airfleets.net
Statistics on the world's airlines and aircraft

Airports
airports.org
Airports Council International statistics on the world's airports

Air safety
aviation-safety.net
Data on air safety and accidents

Air speed records
fai.org/records
The website of the official air speed record governing body

Car manufacture
oica.net
The International Organization of Motor Vehicle Manufacturers' website

Metros
metrobits.org
An exploration of the world's metro systems.

Rail
uic.org
World rail statistics

Railways
railwaygazette.com
The world's railway business in depth from *Railway Gazette International*

Shipwrecks
shipwreckregistry.com
A huge database of the world's wrecked and lost ships

SPORT

Athletics
iaaf.org
The world governing body of athletics

Cricket
cricinfo.com
Cricinfo, launched in 1993, since merged with the online version of *Wisden*

Cycling
uci.ch
The Union Cycliste Internationale, the competitive cycling governing body

FIFA
fifa.com
The official website of FIFA, the world governing body of soccer

Formula One
formula1.com
The official F1 website

Olympics
olympic.org/uk
The official Olympics website

Premier League
premierleague.com
The official website of the Premier League

Rugby
itsrugby.co.uk
Comprehensive rugby site

Skiing
fis-ski.com
Fédèration Internationale de Ski, the world governing body of skiing and snowboarding

Tennis
lta.org.uk
The official site of the British Lawn Tennis Association

ACKNOWLEDGEMENTS

Special research: Ian Morrison (sport); Dafydd Rees (music)

Academy of Motion Picture Arts and Sciences – Oscar statuette is the registered trademark and copyrighted property of the Academy of Motion Picture Arts and Sciences
Air Crashes Record Office
Airports Council International
Alexa
Apple
Applied Animal Behaviour Science
Artnet
Art Newspaper
Association of Tennis Professionals
Audit Bureau of Circulations Ltd
BARB
Barclaycard Mercury Prize
BBC
Roland Bert
Billboard
Peter Bond
Box Office Mojo
BP Statistical Review of World Energy
Richard Braddish
Breeders' Cup
Thomas Brinkhoff
BRIT Awards
British Academy of Songwriters, Composers and Authors (Ivor Novello Awards)
British Film Institute
British Library
British Phonographic Industry
Cameron Mackintosh Ltd
Carbon Dioxide Information Analysis Center
Charities Direct
Checkout
Christie's
Computer Industry Almanac
ComScore.com
Stanley Coren
Crime in England and Wales (Home Office)
Department for Culture, Media and Sport
Department for Environment, Food and Rural Affairs
Department for Transport
Department of Trade and Industry
The Economist
Philip Eden
Emporis
Environmental Performance Index
Ethnologue
Euromonitor International
FA Premier League
Federal Bureau of Investigation
Fédération Internationale de Football Association
Fédération Internationale de Motorcyclisme
Fédération Internationale de Ski
Film Database
Financial Times
Food and Agriculture Organization of the United Nations
Christopher Forbes
Forbes magazine
Forbes Traveler
Forestry Commission
Fortune
General Register Office for Scotland
Global Education Digest (UNESCO)
Global Forest Resources Assessment (FAO)
Gold Survey (Gold Fields Mineral Services Ltd)
Russell E. Gough
Governing Council of the Cat Fancy
Robert Grant
Bob Gulden
highestbridges.com
Home Office
Barney Hooper
Imperial War Museum
Indianapolis Motor Speedway
Interbrand
International Air Transport Association
International Association of Athletics Federations
International Association of Volcanology and Chemistry of the Earth's Interior
International Centre for Prison Studies
International Energy Association
International Federation of Audit Bureaux of Circulations
International Game Fish Association
International Labour Organization
International Obesity Task Force
International Olympic Committee
International Organization of Motor Vehicle Manufacturers
International Paralympic Committee
International Shark Attack File, Florida Museum of Natural History
International Telecommunication Union
International Union for Conservation of Nature and Natural Resources
Internet Movie Database
Internet World Stats
Claire Judd
Kennel Club
Ladies Professional Golf Association
Major League Baseball
Man Booker Prize
Phil Matcham
Chris Mead
The Military Balance (International Institute for Strategic Studies)
MTV
Music Information Database
National Academy of Recording Arts and Sciences (Grammy Awards)
National Aeronautics and Space Administration
National Basketball Association
National Football League
National Gallery, London
National Hockey League
National Statistics
Natural History Museum, London
AC Nielsen
Nielsen Media Research
Nobel Foundation
Northern Ireland Statistics Research Agency
NSS GEO2 Committee on Long and Deep Caves
The Official Charts Company
Organization for Economic Co-operation and Development
Organisation Internationale des Constructeurs d'Automobiles
Roberto Ortiz de Zarate
Professional Bowlers Association
Population Reference Bureau
Professional Golfers' Association
PRS for Music
Railway Gazette International
River Systems of the World
Royal Aeronautical Society
Royal Astronomical Society
Royal Opera House, Covent Garden
Royal Society for the Protection of Birds
Eric Sakowski
Screen Digest
Screen International
Robert Senior
Sotheby's
State of the World's Forests (FAO)
Stores
Sustainable Cities Index (Forum for the Future)
Tate Modern, London
Trades Union Congress
The Tree Register of the British Isles
twitterholic.com
United Nations
United Nations Educational, Scientific and Cultural Organization
United Nations Environment Programme
United Nations Population Division
United Nations Statistics Division
Universal Postal Union
US Census Bureau
US Census Bureau International Data Base
US Geological Survey
Lucy T. Verma
Ward's Motor Vehicle Facts & Figures
World Association of Girl Guides and Girl Scouts
World Association of Newspapers
World Bank
World Broadband Statistics (Point Topic)
World Christian Database
World Development Indicators (World Bank)
World Factbook (Central Intelligence Agency)
World Health Organization
World Metro Database
World Organization of the Scout Movement
World Population Data Sheet (Population Reference Bureau)
World Silver Survey (The Silver Institute/Gold Fields Mineral Services Ltd)
World Resources Institute
World Tennis Association
World Tourism Organization